Economic Theory and
Cognitive Science:
Microexplanation

Economic Theory and Cognitive Science: Microexplanation

Don Ross

A Bradford Book
The MIT Press
Cambridge, Massachusetts
London, England

MIT Press books may be purchased at special quantity discounts for business or sales promotional use. For information, please email special_sales@mitpress.mit.edu or write to Special Sales Department, The MIT Press, 55 Hayward St., Cambridge, MA 02142.

This book was set in Palatino by SNP Best-set Typesetter Ltd., Hong Kong. Printed and bound in the United States of America.

Library of Congress Cataloging-in-Publication Data

Ross, Don, 1962– .
  Economic theory and cognitive science : microexplanation / Don Ross.
    p. cm.
  "A Bradford Book."
  Includes bibliographical references.
  ISBN 0-262-18246-7 (hc : alk. paper)—0-262-68168-4 (pbk : alk. paper)
  ISBN-13 978-0-262-18246-1 (hc : alk. paper)—978-0-262-68168-1 (pbk : alk. paper)
  1. Economics. 2. Cognitive science. I. Title.

HB71.R67   2005
330.1—dc22
                                                                        2004059216

10 9 8 7 6 5 4 3

For Nelleke

Contents

Acknowledgments

An interdisciplinary book, like this one, needs special quality-assurance measures if the author is to avoid looking like a foolish tourist too often. The only possible such mechanism is careful criticism from inside all the represented disciplines. Unfortunately, no amount of such criticism, no matter how careful, will eliminate *all* such gaucherie. Thus, despite the extraordinarily generous assistance I have received from philosophers, economists, and cognitive scientists, I stand ready to be embarrassed. My critics have done their best, to superogatory levels.

Harold Kincaid and David Spurrett read and commented extensively on the entire manuscript. As this is not a short or easy book, this was a mighty investment of their time, for which I am deeply grateful.

One or more draft chapters were read and commented on by the following people (in alphabetical order): George Ainslie, John Collier, Dan Dennett, Paul Dumouchel, Dan Hausman, Yannis Ionides, Brian Kantor, Philip Mirowski, and Alex Rosenberg. Profound thanks indeed go to all of these very busy people. Andy Clark and Robert Frank sent correspondence on, and published responses to, arguments from previous papers that have found their way into the book, and these arguments have been improved by their interventions.

Substantial parts of the book were read, discussed, and criticized by students in my postgraduate seminars in the School of Economics at the University of Cape Town during 2001, 2002, and 2003. They have made a difference that is much and wholly for the better.

Material from the book has been presented to audiences at the American Philosophical Association Eastern Division, the Canadian Philosophical Association, the Philosophical Society of Southern Africa, and the International Conference on Logic, Methodology, and Philosophy of Science, and in invited talks at the Dubrovnik Annual Workshop in the Philosophy of Science, the University of British Columbia, Carleton University, Duke University, the University of KwaZulu-Natal, l'Université du Québec à Montréal, and Rhodes University. I am grateful for the attention and critical questions I received from all these audiences.

Parts of chapter 5 were previously published in *The Stanford Encyclopedia of Philosophy*, entry on "Game Theory," by Don Ross (http://plato.stanford.edu/). I acknowledge the kind permission of the editors of *Philosophical Papers* (vol. 31, no. 2, March 2002) to reprint portions of my "Why People Are Atypical Agents." Permission to reprint portions of my "Sincerity Is Just Consistency: Reply to Robert Frank" was granted by the editors of *Rationality and Society* (vol. 16, 2004, pp. 307–318). Permission to reprint portions of my "Metalinguistic Signaling for Coordination amongst Social Agents" was granted by the editors of *Language Sciences* (vol. 26, 2004, pp. 621–642).

For encouraging the very existence of the project, I thank Dan Dennett, and Tom Stone of The MIT Press.

Many thanks go to Judy Feldmann at The MIT Press for careful and efficient editorial work, and to Jessica Lawrence-Hurt for managing the process.

Finally, my greatest debt by far is to my wife, Professor Nelleke Bak, for (inter alia): proofreading and formatting the entire manuscript; handling editorial correspondence while I wandered around the globe for long periods; putting up with my wandering around the globe for long periods; managing the entire infrastructure of our lives with very little help, but many calls for this and that improvement to it, while I sat in the study thinking about utility maximization. Most of the ideas in this book were first propounded in conversation with Nelleke, and some egregiously bad ones were prevented from going any further by this astute filter. It is to my stubbornness, rather than her gullibility, that blame should be assigned for the ones that got through anyway.

1

Introduction: The Future of Economics and Unified Science

The Philosophical and the Historical

This book is the first of a two-volume study of the science of economics in relation to other branches of behavioral inquiry, which takes the unusual perspective of not assuming, to begin with, that there is or could be any such science.

Obviously, there are numerous activities, which consume very substantial numbers of person hours, that are *called* "economics." Most of this activity consists of practical policy analysis and debate. Much of the rest of it involves attempts to measure social and individual welfare variables of particular sorts, and to measure relationships among these variables. The variables themselves are distinguished from one another, related to observable data, and stabilized for reference from one case to another by a body of theory—as in any other conscious apparatus for trying to generate predictions. The body of theory is the intellectual discipline of economics. One main question addressed by this book is, under what interpretation, if any, is this discipline a sound empirical science?

Let me be as clear as possible about the attitude in which this question is posed. I don't doubt that most economics as practiced is highly worthwhile. For reasons eloquently expressed by Dasgupta (2002), I think that the frequent popular, philosophical, sociological, and ideological assaults on the entire discipline of economics are intellectual frauds perpetrated in ignorance of the extent to which good science, including good economics, is based on empirically trained judgment in task domains, and not on practitioners having philosophically rigorous, objection-proof formulations of background theoretical frameworks. So it is not the aim of this book to try to tell economists they should go about their business in a fundamentally different way than they do. This is not "methodology" in the usual sense of that word in the economics literature. The book is about economic *theory*. It interrogates that theory by asking what sort of sound empirical inquiry it would generate if it were, counterfactually, used as a recipe for determining practice. It is entirely consistent to think that practice could be (often, or usually) running along nicely even if the articulated theory used to frame its interpretation would, if taken very literally, dictate misguided inferences.

This stance is common in the most careful philosophy of science. However, the inquiry here won't be pure philosophy of science—that is, an exercise in rational reconstruction without further, more practical, motives—either. I don't only intend to write another study of the foundations of economic theory. I mean also to explore the relationships between that theory and the theoretical foundations of related disciplines that increasing numbers of *practicing* economists agree to be *practically* relevant to their day-to-day work: the cognitive and behavioral sciences. To the extent that I find illuminating things to say about this relationship, my inquiry may indeed have implications for the kinds of empirical study economists think they should undertake, even if I don't want to advertise myself as promoting—heaven forbid—yet another "paradigm shift."

Broadly speaking, there are two ways in which one can construct a coherent portrait of an entire discipline: the *philosophical* strategy and the *historical-sociological* strategy. In the limiting ideal of the first strategy, one tries to represent the body of theory around which the discipline is organized as a connected system of propositions. Some of the propositions will be about (or at least be intended to be about) the empirical world and others will be about logical and evidential relations among the other propositions. The critical aspect of this sort of work consists in testing answers to questions about which propositions are essential to the discipline's structure and which are optional, and about how much authoritative weight the identified logical and evidential relations can bear in application of the discipline to empirical cases. In the limiting ideal of the second strategy, one tries to construct and present reasons for preferring some particular narrative about the development of the discipline that explains the activities of its practitioners over time. The critical aspect of this sort of work consists in justifying judgments about who count as practitioners and who don't, and about how and why the paradigmatic practitioners and their activities change from one period to another.

In characterizing these two strategies, I described limiting ideals. I assume that any attempt to understand a discipline in a relatively comprehensive manner needs to blend aspects of both. Of course, this leaves wide latitude with respect to the balance of emphasis between them.

The present study gives explanatory priority to the philosophical strategy. This does not reflect an assumption on my part that the histories of disciplines are driven more by logic than by psychology and social dynamics. (Neither do I presume the opposite.) It merely reflects a choice of subject matter: this is a study of what economics is about, if it is about any clear thing at all, and about how its domain differs from others with which it is obviously closely related. It is not a history of how and why the discipline of economics developed as it did, except insofar as that development has been influenced by logical considerations.

Despite this, the first half of the book is a selective chronological narrative. Given that my aims are philosophical rather than historical-sociological, why do I construct the account this way? The answer is as follows. There is a deep tension in recent intellectual history between what might be called "whiggish" and "postmodern" narratives. The former are tales of progress (typically allowing, of course, for cul-de-sacs, garden paths, and episodes of wasted time). Philosophers of science (like me) tend to tell whiggish stories, just because we are trying to unearth logical structures, and logical structures must be broadly coherent to *be* structures; so a story about them is bound to be a story of *construction*. *Telos* just goes with doing this sort of philosophy; and historians or sociologists who assume this is necessarily naïve are either indulging disciplinary arrogance, or relying on the implausible empirical assumption that logical considerations never motivate theorists at all.

However, assuming *telos* with respect to some things doesn't entail allowing it with respect to everything. In the case of economics, it is most natural to tell a whiggish tale about the development of mathematical and analytical technique. There can be little serious argument with the claim that this has grown more sophisticated over time. Furthermore, since it is part of the point of mathematics that relations between well-understood propositions are supposed to be transparent, the relationships between earlier and later analytic technologies aren't typically matters for speculation or hermeneutic interpretation, however much analytic effort their specification might require. The chronological part of my study in this volume will be organized around major steps in the refinement of microeconomic analytical tools.

I will not, however, make a whiggish assumption to the effect that this refinement necessarily involved increasingly good or important or profound empirical science. Instead, I will be asking, as my critical question, whether there *are* any deep empirical regularities to which the increasing refinement of technique has allowed improving access. By "improving" I will for now just mean loosely: more descriptively accurate at a finer level of detail, and facilitative of more powerful explanations. I will return to this philosophical issue more rigorously in the final chapter, after the story has been told.

It is a commonplace in critiques of economic thought, both philosophical and historical-sociological, that those people who have captured the role of paradigm determiners in the discipline have rewarded clarity of mathematical refinement more consistently and unequivocally than they have clarity of responsiveness to empirical phenomena. This is not true of all disciplines. That it is surely true of economics invites my way of organizing the inquiry. Anyone who agrees with the commonplace just stated should find it unsurprising that a whiggish history of the analytical apparatus can be told, and should agree, unless their postmodernism is carried to an extreme degree, that the question of whether the technical refinement represents improvement in any other sense is a natural way of setting up a philosophical inquiry.

By "extreme" postmodernism, I refer to an attitude that denies that philosophical inquiry can ever be a well-justified activity. (Few actual postmodernists are this extreme. I'm merely setting up a limiting case here.) Postmodern narratives contrast with whiggish ones in that, in the former, we neither find nor expect any elements of *telos* except reflections of short-run social power struggles. In such narratives, the philosophical attitude must be a fantasy, since from its perspective all we will find if we try to be honest are random walks across the spaces allowed by power dynamics; so far as *logic* is concerned, intellectual history will be just one damn thing after another. My assumption that the inquiry to come is worth doing presupposes that this extreme postmodernism goes too far, but doesn't argue for this. I take for granted that reason, argument, and sincere curiosity about truth and explanation play roles—indeed, important roles—in causing some ideas and intellectual investments to win out over others.

This does not mean, however, that I dismiss the value of less all-consuming postmodern insights. I will orient my study by the device

of setting it up as a conversation with two recent commentators on economics who have asked questions in the immediate ballpark of mine.
(This does not mean that a reader needs to have studied their work
before trying to follow mine.) One of these is a philosopher who is
deeply skeptical about the idea that the development of economics
encodes any nontechnical or nonpolitical telos, and we'll meet him in
the next section of this chapter. The other is a historian of economics
of postmodern sensibility, Philip Mirowski. I'll introduce him and his
role in the conversation now.

Most mainstream economists, like most mainstream philosophers,
aren't very comfortable with the postmodern stance, and are thus apt
to read a historian like Mirowski with their hair continuously standing
on end. This is because a postmodernist, not believing that any one
governing metaphor for a narrative can be unambiguously true to the
exclusion of other possibilities, chooses one or two by discretion and
then gets on with the business of narrating to see what will happen.[1]
The result can look, to the more traditionally minded, like irresponsible speculation, standing to serious history as tabloid journalism stands
to *The Times* or *The Economist*. (See, for example, Binmore's review of
Mirowski in the *Journal of Economic Methodology*.)[2] I will cite an example
from Mirowski's *Machine Dreams* (2002), the main text of his with which
I will converse in this book. In chapter 6 of *MD*, which is a sociological and intellectual history of the relationship between economic
thought and the development of computation theory and computer
technology since World War II, Mirowski discusses the displacement
of von Neumann and Morgenstern's original approach to game theory
by Nash equilibrium after the 1950s. The latter is presented, following
a trope introduced by Keller (1985), as an expression of paranoia,
wherein "solving" a strategic problem consists in internalizing the
entire social world, including the motivations of all agents over the
whole foreseeable future, inside the head of the analyst. Never mind
the details of this construction, which will not again arise as a topic in
this book. I cite it simply as an illustration of why many economists
have difficulty in taking Mirowski, and postmodern attitudes in
general, as serious contributions to scholarship. Mirowski is careful
(2002, pp. 338–339) to tread with sensitivity when diagnosing paranoia
in a technical idea promoted by a man (Nash, of course) whose life was
wrecked by a terrible psychological disease. Still, Nash equilibrium is
a tremendously powerful mathematical idea in the recent history of
economics. Is it not therefore ridiculous—trivializing and in bad taste—

to characterize it as a manifestation of a personality disorder and/or a disease?

The subject raised by this question is our *attitude* to what we do as analyzers, whether we're philosophers, economists, historians, or behavioral scientists. The postmodern sensibility is willing to play with narrative possibilities, and sees reverence for logic as a form of preciousness. I commend this attitude. Some postmodern texts, especially some Anglo-American ones, are ghastly and self-undermining when they forget the relative capriciousness of their own free choices of metaphor and use them as the basis for political and moral hectoring of those who make other choices. However, narrative metaphors are fundamental devices for organizing and reorganizing our conceptual landscapes in search of new insights. It is helpful that some knowledgeable students of the history of thought, as Mirowski certainly is, exercise freedom to sample the possibilities. I think that more traditional sorts of commentators would be better off if they learned to relax a bit about this.

The guiding epistemology of a postmodernist, however, cannot allow him to object if we in the audience feel equally free to pick and choose among his suggested metaphors with a similar casual justification. I do not, as a matter of fact, find Keller's associating the Nash equilibrium with paranoia to be powerful or illuminating like Mirowski does, which is why it won't crop up again in these pages. I will have other arguments with Mirowski, on ideas of his I take more seriously, throughout the book. The point for the moment is that he is well worth arguing with. I bring him up now, right at the outset of my study, because I find his overarching picture of what economic theory has been trying (at best semi-intentionally most of the time) to achieve over the past half-century interesting and persuasive. Along with the perspective of my other foil, to appear in the next section, Mirowski's work frames a conversational context for mine.

Here, then, is Mirowski's "big idea," which I will follow him in entertaining. Economics is, in some sense to be made precise by any would-be account of it, about optimization *of* something or other *by* something or other. Optimization has been taken to be, at various moments in the discipline's history, of material wealth, or psychological satisfaction, or utility on one of its several interpretations. It might be done or attempted by people, or collectives like households or firms, or by people or firms in special sets of circumstances, or by parts or aspects of people or firms on special interpretations. But when we study economic thought we are studying a part of the theory of optimization. Now, it has become increasingly central to twentieth-century work on optimization that optimization is *computation* under some description. Theorists of previous centuries had only imprecise conceptions of what computation is, when they bothered with the idea at all. However, a defining feature of any contemporary theory—not just of optimization itself, but of evolution, development, or dynamics generally—is that it must, somewhere and in some sense, be explicit about what system is supposed to be computing what information and how.

Most current debates on the foundations, methodology, scope, or justification of economic theory are heavily concerned with its relationships to neighboring domains of inquiry, mainly, where microeconomics is concerned, psychology and evolutionary theory. These, in turn, now come organized together under the rubric of "cognitive science." (Hence my title for the two volumes of this study.) Cognitive science came into being precisely because, after World War II, it became impossible to think about mind or learning or behavioral responses to environmental conditions without resort to the exploding formal and technical understanding of information processing.

Mirowski's history of the role of economists in this wider process depicts them as being dragged, usually with at least one foot planted in the dirt, along behind the advancing arc of what he calls "the cyborg sciences." Because his tone is personal and heavily ironic—often outright comic—his narrative is easily read by the Very Serious as disrespectful to the discipline. Such a reaction confuses medium and message. What it means for something to be a discipline, as Kuhn and Lakatos emphasized, is for its practitioners to constantly try to handle as many new phenomena as they can with as few new theoretical tools as possible. Economists, then, in trying to preserve continuity while new worlds of thought opened around them, behaved just like any other scientists would and should, so "accusing" them of conservatism does not necessarily mock them. This I take to be a more specific justification for my procedure of hanging my critical questions about the current state and future of economics on a structure that *begins* by sketching development that is continuous along at least one dimension (the refinement of mathematical analysis).

I'll conclude this opening section by outlining Mirowski's broad thesis. I will return to it in greater detail toward the end of the book, when it will no longer be premature to contrast my own account with it. For now, I outline it just to provide a point of departure for what is to come.

The hero of Mirowski's story is John von Neumann. This extraordinary polymath, the single greatest engineer of our contemporary scientific and technological environment, is characterized as having discovered the principles that would carry economics forward precisely because, as someone from outside its institutions, and supported by a massive, independent power base (in the Cold War military, among other places), he was under no obligation to revere its history. For Mirowski's von Neumann, the way to do economics was to implement dynamic computational theories in working machines and thereby find out what relative optima could be computed by what principles of system organization under what circumstances. The economics profession is then depicted as following von Neumann down this path, in starts and lurches, while trying in every possible way not to. (This is the source of the comic tone mentioned above.)

In particular, on Mirowski's telling, economists tried to ignore a central result of the theory of computation, Gödel's incompleteness theorem, by ignoring considerations of computational effectiveness and pursuing possibility proofs, after the fashion of Bourbaki, rather than constructive proofs. In this, they are presented as doing their damnedest to preserve neoclassical equilibrium analysis, enriched by powerful new advances in the theory of functions and topology theory. The two great shibboleths of postwar economics are thereby depicted as being general equilibrium and Nash equilibrium, both understood by Mirowski as static rest points that cannot be computed for a large empirical system in real time with finite resources, or even identified uniquely in the relevant, fully general cases by means of constructive and effective techniques.

I am later going to defend the theoretical centrality of both these concepts, and will not be persuaded by Mirowski that the first lesson of a sound twenty-first century economics course should be Gödel's result. However, these are issues for down the road. Here, in setting up the target space for my own inquiry, I want to focus on Mirowski's "five possible futures" for economic theory in light of his analysis as just described. They constitute an imaginative and well-informed way of organizing the terrain represented by current debates, relatively independently of Mirowski's particular argumentative path to them, and I will gratefully use the space they set up for locating the path I'll be developing.

Mirowski's first possible future is playfully called "Judd's revenge," after the econometrician Kenneth Judd. In this future, economics pays essentially no attention to cognitive science. It uses computational technology to study, with increasing intricacy, what would happen to rational agents if they could access and crunch all the information that our newest machines can, at least as quickly as they do (or, for some applications, instantaneously). As Mirowski puts it (2002, p. 451), this future implements the idea of conflating rationality with econometric inference. There isn't much room for doubt, given the allocation of person hours in economics now, that this activity will be at least *part* of the future of economics. To the extent that it dominates that future, it represents the regime in which economics remains most proudly separate from disciplines that might, on other conceptions, be thought to be its neighbors. Mirowski, given his particular critique as sketched above, regards this as the path by which economics could drift most completely away from all relevance to anything outside of itself, including actual human economies.

In this book, I will be defending a conception of economics as separate from its neighbors in a particular and relative sense. A question I will thus want to touch on at various points is the extent to which economics can be separate in the way I suggest without disappearing into the sort of solipsism against which Mirowski warns. I will give reasons for thinking that he is right to regard Judd's revenge as a path to irrelevance, for reasons that have nothing specific to do with Gödel's theorem.

Mirowski names his second possible future "Lewis redux," after the economic theorist Alain Lewis, from whose work Mirowski derives his own emphasis on the critical importance to economics of formal incompleteness. In this future, economists make heavy use of computation theory while largely ignoring other, biologically connected, parts of cognitive science. (This might be glossed as: they treat computation theory as if it *weren't* relevantly integrated into cognitive science.) They use results in the theories of functional relations and of topology to try to engineer their way around the implications of Gödel's proof. Mirowski depicts Kenneth Arrow's current perspective as the leading representation of the view, which takes heart from such results as Scarf's (1973) procedure for computing approximations to general equilibrium under special restricted circumstances.[3]

In this book, I will give arguments as to why this sort of program can indeed be a very useful contributor to progress in economics, though my argument will also suggest that Mirowski is right to think that it will not help if it is as divorced from cognitive science as its "pure" exemplification would have it be. This argument of mine will depend on a particular philosophical interpretation of cognitive science itself, one which Mirowski never considers.

Future number three is called "Simulatin' Simon"; "Simon" here is of course the late Herbert E. In this scenario, economics integrates itself massively with artificial intelligence research, emulating the biography of the program's celebrated inspirer. As Mirowski rightly says, this future is already with us to a substantial extent. He cites Epstein and Axtell's (1996) book on *Growing Artificial Societies* as a representative recent work. The motivation for the approach is straightforward: let us assume that biological brains are the basic causal engines of economic behavior, and then see what they can do under specific constraints by simulating them at various levels of abstraction. In presenting this methodology as involving integration with artificial intelligence (AI), one of course need not have in mind just AI in its narrow, symbol-processing sense, as opposed to connectionist or artificial life models (see Langton 1995; Levy 1992). It is an open question for economics-as-simulation how abstract the simulations must be to be relevant and productive; perhaps they can ignore all natural implementation details, as in traditional AI, or perhaps we can only discover interesting things about economic behavior by inducing artificial agents equipped with neural nets to learn regularities in simulated societies and monitoring what they stumble across.

Mirowski does not doubt that this sort of integration between economics and cognitive science will be an essential *part* of any future in which economics makes progressive contributions to our understanding of behavior. Behavioral science cannot, as a practical matter, thrive on a strict diet of observations of biological systems plus top-down theory. However, Mirowski affirms that economics cannot just consist in such work, since simulation activity by itself tends to generate a plethora of special models and practical design principles for special cases, without promoting much in the way of general understanding. A philosopher of science might try to work up a general epistemological principle to this effect, but this is not the sort of interpretation of his objection Mirowski intends. His point, rather, is that without a strong telos, which in engineering can come from the market's or the

military's demand for products working to specific functional specifications, and (I add here) in science can derive from the search for
explanatory generalizations, simulation work tends to generate diminishing returns in its own terms; simulations make things happen, but
it becomes unclear how to characterize what is happening or why.

I endorse Mirowski's diagnosis here. I would add that an additional
problem with simulation alone, at least as it has often been engineered
in AI and also in some A-life modeling, is that it attempts to find the
basis for behavioral patterns as "emerging" from, or even being decomposable into, the internal dynamics of modular parts of simulated
systems. This is natural for any engineering approach, since we would
learn little from trying to simulate unanalyzable wholes as pure black
boxes even if we could build them.[4] However, in chapter 6 of this book
I will be presenting a radical criticism, grounded in the philosophy of
behavioral science, of individualist models of economic phenomena,
and on the basis of this critique will advance reasons for doubting that
interesting economic generalizations follow straightforwardly from the
ways individual agents are internally governed. Of course, a simulation might be directly of a social system, with individuals in the system
being modeled as relatively unstructured nodes (see Kennedy and
Eberhart 2001). To the extent that economic research is built around
simulations of this kind, however, we slide toward Mirowski's distinct
"fifth future," to be discussed below.

Mirowski's fourth future is inspired by (quoting his labeling practice
again) "Dennett's dangerous idea," after the philosopher of mind and
biology Daniel Dennett. This names the program by which economic
theory is genuinely and fully integrated with the main current research
front in evolutionary cognitive science. Rather than merely using artificial computational devices to simulate biological agents, it involves
modeling these agents as literally *being* specific instances of computational devices. It

proclaims that it is possible to access some algorithms from artificial intelligence, combine them with a particularly tendentious understanding of the
theory of evolution, and arrive at a grand Theory of Everything, all to the ultimate purpose of maintaining that all human endeavor is constrained maximization "all the way down." . . . The theory of rational choice (perhaps simple
optimization, perhaps game theory) is unselfconsciously treated as the very
paradigm of information processing for biological organisms and machines;
consequently, both computers and humans are just a meme's way of making
another meme. . . . [O]nce one takes the death-defying leap . . . and stipulates

that evolution is everywhere and always algorithmic, and that memes can freely soar beyond the surly bounds of bodies, then one can readily extrapolate that the designated task of the economist in the bungee-jump is to explore how the neoclassical instantiation of rational economic man "solves" all the various optimization problems that confront him in everyday economic experience. Neoclassical economics is cozily reabsorbed into a Unified Science that would warm the cockles of a Viennese logical positivist. (Mirowski 2002, pp. 533–534)

If future number three is already upon us, it is surely having to jostle hard for attention with this future number four.[5] The current research streams identified by Mirowski with Dennett's dangerous idea are: modeling games by competitions among finite automata, as in the work of Kalai (1990) and Binmore (1987–1988); evolutionary game theory; experimental and formal forays into so-called "behavioral" economics; modeling of economic dynamics using genetic algorithms or neural networks; and most of what goes on at the Santa Fe Institute, regardless of which exact box it is classified in. All this can hardly be regarded anymore as the activity of a rarified avant-garde; it describes most of the theoretical innovation in microeconomics over the past ten to fifteen years. In calling it a "possible" future, Mirowski alludes to the fact that he doubts it has legs for the long innings—mainly because (he says), he doubts that people trained as economists will prove able to understand cognitive science well enough to make real contributions to it (2002, p. 535).

As Mirowski emphasizes at several points in his book, what really leaves him ambivalent about the logic of this future is that it begins by deconstructing the primacy of the sovereign neoclassical individual— a healthy thing, he thinks, in moderation—but then sails beyond mere correction of an historical exaggeration to promote the wholesale dissolution of the self. The steps by which Ken Binmore (1994, 1998) links his model for applying game theory to the philosophy of agency are cited as the most explicit evidence of how and why this happens (Mirowski 2002, pp. 515–516). In Binmore's model, the decisions of individual agents are irrelevant to system dynamics in the long run: agents are driven by system-level dynamics to fashion selves that play equilibrium strategies *given* the dynamics, rather than the dynamics being contingent functions of the strategies the agents *choose*.

It is extremely interesting, in light of this, that Mirowski names this future after Dennett. Mirowski gives no hint in his book of the fact that revision of the concept of the self has been the abiding undercurrent of

Dennett's otherwise apparently loosely connected work on intentionality, consciousness, evolution, and free will. As I will discuss in detail in chapter 7, once this is understood, all of Dennett's particular projects on these other topics become more plausible than they have seemed to his critics. Furthermore, as I will also document, Dennett's theory of the self has been strongly persuasive, at least in the short run: most cognitive scientists who now write on the self have incorporated and then elaborated on his perspective, whether they fully appreciate this or not.

However, as we will see, to read Dennett as dissolving or annihilating the self is a profound misunderstanding. On the contrary, as I will argue, the best explanation for the success of his view—success that has been unusually unequivocal compared with the usual fate of theses in philosophy—is that it is really the first systematic way of thinking about selves we've ever had that does justice to the richness and subtlety of the range of empirical phenomena associated with the concept. The textual evidence in Mirowski's book suggests that his clearly prodigious reading on many topics (and, I should add, his wonderful detective work through the unpublished archive of letters and other marginalia surrounding the history of recent economic theory) hasn't extended to the burgeoning philosophical literature on what's now called "moral psychology." This is, I think, confirmed by another remark he makes in connection with his evaluation of his future number four. He says that he doubts that the fundamental source of valuation will turn out to "congeal for the purposes of a science of economics . . . within the recesses of the idealized computer situated between the ears of the representative economic agent" (ibid., p. 564). I understand how Dennett's theory of agency and of the locus of intentionality (hence, of valuation) *can* be misread, given its originating context in philosophical debates of the 1970s, in a way consistent with this criticism. However, as we'll begin to see in chapter 2, and as will unfold in full detail in chapters 6 and 7, the reading couldn't be more completely backwards.

If Dennett's idea is supposed to be dangerous because it threatens to deny the self,[6] then the diagnosis of danger in the sense Mirowski intends[7] is going to be decisively confuted in these pages. We'll then be able to ask, in chapter 8, what this implies for the prospects of the kind of economics done by Binmore and company.

One of the things I commend in Mirowski's style of discourse is that it never hides the author's commitments behind a ponderous pretense of his being a disinterested conduit for the Voice of Objective Reason. He tells the reader what he's going to be up to just like a real person in a room would. This will seem gauche to some academic sensibilities—it can actually *be* gauche when it's the expression of a conceit, rather than being, as in Mirowski's case, just what happens naturally if you're a postmodernist in the good French sense instead of the bad Yale sense—but I think the clarity of debate it invites is laudable. So let me now, without my pretending to a full level of comfort with the style on which I can't follow through in practice, at least show respect for it by a clean display of my own cards. This study (both volumes) will promote Mirowski's future number four, though without thereby trying to reduce futures two or three or his own favored future number five (below) out of the picture. And—here is where I take my rhetorical plunge and risk clanging in the ears of those whose norms of academic style I've unfavorably contrasted with Mirowski's—it has a couple of intellectual heroes. They are Dennett and Binmore. There is going to be a dramatic plot in the coming narrative (though at the pace of Henry James compared to Mirowski's Dasheill Hammett), and at the end Dennett and Binmore are going to get up to the top of the mountain and show us how to integrate economic theory with the wider cognitive and behavioral sciences.

It should now be evident why I have opened this book by introducing Mirowski as one of my two conversational foils. To conclude the exercise, we must briefly see the future of economics that he himself favors. His future number five is dubbed "vending von Neumann," after *his* avowed hero. It involves taking fully seriously the idea that *types* of whole markets—Walrasian tatonnement, Shapely-Shubik, one-sided unified quasi auctions of various types, two-sided clearinghouse or double auctions, and so on—implement different formal *types* of computational devices. Just as with the different types of devices sorted into hierarchies with respect to logical power by the mathematical theory of computation, or the different types of grammars sorted into a generative-power hierarchy in Chomsky's work on the foundations of formal linguistics, we can try to develop a generalizing theory that tells us which markets can simulate or beget which others, and compare them with respect to both information-processing capacity, and differential efficiency given particular allocation problems. That is, economic theory could be developed into a computational theory of markets. Mirowski argues persuasively that this vision faithfully reproduces von Neumann's ambition for the discipline arising from the revolution in logic and mathematics of the early twentieth century—although of course von Neumann could not put it in terms of the zoology of market types, mostly developed after his death. (See O'Hara 1995 for a survey of this.)

In the final chapters of this book, I will argue that the von Neumann vision as sketched by Mirowski is not a competitor to Dennett's dangerous idea, as he imagines, but is fully compatible with it. Indeed, by drawing on my own and collaborators' work on the underlying metaphysics necessary to make Dennett's theory of intentional behavior fully consistent with the social and physical sciences (Ross 2000; Ross and Spurrett 2004a; Ross et al. forthcoming), I aim to show that the prospects for successfully vending von Neumann look much better if we are persuaded by Dennett's theories of the self and of intentional behavior, and by Binmore's game-theoretic model of the wider social dynamics in which markets arise. I thereby combine Mirowski's futures four and five into a comprehensive model of economic theory as part of a unified science. And, yes, I hope the cockles of a Viennese logical positivist would thereby be warmed. As long as one doesn't aim for the reduction of empirical knowledge to "sense data," why should that be a bad thing? A coherent picture of the whole world is the greatest thing science is for; or so I will argue later in the present chapter.

All of this will require two volumes to work out. In this first volume my concentration is on the relationship between microeconomics and the theory of intentional behavior. It will thus feature its first hero, Dennett, much more than its second one, Binmore. The next volume will be about the relationship between macroeconomics and the other sciences of social dynamics, and there Binmore's work will be the most powerful element of the engine.

In the discussion to this point, I have self-consciously acknowledged that orienting my inquiry partly in conversation with Mirowski will not immediately recommend it to mainstream economists, while urging the latter to control their trigger fingers. However, as I have also indicated, I am far more loyal than Mirowski is to a whiggish principle for understanding disciplinary histories. I will thus spend two long chapters renarrating the history of microeconomic theory from Jevons through contemporary game theory, in a way designed to show how my eventual comprehensive model can be understood as *recovering* the core neoclassical insights rather than supplanting them. So, my appreciation for elements of its style notwithstanding, this is decidedly *not* going to be a postmodernist exercise. It will be stodgy old philosophy of science. Well, there are other, less recent, heroes in the background to this book, and some of them worked in Vienna.

Science and the Human World

Mirowski's narrative depends on a few normative presuppositions of large moment. One of these is that in a conflict between "scientistic" and "humanistic" images of inquiry, the latter are self-evidently the forces of good. Two subsidiary, and standard, presuppositions are important in buttressing this proposition, and both undergird the irony with which Mirowski describes Dennett's dangerous idea in the passage I quoted a few pages ago. One assumption is that all "logical positivist" hankerings for a unified science have somehow been resolutely discredited among sensible people. This is supposed to be part of the reason for the next presupposition, which is that our manifest view of ourselves as warm intentional actors in moral dramas and comedies, the good old people we've approximately taken ourselves to be since at least Homer's time, does a level of service for the coherence of our worldview that science can't possibly supplant.

I deny all of these presuppositions, quite flatly. Since some reviewers of this book will no doubt want to accuse me of "scientism," I will make things easy for them: the perspective to be defended here is scientistic. In some quarters, saying this is akin to standing up at a town hall meeting in Alabama, where I live, and calling oneself a liberal. I do this second thing without blushing, though, and I feel exactly the same way about the first. Just as I don't think anyone has ever provided sound reasons for regarding liberalism as a path to social degeneration, so I don't think any arguments for scientism as the necessarily nihilistic road to *1984* or *Brave New World* cut any real mustard. This section is about the charms of scientism.

Science constantly furnishes us with astonishing ideas about the nature of reality. Physics tells us that there may be an infinite number of universes, of which ours is just one, and that perhaps two particles in no physical contact with one another can somehow influence each other's properties. From evolutionary biology we learn that birds are the only living descendents of dinosaurs. Geologists reveal that, as a result of the current trajectory of the Earth's tectonic plates, Australia will eventually collide with Alaska. Contemporary educated people have grown used to the idea that, at least where the causal structure of the world uninfluenced by human agency is concerned, our stock of "commonsense" assumptions and principles is systematically unreliable as a guide to the facts. Our everyday scale of perceptions, along both its temporal and its spatial dimensions, is simply too pinched and unrepresentative to be trusted as a direct window onto wider truths, at least about physics, geology, astronomy, microbiology, and so on.

This process, whereby our sense of epistemic comfort about the physical world is regularly mocked and undermined, has been going on for at least four centuries now, and this seems to have been long enough for many people to have become used to it. We continue to be amazed by *particular* scientific discoveries, but we are less apt than our seventeenth-century ancestors to be amazed that we are continuously amazed. In one broad domain, however, much popular and scholarly opinion continues to resist the call to sophisticated skepticism about everyday wisdom. When scientists tell us remarkable and deeply counterintuitive things about our apparent experiences of ourselves and the bases of our own actions, many hesitate or rebel. To be told that space only seems to be Euclidean in its geometry because we live our lives in a tiny arc of it is one thing—rather like being told, if you have lived your whole life in an inland desert, that most of the world is in fact covered with water. But if someone tries to convince us that we, as beings whose very identities are structured around the experience of reflective choice, are fundamentally confused about how minds work or about how behavior is caused, this seems an entirely different sort of thing—epistemically inappropriate *in principle*. After all, we appear to directly experience the causal procedures underlying our own actions. How could a distanced, third-party perspective possibly be better informed about such processes than their very subjects?

It isn't terribly hard to get even diehard believers in the authority of subjective experience onto the upper reaches of slippery slopes here. Many agree that their brains must, in some sense and to at least some degree, be the physical basis of their thoughts. And they will then further admit that their direct experience doesn't encode much information at all about the structure or workings of their brains. To learn about brains we have to assume a third-party perspective, just as we must to learn about the galaxy. And then, if some detached scientist tells you something about your brain that you couldn't know "from inside," it follows immediately that this scientist has told you something about the causal basis of your own actions that you couldn't have discovered through introspection.

The slippery slope is covered with outcrops to grab onto, however: there are sophisticated ways of remaining skeptical about the claims of the sophisticated. The way that is most powerful, and crucially undergirds all other approaches, works as follows. Third-person science regularly trumps common sense when the aspects of the world at issue have the character and structure they do *independently* of our own thought and experience. The universe would have had the properties it does whether anyone had ever been capable of conceiving of them or not; and so there is no deep epistemic mystery as to how beings of limited perceptual reach, however sensible in their reasoning, might turn out to be wrong, even massively wrong, in their conclusions about them. The same is true for the physical brain: we all know that although the existence of our own brains might depend on some fortuitous choices made by our ancestors, these ancestors did not choose our brains' weight or color or basic neurochemical constitution. But where many aspects of the domain of human experience and action are concerned, matters seem (prima facie) fundamentally different. Human minds and selves are personal and social constructions, partly and crucially *constituted* by thoughts and reflections and their causal consequences. The same goes for human economies and political structures. What it *is* to be a democracy, or a jazz lover, or an introvert, is mainly a function of how these concepts of kinds of structures and people feature in our organization of our own experience. To at least some extent, then, their deep nature can only, and in principle, be understood from their insides, and partly in terms of the categories of our everyday experience of ourselves. Or, at least, so many commentators have argued.

This view is by no means restricted to the unsophisticated. It has been explicitly and recently defended by the influential philosopher John Searle, both with respect to the contents of our thoughts (1992) and the meanings of the elements that make up our social structures (1997). Thomas Nagel has also written eloquently in criticism of the possibility of a "view from nowhere," that is, an imagined domain of godlike detachment independent of any special and limited perspective. Nagel (1986) takes this domain to be the epistemic ideal of objective science, and he argues that it is incoherent, even in the case of physics, but especially where minds and their products are concerned (1974). Searle and Nagel have many sympathizers among scholars in the humanities and social sciences. I will refer to the view of this "camp" as "anthropocentric" insofar as it is committed to the idea that where mental contents and many social structures are concerned, "seeming (to us) to be" and "being" amount to the same thing.

Within this humanist empire, however, there are notable pockets of dissent, reaching to constitute the majorities of some whole disciplines. Evolutionary psychologists, many economists, and social scientists of various "structuralist" persuasions—in fact, as Mirowski sees, most of the promoters of Dennett's dangerous idea—widely doubt that pursuit of mainly subjective (including intersubjective) insight is a fruitful road to understanding social processes or behavior.

In this book and its successor volume I will be laying out and defending a comprehensive antianthropocentric view, uniting core insights of neoclassical economics with evolutionary cognitive and behavioral science. A fundamental implication of this picture is that our conventional, "folk" schema for sorting intentional, behavioral and social reality will not generally be preserved through transformations to adequate scientific descriptions.[8]

I indicated in the previous section that I'd be orienting the inquiry initially as a conversation with two rival perspectives. One of them, Mirowski, we've met. The other is a purer foil, in that disagreement with him is much more straightforward and across-the-board. It is helpful when one is dividing terrain at so grand a level as I am here, to be able to contrast it with a clearly articulated perspective that sees the fundamental division as lying in the same place, and then makes the opposite assessment of it. This, at the very least, provides some reassurance that one's critical target is not a straw man. (Mirowski, of course, performs a similar but more nuanced service of this kind.) The philosopher John Dupré (2001) has recently published a book in which he begins by seeing just what I do, namely, that evolutionary behavioral science and mainstream economics are deeply complementary disciplines, united by their allegiance to an nonanthropocentric model of explanation—which Dupré calls, sure enough, "scientism"—and trying to furnish understanding just where, respectively, their partner discipline's resources run out. The whole point of Dupré's book is to deplore this alliance as bad science driven by confused metaphysics, and as ethically dangerous to boot. Dupré at least agrees with me that the alliance is both natural and important. The aim of this book is to show *why* and exactly *how* it is both natural and important, and, in exact opposition to Dupré, to justify and celebrate its scientific and (to a lesser extent) metaphysical virtues. (Its normative virtues will be postponed until the next volume, *Macroexplanation*.)

I do not mean to suggest that this book is mainly a response to Dupré (or to Mirowski). I will reply, in the course of things, to those of their particular arguments that have conclusions directly germane to mine, just as I will to the arguments of many other people. Dupré's core case against the complementary extension of evolutionary cognitive science and economics ultimately rests on a metaphysical thesis about the degree to which the world has a unified causal structure; and although I will discuss metaphysical issues throughout the book, I won't be starting from metaphysical ground zero.[9] I bring up my foil early on because Dupré and I stand on opposite sides of a divide over the appropriate relationship between science and the world of human phenomenal experience that is absolutely fundamental. Arguments that will preoccupy us in later chapters focused specifically on economic theory will depend on prior explicit attention to this issue.

A long tradition in philosophy sees the deep task of scientific inquiry as that of achieving insight into *essences* of structures and processes. Now, the term "essence" means a number of different things in different contexts. With respect to important uses of the concept in the biological sciences, I am critical of essentialism. However, there is an aspect of essentialism, in its widest sense, on which my whole inquiry rests. This is the view according to which the job of scientific theory is to organize our perspective on general reality by isolating real causal and structural relationships that, because of their very generality relative to particular human concerns and purposes, tend to be invisible to casual observation. Let us take biological taxonomy—one of Dupré's favorite subjects—as an example. It would never occur to most non-scientists that onions and garlics might be types of lilies (as in fact they are). As Dupré points out at length (1993, pp. 17–36), this is because very few particular, practical human goals need be sensitive to this fact; it is irrelevant to the farmer, the chef, and the gardener. The categories of everyday language therefore do not respect this fact; the proprietor of a seed shop who produced a bag of onion seed in response to a customer's request for lilies would rightly be thought an obtuse and antisocial user of English (and of communicative conventions more generally). However, the inclusion of onions among the lilies is everything to the biological taxonomist concerned with that group of plants. Because of this sort of attitude among scientists, the popular stereotype views them as fanatics about the truth of arcane "factoids." But what makes the biologist's classification true in some way that the gardener's isn't? After all, the gardener's use encodes a perfectly respectable fact about everyday English semantics. The answer to the question is as follows. Grouping onions and garlics among the lilies tells us something about the processes of evolution, and the evolutionary perspective in turn systematically organizes almost all the structural regularities in biology. The gardener's classification entirely ignores these regularities because they don't matter to her purposes.

The word "systematically" is doing important work here. In one sense, the gardener's classification follows a system. She is motivated to group together plants that have flowers of similar appearance, grow in similar soil conditions, need similar amounts of irrigation to prosper, and perhaps have similar prices. But it is not "systematic" as I am using the term here. What this means is that these different dimensions of similarity are not all products of an underlying, informationally compressible structural pattern *about the plants themselves*. They *are* products of informationally compressible patterns about the sociology and psychology of gardening; but this makes them relevant to the social scientist's system rather than the biologist's. The former is interested in the behavior of gardeners, whereas the latter is interested in plants. The *gardener's* system, therefore, as defined by reference to its objects of organization—that is, plants—is shared by *no* part of science.

I am going to mark this distinction, throughout this book, by using "system" as a technical term. That is, I am going to reserve use of the term "system," when applied to principles for organizing suggested structural regularities, for those sets of such principles as are intended to be candidates for survival under any transformation of human psychological and social purposes continuous with actual human history, however radical, just as long as the transformation in question did not eradicate concern with knowing about the objective causal and structural relations among all facts. By the terms of this formulation, a system is something vulnerable to a criticism that it is anthropocentric and merely practical. The gardener's classification scheme, by contrast, faces no such criticism.

Systematicity avoids being an entirely quixotic ambition only if it is accepted that there *are* objective facts independent of any particular human purposes. This is something for which I will not argue in this book; every exercise in philosophy can't be an exercise of every philosophical issue, and *basic* realism is something I'm simply going to take for granted. Readers interested in defense and articulation of this basic realism that I presuppose are referred to Hacking (1983) and Miller (1987). Hacking (1999) has sensible things to say about how to prevent affirmation of basic realism from turning into dogmatic and silly denial of obvious facts about the social construction of many kinds of things. I will not be denying these sorts of facts.

An example will help to clarify the special meaning I'm attaching to "systematic" thinking. Einstein's redefinition of space and time was largely driven by the need to make these ideas nonanthropocentric, that is, to disassociate them from a folk conceptual basis in the experience of a spatially centered agent changing its locations relative to other bodies and bookkeeping these changes in units of elapsed time. In relativity theory, space and time are defined by axiomatic postulates that render their application insensitive to particular reference points. Einstein's analyses might someday be modified or abandoned as physics develops. However, no merely psychological or social changes (developmentally continuous with our current standpoint) not themselves caused by scientifically motivated adjustments to physical theory are supposed to influence such revisions. That we might violate this regulative ideal, or even be unable to avoid violating it because we are incorrigibly fixated on our social relations, is a familiar point stressed by social theorists of science. This thesis is entirely compatible with the claim that objectivity nevertheless is the appropriate regulative ideal that science, in its institutionally imperfect way, tries to respect. So long as Einstein's analyses remain canonical among physicists, to the extent that anyone uses concepts called "space" and "time" incompatible with Einstein's, they are failing to use the concepts systematically.[10]

Why do I want to define the idea of a system in so roundabout a way? Why not just say that systems are those structures we would identify if we had no specially human purposes? The answer is that the notion of an intelligence without *any* special purposes is impossible. Intelligent clouds of particles half a light-year in extent would not and could not notice many of the patterns we do, because their purposes—the saliences shaped by the selection conditions under which they evolved—would be so different from ours. To this (strictly limited) extent, I endorse Nagel's view that we cannot literally aspire to utter perspectivelessness, of the sort sometimes imagined for God. In this book, I will be heavily concerned with economic patterns, and these might be invisible to creatures who experienced little significant scarcity with respect to the resources they liked to consume (though I cannot imagine how intelligence might evolve without such scarcity, since it seems unlikely that intelligence could arise unless at least its original instance evolved under selection pressures). The "view from no particular human place" might thus not quite be the "view from nowhere"; at any rate, the former is all that I will need to appeal to in this book. This is simply the idea that although all inquiry has a history rooted in practical concerns, genuine detachment from such concerns is a regulative ideal that we can design institutions to try to honor. (Someone who normatively dislikes science or its effects might think that we shouldn't design such institutions; but that is a different claim.) The basic institutional mechanism we have built in pursuit of this ideal is the system of anonymous peer-review guardianship against attempts to add new evidence and claims about theoretical justification to the record of scientific literature.

Linked to this basic institutional mechanism is a secondary, but very important, additional one. Scientists, famously, use a lot of mathematics, at least in many disciplines (including both cognitive science and economics). Much of this is simply statistics, and derives from the importance of exact measurement. But that is not the whole story. Natural languages and the distinctions they draw are evolutionary products shaped by the interaction of cultural and genetic selection. They therefore encode, in deeply embedded and mutually reinforcing levels, distinctions important to *folk theories*—that is, the nonscientific social-cognitive structures that organize relationships important to special human purposes. Mathematical language is quite different, and this reflects differences between the nature of mathematical and of practical reasoning. Mathematical reasoning begins from sets of rigorously fixed procedural concepts, and these fixed points then have absolute authority, relative to special purposes in application, over what can and cannot be stated in the language. If we suspect there may be some particular structural fact but cannot figure out how to express it mathematically, this does not show that there is no such fact; but it implies that we must do some more work, either logical or empirical or both, before we can say that we are quite sure just what the putative structural fact is that we are trying to claim.

This feature of science implies some real constraints on what can and cannot count as a system in the sense I will intend here. For something to be a system in this sense, the internal and external causal relationships it encodes must be measurable in principle by some *explicitly conceived*, physically possible (hence finite) measuring apparatus, where "explicit conception" means: describable in a mathematical language sufficiently abstract from natural language that the description could be used as a blueprint for (relatively) faithfully building the apparatus by anyone fluent in the language. Notice that this does not say: describable in literally and purely *formal* language; I am not trying to avow logical positivism here. The idea is more modest than that. It is merely that our best test of the clarity of any attempt at communicating information lies in the extent to which the recipient of such information can go on to *do* something she could not do without it. In science, the primary extracommunicative activity is the development of protocols for measuring causal capacities[11] that produce agreement from one occasion of measurement to another. Insofar, then, as people embedded in different cultures can swap recipes for measuring such capacities, and verify the effectiveness of such information transfers by achieving shared abilities to move bits of the world around, they can have the satisfaction of getting evidence that they are communicating at least some noise-free information.

This view would be hard to distinguish from positivism if, like the positivists, we were subjectivists about meaning. However, following the *semantic externalism* that has become a nearly universal doctrine among philosophers of mind these days, and which I will explain in the next chapter, I maintain that people's abilities to know that they are communicating relatively noise-free information to themselves is parasitic on their abilities to know that they are communicating relatively noiselessly to others.[12] If one now adds that intersubjective agreement is the best—perhaps, ultimately, even the only—test of objectivity there is, then the grounds for the importance of mathematical expressibility in achieving systematic description should be clear.

This constraint on what can be regarded as a system is an operational principle of epistemological caution, not a statement of some metaphysical idea about "the world being mathematical." (I don't understand what putative facts of that sort are really supposed to mean in the first place; perhaps Plato scholars understand.) However, it imposes practically important restrictions on what does and doesn't count as a scientific idea. For example, many social scientists talk quite a lot about systems of power relations. Now, I don't doubt that talk about social power is useful and important. We need to be able to say that Stalin craved power, that white South Africans have demographically disproportionate economic power relative to black South Africans, and so forth. These claims are true, in the context of systems (real, measurable systems) of *discourse* relative to important human purposes. But whereas I'm sure that systems of communication are real systems, on which the sciences of information are getting an increasingly good grip, I have no idea whether systems of power relations are real systems, because no one has ever given us a comprehensive, explicitly conceived apparatus for measuring them and their causal consequences. (Bargaining power, as modeled by game theorists, is a more restricted idea than the sociologist's "power" concept.) This might yet happen. But I want to say that, for now, social science that takes power relations to be fundamental structures isn't systematic.

What is supposed to be the point of this quibbling over what is and isn't "systematic"? I am not trying to say that everything nonsystematic is useless, or less useful than what I call systematic, or that social scientists who talk about irreducible power relations should necessarily be accorded less prestige and money than physicists. I am (here) just trying to mark a distinction, one central to the purposes of this book. I can best indicate its import by turning again to my foil, Dupré.

Dupré is hostile to evolutionary cognitive science and economics, especially in conjunction, because he is hostile to the general project of trying to provide systematic (in my sense above) accounts of human behavior. This point is more subtle than it might look. Dupré would not object (given what he says) to systematic accounts of *aspects* of human behavior, so long as such accounts are not deliberately unified in such a way that they comprehensively contradict our general, folk understandings of that behavior, as driven by special human purposes. The use of "unified" and "comprehensively" here is crucial. So long as we merely systematized aspects of behavior piecemeal, we could not be claiming priority over folk doctrines of self-understanding whose whole point is logical unity under general, rule-of-thumb, useful concepts. Piecemeal systematization might incrementally change such self-understandings, in inherently unpredictable ways, but Dupré doesn't say that he has a problem with this. (I suspect that many who find his sort of perspective attractive *do* fear and dislike such change, however.) What Dupré objects to are deliberate, philosophically motivated attempts to construct overarching systematizations of behavior *for the sake of* revisionist unification. He calls this "imperialism"; and he argues that such imperialism represents misguided metaphysics, dodgy science, and ethically nasty politics, all at once. Anyone who has spent much time among humanists will know that this set of claims finds many sympathizers.

As noted above, the two bodies of scientific activity indicted by Dupré as the (currently) most dangerous vehicles of imperialism are evolutionary cognitive science and neoclassical economics. They are most dangerous of all, he thinks, when they combine forces, since neither can plausibly claim, all by itself, to be the basis for a truly universal empire. Together, however, they can entertain a pretense of true hegemony; or so Dupré fears. This is his broad reason for regarding what Mirowski calls Dennett's idea as "dangerous." (Mirowski's main reason, although related to this, is, as we've seen, more specifically centered in worries about violence to the concept of the human self.)

Dupré's own case for the conjunctive power of cognitive science and economics is relatively brief and impressionistic. It rests mainly on the fact that evolutionary cognitive science and neoclassical economics share a debunking attitude to the humanistic self-image as it depicts social motivation and the value of moral willpower, and that they similarly express this attitude in the technical language of a restricted optimization calculus, in which predicates denoting moral evaluation play no proper or direct roles. Economists, classically, treat agents as found bundles of preferences that relentlessly optimize as best they can, subject to the limitations imposed by their own information-processing and energy constraints, and to external constraints imposed by their environments (including the optimizing efforts of other agents). The enterprise of filling in the details of this vision, however, falls short of the full imperialist's reach because economists have traditionally forced themselves into professional silence on the question of how these bundles of found preferences arise in the first place. Furthermore, economists typically treat the machinery that carries out the derivation of behavioral policies from preferences and optimization schemes as housed inside black boxes (according to Mirowski, black boxes with impossible internal mechanisms); so here lies another check on the limitlessness of their imperialism. But if the economist therefore admits that she can't rule the world of behavioral explanation alone, evolutionary cognitive science may furnish just the partner she needs to reign as half of a duopoly. For evolutionary cognitive scientists claim to have found a single family of explanatory schemata for handling just those regions the economist can't conquer. That is, they will tell us how patterns of preference arise, and "how the mind works" (Pinker 1997). And they aim to do so using the very logic of optimization, here in the context of evolution's running fitness tournaments, by which the economist lives and breathes.

The foregoing is a persuasive first impression of the hegemony. In this book, I am going to argue that it is broadly correct. However, I begin from the premise that we have no hope of accurately evaluating its promises or threats, epistemic or moral, until and unless we get the details of its tactics right. The broad conception sketched above leaves room for a plethora of internal disagreements and tensions, with which many particular resolutions and reconcilations are logically compatible. Which path we choose through this labyrinth of possible systems is not just important to the plausibility and desirability of the general imperialistic partnership—it is everything. Some of the logically possible paths fail epistemically, others may indeed blind us to possibilities for improving the human condition that are not actually closed, and still others disappoint on both counts. This is why it is possible for Dupré to see the imperial legions coming, just as I do, but to then think that they had best be fought, whereas I'm inclined to celebrate their coming arrival. (Mirowski, it seems, prefers to laugh at them, since he expects them to self-destruct.)

In this study, I will defer overarching evaluation of the partnership between economics and evolutionary cognitive science until my account of how it might best work is well along in development. The full positive assessment thus happens only at the end of the second volume, though its opening sketch will be seen near the end of the present volume. So it is going to be a long wait before full answers to Dupré and Mirowski are on the table. However, I hope that there is plenty to sustain interest along the way in terms of light that will be shed on philosophical problems internal to the two enterprises this book brings together.

Before I shift my foils toward the back of the stage for awhile, let me say something about preferences over figurative tropes. In accepting Dupré's metaphor of imperialism over the last few paragraphs, I have deliberately been talking a bit playfully and ironically. The reverse gestalt in which to view the same phenomenon is based in the concept of *cosmopolitanism*. For many people, this is just as much an ideal as its reversing image, imperialism, is a thing to be feared and resisted. Systems are bad—they are imperialisms—when their main effect and sustaining motivation is the exclusion of otherwise viable and productive alternatives. But systems can also be liberating when they lift us out of mutually excluding pits of confusion into which groups of us have separately fallen, when they show us how problems that have no evident solutions taken one by one find productive recourse when seen as expressions of more fundamental and common challenges. The ultimate aim of this book is to promote such a cosmopolitan basis for progress in our understanding of behavior.

I have spun the account to come as an updating and defense of neoclassicism in the light of cognitive science. Many economists are likely to find this distinctly eccentric, in that the picture that will emerge by the end of this volume will look strikingly different from the one usually associated with neoclassicism, and will jettison a number of theses to which neoclassicists are widely regarded as committed. I will reject the idea that individual people are (in general) rational maximizers of expected utility. I will, indeed, reject individualism, both methodological and ontological, altogether. People will not be depicted as generally selfish. Evolutionary dynamics will be accorded far more weight as a causal determinant of economic behavior than deliberate, rational calculation of plans going on in the heads of economic agents. All of this will sound exactly like the sort of program presented by current advocates of "behavioral" and "evolutionary" economics (e.g., Bowles 2003) as being the essence of *anti*-neoclassicism. So surely I am just being perverse in selling my argument as a vindication of neoclassicism. Or perhaps, even worse, I just want to pretend that I am on the side of the people with the big guns—or the big grants—while actually co-opting all the theses of the more honest rebels.

The philosophical attitude I have explained in this section provides the key to understanding my apparently odd rhetorical preferences. As I will explain in detail throughout the book, the currently justified enthusiasm for new experimental, behavioral and evolutionary approaches in economics—the very enthusiasm that brings economic theory into natural alliance with cognitive science—seems to be revolutionary for two reasons. First, it tends to be sold by comparative reference to a picture of neoclassicism that is a historical caricature. Second, to the extent that the caricature isn't persuasive to thoughtful economists, the current "paradigm shift" is often associated with rhetoric that denies the importance of systematicity. That is, there is a tendency for new behavioral economists to suggest, either deliberately or in philosophical innocence, hyperempiricist methodological principles, according to which the best new work simply piles up new facts about what people do in economic settings. To the extent that this polemically succeeds, it must ultimately undermine economics as a discipline, turning it into a branch of applied social psychology. That outcome really would represent a rejection of everything important in neoclassicism; but it is an outcome I will be giving arguments for resisting.

What's to come, therefore, is a defense of neoclassicism in two senses. First, I will offer a philosophical interpretation of the history of neoclassicism insofar as it relates to psychology—which is why this history is almost exclusively about neoclassical consumer theory—that combats the caricature. I will try to explain how neoclassicism (in the version I will call "mature") came to be associated with individualism; but I will give grounds for regarding this as based on a single philosophical error—taking people as the prototypical agents—that cognitive science more or less naturally corrects. Second, I will argue explicitly that the core neoclassical commitment to economics as the systematic science of maximization under scarcity comports *better* with the most sophisticated philosophy of cognitive science than does emphasis on unsystematic hyperempiricism.

In my historical treatment of neoclassicism in chapter 3, the most systematic of the neoclassical founding fathers, Leon Walras, receives little mention by comparison with his rather more muddled contemporary, W. S. Jevons. This is just because this is a book about economics and cognitive science, and Jevons is much more responsible than Walras for economic theorists' attitudes to psychology over the years. But it will help to substantiate my choice of neoclassical colors for the team shirt to point out briefly how closely the philosophical starting principles I have outlined in this section echo those articulated by Walras.

Walras devotes the opening four chapters ("lessons") of his *Elements of Pure Economics* (1874/1954) to themes in the philosophy of science. Here is what he does there. First, he criticizes conceptions of the scope of economics given by Smith and Say as appropriate to practical and normative enterprises but not to a systematic science. I will echo and expand on this point in chapter 3. Then he distinguishes between "sciences," "arts," and "ethical inquiries," the scheme I have basically defended in this section using more contemporary jargon. In drawing the distinction between sciences and ethical inquiries, he insists on a prior distinction, taken to be even more fundamental, between the study of relationships among rational agents and things (parametric relations, in contemporary terms) and among rational agents and other rational agents (nonparametric relations). This distinction, and the philosophical use to which it is put, will also find updated expression and emphasis here, when in chapter 8 I discuss the differences between the economic modeling of brains and the economic modeling of human selves, and the way in which this distinction preserves an essential role for the concept of rationality even within a resolutely naturalistic world view. Finally, Walras defends the efficacy of a "pure" theoretical typology for economics that avoids tethering itself to folk terminologies or intuitions about people and societies, and that grounds its concepts in mathematical analysis. These preferences will also find strong advocacy in this book.

It is now fashionable among the advocates of the behavioral, experimental, and evolutionary approach to economics to refer to their intellectual orientation as "post-Walrasian." For reasons that will now be clear, though I promote the importance to economic theory of behavioral evidence and evolutionary reasoning as wholeheartedly as any of them, I am not sympathetic to their labeling preference, or to the attitude to the history of economic theory it encourages.

Expository Strategy

Anyone writing an interdisciplinary book that advances a novel, polemical thesis (rather than being a bridge-building survey) faces delicate problems of audience location. Science is organized into disciplines partly for reasons of efficiency. Economists would not get as much economics done as we'd like if they were expected to be cognitive scientists as well, and vice versa. If I were aiming to reform economics by application of cognitive science, it would be obvious that I should first summarize the relevant cognitive science for economists, and then get to work using their conceptual framework and vocabulary. If my objective were instead to address cognitive scientists from the perspective of economic theory, then the reverse procedure would be appropriate. However, I'm attempting something more ambitious than either of those tasks, namely, trying to illuminate theories in *both* domains by reflecting on their borderlands. It might seem as if this aim would require first writing a primer on cognitive science for economists, then writing a primer on economic theory for cognitive scientists, and only after doing both of those things getting down to the main work. This, however, would entail my asking both groups for a level of upfront investment that would require so much faith in eventual payoffs as to be megalomaniacal on my part.

Fortunately, there is a third available disciplinary perspective from which I can try to address my two audiences. This discipline is the philosophy of science. Now, many economists and cognitive scientists will doubt that philosophers have earned any authority to talk usefully to them about either subject. I share the view, widespread among scientists, that philosophers often have a dubious tendency to try to reform science on the basis of supposed metaphysical and/or epistemological special insights that are in fact mixtures of arrogance, ignorance about real scientific practice, and failures of imagination. (See Ross and Spurrett 2004b for discussion of this [minor] social problem.) This, however, mainly just tells us something about the particular way in which work in philosophy of science, when it isn't very good, tends not to be very good. It remains the case that the very point of *good* philosophy of science is to examine the wider landscape of separated disciplinary silos in search of potentially unifying themes.

If all we wanted from science were enhanced capacities to predict and control our practical environment, unification of science might not matter. Indeed, to relentlessly pragmatic people, pursuit of philosophical unification often appears to be nuisance activity, raising concerns and proposing constraints that impede freewheeling empirical investigation. However, I submit that most people would be justifiably disappointed in a science that held out no hope of furnishing us with a general, albeit provisional and continuously revised, *world view*. I won't here try to mount an argument against the convinced pure pragmatist that she should feel otherwise. So a reader who genuinely doesn't care about whether, or how, the separate systems of knowledge provided by the various sciences might yield a sum greater than their parts should probably put this book down now; for such a reader, I doubt that the opportunity cost of the work ahead could be justified. However, I suggest to other readers, those who hope that science can tell us genuinely enlightening things about the nature of reality in general, that their hope is not forlorn if and only if it is actually possible for philosophy of science to be done responsibly. Gesturing at a list of some exemplary historical and contemporary practitioners—Aristotle, Hume, Reichenbach, Carnap, Michael Friedman, Wesley Salmon, Philip Kitcher—I insist that it is.

The key requirement that distinguishes responsible from annoying philosophy is that the philosopher must care primarily about facilitating the growth of scientific knowledge itself, rather than the promotion of this or that neat, preconceived philosophical "ism." Commitment to this order of priorities is the important common property of the philosophers I just listed, along with many others I risk insulting by arbitrarily and idiosyncratically not including them in the list. (They will, I hope, understand that a long list of philosophers' names would be an agonizing device with which to open a book.)

I will speak, then, to both economists and cognitive scientists as a philosopher. This suggests a general order of presentation. I will establish, in the next chapter, the specific philosophical setting from which the argument will be conducted, and thereafter outline the necessary economics to cognitive scientists, and the other way around, as I go along. Even with the preestablished superdisciplinary position at hand, however, this will still be a tricky and delicate business. The book would be too long and too recurrently dull for anyone to read if I tried to explain every potentially opaque economic concept for cognitive scientists, and vice versa, each time a new one had to be brought into the argument. On the other hand, neither economists nor cognitive scientists will find my argument persuasive if they each see, when watching me use the concepts on which they are experts, that I'm boiling out the subtlety of these concepts by resorting to cartoon simplifications of them. Faced with this tension, what I do in the chapters to follow amounts to a running series of implemented judgment calls. Sometimes I will talk mainly to economists and urge cognitive scientists to skim, asking them to trust my assurance that if some fiddly technical distinctions of economics will be left a bit opaque to them, nothing in the main logic of the argument will thereby be hidden. At other points I will ask economists to be casual tourists while cognitive scientists are being reassured that I'm not fudging important inside issues. I am, though, going to assume throughout, with confidence I know to be often justified, that both economists and cognitive scientists are smart people who can correctly infer a lot from contextual clues.

The chapters to follow will vary in their levels of accessibility to different groups of readers. So as to give everyone some warning about where their own zones of difficulty—and perhaps boredom—are to be expected, as well as promise of easier times ahead that might justify perseverance through the tough bits, here is a schematization of the chapter-by-chapter organization.

Chapter 2 provides all of the purely philosophical theory and terminology on which my subsequent argument will depend. Professional philosophers of mind and science will be able to skim it briskly, but all others are apt to find it a somewhat dismaying blizzard of special language. Unfortunately, the fact that folk concepts of people, mind, and action are not evolved for purposes of systematic inquiry makes the need for such terminology inevitable. I thus make no apology for it. I have tried to help nonphilosophical readers by putting each occurrence of a term that will be put to essential use later in the book in bold type. This device perhaps makes for ugly-looking pages, but it will permit a reader who can't remember the exact meaning of an obscure term when it's invoked later on to easily page back and find its role in the framework. I have not tried to define the terms in explicit bullets because I think that this causes more semantic distortion than not. Meaning is use, as Wittgenstein emphasized. That is why I have bolded *every* use (just in chapter 2) of the key philosophical terms, instead of just their first uses. But the chapter is self-contained in grounding the vocabulary in its pure philosophical home district, which is the appropriate point of reference when it travels out for application to economics and cognitive science.

Chapter 3 is about economic theory and its history. This, along with chapter 5, will be the most difficult part of the book for noneconomists. I doubt that any cognitive scientist or philosopher will handle the whole chapter with complete ease. However, I hope they will appreciate that I have had to make pragmatic trade-offs here between the good of interdisciplinary transparency and the evils of impossible length and continuous expository digressions. I certainly don't claim that this balance has been perfectly achieved. Economists will no doubt find some of the digressions I *have* allowed to be dull and unnecessary. Cognitive scientists and philosophers will sometimes be annoyed by how much work I am asking of them. If, as a result, *nobody* finds the pedagogy of the chapter ideal, I can only enter pleas about the compromises that come with cosmopolitanism.

Chapter 4 returns to philosophical argumentation. Both economists and cognitive scientists may find it a bit ponderous at times, and neither group is likely to find its arguments wholly convincing. However, they are not really supposed to be. I don't think that philosophy *by itself* can ever establish anything of empirical significance, and this book is about topics of science. Nevertheless, the chapter is essential, and everything that follows will be misunderstood by a reader who skips it. What philosophy *is* for is establishing clear conceptual frames. This book advances a highly unusual and tendentious view of economic theory and its relationships to its cognate disciplines. In doing so, it relies on an interconnected battery of novel conceptual distinctions. If these were not made carefully, and with reference to the historical context built up in chapter 3, my main theses will seem much wilder than I think they really are. Chapter 4 might thus leave many readers impatient, but it represents an upfront investment without which later returns just can't be had.

Chapter 5 returns to economics, but to behavioral, experimental, and evolutionary economics specifically. Here is where readers familiar with the leading current debates in theory, whatever their disciplinary orientation, will at last find familiar themes joined. A certain amount of technical vocabulary from economics will arise here, and readers who are not experimental economists or game theorists might find it useful to have a copy of Thaler's *The Winner's Curse* (1992) and Dixit and Skeath's *Games of Strategy* (1999) at hand for reference.

Chapters 6, 7, and 8 apply theses from the philosophy of cognitive science to the range of foundational problems for economic theory that have been gathered by the end of chapter 5. From the beginning of chapter 6 through to the end there is no more purely conceptual material that makes differential demands on different groups of readers. These chapters are the argumentative heart of the book. Here is where everybody's investments in the earlier chapters is supposed to pay off. It is where I hope that economists will encounter a genuinely new way of thinking about the implications of evolutionary cognitive science for their conception of their subject, and where cognitive scientists and philosophers will find a new testing site—analysis of economic behavior—for a perspective on cognitive-scientific explanation with which most will have been antecedently familiar.

The brief chapter 9 aims for symmetry by returning explicitly to my two foils from the present chapter, and presenting the book's general conclusion by comparison with their views. It does so in a way that looks forward to the second volume of the study, in which the account is completed by relating macroeconomics to the cognitive and behavioral sciences of the social.

What lies ahead is thus a long road, with some difficult slogging right at the beginning for most readers. I hope that they will find this justified by the interest of the places we're going to, and the unusual synthetic view we'll be taking of them.

2 Philosophical Primer: Intentional-Stance Functionalism and Real Patterns

Intentionality

As indicated in the previous chapter, Mirowski associates consequences with Dennett's views on evolution and the self that I deny it has. I will diagnose our disagreement by reference to the actual implications of Dennett's theory of **intentionality**, a subject of primary concern to philosophers that Mirowski doesn't discuss. Dupré is a philosopher, who has himself written (1993) on intentionality; yet he shares Mirowski's view. I think this is because he has a mistaken theory about a second philosophers' subject, **mereology**. (In particular, I think that he wrongly conflates unification and reduction.) I will discuss each of these topics in turn. They are closely related to each other, so while each will have a section named after it, the seam between the discussions won't be crisp and neat.

Dennett has produced separable but entangled theories of **intentionality** and consciousness. These theories are each partly philosophical analyses of the concepts, and partly empirical, Darwinian accounts of how such phenomena can arise in the natural world. The theories of **intentionality** and consciousness are used to generate a theory of **intentional** behavior, or, in the jargon more directly associated with economics, of *agency*. All of this then forms the logical background to a series of empirical hypotheses about which sorts of agents have *selves*. A distinctive aspect of Dennett's general philosophical view is that although agency is a very widespread phenomenon in nature, extending far more broadly than the domain of human action, agents-with-selves form a distinctive, numerically small, and unusual subclass: approximately, the subclass is made up of cognitively typical, non-infant individuals of the species *H. sapiens*. Furthermore, agents-with-selves can themselves be participants in larger patterns of selfless agency of which they may or may not be aware, and are also themselves patterns of interaction among yet other selfless agents of which they are usually not aware. The relevance of the topic of **mereology** enters into all this in that the relationships among these different strata of agency are not, as one might expect, relations of interlevel reduction or decomposition.

The above paragraph is a compact outline of the background conceptual package that will be used in this volume and its successor. It is not all due just to Dennett; furthermore no specific claim should be presumed to be endorsed as part of my argument just because Dennett said it somewhere. When I borrow a claim or argument specifically from Dennett, as from anyone else, I will say so. Nevertheless, it is appropriate to call the package in general "Dennettian" because, as a recent collection of papers (Brook and Ross 2002) attests, it has expressed itself not just within philosophy through Dennett's influence on debates there, but has been put to work across the cognitive sciences—especially in AI, ethology, consciousness studies, and developmental and personality psychology—as a result of the fact that Dennett has been more directly influential on methodology in these fields than any other philosopher. I will make further, more specific, comments on paths of influence parenthetically as the discussion moves along.

What I'm calling "the Dennettian package" is, as noted, a dense weave of conceptual and empirical theses. In accordance with the philosophical naturalism promoted most directly by W. V. O. Quine in the 1950s and 1960s, and presumed by Dennett and by me, any attempt to strictly separate the conceptual and the empirical elements would be arbitrary; an important aspect of empirical science is conceptual clarification, and any philosophical thesis of interest to a naturalist had better have some specific empirical consequences. Nevertheless, what has been chosen for inclusion in this chapter is based on a rough-and-ready separation of more purely philosophical material from that which is located substantially in cognitive science. This chapter will therefore not discuss the Dennettian views of consciousness, selfhood, or agency, no one of which can adequately be treated by a narrowly philosophical approach. What the reader should expect in this chapter are introductions to some conceptual tools forged in the workshop of philosophical argument.

Outside the precincts of professional philosophy, to say that a bit of behavior is **intentional** is to say that an agent engaged in it for a reason, and that the reason in question was *her* reason. We will not be able to use the concept of **intentionality** this loosely here, because resolution of various ambiguities, reifications, and equivocations in everyday notions of agency, reasons, and reasons-to-and-of-subjects are all going to be needed at later stages of the book. Philosophers analyze **intentionality** as a technical, noneveryday notion by initially focusing on a diagnostic feature of it, namely, that the domain of the **intentional** is coextensive with the domain in which explanations and predictions appeal to beliefs, desires, and other so-called **propositional attitudes**.[1] This terminology expresses the point that to attribute to a subject a belief or desire that x (some particular proposition) is to claim that the subject represents some state of affairs x, and stands in a particular attitudinal relation to x, namely, the attitude of believing or desiring that x.

For example, one might explain or predict a delivery person's leaving a package outside the front gate, instead of on the doorstep, by saying "She believes that the dog is vicious; and she doesn't want (desire) to get bitten." Or, to use a polemically important example due to Dennett, one might explain a chess-playing computer's move by saying "It wants to get its queen out early, and believes that if it now advances this pawn it will then be able to move the queen." To predict the behavior of the machine, one must ascribe to it a standing desire to play winning chess, plus some further beliefs about chess rules, good strategies, and the probable reactions of opponents. The practice of explaining and predicting behaviors and/or states of systems by invoking interacting networks of beliefs and desires is often referred to by philosophers as "folk psychology," which is typically modeled as a theory or theory analogue. That is, we can try to summarize folk psychology as implicitly deploying theoretical generalizations of the following sort: if a person *desires* outcome x, and *believes* that doing y is a good way to bring about x, and *fears* no other consequences of doing y to an extent that outweighs the desirability of x, and *believes* that she can do y, then she will do y.

It has often been suggested, by both philosophers and economists, that the axioms of microeconomics are necessarily elaborated versions of folk-psychological generalizations of this kind. The neoclassical economist's "preferences" look like technical regimentations of "desires," and her "expectations" seem to be beliefs with explicit probability values attached (Rosenberg 1992). And it should just be obvious that the scientific status of generalizations over beliefs and desires must be an important background issue in cognitive science, insofar as psychology is one of its core disciplines. Readers should thus not be surprised that arguments about intentionality will play an important role in a book about economics and cognitive science.

Now, to the explicit Dennettian position on **intentionality**. Many people, including many philosophers, think that in the case of the chess-playing computer above, the assumption that the machine has beliefs and desires is just a practical pretense, like assuming that the actor in a film really does fear being eaten by the surrounding aliens. The pretenses might be necessary in both cases—you can't enjoy the film if you insist on reminding yourself that the actor is in no danger, and you can't predict what the computer will do if you don't treat it like a real chess player—but, one might think, to take either pretense too literally would be to lose touch with reality. In the case of the computer, this view is closely related to the conviction that the machine lacks introspective consciousness, and that "real" **intentionality** is inextricably associated with such consciousness. In particular, supposing that explicit consciousness by an agent of a belief or desire is crucially associated with its being **intentional** is one very traditional and common way of starting to unpack the folk idea that an **intentional** reason must be the agent's "own" reason. However, Dennett rejects this entire approach, arguing that, if the chess-playing computer is complicated enough, we can and should truthfully and nonmetaphorically attribute **intentionality** to it. (In his language, we should "take the intentional stance" toward it.) He recognizes that this claim will seem incredible in the absence of some surprising but persuasive analyses of the concept of consciousness as well as **intentionality** itself. His main career project has thus been the development of complementary theories of these two concepts.

It will likely startle economists to be told that understanding main disputes in the foundations of their discipline requires attention to implicit assumptions about the nature of consciousness. If any subjects are none of their proper business, they might suppose, this is surely one of them. However, as we will see in detail in later chapters, unearthing unexamined assumptions about consciousness, and their influence on conceptions of personhood and agency, turns out to be the key that unlocks the door to a host of puzzles in the history of theoretical and methodological controversies in economics. Perhaps this will seem less surprising if I add a pair of rhetorical questions here. Where would one think of looking for such a key *except* among unexamined assumptions? And would assumptions more likely go unexamined with respect to a subject economists *did* often regard as their business?

Though philosophers can claim to be the experts on highly abstract concepts like intentionality, it would not be reasonable for them to say this about consciousness. Here, it will surely be agreed, carefully theorized empirical science must ultimately supply most of the facts. In developing any potentially satisfying theory of consciousness, therefore, we must pass gradually from the domain of philosophy to that of cognitive science. This is why, as I said above, I will defer consideration of issues about consciousness until chapter 6.

For now, the focus remains on **intentionality**, and on the background to Dennett's theory of it. The main context for this background is the history of attempts to understand the place of mind in nature. Most philosophers prior to the twentieth century believed that minds were nonphysical entities of one sort or another. On this view, beliefs and desires could be thought of as real states of "mental spirit." However, as mind–body dualism began to be rejected by philosophers and psychologists, it seemed necessary to replace the dualist's spiritual states by physical ones. One obvious possible idea here is that every particular **intentional** state—that is, every particular **propositional-attitude** state or "mental state"—might be identical with a particular brain state, directly identifiable and describable in the language of neuroscience. A stronger extrapolation of this idea, one that would more directly facilitate the unification of folk psychology with scientific theory, would be an ambition to map each *type* of **intentional** state onto a *type* of neuroscientific state. This hope has always faced some prior logical and conceptual difficulties. How could a kind of brain state be "about" an indefinite class of objects, say, "orange things," or, perhaps worse, an indefinite class of abstract objects, say, "democratic countries"? After all, nothing in a brain is orange; and it seems prima facie absurd to suppose that the brain's available array of potential coding vehicles—synaptic potentials, neuroreceptors, and chemicals—could directly symbolically represent the constituent aspects and internal structural relations of the concept of "democracy," the meaning of which is socially controlled, and which lacks clear boundary conditions. (To see the point of this worry: could it possibly make sense to try to find out what "democracy" *means* by studying people's *brains*?) Moreover, people, who have gotten on quite well explaining and understanding each other in **intentional** terms for millennia, do not (generally) directly observe brain states, including their own.

In 1949, the philosopher Gilbert Ryle sought to resolve this impasse by arguing that the concept of mind and all the mental subconcepts that flesh it out, including the **intentional** concepts, are constructs out of observable patterns in behavior. The mental states that we think we directly perceive as inner states in our own cases are in fact, according to Ryle, *judgments* about our behavioral dispositions, at which we are so efficient, and which are so natural, that they feel like inner perceptions. This so-called logical behaviorism was naturally interpreted, in the 1950s, as the appropriate philosophical partner to the operational behaviorism then dominant in psychology—and, as we will discuss in the next chapter, then being promoted in economics by Samuelson. One of Ryle's foremost students was Dennett. One way of understanding Dennett's career is as showing how to reconcile the core insight of logical behaviorism with the idea that the mind is a kind of information processor. Mirowski should be smiling here, for it seems we have a perfect exemplification of his theme: another attempt, this time in the heartland of analytic philosophy, to preserve a principle dear to the intuitions of neoclassical economics under pressure from the cyborg sciences. As we'll see later, however, I part from Mirowski by believing that this attempt has been a success.

Staying with Mirowski's principle for plotting the narrative: the campaign of the cyborgs in philosophy was expressed by the doctrine known as **functionalism**. Around the time (1969) that Dennett published his first book, **functionalism** was battering away at the view that types of **intentional** states could be identical to types of brain states. If mind-brain identity theory were true, the **functionalists** argued, then no two creatures with significantly different brains could, *by definition*, ever share the same belief—for example, that two and two are four. This objection is less vague and more direct than the traditional concerns mentioned above over our imaginative problems with seeing neural elements as direct symbolic vehicles. Surely it cannot be a *conceptual* truth that dolphins, or any possible aliens—or cyborgs—could not grasp the proposition that "$2 + 2 = 4$" unless they had just the same types of neural states as people. (Why couldn't a brain be made of silicon instead of protoplasm?) The **propositional content** of a given belief, the **functionalists** argued, must be a function of that belief's role in a general network of intentional states. Similarly with words: the meaning of "democracy" is a function of the *uses* that are made of it in whole conceptual systems (which of course vary somewhat among different communities of users). It helps in grasping this point to ask another rhetorical question: could anyone be said to have mastery of the concept "democracy" if they had *no* conception at all of autocracy or oligarchy?[2]

The great philosophical issue for the **functionalists** has been the problem of **representation**. The extraordinary property of **propositional attitudes**, indeed of mental states generally, is that they are somehow "about" states of affairs in the world. The main task of an adequate philosophy of mind, it has been generally assumed, is to explain what this "aboutness"—which philosophers just call by the word "**intentionality**" itself—amounts to. Such an analysis, to be satisfying, must comport with a plausible empirical story about how it arises in the natural world. In the early **functionalist** accounts, it was usually taken for granted that the problem of representation needed to be addressed against a background assumption of so-called **internalism**. How could networks of interacting entities, of whatever possible sort, be bearers of intentional meaning unless their constituent entities were themselves invested with symbolic content independently of their contexts at some basic level? If mental states play a causally significant role in behavior—that is, if bodies sometimes do things because minds desire them to, under some description meaningful to themselves—then how can this work unless some basic *representational* (semantic, meaning-bestowing) properties of internal states are intrinsic to some of their physical states? How can *any* states have causal powers *because* of their intentional properties, unless those properties are identical with some physical properties after all (Kim 1998)? The denial of dualism just *is* the thesis that there are no superphysical causes, that is, that physics is causally complete. The thesis of **internalism** is the view that because **intentional** properties must be lawfully attached (by some specific relation or other) to some physical properties if they are to do causal work, and because physical properties must have context-independent identity conditions, at least some core **representational** states must have the meanings they do by virtue of conditions strictly **internal** to the psychological dynamics of thinking agents, invariant under changes of outside environmental (including social) circumstances. Before we move on, carefully note two facts about **internalism**: (i) its underlying rationale relies on metaphysical atomism about physical causation; and (ii) it is straightforwardly incompatible with logical behaviorism.

The integration of work in AI with cognitive science more generally during the 1970s provided a stimulating focus for the problem. (The Mirowski story continues: cyborgs to the rescue.) When we build computers (of the conventional, symbol-processing, kind), we make machines that seem to produce regular physical behavior, meaningful as the execution of tasks, by virtue of the relations among their atomic electronic states. How this works isn't mysterious: computers are controlled by programs designed to model relationships among internal and external conditions in networks of electronic *syntactic* states that are only individually symbolic *in virtue of* the isomorphisms captured in the overall **functional** relations that describe input-output transitions at the system level. In a series of classic papers (most gathered together in Putnam 1975) Hilary Putnam argued that we can solve the problem of **intentionality** by understanding minds as programs. The key test passed by this proposal, Putnam argued, is that it handles the specific problem of the *multiple realizability* of **intentional** states mentioned above. That is, we can understand how two systems with different sorts of physical constitution—for example, a human brain and a unit of cyborg executive hardware—could share common **intentional** states if we recognize that they implement the same network of functional isomorphisms: they run the same syntactic program.

Putnam's specific version of computational **functionalism**, known as "Turing-machine functionalism," was soon exposed to a battery of criticisms based on empirical work in both AI and neuroscience. Biological brains are unlike electronic computers in being massively parallel processors, rather than hierarchically stacked, serial executors of condition-action specifications. Their state transitions are better modeled as vector transformations across multidimensional coding spaces, rather than digital, symbol-by-symbol, replacements of syntactic atoms. (See Churchland 1995 for a polemical survey.) These empirically guided modifications since the 1970s to Putnam's thesis that minds are programs are not just technical fiddles, since they are of direct relevance to the kind of agent that a real biological system could implement. (Mirowski smiles yet again.) However, they do not necessarily impugn the core idea of explaining **intentionality** by reference to functional isomorphisms between patterns of brain states and networks of physical-causal regularities in environments—that is, to understanding minds as programs, under a suitably catholic interpretation of "program." This core idea is what **functionalism** has come to denote among philosophers; and **functionalism**, so construed, remains the dominant working hypothesis in the philosophy of mind.

I noted earlier that a satisfying analysis of **intentionality** must be stapled to a plausible empirical hypothesis about the natural origins of meaning. In presenting Putnam's answer to the problem of representation, I bypassed a question that will have occurred to many readers, including novices to the issues. I noted that we have no practical difficulty—indeed, find essential practical utility—in attributing intentional meaning to global state transitions, and to some local state transitions,[3] of our designed computational devices. However, it has been objected from the early days of the functionalist tradition, but most directly and famously by Searle (1980), that this fact cannot explain **intentionality** because our attribution of intentional meaning to states of artifacts is parasitic on the fact that we are already intentional interpreters. Our machines themselves know nothing of such interpretation, and in this crucial respect they are not models of us. Their **intentionality**, the objection says, is derivative of our own. But an explanation of **intentionality** must tell us how it arises in the first place, not how it can be modeled once we already have it in the world. Thus, the objection concludes, we do not explain what minds are by regarding them as programs.

In my view, the essential first step in answering this objection is due to Dennett (1987, chapter 8). Natural selection, like a human engineer, *is* a designer, though it differs from the engineer in having no foresight. Darwin's work transformed our understanding of all biological processes precisely *because* it showed us how mindless processes can build functional machines—eyes, lungs, and intentional systems alike. Natural programs—minds—evolved under selection pressure because, in environments subject to unpredictable changes in parameters important to the maintenance of complex living systems, the strategic flexibility and learning made possible by intentional representation is a frequently effective adaptation. There are of course widespread instances of alternative adaptive strategies: clams build fortresses good against most intrusive fluctuations; insects and fish constantly flood the environment with waves of copies so that even though most perish, enough reproduce by good luck to keep the genotype going; and so on. However, if it is accepted that natural selection, given world enough and time, can build highly complex, integrated adaptive machines, there is no *principled* reason it cannot build computers along with cameras and oxygen pumps.

Many philosophers (e.g., Fodor 1996) think that this response misses the crux of the problem. If we are natural computers and that's all there is to be said, they object, then the intentional meaning we seem to find in our own states is just a kind of illusion. We imagine that some state of ourselves means "There's an elephant in the road"; but, on Dennett's story, it seems that no state of ours could really mean anything more specific than what states of this type evolved to mean. Furthermore, the meanings of states can no longer be thought to be intrinsic; they must instead just be attributed by interpreters. Since natural selection itself has no intentions, there is no natural fact of the matter as to whether the meaning of the state in question is "There's an elephant in the road," or "There's a big animal in the road," or "There's a large, dangerous obstacle in the road I can't move" *if* these interpretations are all equally relevant to control of behavior for optimization of expected biological fitness. (The reader will see that these variations just scratch the surface by performing a similar exercise on the possible informational parsings of "road.") What we want a theory of intentionality to do, the objection continues, is be able to differentiate one state from another as finely as our actual, semantically nuanced, thought allows; anything less has missed the point of our philosophical question. A story that tells us how, in general, we manage to avoid large, dangerous objects doesn't tell us anything about how a thought can be about, exactly, elephants, or about an individual as an elephant. Furthermore, it seems to make **intentionality** epiphenomenal, (that is, incapable of doing causal work in a physical world) since, in denying that meanings attach intrinsically to some physical, context-independent states of systems, it violates **internalism**.

Of course, Dennett's theory is *supposed to* violate internalism. It has to if it is to ground an understanding of **intentionality** that is compatible with logical behaviorism, as I pointed out. Dennett's so-called **intentional-stance functionalism** answers Searle's objection by turning its starting premise on its head: instead of explaining how cyborgs can have intentional states like people do by figuring out some way in which their intentions could be intrinsic to their internal states, we set out to explain how our intentional states could be merely attributed by interpreters, just like those of cyborgs. Now Mirowski is pleased as pie. Sure enough, it seems, Dennett's dangerous idea rests on the assumption that people are literally cyborgs. The annihilation of the self surely can't be far behind, if it hasn't happened by implication already—no?

I want to pause for a moment here to address again those economists who think that Mirowski's "cyborg history" of postwar economics is crazy. I will be arguing in this book, in a much more traditional and less racy way than he does, that his core insight is correct in one sense: the question of whether people are (sophisticated, complex) machines is central to any attempt to understand and try to justify contemporary economic theory. I don't ask the skeptical economist, who is, by assumption here, unpersuaded by Mirowski, to accept this on the basis of my declaration. How and why I think the claim is true is something that will, perforce, emerge only gradually. However, let me start by setting it in its philosophical context as follows. The **internalist's** objection to traditional **functionalism** is logically valid: if **functionalism** depends on finding intrinsic, context-independent **intentional** meaning in atomic physical states, then **functionalism** must fail because the idea of an intrinsically meaningful physical state is entirely mysterious. Indeed, Dennett's crucial claim (see again his 1987, chapter 8) is that the idea of an intrinsically meaningful state in general is necessarily and hopelessly mysterious. The great challenge that his **intentional-stance functionalism** has faced is to explain—not, contra Mirowski, to dissolve—consciousness and the self without an appeal to intrinsic meaning. For reasons that will emerge, I believe Dennett has (with, as he once put it, a little help from his friends) risen to both challenges.

We will see in chapter 5 that contemporary currents of lively theoretical debate among some leading economists are in fact wrestling with the same challenge that Dennett has faced, though they have arrived at it by a different path and state it in terms that obscure the logical connection. This will constitute additional evidence for the validity of Mirowski's perspective. Economists, we will see, have lately been drifting into an internal debate between a traditional humanistic conception of the agent that presupposes **internalism**, and the other possible response (that is, other than **intentional-stance functionalism**) to the failure of **internalism** that has been articulated by philosophers. This is the position known as **eliminative materialism**, or just **eliminativism** for short. This thesis, to put it as briskly as possible, is the view that there are no such things as propositional attitudes after all. I will be showing, in chapters 4 and 5, that these generic options in the philosophy of **intentionality** express themselves quite exactly in current rival programs among economists for understanding what economics is about. **Eliminativism** *is* a metaphysic that shatters the self in the way Mirowski worries about, so a possible future for economics that is "dangerous" in his sense really might be on the cards. It is because Mirowski makes no acknowledgement of the difference between **eliminativism** and **intentional-stance functionalism** that he mistakenly associates Dennett (and Binmore, and evolutionary game theory) with his "dangerous" future. Unlike Mirowski, I have no normative commitment to humanism, which is why I've been putting scare quotes around "dangerous" here. However, I'll ultimately argue that, as a matter of fact, **eliminativism** won't work to legitimatize an economic science, but Dennett's theory will. Mirowski and other humanists will thereby be given reasons for breathing easier.

The logic of my approach will thus involve presenting the economic theorist with a choice between underlying philosophies of **intentional-stance functionalism** and **eliminativism**, and then tracing out the consequences of each choice for economic analysis. This choice is forced only on the assumption that an **internalist** account of **intentionality** won't work. Explaining why **internalism** fails is important for an additional reason: current defenses of humanism in economics rely on **internalism**, as we'll see in detail in chapter 4. Finally, the critique of **internalism** will play a necessary background role to my showing, in chapter 6, why Dennett's dangerous idea is incompatible with individualism, contrary to Mirowski's understanding. Here, then, we have an exercise in philosophical explanation that needs to be done up front.

So: what is wrong with **internalism** about **intentional** content? As noted above, the atomistic tradition in modern scientific metaphysics has encouraged the idea that the meanings of sentences and longer vehicles of content must be composed out of meanings of basic constituents and relations among them—words, for example, in the case of sentences. In the context of the contemporary philosophy of cognitive science, this idea was given a new twist. If individual thoughts can be causally efficacious in virtue of their meaning, it has been argued, then an individual brain event must contribute to the computational programs in which it functions as a syntactic token by virtue of some intrinsic properties it has, on which some systematic semantic properties lawfully "supervene."[4] To reiterate the basic argument, it depends fundamentally on the premise that a *causal* capacity must be intrinsic to the entity doing the causing. It follows from this that if intentions can cause behavior, it must be true that at least some semantic properties are what they are by virtue just of internal, psychological facts, depending in no way on external, environmental, context—in particular, on social facts. Otherwise, no intentional states could cause anything at all. Kim (1998) provides the clearest and most sustained defense of this argument.

Internalism thus defended is a metaphysical restriction on the individuating conditions for basic intentional properties. It becomes most directly relevant to behavioral science if it is taken to license a program of explanation in cognitive science that Fodor (1980) dubbed "**methodological solipsism.**"[5] This is an operational expression of **internalism.** If some brain states can be causally significant to behavior in virtue of their semantic properties, then we ought to be able, in principle, to identify these properties by studying that brain in isolation from its environment. In Fodor's favored version, the brain would be studied at the level of computational—that is, software—description, where we would look for syntactic (formal) properties sufficient to determine basic semantic properties. An alternative, more directly reductionist, version of **methodological solipsism** would suppose that we could determine semantic properties on the basis of neural properties— vector-transformational properties in connected synaptic regions, perhaps.

From the mid-1970s, **internalists** generally did not try to argue that *all* semantic properties must be internal. As a result of arguments given by Putnam (1975), and independently by Kripke (1972), it came to be generally accepted among philosophers of language that one aspect of linguistic meaning, reference, could not be determined entirely "in the head" of an individual speaker. At least, this was generally accepted with respect to proper names, and, more importantly for our purposes, the so-called "natural kind" terms supposedly important to science. The term "elm tree" refers to all and only the trees that have a certain genetic structure, and most speakers of English believe this. But most speakers have no idea what this genetic structure is, and can't even infer it from other properties of elms they can distinguish—that is, one can be a competent user of the term "elm" without being able to tell elms apart from, say, beeches. In that case, part of what determines the referential meaning of the term "elm" is stored socially—in the authority of botanists, on which we rely whenever picking out the elms matters for some purpose—rather than psychologically. Thus individual people can have beliefs that are *about* elms even though they don't know what elms exactly are, so long as, and just because, their community as a whole, so to speak, knows what elms are. No one who finds this argument persuasive can be a *total* **internalist,** and by 1980 or so most philosophers had come to accept some version of the argument.

Fodor (1987) attempted to hang on to **internalism** by detaching referential meaning from other semantic properties, and then holding that these other properties are the ones relevant to **intentional** causation of individual behavior. However, this position proved to be unstable. In a series of influential papers (especially his 1986), Tyler Burge extended some arguments originally traceable to Wittgenstein (1953) against semantic **internalism** *in general.* Wittgenstein had argued that the very idea of the correct use of a word depends on the existence of social rules, because in the absence of such rules an individual speaker wouldn't be able to judge, in general or on any specific occasion, whether she was applying one rule R with exceptions $E_1, \ldots, E_n$ or another rule R' with exceptions $E_1, \ldots, E_{n+1}$; only something external to the speaker's private standards of correctness can stabilize her judgments.[6] Burge's contribution is then to notice that this implies the extension of semantic **externalism** (the denial of **internalism**) to elements of language generally, and not just to names and terms referring to natural kinds. Then, insofar as the semantics of public language are relevant to determining the contents of **intentional** states—which they surely are because we individuate **intentional** states in the first place, including our own, by picking out their content using public language—**methodological solipsism** will be unviable in behavioral science generally, at least to the extent that semantically distinguished **intentions** are relevant to the explanation of behavior.[7] It is a rare argument that actually gives rise to near consensus among philosophers, but this turned out to be one of those unusual cases. Even Fodor (1994) finally abandoned **methodological solipsism**, and McClamrock (1995) gives general grounds for regarding it as a substantially dead thesis. (See in addition Ross 1997.)

Note that rejection of **methodological solipsism** doesn't in itself imply the falsehood of *metaphysical* **internalism**. It might be that although a scientist could not individuate an **intentional** state without attention to environmental (especially social) variables, it might nevertheless be true, because of the worries about causal efficacy discussed above, that some **intentional** properties must be lawfully coextensive with (supervene on or reduce to) some systematic sets of intrinsic, internal properties. This is the position of Kim (1998). It is difficult to see, however, how this kind of **internalism** could possibly be relevant to any science. An argument can be made out that it suggests **eliminativism**: if social and other behavioral sciences must individuate states by reference to **intentional** properties but **methodological solipsism** fails, then it seems unlikely that the types of states presumed in social science explanations will map onto states that are in fact causally efficacious. Kim (1998) denies that this argument holds in general, but Marras (2002) decisively refutes his denial. However, no scientists are going to take prospects for **eliminativism** seriously on the basis of a purely metaphysical argument; they would need to be persuaded by actual improvements it gave them in terms of explanatory and/or predictive success, or at least in terms of local conceptual unification, within their sciences.[8] In any case, Ross and Spurrett (2004a) show that Kim's metaphysical argument for **internalism** depends on folk assumptions about the nature of causation that find no support in any science, including the science that ought to have to justify them if they have any sound basis, namely, fundamental physics.

I will therefore not spend more time here attacking purely metaphysical **internalism**. There will be an opportunity later in this chapter to undermine it further, without an additional digression, when I'm discussing issues around **mereology** that are independently on the agenda. For the moment, I will continue the discussion of **intentionality** on the presumption that **internalism**, as a thesis relevant to the behavioral and cognitive sciences, ceases to be a serious prospect with the collapse of **methodological solipsism**.

The denial of **internalism** regarding the contents of intentional states must not be carried all the way to the encouragement of mystical theories of behavioral causation: an agent's behavior can't be sensitive to information she doesn't—herself, physically—have in *any* sense. We'll need to pay attention to this requirement when producing a theory of economic agency in chapters 7 and 8. The point of **externalism**, rather, is that the contents of intentional states, insofar as these are indexed by **propositional attitudes**, can't be read directly off properties of neural (or purely syntactically individuated) states, even in principle. A **propositional-attitude** attribution, if it gets at anything of scientific importance, must be trying to pick out triangulated regularities among a subject, features of her environment, and patterns of expectation in her interpreters. For example, if I tell you that "Bill believes it's raining," what I'm doing is using the public referential apparatus I share with you to enable you to predict, and perhaps explain, that Bill picks up his umbrella before going outside. I'm helping you to *situate* Bill in the part of his environment that controls the aspects of his behavior that presently interest us. It is crucial to this communication that you and I share an externally developed semantics that neither of us controls. (Note that Bill himself need not be a user of this language.)

Dennett's **intentional-stance functionalism** is the conceptual account of mind that comports most coherently with **externalism** about the contents of **propositional attitudes**. We can thus now start to see why

Mirowski's association of Dennett and his followers on this philo-sophical issue with the view that the fundamental source of valuation will turn out to "congeal for the purposes of a science of economics . . . within the recesses of the idealized computer situated between the ears of the representative economic agent" (2002, p. 564) is backwards, as I claimed earlier. What Mirowski describes is the **internalist's** view. But Dennett is the original and most influential proponent of **externalism** in the philosophy of cognitive science. This will turn out to matter a great deal to the correct application of his theories of mind, agency, and selfhood to economics.

Dennett refers to the practice of attributing triangulated **intentional** relations for the purposes of behavioral prediction and explanation as "taking the **intentional stance**" toward the system in the subject role. Now, no one seriously doubts that taking the **intentional stance** to people, and to some animals, is often predictively useful, at least up to a point. This is, quite obviously, the main way in which people coordinate their plans and expectations every day. However, Churchland (1981) and other **eliminativists** point out that (1) this predictive leverage may be strictly parochial among a particular species of animals, *H. sapiens*, at a particular time and place and over a strictly delimited subset of tasks and purposes, because (2) it fails to carve nature at any general causal joints, as a result of which (3) it contributes to no genuine scientific explanations. Folk psychology based on the deployment of the **intentional stance** has the same status, according to **eliminativists**, as folk (or Aristotelian) physics: it is useful, up to strict limits, in restricted domains derived from common human purposes, but in failing to generalize beyond this domain it is *false* as an account of the structure of the world. (One of the tasks of a true theory will be to explain why the folk account is successful in its domain; but this account will inevitably have to draw on neuroscience and evolutionary history.) **Eliminativists** are fond of an analogy between folk psychology and "demonic possession theory" as a device for describing the behavior of socially marginalized, unmarried women in some pre-scientific European communities. That theory provided better predictive leverage than no special theory at all, but its ontology is just mistaken: there are no witches. Similarly, according to **eliminativists**, there aren't really beliefs or desires.

Eliminativism strikes most people, on first acquaintance with it, as an incredible view. Some philosophers have attempted to refute it on a priori logical grounds. (For example: **eliminativists** appear to be trying to believe that there are no beliefs. See Churchland 1979 for an entirely persuasive response to such cavils.) Such strategies are incompatible with the stance presupposed in this book, and discussed in the second section of this chapter above. It is an empirical question whether there is or isn't a way of systematizing reality that could deliver better predictive and explanatory success than **intentional-stance** theory, or that could do almost as well while being better unified with the rest of science. If there is such a theory to be had, then **eliminativists** are right, regardless of whether people will or could, given their social psychology and history, actually stop using the **intentional stance**. (Exactly analogously, the justifiable semantic stubbornness of gardeners as discussed in chapter 1 is irrelevant to the question of whether onions are lilies.) If there is a persuasive case to be made against **eliminativism**, it must be empirical. (Normative presumptions against **eliminativism**, such as Mirowski seems to take for granted, won't do any more than a priori logical ones. Who knows whether we wouldn't be better off with replacements for folk concepts of beliefs, minds, persons, and selves, if they're possible?)

Economists used to theories that traffic in preferences, beliefs, and information might suppose that **eliminativism** would be a disastrous theory for their enterprise. We will see in chapter 5, however, that **eliminativism** has lately been seen as a tempting thesis by some important economists anxious to purge their discipline of commitment to an implausible mapping of a folk conception of rational agency onto biological people. As I noted above, this substantiates Mirowski's contention that an economics without selves is a serious prospect, even if he is wrong, as we'll see, to associate Dennett, Binmore, or evolutionary game theory with it. Though I will ultimately resist the **eliminativist** recourse, I will travel considerable distance along the road to it before turning off. On empirical grounds, I will argue that folk psychology does track some important regularities, but that it is indeed false as a direct model of people. Insofar as some applications of economic theory treat rational economic agency as an idealization of aspects of personhood, I will give grounds for skepticism about the power of these applications to track reality.

With Dennett, however, I am not an **eliminativist**. Though the basic grounds for rejection of **eliminativism** must be, as noted above, empirical, some conceptual diagnosis of the differences in emphasis that lead Dennett away from **eliminativism** is an efficient way to complete the presentation of his position for nonphilosophers. In Dennett's view,

eliminativists share one mistake with **internalists** about propositional content: overcommitment to the idea that a true theory of any phenomena must yield *determinate* measures of all key variables at all scales of measurement. Explanation of this point requires us to first survey the other main philosophical background topic I promised to survey in this chapter, namely, *mereology*.

Mereology

We will lead into this topic by way of further reflections on Fodor's objection that trying to explain **intentionality** by Darwinian means leaves the semantic contents of **intentional** states underspecified. Let us return to the case of the person who's said to believe there's an elephant in the road. To use the case as what Dennett calls an "intuition pump" for exposing different philosophical presuppositions, we'll add some further imagined details. Suppose that you and I are standing on a kopje overlooking the road, from which we can both see a landrover moving along it. From my position, I can also see, before the driver can, an elephant in the road ahead of the vehicle. The animal is blocked from your sight altogether by a copse of bushes beside you. Now, we both see the driver suddenly brake as she rounds a corner in the road. "What's the matter?" you ask, "Why did she stop?" "She just saw that there's an elephant standing in the middle of the road," I reply. You, let us suppose, are sufficiently satisfied with this answer to ask no further questions (at least about the driver's motivation).

It's crucial to your satisfaction here that you know that the driver is a person, and that you know something about people. If the car were being driven by an autopilot rigged to a camera for keeping it on the road, my merely reporting that the elephant had been perceptually registered should provoke further questions from you about the interesting AI program that must be relating the robot's perceptions to goals more complicated than just following the road. If a philosopher pestered you concerning what it is you know about people that makes my report a satisfactory explanation for you, the philosopher would likely pry out of you some low-level generalizations about people usually believing the evidence of their senses in good light and sobriety, and about people believing that driving up to elephants invites injury and destruction, and about people usually having strong desires to avoid these things. That is, you'd make explicit some folk-psychological relations between typical people and a kind of situation, and you'd do so by attributing a variety of **propositional attitudes,** both to typical people in general and to this driver as a presumed instance of a typical person.

Let us focus on just one of these attributions. "She believed there was an elephant in the road," you said to the philosopher at one point. You said this because you think it truly describes the facts. Which fact does it describe? And a fact about what? You certainly don't think that the truth of the fact depends on the driver's having said aloud to herself, in English, "There's an elephant in the road," or on that English sentence having "flashed in her introspective consciousness" (whatever exactly that might be taken to mean). After all, you'd be fully as happy with the truth of your **propositional-attitude** ascription even if you know that the driver is a unilingual Zulu speaker. This is why, if you were an **internalist** about **intentional** content, you'd need to suppose, following Fodor (1975) and many others, that what happens in the driver's brain was a tokening in her neural program of a sentence in a nonpublic "language of thought" that expresses the same proposition as both "There's an elephant in the road" and "Kukho indlovu emgwaqini."

However, let us suppose that you're familiar with the literature in philosophy of cognitive science from the 1980s and 1990s, so, for the reasons we've surveyed, you're not an **internalist**. You think your attribution to the driver is true because there's a network of social facts about language *and* a standing set of behavioral regularities involving people and elephants, *and* your attribution picks out a recurring node in this network, which the situation as a whole is overwhelmingly likely to instantiate, *and* the philosopher who's bothering you knows enough about the relevant network to pick out that same node when you draw his attention to it.

If the philosopher is an **eliminativist,** he'll approve of every part of the story above except your use of the word "true." In direct opposition to Dennett, he'll insist that you should replace it with something less metaphysically ambitious, like "useful for communication." After all, you, as a good **externalist,** will admit that it doesn't matter to the utility of your **attitude** ascription exactly which of a host of neural microstates the driver was in; you're not talking directly about the driver in isolation from the environment, let alone about the driver's brain in isolation, anyway. But, then, the eliminativist goes on, the *particular* attribution, "She believes that there's an elephant in the road," aims at a level of precision that outruns your evidence. Why not replace "elephant" with "big animal" or "in the road" with "ahead"? Indeed, if the driver is, ex hypothesi, a unilingual Zulu speaker, then you should appreciate that your attribution falsely reads out some special, culturally specific, Zulu ontological notions about objects like elephants and roads that, as a good **externalist**, you have no grounds for excluding as irrelevant to the *semantics* of the relevant **intentional** relation.[9] Your attribution is at once too precise given your evidence, and not precise enough given what you know about the general dynamics of meaning, thought, and behavior. It fails to carve nature at its joints. It's good enough for some rough practical purposes, but it isn't true.

This response recapitulates Fodor's objection to Dennett's evolutionary account of the original source of **intentionality**. Fodor, of course, does not take his objection to imply **eliminativism**. But this suggests that the dirigiste **internalist**[10] and the **eliminativist** share an important hunch in common that Dennett doesn't. This hunch is that there's an ultimate, real, micro, level of description of reality at which all true facts are determinate. Perhaps we never quite reach this level in our actual descriptions, but this is just because our measurements can't be infinitely fine. However, it is often supposed, they can get progressively finer; indeed, this is what scientific progress partly consists in. If we use the right ontological categories to begin with, it is imagined, then refinement of our measurement capacities will be tracked in refinement of, but never recategorization of, our set of descriptive categories. **Internalists** think that beliefs and desires will pass this refinement test as we learn more and more about brains. **Eliminativists**—along with Dennett—are sure they won't. But because **eliminativists**, unlike Dennett, consider the refinement test to be based on a sound metaphysical principle, the failure of **propositional attitudes** to pass it leads them to deny the truth of **propositional-attitude** ascriptions.

Western philosophy began with pre-Socratic thinkers whose leading idea was that, appearances notwithstanding, reality is unified by virtue of the fact that, at bottom, it's all made of one fundamental kind of stuff. Water, air, and fire were early candidates. Modern science preferred something a bit more abstract; matter, and, eventually, matter-energy. The study of reality as a boiling down to fundamental unity in one underlying kind of stuff, of which special manifestations are "modes," is **mereology**. It is, as noted, the core of Western metaphysics. So **eliminativists**, in interpreting realism in terms of it, are in good company. If the content of all propositionally identified beliefs and desires is impermeable to closer determination as more microfacts are gathered—even wide, soundly **externalist**, arrays of microfacts about brains *and* histories of languages *and* behavioral dispositions—then **propositional attitudes** look like what philosophers call "**mereological** danglers." As we learn more, their failure to reduce to something more definitely measurable leaves them stranded ever further outside of inclusion in unified science.

In my view, issues associated with the **mereological** urge are about as deep as philosophy goes. Those readers who have picked up this book in hopes of learning about economics and cognitive science are therefore apt to be alarmed. It looks as if a good deal of controversial, maximally deep, metaphysics will have to precede any attempt to choose between **intentional-stance** theory and **eliminativism**. And I've said, several times now, that this choice will turn out to be crucial to the foundations of economics and to its relationship with cognitive science. Oh oh.

There is, I'm afraid, no hope of saying clear and useful things about the general relationships between two special sciences, like economics and cognitive science, in the absence of a clear view on questions concerning **mereological** and intertheoretic **reductionism**. Somehow, this must be done without recourse to a chapter or more of metaphysical argument. What I will do here, therefore, is provide both a conceptual summary for nonphilosophers, and a statement of my own position (one that incorporates, but extends beyond, Dennett's). I will merely characterize, rather than provide, the arguments for this position. Readers who want to see the arguments will be referred elsewhere, to other places where I have published them.

We must first distinguish between two related senses of **reduction**. A **mereological reduction** shows how one ontological domain, one network of kinds of objects, events, and relations, is in fact *constituted by* another—typically, by one at a "lower level." For example, one might try to reduce types of objects, events, and relations studied in chemistry to objects, events, and relations studied in microphysics. An aspect of this endeavor, in any particular case, might involve **intertheoretic reduction**—for example, showing that some well-confirmed theories of chemistry can be restated in the language of microphysics, or shown to be logically derivable consequences of well-confirmed microphysical theories. (Note that **mereological reductionism** is a directly metaphysical thesis, whereas **intertheoretic reductionism** is a logical-linguistic program.) If all well-confirmed theories of objects, events, and relations in a given domain were **intertheoretically reduced** to theories of another domain, this might itself constitute an argument for the corresponding **mereological reduction**. For a **logical empiricist**, who believes that theoretical summaries of experience provide our only means of systematic access to truth, adding the **mereological** spin to an **intertheoretic reduction** is gratuitous. By contrast, a **scientific realist**, who allows that we can justifiably believe in the independent existence of networks of objects, events, and relations based on inference to the best explanation, will allow the possibility that we might have a good metaphysical argument for a **mereological reduction** *without* being able to achieve the corresponding **intertheoretic reductions**. This is the case in which we get **elimination**: the objects, events, and relations of the theory that won't **intertheoretically reduce** in accordance with our well-grounded metaphysical convictions become **mereological** danglers, and are thus banished from our ontology.

We can explicate these distinctions using an example familiar from the **eliminativist** literature. Consider, again, a demonic-possession theory of some types of human behavior. A **logical empiricist** could reject the theory, and use of its theoretical term "witch," for one or both of two reasons: the theory is irredeemably internally inconsistent, or "witch" cannot be operationalized in observational terms. A **realist** might eliminate "witch" as a designator of a real kind for the first reason—though not for the second—but has additional, and more typical, grounds of argument. The **realist** can point out that no supernatural entities in general are compatible with the existing, relatively unified, body of accepted science, so that if "witch" necessarily designates a supernatural entity, then witches aren't fit *kinds* of objects of belief. Some philosophers would argue that if the body of theoretical claims about witches could be recovered (by **intertheoretic reduction**) in terms of a theory making no reference to putatively supernatural entities, then we could say that witches had been redeemed as a kind by being shown not to be supernatural after all. However, the actual fact is that the kind "witch" doesn't so reduce to any well-confirmed theory. Once you get rid of the property of being possessed by demons, it turns out that you're left with no generalizations you can state at all that you think apply to all and only witches. Therefore, we **eliminate** the kind: "witch" carves nature at no real joints; there are no witches. This is the kind of story Churchland advocates with respect to **propositional-attitude** states.

As noted previously, one philosophical stance I'm going to presuppose in this book is **realism**. I'll therefore simplify the discussion of **mereology** from here on by saying no more about the **logical empiricist** view. It will be relevant to my discussion of economic theory in chapter 3, however, that **logical empiricists** *can* be **eliminativists** in the sense described above. Thus when I argue that Samuelson, who had a loosely **logical empiricist** philosophical attitude, should have been an **eliminativist** about **propositional attitudes** for the sake of maximum internal consistency, this should be read as meaning that he should have rejected beliefs as being impossible to operationalize. Here, however, I am primarily concerned with the relationship between Dennett's theory of mind and Churchland's version of **eliminativism**. Both views depend on **realism**; so the presumption of this framework will help to keep things simpler.

I'm also going to bypass detailed discussion of **intertheoretic reduction**. Philosophers have entertained different theories of what, logically, this comes to (see Marras 2002). Partly because of these complications, it is controversial among philosophers as to whether the history and practice of science features any, some, or many cases of **intertheoretic reduction**. Different exact formulations of the concept allow for varying degrees of tolerance about partial failures of fit in putative **reductions**. For example, whether classical mechanics **reduces** or doesn't **reduce** to relativity theory partly depends on whether one thinks that classical physics requires a substantival ether, and if so then on whether it decisively matters that relativity theory discards the notion.

The reason I can bypass all this here is because neither **eliminativists** nor **intentional-stance functionalists** depend, in general, on any view at all about the frequency of **intertheoretic reductions**. Perhaps they are common, perhaps they are rare; it doesn't matter. What *does* matter to their disagreement is whether one thinks that scientific unification ought to consist in progress toward *general* **mereological reduction**. This is a metaphysical issue, unlike the primarily epistemological and logical issues surrounding **intertheoretic reduction**.

As noted above, much of Western philosophy is dominated by a presumption that the achievement of a unified worldview must consist in progressive **mereological** simplification. The classic statement of this view in postwar philosophy of science is a 1958 paper by Paul Oppenheim and Hilary Putnam. They, rightly, try to substantiate the hunch that the world is built in natural levels by appeal to empirical evidence furnished by the history of scientific progress. Influenced by the prevailing **logical empiricism** of their time, they interpret this evidence in terms of **intertheoretic reduction**, but for present purposes this aspect of their claim is incidental. The crucial point is that, as of 1958, it seemed to them empirically correct that science seemed to promise, and to be delivering on, a cascade of **reductions** in which properties of social groups would be shown to decompose into properties of multicellular organisms, properties of multicellular organisms into properties of cells, properties of cells to properties of molecules, properties of molecules to properties of atoms, and properties of atoms to properties of subatomic particles. It is useful to illustrate this conviction directly by reference to the topics of this book. Macroeconomics, being about social groups, should, on the Oppenheim–Putnam hypothesis, **mereologically reduce** to psychology, a science of multicellular organisms. **Reductions** *within* fundamental levels were also of course to be expected here and there; so if there is a distinct science of microeconomics, this should also find its domain in the second level from the top, in which case macroeconomics will **reduce** to psychology by way of an intermediate **reduction** to microeconomics.

I take it that this picture will be familiar to almost all readers. It remains the dominant popular view of the basis of the unity of science (though it is perhaps now being displaced by a wave of faddish journalism on complexity and "emergence"). It is also the picture on which **eliminativists** (and **internalists**) depend. In chapter 3 we will encounter the arguments of a group of prominent **eliminativists** in economics who implicitly suppose that both microeconomics and **propositional-attitude** psychology should face **elimination** because macroeconomic generalizations will be cashed out directly in terms of biological concepts. These arguments depend on combining belief in the **mereological** cascade down the Oppenheim–Putnam levels with the view that **intertheoretic reduction** fails as between established theories in both microeconomics and **propositional-attitude** psychology and anything at a lower level. As previously described, this is the standard logic of the **realistic eliminativist**.

With Dennett, however, I am a skeptic about the Oppenheim–Putnam cascade. The basis of this skepticism is straightforwardly empirical. It seems to me, and to Dennett, that the progress of the various sciences since Oppenheim and Putnam wrote has failed to substantiate **mereological** (or **intertheoretic**) **reductions** among *any* of their levels. The prospects of **reducing** population biology (including evolutionary macrobiology) to cellular biology look hopeless (Keller 2001; Kitcher 1984), thus blocking **mereological reduction** of the domain of multicellular organisms to that of cells. At the next level, Kincaid (1997) argues that key phenomena in cellular biology, such as signal sequences, are multiply realized in different sequences of amino acids, and that these sequences play different roles in different contexts; thus the network of properties and relations at the level of cell biology isn't fully explicable by reference to properties and relations at the level of molecular biology. Deeply destructive to the **mereological reductionist's** hypothesis, because it undermines her literature's favorite presumed case, is the collapse of prospects for **reduction** of chemistry to physics (molecular level to atomic level). **Mereological reductionists** are fond of assuring us that the property of being a water molecule is identical to the property of having two hydrogen atoms and one oxygen atom in a certain bonding relationship (see, e.g., Kim 1998, p. 84). However, it turns out that a sample of liquid water does not consist only of H_2O monomer molecules, but also, at any moment, of various polymerous molecules such as $(H_2O)_2$, and $(H_2O)_3$, in a condition of statistical equilibrium involving rapid reciprocating transformations (van Brakel 2000; Millero 2001; Ponce 2003). If we allow polymeric forms of H_2O to count as water, then water is multiply realized. Worse for the **reductionist**, what chemists recognize as procedures for determining homogeneity or heterogeneity of substance, or establishing whether something is a pure element or a compound, are a variety of tests of which the most crucial involve attempts to separate a sample into its different constituents, and to determine whether it is hylotropic under phase shifts (Needham 2002; Ponce 2003). These procedures track relational, or dispositional properties—what it is that a sample does rather than what exactly it is made of. Following an account of these procedures, Ponce (2003, p. 145) concludes that "chemical kinds are not, within chemical thermodynamics, individuated by reference to their microstructure or micro-composition, but rather by reference to their macroscopic physical properties, including their behavioral or dispositional properties."

No background assumption is more fundamental to the arguments in this book than the conviction that if empirical science and metaphysical hunches conflict, it is the latter that must be surrendered. I thus claim that the facts above, and a parade of others like them, refute **mereological reductionism**. The sample deliberately includes no instances touching on the relationships between or among domains in Oppenheim and Putnam's top two levels (social groups and multicellular organisms), because the book as a whole will constitute an extended case study of that. But the reader may now gather where the argument is going to take her in that respect.

The empirical case against **mereological reductionism** has been grist for the mill of my second foil, Dupré. If the only way to unify science were by means of **mereological reductionism**, and that then fails, are we not necessarily left with a metaphysically disunified world view? And in that case, when the biologist tells the gardener that he's saying something false about plants in denying that onions are lilies, is not the former just presuming an authority based on unjustified **reductionist** assumptions? In the gardener's wide context of use, different from the biologist's, lilies are kinds of colorful flowers, onions aren't, and so onions aren't lilies. This way of interpreting the failure of **mereological reductionism** resonates with the nineteenth-century doctrine of "emergentism" that is lately becoming popular in science journalism. (See, e.g., Johnson 2001.) On this view, organization and increased complexity at "higher levels" bring new networks of properties and relations, including causal relations, into the world that have no determinate basis outside of the contexts relevant at those higher levels. In both its nineteenth-century and currently popular versions, emergentism is often taken to violate the causal closure of physics, that is, the principle that there is no such thing as change or action that does not involve physical change or action, since this principle is often taken to be nothing more than a consequence of general **reductionism**. (See Spurrett 2000 for a survey—leading to a refutation—of this view.)

It is a key part of Dupré's (1993) argument strategy to try to force a choice between radical disunity of science and **eliminativism** about *all* higher-level phenomena. Since the latter would be a bogglingly radical form of **eliminativism**—holding that every empirical claim made outside of subatomic physics is *false*—the disunity hypothesis then emerges (pun intended) as the most plausible metaphysical hypothesis. This strategy, however, simply ignores the alternative to both of these positions promoted by Dennett (1991a), and since extended in a body of work by me and a number of others (to be described and cited below). What this dialectic does show, however, is that Dennett's theory of **intentionality** rises or falls with a metaphysical thesis about **mereology**. If concern for the unity of science compels us to pursue **mereological reduction** of psychological states, then Fodor's objection to Dennett's theory of **intentionality** will be decisive—even if it leads, contrary to Fodor's intentions, to **eliminativism** instead of partial **internalism**. If, on the other hand, the **mereological** urge is not so compelling, then we have no reason to think that our attribution of a belief about elephants needs to find its precise content mirrored inside a brain for that attribution to be true. Natural selection could explain why our subject has beliefs about anything, and then social facts would do all the work in explaining why some of these beliefs are (truly) about elephants, rather than just large animals. Her belief is a belief about, specifically, elephants, *because* attributing *that* belief—not just a belief about large animals, but also not a belief packed with biological distinctions she doesn't draw—predicts her behavioral patterns with maximum efficiency. This is so because "elephants in roads" gets at the semantic grain around which the community of explainers and predictors has historically converged and that's the whole (relevant) fact for **intentional-stance** characterization. Don't ask which facts about her *brain* make "elephant" a better description than "large animal" because none do. Refine **intentional** attributions not by drilling down, but by going wide—into the social environment and into biological and cultural history. **Intentional-stance functionalism** holds **propositional attitudes** to be real not as descriptions of patterns in brains, but as descriptions in patterns of social communication. This fact is obscured, according to Dennett, by the fact that people regularly take the **intentional stance** toward themselves, and misinterpret this as inner perception, that is, introspection. They thus miss the fact that they're constructing themselves by reference to a background network of social relations. As long as we're not committed to **mereological reduction**, there's no reason in principle why such relations can't be logically and causally prior to properties of individuals.

But we will go from Fodor's frying pan to Dupré's fire if, in shrugging off insistence on **mereological reduction**, we give up concern for **scientific unity**. In the next, final, section of philosophical preliminaries, I will explain how to save the baby when the bathwater is dumped.

Real Patterns and the Intentional Stance

Suppose you were trying to construct a mind. The point of doing this would, presumably, be similar to the structural pressures that led natural selection to do it: you want a control mechanism that can flexibly guide a complex system—a robot—through environmental contingencies you can't anticipate in advance. If you were an **internalist**, you might suppose that you'd need to deliberately build in, one by one, the many beliefs and desires you think the robot will need if it is to successfully cope. Or, if you thought the system could ultimately build these for itself using some general axioms and a learning program, you'd suppose that in doing so it would have to *come to* possess a large array of physically distinct symbolic tokens, one for every primitive **intentional** state (from which others will be composed), that it can then internally manipulate.[11] **Anti-internalists**, both **intentional-stance functionalists** and **eliminativists**, argue that neither approach is a plausible model of human intelligence, since both require closer anticipation of possible environmental contingencies than human plasticity suggests. **Externalists** emphasize that the external world stores plenty of information. A system that can just be *disposed* to react appropriately given various input patterns can achieve complex behavioral capacities using less rigid representational principles (Clark 1998). And if a system's reaction patterns can be shaped by its environment over time, so that it acquires new dispositions as it learns, then, if it has a symbolic bookkeeping system like a language, it might want to try to keep track of these shifting systems of dispositions in its own dynamics by labeling (some of) them. The labels themselves can be stored in the world—in texts, and in networks of other systems' dispositions. (This is just the externalist thesis implemented.) And then the labels themselves can be triggers of further dispositions. Thus, for example, I can cause you to judge, explicitly in English, that you believe that Winston Churchill liked brandy by saying "Winston Churchill liked brandy." In fact, reader out there, I just did that very thing. If you'd never had exactly that thought before, there may previously have been no fact of the matter about whether you had a belief whose content was precisely captured by that sentence. But now you do, and we can know it.

Many artificial intelligence products, especially those running on so-called *connectionist* architectures, do not store each of the beliefs by which we can reliably explain and predict their dispositions separately, at distinct physical addresses in their internal circuits. Instead, these dispositions are consequences of the interactions of patterns of informational activity *distributed* across the whole system. The rapidly mounting evidence from neuroscience suggests that, at least in what we think of as their general cognitive functions, brains work in this way too. If this is so, then there is no particular state of your brain, of the sort a neuroscientist could pin down and point to, which codes a belief about Churchill and brandy. The **eliminativist**, as we have seen, concludes from this that you have no beliefs. Dennett, by contrast, argues that your belief just consists in the fact that your whole system of dispositions is such that your behavior is consistent with that belief, and inconsistent with its denial. When you wonder whether you have that belief, you take the **intentional stance** toward yourself, and, on the basis of a very simple bit of behavior—asking yourself a question in English—you rightly judge that you do. This is the same sort of procedure by which we judge that the computer believes appropriate things about chess: we put it into a game situation and look for the right sorts of patterns in its behavior. The main (relevant to present issues) difference between existing chess-playing machines and human chess players is that the latter do, and the former don't, take the **intentional stance** toward *themselves*. This, according to Dennett, has implications for whether the chess machine is **conscious**—we postpone this issue to chapter 6—but it does *not* imply that the machine doesn't have real **intentional** states. What it is to have **intentional** states—real ones, in the only sense of "real" that attaches to any intentional states—is to exhibit behavioral patterns that can't be predicted or explained without recognition of the patterns indexed by the **intentional** states in question.

The last sentence directly states the core thesis of **intentional-stance functionalism**. To link it to the issues about **mereology** discussed in the previous section, we must emphasize that the "can't" in the sentence has to be read with metaphysical force. If the only reason we take the **intentional stance** toward complex systems is because the network of causal relations between their behavioral responses to environments and their internal microprocessing details is too complicated for *us* to work out, then we have not avoided Dupré's disjunction between **eliminativism** and **disunity**. To see this, suppose that our use of the **intentional stance** was necessitated just by our epistemic limitations. Then concern for the scientific ideal of objectivity—perspective independence—might lead us to regard anything so motivated, however indispensable for practical purposes, as separate from genuine scientific description. This would be **eliminativism**. Alternatively, we could follow Dupré in regarding this sort of restriction on "genuine" science as putting philosophical carts before social-institutional horses. If people can adopt a scientific institutional attitude toward **intentional** phenomena to useful effect, as they can, then we should regard **intentional** psychology as a science. However, since we can't reduce it to our other sciences, we get **disunity**, and should learn to live with, even revel in, ontological pluralism. (Dupré makes this sound more fun by calling it "promiscuity.")

How, then, and on what grounds, can one read the indispensability of the **intentional stance** in a way stronger than the epistemic-practical sense? This issue has been a source of difficult adventures for Dennett over the years. His position has regularly been associated with **instrumentalism**—a view that will be familiar to economists who have studied Milton Friedman's (1953) famous essay on methodology.[12] **Instrumentalism** is the view that it doesn't matter to the evaluation of theories whether they're based on plausible ontologies—whether, for example, they generalize over beliefs and desires even though these are **mereological** danglers. Theories are instead just supposed to be reliable instruments for generating correct predictions. **Instrumentalism** is no basis for a response to Dupré's disjunction; it just begs the question against it, by shrugging off all concern with metaphysics altogether. Dennett, in any case, disavows **instrumentalism**,[13] since **instrumentalists** must deny the significance of explanation to evaluations of theories, and part of what is supposed to make the **intentional stance** essential, according to Dennett, is its explanatory power.

I have argued elsewhere (Ross 2000) that although Dennett clearly both wants and needs to avoid Dupré's disjunction, his own efforts to do so have never been entirely successful. He comes close, however—finding a crucial insight, but then failing to exploit it fully systematically—in his paper "Real Patterns" (Dennett 1991a). In Ross (2000), Ross and Spurrett (2004a), and Ross et al. (forthcoming), I and some coauthors have fleshed out Dennett's insight so as to render it a complete alternative to the components of Dupré's disjunction. Here, I will ignore the fine in-house argument details that mark the passage from Dennett's own view to mine. I will just directly describe the position and summarize its specific motivations.

What I called "Dennett's crucial insight" above is his recognition that **eliminativism** rests on taking causal concepts as metaphysically fundamental, whereas *informational* concepts may be more so—and may offer promise for **unification**. Suppose the chair of the Federal Reserve caused the stock market to fall (on purpose) by hinting here and there for a few days that he was going to raise interest rates. The cause of the market's fall is, surely, not mysterious. It rests on the fact that information about the chair's hints is acquired by various traders. This information is more abstract in its content than what was specifically communicated by any of the chair's particular remarks; furthermore, it would have made no difference had the chair said slightly different things to different people instead. We gain our best predictive *and* explanatory leverage over the phenomenon of the market dip by getting the information that the chair has spread hints about a general intention, hints he knew would in turn reach enough key traders, by one route or another, to bring about his desired effects. Both *more* specific information and *less* specific information about what he said to whom would explain and predict somewhat different causal consequences from the ones we observe. And now the key point: this last fact has nothing to do with any epistemic limitations on the parts of the explainers and predictors. A Martian with a superior physics or neuroscience to ours would—since **mereological reductionism** is false—miss a **real pattern** necessary for the *best* available prediction and explanation if she didn't acquire information about the chair's **intentional** behavior at the right grain of content (and about macroeconomic patterns relating interest rates to investment behavior). What makes one grain "right" and another "wrong" are facts about the structure of the world, not facts about the Martian's epistemic capacities.

Thanks to the work of Shannon (1948), we can understand the concept of information in physically measurable terms. (There are a variety of alternative detailed interpretations derived as modifications from Shannon's basic idea, over which we will not fuss here; see Barwise and Seligman 1997, and then Ross et al. forthcoming for the exact interpretation presupposed in the claims below.) That the chair will raise interest rates by 1 percent on January 6 carries more bits of information than the news that he will raise rates by some indefinite amount sometime this month, because the former excludes more states of affairs that are consistent with the full state of the world on, for example, January 3. (That is, the prior conditional probability of the former is lower.) Information, to travel from a source to a receiver, must pass along some real channel and involve a real process in space-time. How many bits of information a channel can carry is a function of the noise on it, and noise is likewise measurable in bits. There is fact of the matter concerning what information about a given source is available at the receiving end of a channel—objectively available, that is, whether or not it is extracted by the receiver to do further work.

Various objective facts about networks of informational channels are determined by the overall structure of spacetime. Thus, for example, no possible informational channels link non-timelike connected regions of spacetime[14]—I cannot receive any information from outside my light cone. Nor can anything or anyone receive information from inside black holes or from the other side of the big bang, if these are what physicists call "singularities."[15] Some information is irretrievably dissipated for possible reception outside particular spacetime regions; thus, perhaps no one in the twenty-first century can ever get any information about whether Napoleon had more or fewer than 1,200 hairs on his head at Waterloo. No informational channel could connect a source and a receiver if the computation necessary for extraction required more time than the life span of the universe. And so on. Facts about informational availability—availability *period*, not just availability relative to practical costs and benefits of extraction given some receiver's utility function—are thus physical facts, and the fact that they are physical facts is itself a metaphysical fact. *Entropy* is the name for the measure of information dissipation; *negative entropy*, or, *negentropy*, refers to work that some systems (e.g., living systems) do to reduce entropy in their local environments.

Since information is physically meaningful, we can (and do) have a theory of it that is not disunified from physics. Among the things this theory can tell us are the limits on *algorithmic compressibility* of given strings of bits. So, for example, a rambling description in English of my current physical location can be compressed into a string of four spacetime coordinates on a relativistic metric; but it cannot be compressed into representation by just two or three coordinates. This is a fact, not a perspective-dependent interpretation. The theory of computation looks at, among other things, the general properties and limits of compressibility of various kinds of patterns of information. (Economics as conceived under Mirowski's preferred future for it would thus be a branch of objective inquiry, because it would study these general properties and limits as they apply to different kinds of markets, understood as kinds of information processors.)

A highly suggestive philosophical extension can be given to these conceptual relations by noting that causation has often been analyzed in terms of transmission of information. Certain processes transmit information about their antecedent stages while others do not. Salmon (1984) argues that only the former are genuine candidates to be causal processes. Following Reichenbach (1957), we can put this in terms of the transmission of marks. In the absence of specific structure-preserving (and, ultimately, structure-constituting) activity, entropy will eliminate marks on objects that carry information about their histories. A structure is, by definition, something that resists entropy, however briefly. Therefore, wherever marks are preserved we have structure. The goal of science is to discover the structures in nature. We can discover such structures because, as fairly sophisticated information-transducing and -processing systems, we can detect, record, and systematically measure mark-transmitting processes. This is intended by Salmon as an *analysis* of causation—that is, as a theory of what causation *is*, in terms of something more general.

This philosophical extension allows us to use the concept of objective information to articulate an idea of **unification** without **mereological reduction**. Try to imagine the whole physical universe as a network of informational channels on one topology that can be examined at different scales. In our earlier example, a variety of informational channels link the Reserve chair's hints to the falling stock market. We can establish the causal consequences of the hints not by examining the microprocesses underlying his specific utterances, but by comparing the channels in the actual world with those in a possible world where he would instead, say, announce a specific rate change at a press conference. Such an action would open channels to a different set of events.

What allows us to get **unification** from this sort of conception is the fact that we must find all empirically possible information channels on *one* topology. Thus physics, describing for us the general, contingent, topology of the universe, constrains all other sciences by identifying and excluding an infinite set of impossible channels. This kind of constraining relation conforms with the institutional and historical facts about science: no special sciences are allowed to contradict (at time *t*) whatever has become a matter of approximate consensus among physicists (at *t*); but accounts in special sciences have never, actually, been *required* to facilitate **mereological reduction**. Why does the requirement of a single consistent topology not imply **mereological reduction**? The answer is that informational channels at one scale are not, in general, composed out of channels at smaller scales. What is noise at one scale may be information at another, and vice versa. Suppose the Reserve chair coughed while passing one of his hints. His words and his cough are part of the same microprocess at one scale, and both supply some information about the tension in his vocal chords, which might in turn enable some predictions about whether he'll have flu symptoms on January 6. But for predictors of the consequences of his intentions about the market, the same cough is noise. Requiring a single consistent informational topology at all scales does not even impose an assumption that boundary conditions on channels across given regions of the topology must line up at all scales. Thus different sciences can cross-classify physical processes without falling into conflict with each other. But cross-classification blocks **mereological reduction**.

Note that what I have said here does not *solve* philosophical problems about how abstract processes like the communication of **propositional content** can be *causes* of "concrete" events like pushing a button. Solving this problem demands lengthy analysis of what is intended by various causal concepts in the first place; for this the reader is referred to Ross and Spurrett 2004a, and to Ross et al. forthcoming. Note that although, in these analyses, we take Salmon's theory of causation mentioned above to supply an important insight, we don't accept it as the complete story. I mentioned Salmon's analysis in the course of explaining some conceptual relations; I didn't assert its truth as a premise on which arguments in this book will depend. Here, I am concerned just to indicate what my working attitude to **reductionism** in this book will be, and on what grounds, in general, I take this attitude. It is thus adequate for present purposes to say just this much about causation: the single-topology requirement rules out *supernatural* causation, which would imply informational channels that leave the surface of the topology (flying above it or tunneling beneath it). The possible causal relations are a subset of the set of possible informational relations, and the actual causal relations are a subset of the set of actual informational relations. Without stating and motivating principles for demarcating these subsets, I have not provided an *analysis* of causation (something I have done, with coauthors, elsewhere). All I have done is described what I will take to be my license for allowing, in the arguments to come, causal relations that need not decompose into microphysical ones. This is, of course, altogether consistent with how special scientists, including both economists and noninternalist cognitive scientists, talk about causation; and that is the point.

We now have enough concepts on the table to state the "Dennettian" theory of existence that is introduced and defended in Ross 2000. This theory says:

To be is to be a real pattern, and a pattern is real iff

(i) it is projectible under at least one physically possible perspective and

(ii) it encodes information about at least one structure of events or entities S where that encoding is more efficient, in information-theoretic
terms, than the bit-map encoding of S, and where for at least one of the
physically possible perspectives under which the pattern is projectible,
there exists an aspect of S that cannot be tracked unless the encoding
is recovered from the perspective in question.

This theory makes it a contingent and empirical matter whether any
particular **pattern** we believe at some point to be **real** is **reducible** to
another, and, crucially, insists that the question of the reality of any
pattern is not to be decided on anthropocentric grounds. This is so
because **patterns** are required to be projectible under a *physically possible* perspective, rather than a perspective that is an artifact of human
perceptual or cognitive capacities, so if there is a physically possible
perspective from which some phenomenon recognized by our current
working ontology could be more efficiently represented under an alternative ontology, then our current ontology is false, regardless of
whether we are or are not, or shall ever be, aware of the existence of
the alternative possible perspective in question.

This is the basis on which I reject Dupré's **disunity** hypothesis,
based as it is on allowing anthropocentrically motivated and useful
patterns—but which can't be unified—to count as **real**. My view makes
eliminativism an empirical hypothesis, as it should be. Our current
intentional psychology, or our current economics, could and should be
eliminated if and only if there are other **real patterns** out there for us
to discover that render theories cast in terms of their ontologies redundant. Because the theory of existence demands **unification**, it legiti-
mates our worrying about how economic theory and cognitive science
relate to and mutually constrain one another. However, because it does
not require **unification** by **mereological reduction**, it does not urge us
to explain the interdomain relations by directly mapping the ontology
of one domain onto that of the other; and it will not call on us to **eliminate** a given microeconomic theory just because it can't sustain such
a mapping. Finally, my stating of the theory as my underlying philosophical commitment will allow the reader to understand how I can
talk about **intentional** states—beliefs and desires—as real objects for
scientific investigation, without having to suppose that they pick out
internal states of individual people.

I will conclude this conceptual primer by summarizing the upshot
of the philosophical stage setting for the work to come. First, I have

broadly agreed with Mirowski that the crucial questions for economic theory here in the early twenty-first century concern the way in which it logically connects with cognitive science. Like Mirowski, I will look for the connection in the conceptual space provided by formal theories of information and computation. Unlike Mirowski, I will promote the program for economics that he associates with Dennett, Binmore, and evolutionary game theory (while identifying useful supporting roles for the other programs he considers). I will agree with him that this program preserves rather than displaces the core philosophical assumptions of neoclassicism, although this is a largely empty claim in advance of considerable work to locate the contested content of that core. (This work will occupy chapters 3 and 4.) Since my account thus emphasizes continuity, it will be Whiggish rather than postmodern. Postmodernism will also be resisted in a second sense: instead of fracturing the domains of behavioral and other scientific inquiry and explanation, like Dupré, I will insist that if economics is to be vindicated as a science it must be unified with its cognate enterprises. However, I will not seek such unity by pursuing relations of reduction or supervenience. Instead, I will look for possible real patterns as the objects of economic theory, where a constraint on such patterns is that they comport naturally with current trends in cognitive and behavioral science. Finally, though I will differ from both Mirowski and Dupré in making no normative presumption in favor of humanism, it will emerge that, in the framework that nonreductively unifies cognitive science and economic theory, the concept of the self is explained and substantiated rather than sacrificed.

A Separate Science of Economics

The philosopher Daniel Hausman (1992), following John Stuart Mill, has emphasized that practitioners of economics regard it as a distinct science *separate from* other disciplines that study human behavior (and behavior in general). This attitude of economists might not strike us as peculiar so long as our perspective is immersed in the practical world of modern industrial society. We all know that the causal flux of production and consumption activities in such societies is terrifically complex, and that most of the activities of nearly all people are substantially governed by it. However, from this perspective economics seems more like a branch of engineering than of science properly speaking. We, and our ancestors, have built, by design or accident, a complicated machine and have chosen or allowed our lives and social structures to be regulated by it. Naturally, in this situation, we are deeply interested in trying to monitor, predict and, as best we can, control its operation. This sort of concern seems at bottom *practical* rather than fundamentally scientific. It might lead us to expect that economics should stand in relation to *basic* behavioral sciences—psychology, sociology, and ethology—as engineering stands to physics and chemistry; that is, a body of applied lore consistent with basic sciences but separated only for the sake of achieving control in a domain individuated by reference to our parochial purposes.

The interpretation of economics as social engineering is widespread in the popular literature. Those who protest inchoately against the influences of economics on politics, forlornly seeking someone in control of "the system" *to* whom their complaints can be directed, are quite obviously transfixed by the engineering image. Their spokespeople often make explicit their conviction that, since the economy is a machine of human construction, we could, if only we maintained sufficient willpower and political coherence, fundamentally redesign it or even escape from its demands altogether. The opposing view, according to which "economic reality" exerts an independent controlling grip analogous to the structures of physical nature, is derided by such people as "economic determinism," which in their eyes is a kind of moral failure.

Of course, denial of the claim that economic processes are controllable by sheer willpower does not imply economic determinism, any more than physical determinism (in the metaphysical sense) is implied by acknowledgement that engineers can't simply direct the physical universe to operate differently. This simple logical point is too obvious to need argument, or to be of much interest except in the purely political sense. But the perspective of most economists differs from the popular one just sketched in a deeper way. For economists, there are, as a matter of objective fact, distinctive causal regularities that govern relations among equally distinctive economic variables, in the scientific—or, to use the terminology defined in chapter 1, *systematic*—sense of "govern." This need not entail the claim that the processes described by these regularities are "universal" in the sense of having actual informational (causal) consequences on the topology of every possible world, since there may be possible worlds in which none of the relevant variables are instantiated. But the regularities are taken to be universal in the sense that for any system over which a generalization of the form "If x then y" is true, then in that system information that x obtains carries information relevant to the probability of y, regardless of anyone's wishes to the contrary.[1]

In terms of the metaphysical framework sketched in the previous chapter, this claim to objectivity must commit whoever makes it to the defense of two components: some economic generalizations must be both *true*, and *metaphysically nonredundant*.[2] I will focus for now on the second requirement. It is far from obvious that *separate* generalizations, at the fundamental level of the metaphysical organization of the world, govern a distinctive economic domain. That resources are lavished on measuring economic variables is not evidence for this. After all, lots of people occupy their lives with learning and applying knowledge of the regularities that govern the operations of car engines, for obvious and sound practical reasons; yet nobody supposes that there is a distinctive metaphysics of automotive science. Why should matters be any different where economic machines are concerned? Why should economics not just be a grab bag of applied psychology and applied sociology?

Although I intend this question as a philosophical one, answerable to the demands of normative (logical and empirical) justification, for reasons discussed in the previous chapter the philosophical evaluation needs to be sensitive to the answers economists have given to themselves over time. I will therefore proceed by offering a brief intellectual history of the separateness thesis, adding some philosophically relevant asides along the way, but mainly deferring external evaluation until later. Furthermore, I will here just be concerned with the separateness thesis only as it applies to the relationship between economics and psychology—that is, the view that microeconomics is not just a special branch of some more general theory of individual behavior. (Evaluation of the relationships between economics and sociology will be a concern of the second volume of this study.) For this reason, my philosophical history will not try to describe the whole body of economic theory as it was at any point in history. In particular, I will concentrate on economic theory as it has modeled consumers and consumption. The other side of the economic process, production, will come up only incidentally.

Before Economics

Induction on the history of science suggests that one contrastive diagnostic trait of a proper metaphysical domain is its nonobviousness. In the case of practical domains, as soon as a new technology is evidently important to human purposes, work will begin on isolating and improving the engineering expertise relevant to controlling it. By contrast, real scientific domains can and in every case were for some time invisible to inquirers. If at some point in the past people thought that all causation was animated, then we can say that during that period neither of the metaphysical domains of physics or biology had been picked out. To take another example, Julian Jaynes (1976) has famously argued that at the time of Homer no one in the classical Western world had yet latched on to the domain of psychological causation; and although his claim may well not be historically true—I take no stand on this—it is at least coherent enough to be worth debating. Precisely *because* proper scientific domains are general—if not necessarily logically "universal" under some interpretation—they tend to be invisible from the practical, situated perspectives of folk conceptual organization. We spot them only when we go abstract and start tracking homologies of pattern.

This point holds, as a fact about human intellectual history, for the economic domain as contemporary economists understand it. Ancient Western societies did not clearly glimpse the abstract domain. As I have discussed elsewhere (Ross 1994b), for example, the ancient Romans during the time of Emperor Diocletian were puzzled by price inflation, never linking it to the expansion of the money supply that resulted from the minting of new coin to pay off mutinous soldiers. Nor did they appreciate the causal connection between decreed price controls and subsequent scarcities of goods on the market. Of course, this is a suggestion about ancient perceptions, or lack of them, concerning *macroeconomic* patterns. Can a similar point be justified regarding *microeconomic* relationships?

Aristotle uses and says much about a concept that is translated as, and is etymologically related to, "economics."[3] However, the meaning of this concept is substantially different from that intended by the contemporary economist. Aristotle, along with (presumably) everyone else since the birth of digitalized thought, saw clearly enough that people want things, and that under normal circumstances they expend some resources, including time, to get them.[4] His society had a well-developed and quasi-legal notion of property, and he recognized that property maintenance is an important practical activity because various forces, not least the acquisitiveness of other people, work to undermine it in any particular case. However, there is nothing in Aristotle's discussion to suggest that he thinks of the economic domain as involving a distinct logic of its own. His reflections on it are strictly practical; in particular, he is concerned to determine how a sensible citizen might best devote prudent attention to maintenance of his property without allowing anxiety about this to unduly dominate his life. If Aristotle's thoughts on economics were published today, they would belong more appropriately on the business or "self-help" shelves than on those dedicated to economic science.

Scott Meikle (1995, 2001), a leading authority on Aristotle's economic writings,[5] has plausibly isolated the central metaphysical difference between Aristotle's way of conceptualizing the economic realm and the contemporary economist's. For Aristotle, Meikle argues, only a specialized subset of human activities is directed to the pursuit of economic ends, and these ends are in turn distinguished by their association with the maintenance of material comfort and property. In this context, if we think of the concept "money" as broadly denoting the set of vehicles that conventionally store wealth in a given society (as opposed to the various narrower concepts of money used in modern monetary economics), then it is appropriate to say that for Aristotle economics is "the science of money." As Aristotle would have agreed, this phrase is a metaphor; there is and can be no proper "science" of money in this broad sense, but only a practical art.

Contemporary popular usage of the concept of economics is—as in many other domains, including physics, biology, and psychology—still in substantial accord with Aristotle's here. The voices of economists are omnipresent in popular media, and the overwhelming subject of their opinions and advice is the maximization of private and public material wealth. Since most professional economists earn their livelihoods by furnishing such advice, even they may typically share in this Aristotelian conception, at least in their less reflective moments. As Meikle (2001) notes, however, modern economic theory implies a profoundly different view of the subject's scope and domain, one that differs sharply from the everyday ontological presuppositions of common social life. (Meikle also deplores this difference, for reasons broadly similar to Dupré's.) Understanding of its basis is best achieved by briefly tracing its evolution in intellectual history. The history in question is a complex and much-contested business, so care is needed here; but, since this book is not a historical treatise, I must try to be brisk at the same time. The reader is warned that, since my purposes here are philosophical, I will be imposing a more logical and linear order on developments than a pure concern for documentary accuracy would legitimize. In this chapter and those to follow I'll be defending a particular thesis about the scope and proper objects of microeconomics. For this thesis to be truly clear—especially to economists themselves—it has to be built on a foundation of historical reference points. What's coming, then, is history with a spin. (Mirowski, standing off in the wings, might remind us that there's no other kind anyway.)

Bentham and Sensationalism

As Meikle emphasizes, for Aristotle there are numerous sources of value, many of them—and the most important of them—sui generis. Furthermore, the values people attach to both actions and objects are determined by the uses to which they are intended to be put. By contrast, for the contemporary economist value is a homogenous variable, denoted by "utility" and instantiated in particular arguments by whatever an agent tries to maximize. The basic conceptual shift occurred (though as we shall see, incompletely) at the so-called marginalist revolution of the late nineteenth century that gave rise to neoclassical economics. This is what makes its classicism "neo."

The so-called classical political economists—Smith, Hume, Ricardo, Say, Malthus, Mill, and Marx, to name the leading lights—did not share a clear and common view on the sources of value. There is thus no such thing as "the" classical position, to be neatly contrasted with Aristotle's or the neoclassical view, on what marks economic activity off from other sorts of behavior. The classicists all believed that an overriding preoccupation of political activity was and had to be the preservation of some minimal level of societal material wealth necessary for general stability and order, and their work was mainly motivated by the conviction that in the modern state this purpose was qualitatively more complex than it had been in the context of ancient city-states or feudal princedoms. Because they emphasized the organization of whole societies rather than of individual households, their analyses look much less like exercises in applied folk psychology than do Aristotle's.[6] Furthermore, as Mirowski (1989) emphasizes, they began the process of rendering economics scientific, in the modern sense, by concentrating attention on whether there is a conserved quantity in economic processes; for them the possible quantity in question was exchange value. However, being preoccupied with the special features of material wealth and its maintenance, they were Aristotelians with regard to the empirical *scope* of economics. Contemporary economic theory is the product of two major philosophical shifts away from this perspective. The first occurred in and took root, with much lurching and backsliding, over three decades following the 1870s. The second was articulated by leading economists in the 1930s and 1940s.

The story typically starts with Jeremy Bentham, whose work is the basic proximate fountainhead of the philosophy of neoclassicism.[7] Bentham's radical subjectivism on the sources of value is, of course, enough to mark him off sharply from both Aristotle and most of the classical economists (though its relationship to Smith's philosophy of value, in particular, is complex). That neoclassical economics relies on subjectivism about value as its overarching philosophical commitment is too obvious to need argument, either philosophical or historical. Subjectivism can be expressed either as the metaphysical thesis that, in fact, there *are* no objective values, and/or as the psychological thesis that human behavior is mainly motivated by subjectively derived and entertained sources of valuation rather than by objectively given ones. Bentham was certainly a subjectivist in both of these senses,[8] whereas most neoclassical economists have been professionally agnostic on the metaphysical thesis while (as we shall shortly see) differing in their interpretations of the psychological thesis. Philosophically, the two theses of course have important and deep relationships. For the moment, since our concern is with the separation of economics from psychology, attention will be restricted to subjectivism as a descriptive hypothesis about motivation.

Bentham and his fellow utilitarians famously argued that all purposeful human activity is fundamentally motivated by efforts to maximize pleasure and minimize pain. This claim also admits of two interpretations: it can be taken as an empirical hypothesis about human psychology or as a logical proposal concerning the meaning of purposive action. That is, one can read the Benthamite view as an endorsement of the hedonist's claim that people are driven about by their urges for and aversions to various *sensations*; or one can read it mainly as *just* a special way of avowing motivational subjectivism, with "pleasure" and "pain" simply standing in as labels or placeholders for whatever distinguishes a given person's objects of value from her objects of resentment. Sensationalistic hedonism as a psychological theory is a more specific thesis than motivational subjectivism, and, being descriptive rather than normative, is logically independent of normative subjectivism. As a democratic agitator first and foremost, Bentham's deepest concern was for the latter, since he took political respect for normative subjectivism to be partly constitutive of democracy. With respect to the specificity of the psychological subjectivism he endorsed, Bentham is more cautious.

In his personal views Bentham certainly *was* a sensationalist, in the sense that he was an empiricist of the Humean type. For such empiricists, minds can't respond at all to anything that isn't ultimately reducible to a sensation. It is important to stress just how literally Hume took causal sensationalism. Hume's model of mind is inspired by Newtonian mechanics. When he says that all ideas—which, in his case, means all mental contents—are ultimately caused by impacts on sensory surfaces, this should not be read metaphorically. The Humean mind really is supposed to be a sort of resonance chamber in which forces transferred from sensory impacts collide, and in which regularities in the aggregate effects of these collisions are in principle sufficient for explaining and predicting all thought.[9] Bentham took over this model of mind as part of the general empiricist philosophical package he endorsed (though, as Mirowski [1989] stresses, he may not have really understood the implications of its intended basis in classical physics).

Hume viewed his work as the framework for an ultimate science of the mind that would be scientific in, again, the specific sense of Newton. That is, it would involve systems of equations that would permit derivations of the ideational (i.e., semantic, in contemporary terms) consequences of sequences of sensory impacts, using some standard metric for quantification of forces. Were such a system to be achieved, we would then be able to comparatively measure the relative forces—or "degrees of vivacity," to use Hume's own language—of different people's mental contents, including their motivations. A full Humean psychology would thus have permitted quantitatively exact interpersonal comparisons of utility, that is, precise measurements of the relative strengths of people's desires for and aversions to various perceptible outcomes.

To what extent Bentham shared Hume's speculative confidence about future scientific psychology is a matter for debate. However, what most needs emphasis in the present context is that although Bentham took the approximate Humean model of mind for granted, in his discussion of the psychology relevant to economics he carefully avoided helping himself to the resources of a science that hadn't yet come about. In his posthumously published analysis of the components of utility (1859/1954), Bentham decomposes it into five "elements" or "dimensions of value": intensity, duration, propinquity, certainty, and extent. Despite claiming that intensity is the most important of these with respect to its role in guiding behavior, he says "Of these five, the first, it is true, is not susceptible of precise expression; it *not* being susceptible of measurement. But the four others *are*" (p. 443). He then sets off into a long justification of the second part of this claim, and never returns to the implicit problem raised by the first part;[10] we might presume on the basis of this that Bentham took its truth to be obvious, at least as a fact about then-existing scientific knowledge and technology.

Bentham thus believed, on the one hand, that an individual's purposeful behavior is guided by responses to *cardinally* experienced utility—that is, utility levels subjectively experienced as differentiable with respect to their intensity—but simultaneously believed, on the other hand, that these cardinal differences could not be comparatively measured through introspection or observations of choice behavior. The most natural interpretation of his remarks quoted above is that he was deliberately scientifically agnostic on the question of whether they could be objectively measured at all, regardless of such speculative hopes along (poorly understood) Humean lines as he may have personally entertained.

The Early Neoclassical Economists and "Semi-Aristotelianism"

Mandler (1999, pp. 112–117) reflects the common view in stressing that this attitude of Bentham's was exactly the one taken up by the founders of neoclassical economics after 1870.[11] This is not surprising. As Robbins (1998) notes, the leading British source of the new economics, William Stanley Jevons, clearly had his copy of Bowering's *Works of Jeremy Bentham*, containing the "Psychology of Economic Man," close to hand when he wrote his chapter on the psychological foundations of his study. (Jevons exactly follows Bentham's topic order as found in that essay.) On the subject of the motivational importance of preference intensity, he echoes Bentham almost exactly. "Far be it from me," he says, "to say that we shall ever have the means of measuring directly the feelings of the human heart. A unit of pleasure or of pain is difficult even to conceive; but it is the amount of these feelings which is continually prompting us to buying and selling, borrowing and lending, laboring and resting, producing and consuming" (Jevons 1871, p. 13).

Jevons's project—the project that launched economics as we have known it since—was to find a way of applying calculus to model quantitative relationships among demand levels, scarcity conditions, and production possibilities in the case of a given single agent. This is still what mainstream, core microeconomics, so far as its relationship to psychology is concerned, is all about.[12] In this context, Jevons's problem, given the Benthamite psychology he presumed, was to somehow engineer his way around the fact that people respond to *cardinal* utility—the varying intensity levels of the pleasures and pains associated with different outcomes—but from their behavior alone we can infer only *ordinal* utility measures, that is, mere rankings of their preferences over outcomes. The key to unlocking this problem, for Jevons, was the marginal principle, the idea that a rational agent will apportion her expenditures of resources in such a way that she could not make herself better off, given her budget constraint, by giving up a marginal increment of any one source of utility for a marginal increment of another source. Jevons's system relies, in particular, on an independently defended principle of *diminishing* marginal utility. In most of Jevons's formulations this depends on an introspective inference, one that Jevons thought had been established by the scientific psychology of his day. Much of the subsequent history of work in the foundations of economics was dominated by the question of how much of agents' behavior could be predicted and explained on the basis of the assumption of the marginal principle, with or without diminishing marginal utility, plus observations of choices.

Jevons's casual trust in the fairly primitive empirical psychology of his time was portentous for the development of views on the separateness question. As we have seen, for Aristotle and for the classical economists economics is concerned with those aspects of behavior related to the acquisition and maintenance of material comfort and wealth, where such acquisition is held to be just one (inferior) member of the set of objectively valuable human goals. Thus for Aristotle some activities are economic, or have economic aspects, whereas others aren't or don't. By contrast, in conceptualizing all ends as homogenously reducible to the universal goal of utility maximization, in which consumption by anyone of anything that she subjectively values enhances her utility by definition, Jevons and the early marginalists implicitly widened the scope of economics to encompass the whole of purposive activity. Bentham had explicitly drawn attention to his intended "wide and expansive" sense of utility as encompassing all *possible* motives. Jevons extends this theme when he turns to defining the ends of economic activity, which he calls "commodities": "By a *commodity*," he says, "we shall understand any object, substance, action or service, which can afford pleasure or ward off pain" (ibid., p. 41). This notion of commodity is not *restricted to*, though of course it includes, material goods. Since the scope of economics is the study of all commodity exchanges and distributions, according to Jevons, it is thus not limited to narrowly material transactions. Since Jevons follows Bentham in *identifying* value with subjective utility, value on his view cannot reside solely in any single kind of material input, such as land or labor, the typically privileged sources of value in classical treatments such as those of Smith, Ricardo, and Marx.

As Mandler (1999) documents, it took the early neoclassical tradition some time to grasp the full implications of this. Jevons is aware—

inevitably, since Bentham is transparent on the point—that one could "call any motive which attracts us to a certain action pleasure and that which deters pain" (1871, p. 31). But he then immediately raises for himself the problem that remains a favorite concern of skeptics (e.g., Sen 1987) about the psychological adequacy of neoclassically derived microeconomics: the tautology objection. If one follows Bentham too literally here, Jevons worries, then "it becomes impossible to deny that all actions are prompted by pleasure or by pain" (1871, p. 32), and, in that case, citing someone's will to maximize their utility as an explanation for their actions would be empty. He therefore retreats to a semi-Aristotelian position and divides pleasures into "higher" and "lower" categories, in which the former include those that involve moralized or altruistic motivations, while the latter are restricted to the satisfaction of "material" sensations. The aspect of behavior concerned with such material well-being is then taken to be the proper domain of the economist. Jevons's great successor, Marshall, follows him in this; and since Marshall's *Principles of Economics* (1890) became the standard foundational text of the discipline for decades, there is much justification for taking the semi-Aristotelian view of economic psychology as the neoclassical orthodoxy up to the 1930s. Notice that this view suggests a *rejection* of metaphysical subjectivism, along with, at least, agnosticism on the question of whether psychological subjectivism universalizes to all behavior in the way that Bentham had supposed.

Orthodox though it might have been, however, this semi-Aristotelian position was not without its dissenters during the early neoclassical period. Some philosophically alert commentators noticed that the semi-Aristotelian view, since it defers to the vague idea that "noble" or "higher" aspirations are somehow metaphysically special, is incompatible with the thorough-going naturalism about motivation that had been urged by Hume and taken up by Bentham. One leading neoclassical theorist, Wicksteed (1910), explicitly recognized that the position is unstable, since, for an empiricist, the distinction between higher and lower pleasures is completely ad hoc. Unlike Jevons, though, Wicksteed does not equivocate. The scope of motivations encompassed by the principle of marginal-utility maximization, he says, includes "all the heterogeneous impulses of desire or aversion which appeal to any individual, whether material or spiritual, personal or communal, present or future, actual or ideal" (Wicksteed 1910, p. 32). Here, we at last see a clean and decisive shift away from the Aristotelian conception of the scope of economics, just the one emphasized by Meikle.

This shift is crucial to an understanding of the historical interpretation of the separateness thesis. According to a well-established and
very broad philosophical tradition—one including Kant, much postpositivist analytic work,[13] and, as I will later argue, the contemporary
metaphysics of behavior and cognition—the domain of "action" in
general is the appropriate object of a distinct analytical science in a way
that the study of the pursuit of a particular end, such as material
wealth, could not be. That is, the wider domain is a suitable candidate
for the application of a body of systematic logical relations, whereas
the narrower domain of action aimed at satisfaction of material wants
is a metaphysically arbitrary concatenation yoked together by reference
to practical human purposes. Many economists have clung to the idea
that agency in general is a fit subject for distinct logical analysis, and
have taken this fact to provide deep justification for separateness. They
are now often shy about explicitly saying so, however, following a full
century of relentless criticism of this conviction. In the chapters to
come, I will be defending their stubbornness, and encouraging open
acknowledgment of the idea that there is a possible systematic science
of intentional action and that economics is that science.

But we are getting ahead of ourselves. The view that purposive
behavior can be interpreted as a homogenous and sui generis process
needs to be distinguished from particular views as to what might
causally generate such a process. Wicksteed and those among his contemporaries who shared his view were still Humean in their psychology. That is, they took it that the relative intensity of preference and
desire is a real psychic force governing the causation of purposive
activity, even if this force could not be measured practically. This view,
in the early twentieth century, was highly vulnerable to the gathering
forces of positivism and psychological behaviorism, which had no time
for unmeasurable causal principles—or, in the case of positivism at its
most pure, for any causal principles at all. Furthermore, progress
during this time by economists in sharpening the logical instruments
of marginal analysis steadily isolated the epistemological role of cardinal utility in economic theory, and helped to prime it for elimination.

We cannot try to follow all the details of this development here, but
one milestone along the path should be noted.[14] As early as 1881, Edgeworth had shown how to represent Jevonsian marginal analysis using
the device of indifference curves. The idea behind their use is that if an
agent can consistently rank her preferences, and can tell when she is
indifferent with respect to certain outcomes, then we can graph a part

of her utility function by placing her demand level for one scarce utility-satisfying commodity on the y-axis and the demand level for another such commodity, to be traded off against it, on the x-axis. The technique will be familiar to anyone who has taken a first-year course in economics. Each point in the space of the graph represents a ratio of consumption between the two commodities. Among some subsets of these points, the relationship of indifference will hold; that is, the agent would expend no energy or other costs in trying to get from one point in the subset to another. If we assume diminishing marginal utility, that is, that for any commodity an agent's utility from consuming further increments of it decreases on the margin, then each curve through any one of these indifference subsets of points will be convex to the origin. Which indifference curve, as between any two commodities, the agent will actually situate her consumption along will be sensitive to their value to her relative to the total stock of *other* commodities she could consume, and to her income. Suppose we could find some one commodity for which our agent's demand on the margin incorporated both her expectations about total income, and all her pairwise indifference curves over the total set of utility-satisfying commodities. Available energy or time might be plausible idealizations here,[15] but for practical purposes of measurement money is typically used as this idealized "numeraire." If we then substitute money for one of the two commodities on our graph, the resulting set of indifference curves will, up to the limits of our idealization (i.e., up to the limits of the idea that all information about all of our agent's wants are expressible in money prices), capture her demand for the other commodity for each possible income level she might have, the different income levels corresponding to different indifference curves. (Note that, however economists might sometimes express themselves, there is nothing essential about the use of money as the numeraire in constructing indifference curves, so their use need not represent endorsement of semi-Aristotelian assumptions, though it has doubtless often been intended with that in mind. Mirowski [1989] stresses that before many economists forgot their own history, they never would have had this in mind—so Edgeworth certainly didn't.)

For present purposes the crucial point about Edgeworth's indifference curve technology, which was first systematically exploited in the work of Fisher (1892), is that their use incorporates no assumptions about cardinal utility beyond the indifference judgment itself (which is treated as primitive). That is, their construction assumes that we can compare *signs* of marginal utility, but presumes no measurements of any quantitative sums or totals of these utilities.[16] Fisher showed that relative price levels at equilibria—points where agents could not improve their satisfaction by shifting their consumption—can be determined strictly by the gradients of indifference curves. Therefore, if we can derive families of indifference curves for all consumers and all consumption bundles, then we can do our economic analysis without having to know anything at all about cardinal magnitudes. Pareto (1909/1971) took this analysis one step further, arguing that since indifference curves can be constructed on the basis of sequences of observed choices by agents, we need not begin microeconomic analyses from *any* independent measurements of utility, if utility is interpreted as some sort of psychological aspect or coefficient.

As Mandler (1999) shows, neither Fisher nor Pareto was consistently antirealist in their attitude toward utility as a psychological force. Fisher's specific analysis presupposed that the utility an agent derives from a particular commodity is often meaningfully separable from the utility she derives from other commodities; and if utilities can be separated then they must represent real forces.[17] Pareto does the same thing, and, at at least one point, actually asserts a cardinalist interpretation of the meaning of indifference indices (Mandler 1999, p. 121). Mirowski (1989, pp. 222–241) plausibly puts his finger on the deep problem here when he notes that Fisher, on the one hand, was under pressure to dissolve individuals as substantial psychological entities altogether, because with the appropriation of field metaphors from physics, preference profiles simply become fluctuations in uniform utility fields over commodity spaces and there is no endogenous basis for drawing boundaries between individuals. On the other hand, because the early neoclassicals wanted room for general welfare improvements (speaking anachronistically), they interpreted disutility by reference to a psychological resentment of labor. (This, Mirowski argues, ruined the exactness of the analogy between utility and energy, since the key property of energy in the physical models being borrowed was that it was conserved. Fisher thus obtained mathematical closure, as Mirowski explains, by imposition of the law of one price, which amounted to banning motion in the system.) It thus seems likely that their innovations were not driven mainly, if at all, either by intuitions about psychology and agency or by philosophical scruples concerning unobservable motivational states, but by concern for representational parsimony (often expressed as an aesthetic attraction to mathematical elegance). In the positivist atmosphere of the early twentieth century, however, any step along a road to representational simplicity was bound to be understood as an achievement in the direction of *ontological* simplicity, since the positivist rejection of "metaphysics" amounted, in part, to the view that *no* attempt at ontological interpretation going beyond and outside of representational conventions could ever be justified. This way of understanding matters ripped through economic theory with immense force in the 1930s.

As in many other sciences, that decade in economics was one of methodological manifestos. Nearly every leading economic theorist published, at least once, a review of reasons for supposing that economics could and should break decisively with "utilitarianism."[18] This way of expressing the point has generated considerable confusion. By "utilitarianism" the economists of the 1930s usually meant (roughly) sensationalistic hedonism. The real thrust of their campaign, however, was against psychological cardinalism, that is, against any incorporation into economic theory of the idea that agents necessarily guide their consumptive behavior by comparing varying levels of experienced cardinal utility. The confusion to which I just referred arises on at least two fronts. First, as discussed above, Bentham had tried his best to be scientifically cautious about the role that sensationalism could or should play in applied economics. I therefore take his sensationalist assumptions to have been somewhat incidental to his main concerns. The essence of utilitarianism is its linking of radical subjectivism about value with a conception of democracy as requiring moral antipaternalism and equal weighting of preferences in computing the social good. Since these normative theses were clearly still central to the new welfare economics that arose directly from the theoretical ferment of the 1930s, it is misleading to describe the methodological revolt against sensationalism and/or psychological cardinalism as amounting to a rejection of utilitarianism.[19] Second, as we saw in the case of Wicksteed, it is possible to be a cardinalist about utility without being a sensationalistic hedonist; but many writers of the 1930s (and after) seem to suppose that considerations against the latter tell automatically against the former. It has been a long time since anyone seriously defended sensationalistic hedonism as a viable general psychology, so arguments against *it* are easy to make and to sustain. But this has obscured the case against the real target of 1930s polemics, psychological cardinalism, and so it has also obscured the actual positive commitments of different post-1930s theorists.

The pivotal technical accomplishment of the 1930s was contributed by Hicks and Allen (1934). They began from Pareto's discovery, mentioned above, that preference maps sufficient for the prediction of consumption can be based on indifference curves that need not themselves be derived from utility functions. Since, as explained earlier, indifference curves incorporate no presumption of cardinal comparability beyond primitive indifference judgments, any analytic use of utility functions built only out of the elements necessary and sufficient for the construction of indifference curves could be interpreted as harmless from the anticardinalist perspective. Furthermore, Hicks and Allen showed that convexity of the demand function does not require the substantive psychological hypothesis of diminishing marginal utility. It will hold as long as the alternative property of diminishing marginal rates of substitution applies; that is, as long as the amount of commodity x an agent will exchange for a marginal increment of her stock of y declines with her stock of x. Two aspects of this basis for convexity will be important later. First, it is at least in principle testable on behavioral principles alone, since it makes no direct reference to levels of inner satisfaction. Second, it is sometimes justified by a logical rather than a psychological argument. Its violation is consistent with the possibility that an agent could rationally decide to consume only one commodity; and this is supposed to be a reductio ad absurdum on the violation. For reasons that will later be apparent, this is not an ultimately helpful argument if it is interpreted so as to shift the burden of assumption from a psychologically substantive concept of utility to an equally psychologically substantive concept of rationality. However, for the moment its importance simply lies in its exemplary standing as a sign of economists' conviction that theoretical *progress* consisted, to a large extent, in finding justifications for their favorite axioms that do not rest on sensationalism.

This last point helps to show that although "antiutilitarianism" poorly describes the philosophical ambitions of the 1930s theorists, these nevertheless went deeper than a mere concern for representational parsimony. As we saw, skepticism about the measurement of relative intensities had been expressed even by Bentham and Jevons, so adoption of indifference-curve technology need not by itself have been taken as marking an important philosophical shift. The makers of the so-called anti-utilitarian revolt of the 1930s—which continued through the 1940s and 1950s—were, to one degree or another, logical positivists. This is a familiar claim, especially to critics of current neoclassicism. It is often made, however, in ignorance of the extent to which positivism is a complex set of philosophical commitments that underwent systematic internal development during its history and therefore comes in varying degrees of sophistication and scholarly responsibility.[20] Furthermore, the various theses commonly associated with positivism do not all have a common philosophical motivation, and so they do not all rise and fall together. Economists influenced by positivism in the 1930s and 1940s themselves grasped these complexities to different degrees, and so their own conceptions of the epistemological foundations of their joint project to reform their discipline varied as well. I stress again that I am not here engaged in trying to make an original contribution to the history of economic thought, but am merely building a platform that will connect a set of new philosophical theses with the background familiar to economic theorists and their critics. Abjuring pretense to the historian's scruples, therefore, I will simplify examination of the positivist roots of anti-utilitarianism— henceforth, to be more accurately called "ordinalism"—by focusing exclusively on the thought of its two most famous and influential methodological proponents: Lionel Robbins and Paul Samuelson. For both historical and logical reasons, I will start with Robbins.

Positivist Foundations: Lionel Robbins

What is still, for many economists, the "official" statement of the general ontology and epistemology of the discipline was articulated by Robbins in his *Essay on the Nature and Significance of Economic Science* (1935).[21] Robbins's *Essay* is organized around defense of his definition of economics as "the science which studies human behavior as a relationship between ends and scarce means which have alternative uses" (p. 16). It will help orient the reader through the coming discussion if I say up front that in this book I will defend this definition as being the correct one after all, amending it only by dropping the word "human" from it. But this is, again, a project of the whole book. For now, the focus will be on Robbins's own particular interpretation of the definition's basis and implications.

The first philosophical principle on which Robbins mainly relies is very clear: he assumes that a genuine science must have the widest logical scope compatible with the possibility of using it as a basis for deriving testable predictions. It is on this ground that he strenuously rejects what I called the "semi-Aristotelian" position of Jevons and

Marshall, according to which economic generalizations apply only to a class of preferences restricted as to content. Robbins thus follows Wicksteed in endorsing the doctrine that actions are homogenous with respect to their describability in terms of economic logic. Unfortunately for the clarity of subsequent—including contemporary—debate, the basis of this endorsement by Robbins is a set of positivist theses about the epistemology of science.

Calling Robbins a positivist is controversial. Caldwell (1982), for example, structures his historical review of twentieth-century economic methodology by setting up Robbins as a contrastive *foil* for the "positivist" account he associates with Terence Hutchison. This exemplifies, however, my point about taking the dynamic complexity of positivism seriously. I follow Michael Friedman (1999) in emphasizing the Kantian roots of early positivism, with its stress on the axiomatic organization of pure phenomena as the logical basis for science. Caldwell turns Robbins into a foil for positivism by instead emphasizing its empiricist commitments[22]—far too exclusively, in my view. The kind of positivism expressed by economists developed, just as did positivism in general among philosophers, in a more empiricist and less Kantian direction as time went on. This will be revisited in my discussion of Samuelson later in this chapter; and the issue is in turn an important prologue to the epistemological and metaphysical theses I will defend in chapter 4.

The positivist basis of Robbins's criticism of the semi-Aristotelian view is made clearest in his attack on one particular set of opponents, namely, advocates of historicist interpretations of economics who sought to assimilate it to narrative sociology. Robbins's early career confronted him with a campaign for historicism and institutionalism in economics, coming mainly from Germany. The basis for his rejection of this campaign is the essence of (that is, the one core thesis never abandoned during the history of) positivism: a body of claims is scientific, he asserts, only to the extent that it reflects the discovery of logically transparent relations between broad assumptions and specific, testable predictions. (Institutionalism was criticized by Robbins as failing to meet the breadth-of-scope criterion.) This idea will be familiar from chapter 1; it is just the claim that science aims at systematicity. Positivists typically interpreted this as requiring that a theory, to be scientific, had to be capable of expression as a formally axiomatized system of generalizations. Nowhere in the *Essay* does Robbins explicitly go quite this far. However, he often hints that full axiomatization and universality of generalizations is an appropriate limiting ideal.[23]

Because, Robbins argues at great length, many scarce things wanted by people are not material, and do not serve their selfish interests in material wealth, an economics of narrow Aristotelian scope could not rest on any generalizations that are simultaneously broad and distinct enough in their implications to figure in the generation of precise predictions. Economics therefore cannot be the study of the causes of material welfare, except incidentally. There is no question that, for Robbins, this is the overwhelming basis of the need to reject classicism, and for him what distinguishes scientific economics from its ancestor investigations in political economy.

Where does this leave Robbins with respect to the relationship between economics and psychology? Again, firmly in the heartland of early (Kantian) positivism. The two key facts on which the possibility of economics depends are identified as (i) the fact that people can and do order their preferences, and maintain these orderings for nontrivial lengths of time relative to sequences of behavioral choices, and (ii) scarcity, the fact that not all the ordered preferences can generally be satisfied. With respect to the role of psychology in Robbins's conception of economics, the first fact is the relevant one. It is thanks to it that indifference curves for agents can be drawn, and this is true regardless of whether indifference curves are derived from or interpreted by means of utility functions. Robbins is consistently coy on the question of whether the agent herself, or only the economist analyzing her, needs to be aware of the fact that she has a dynamically stable preference ordering. He is, however, explicit in claiming that our basis for knowing the fact is not strictly behavioral, but derives primarily from introspection. Behaviorism is referred to as "a queer cult" (Robbins 1935, p. 87), the strictures of which would cripple epistemological access to essential facts if they were insisted on. This is because, Robbins argues, the relationship between preference and scarcity that comprises the subject matter of economics is embodied in introspectively evident processes of *choice* (ibid., pp. 85–90). It is because we all have regular awareness of inner psychic experiences of deliberately choosing among scarce objects of preference that we can know that economic analysis applies to a real set of empirical phenomena. On this same basis we are said to know that hedonism is descriptively false (ibid., pp. 84–86).

Robbins does not take this to imply that economic analysis aims at describing the *causal* mechanics of choice, which is held to be the proper province of psychology. Economics studies instead the *abstract logic* of choice, identifying by formal deduction the constraints on behavior that must follow from the *mere* fact that choice among scarce objects of preference goes on. Hedonism, if it were true, would be a thesis about the causal basis of choice rather than about its logic, and so interpretations of economics as resting on hedonic foundations involve, according to Robbins, both a factual mistake and a conceptual one. The conclusions of economic analysis, he argues, are not hostage to any particular theory of the mechanics of choice, and herein lies the proper basis of its separateness as a science (ibid., pp. 83–84).

This conception precisely conforms, as I have said, to the positivist idea of a properly grounded science. A science, according to that view, should consist of a series of logically derived consequences of observationally evident facts. Furthermore, the ultimate positivist justification of observational facts *as facts* must be introspective, since the only observational contents to which we are supposed to have direct and unmediated access are inner experiences. The positivist philosopher Schlick (1933/1979) had argued in a classic exposition of this view that any projection of the contents of inner experience to claims about the existence or nonexistence of external, self-subsistent properties and processes involves an inferential leap that rests on a nondemonstrable metaphysical hypothesis to the effect that experiences are caused by external objects and processes, and so cannot be a proper part of science. Here, exactly, is the Kantian core of positivism. In the purest expressions of the view, it comports with a suspicion of the scientific significance of *any* causal claims, a thesis that goes back to Hume and persists in contemporary, sophisticated forms of neopositivism (e.g., van Fraassen 1980, who describes causal hypotheses as "flights of fancy").

There is no reason to believe that Robbins was directly influenced by the positivists of the Vienna Circle. However, I am doing philosophy here, not intellectual history.[24] Robbins articulates a conception of economics according to which it exactly fits the early positivist ideal for science. That is, economics cooked to Robbins's recipe is a self-contained deductive structure resting on an introspective foundation that is taken to be maximally epistemologically modest. Note that since psychology is supposed by Robbins to be concerned with causal mechanisms and relations, a strict positivist might take such psychology to be of dubious scientific status by comparison with economics. Seen in this light, the separateness thesis as justified by Robbins emerges as not merely a methodological policy, but as a philosophical necessity.

To see what is at stake for contemporary issues here, let us relax our tight focus on Robbins for a moment. One might suppose that if economics is seen as the science of the abstract logic of choice, then the natural way to refine and deepen it would be by means of the elaboration of formal rational choice theory. This comports naturally with the factual observation that economists have been, along with philosophers, the major contributors to this elaboration, which has progressed since the 1940s to a level of sophistication Robbins surely did not foresee. Economists and philosophers have tended to base their respective involvements in the rational choice industry on different motivations. Generalizing very broadly, for philosophers rational choice theory is a branch of normative inquiry, part of the answer to questions about what an ideally rational agent *ought* to do. For economists, by comparison, rational choice theory is often viewed as contributing to *descriptive* science, offering analysis of what economic agents *in fact* do given the assumption that they are rational. Economists' use of rational choice theory is thus exposed to criticisms of a sort that philosophers can shrug off, namely, attacks based on evidence that people are not, as a matter of fact, rational in the way they assume. On the other hand, rational choice philosophers, but not economists, must answer worries about the normative appropriateness of being ideally rational, in the relevant sense, in the first place. (These two sorts of criticisms can converge if one is persuaded by studies such as that of Frank et al. 1993 that teaching people rational choice theory as a descriptive tool encourages them to feel normatively inclined to conform their behavior to it.)

These issues will be the subject of chapter 5. For the moment, our concern is with their relationship to Robbins's conception of the domain of economics. This is important because an economist who *does* view formal rational choice theory as a part of the descriptive content of behavioral economics could easily view herself as working within Robbins's conception, just given what has been said about that conception so far. This would be hasty, however. The implication of the separateness thesis as Robbins justifies it is that choice, as a psychological process, is a black box that, so far as economics is concerned, is supposed to be deliberately left shut. Robbins's economist is not advised to proceed by continued introspection of her own deliberative processes, but by logically determining which behaviors would maximize a given agent's preference satisfaction relative to a preference ordering, an environment, and a budget of resources. For Robbins, the only psychological fact (delivered by introspection) that is relevant to economics is that people *do* deliberately choose. Robbins simply asserts (though at some length), rather than argues for, his claim that the existence of real deliberative choice is necessary if economics is to be about anything empirical. It is consistent with everything Robbins says in the *Essay*, and elsewhere, to suppose that he simply took it as self-evident that deliberative choice must be the process linking ordered preferences to behavior because he couldn't think of anything else that might do the job.

As will be extensively discussed in later chapters, contemporary cognitive science is not sympathetic to the idea that the arcane principles of formal rational choice, any more than the refined discoveries of economic analysis in general, are to be determined by continued and careful introspection. One might therefore try to ground the economic use of rational choice theory on Robbins's positivist foundations by means of the following argument. Economics, to be empirically relevant, relies on the assumption that people are, at least approximately, maximizers of their preference orderings. An agent can expect to maximize satisfaction of her preferences only to the extent that her behavior conforms to the axioms of the best normative theory of rational choice that is available. Therefore, the (positivist) economist can and should assume that people are motivated to learn this theory, will do so insofar as their computational limitations can be overcome by practice or formal education, and will then conform their behavior to as much of this theory as they can understand. They might monitor their success partly by introspecting their own choice processes, but they might equally well do so by taking a behavioristic attitude to themselves, simply comparing their self-observed behaviors with the recommendations of normative rational choice theory and making pseudorandom adjustments to their patterns of choice whenever they spot a mismatch, so that they incrementally bring their behavior and ideal rationality into closer conformity.

This argument would undermine Robbins's version of the separateness thesis, since its conclusion invites empirical psychologists to test the prediction that people try to conform to an ideal of rationality by one means or the other. Indeed, Robbins is sometimes interpreted as *potentially* undermining his separateness thesis in just this way. That is, he has been interpreted as asserting that everyday observation regularly reassures us that people try to be genuinely rational in their pursuit of preference maximization. If this *were* Robbins's view then it would hold scientific or novel psychology apart from economics only so long as that psychology did not undermine the conclusions of everyday observation. Few psychologists or philosophers, however friendly some of them might be to the basic conceptual apparatus of folk psychology, nowadays believe that scientific psychology generally vindicates folk generalizations. So on this interpretation of Robbins, he undermines his separateness thesis in a way he wasn't in a position to recognize given his beliefs about psychology.

However, the interpretation does not survive close inspection of Robbins's position. He explicitly insists (1935, pp. 92–94) that economics does not depend on, and should not suppose, that people are competent rational maximizers of utility:

Means may be scarce in relation to ends, even though the ends be inconsistent. Exchange, production, fluctuation—all take place in a world in which people do not know the full implications of what they are doing. It is often inconsistent (i.e., irrational in this sense) to wish at once for the fullest satisfaction of consumers' demands, and at the same time to impede the import of foreign goods by tariffs or suchlike obstacles. Yet it is frequently done: and who shall say that economic science is not competent to explain the situation resulting? (Ibid., pp. 92–93)

One might object here that Robbins's example does not prove his point, since people who favor tariffs might value things other than, and competing with, "the fullest satisfaction of consumers' demands." However, what matters for the moment is Robbins's belief itself, which is that economic analysis does not presume the capacity of its subjects to rationally maximize whatever it is they *do* want.

Robbins considers two other, less demanding, conceptions of rationality that might be thought to be built into economic analysis. "In so far," he says,

as the term rational is taken to mean merely "consistent," then it is true that an assumption of this sort does enter into certain analytical constructions. The celebrated generalization that in a state of equilibrium the relative significance of divisible commodities is equal to their price does involve the assumption that each final choice is consistent with every other, in the sense that if I prefer A to B and B to C, I also prefer A to C: in short, that in a state of perfect equilibrium the possibility of further advantage from "internal arbitrage operations" is excluded. (Ibid., p. 92)

This, of course, expresses the famous idea that a core aspect of minimal economic rationality is transitivity of preferences. It is misleadingly coy of Robbins to say only that these commitments "enter into certain analytical constructions." After all, transitivity of preference is a necessary property if preferences are to be *ordered* at all; and Robbins has enshrined the *fact* that preferences are, at least often, ordered as one of the two foundational assumptions for the possibility and empirical significance of economics. For the moment, however, let us just note that Robbins is trying as hard as he can—indeed, harder than he perhaps can—to minimize the economist's commitment to rationality.

After thus dodging the precise extent of the necessity of consistency assumptions, Robbins finally settles on what he grants as the truly minimal necessary condition:

Of course there is a sense in which the word rationality can be used which renders it legitimate to argue that at least some rationality is assumed before human behavior has an economic aspect—the sense, namely, in which it is equivalent to "purposive". . . . [I]t is arguable that if behavior is not conceived as purposive, then the conception of the means-end relationships which economics studies has no meaning. So if there were no purposive action it could be argued that there were no economic phenomena. But to say this is not to say in the least that all purposive action is completely consistent. (Ibid., p. 93)

This passage is dense with philosophical significance. First, note that it is spun ontologically rather than epistemically. That is, if purposive actions did not *exist* then there would ("arguabl[y]") not *be* any economic phenomena. Since there could presumably still be psychological phenomena (at least on Robbins's introspectionist conception of the psychological) in the absence of purposiveness, the separateness thesis is thus given an ontological, as opposed to merely methodological, twist. But if we are to make the passage as a whole consistent with the previous one quoted above, then we need to ask how the existence of economic phenomena could depend on the existence of purposive behavior without thereby depending on the minimal behavioral consistency represented by transitivity of preferences. Raising this issue does not require any quibble with Robbins's final sentence, since purposive action could clearly go on in the absence of "complete" consistency (about which more will be said in the next section). But how could one ever discern purposiveness in action if behavior did not even manifest (at least through the course of the behavioral sequence under analysis) merely transitive preference structure? After all, if one takes, for example, rocks to be exemplars of systems without purposes, the behavioral evidence for this just consists in the fact that if one *did* ascribe desires to a rock, about, for example, where to sit, on the basis of its sequence of locations, then the resulting system would show no transitivity (except, briefly and occasionally, coincidentally) once the influence of gravitational force was factored out. That is: the influence of gravitational force explains *all* apparent transitivity in rock behavior; and given that fact there is no temptation at all to treat rocks as agents.

But, as we have seen, Robbins disavows behaviorism; and we can now view this disavowal as essential, rather than incidental to, his own understanding of his definition of economics. The set of his claims we have been reviewing can only be made consistent with one another if we take him to suppose at least the bare logical possibility that a person could be introspectively aware of entertaining purposes—indeed, of having ordered preferences—while failing to find expression of this in any transitivity with respect to the rationalization of their own behavior. Because, for Robbins, there are facts about purposes rooted in consciousness and independent of behavior, purposeless behavior is taken to be conceptually compatible with the presence of purposes expressed in ordered preferences. Then our grounds for believing that rocks lack purposes would not be essentially behavioral, but would rest on a factual belief to the effect that rocks lack consciousness.

This interpretation coheres nicely with what Robbins says immediately following the last passage quoted: "It may indeed be urged that the more that purposive action becomes conscious of itself, the more it necessarily becomes consistent."[25] One could hardly frame a more Kantian sentiment—as we might expect from a positivist, given that historical logical positivism *is* the reconciliation of Kantian metaphysics and epistemology with Humean skepticism about causation (Friedman 1999). The sentiment is equally deeply at odds with contemporary cognitive and behavioral science—not to mention ethological facts. However we might define "consciousness," we are likely to think that people have substantially more of it than wasps. However, if one's approach to behavioral prediction is to derive it from mere consequences of assumptions about preference consistency, then one's track record will be vastly better with wasps than with people (Ross 2002c). Indeed, insects make nearly ideal subjects for neoclassical microeconomic analysis. Because the relations between an insect's goals and its behavioral responses are hardwired and sensitive to environmental variations only along finitely specifiable and tightly stereotyped dimensions, location of these dimensions by empirical means picks out a nice set of stable variables for subsequent application of the logical relations that the economist studies. The control regularities discovered by the entomologist *constitute* the insect's budget constraint and condition-action repertoire, from which the derivation of its utility-maximization function is then a straightforward technical matter. We thus have a one-to-one mapping between the biological individual insect and a well-behaved economic agent, and we will never be tempted to explain disappointments in its career of utility maximization as resulting from preference reversal.

Of course, we are under little temptation to suppose that insects experience anything like the phenomena associated with deliberative choice—and this is just the point. Robbins' introspectionist epistemological foundations for economics are almost precisely wrong with respect to picking out the conditions under which microeconomics—as the mere application of logical analysis of consistency assumptions in behavior—works *best*. I will return to this theme in detail in chapter 6. For the moment, I want to highlight two points. First, the reversal of Robbins's Kantian intuition undermines only one aspect of his definition of the scope of economics: it removes his grounds for restricting it to analysis of *human* action. Second, it carries us in the direction of behaviorism, over Robbins's explicit protest as quoted earlier. This draws attention toward some important tensions within the generic positivist attitudes that partly inspired the ordinalist revolt. As noted, classical positivism was deeply Kantian in both its attitude to metaphysics and in its philosophical psychology. Simultaneously, however, its commitment to epistemic verificationism lent it natural affinities with psychological behaviorism, which flourished in the most important postpositivist contributions to the epistemology of the 1940s and 1950s, those of Ryle (1949), Wittgenstein (1953), and Quine (1953). This rival current within positivism is also present in Robbins's *Essay*, and was at least as great an aspect of the *Essay*'s subsequent influence as his affinities with more "classical" positivism.

I noted earlier that in the casual methodological lore of neoclassical economics, the rejection of hedonistic sensationalism and the campaign for ordinalism in the interpretation of utility functions are typically run together as two aspects of the same view. We have seen how Robbins's classical positivism justifies his antihedonism: the latter is a thesis about specific psychological *causation*, which is supposed to be none of the positivist economist's business. However, nothing in the first four chapters of Robbins's *Essay*, to which our attention has so far been confined, validly tells against cardinal interpretations of utility. After all, if the empirical significance of economic analysis rests on people's introspective awareness of processes of deliberative choice phenomena, why should the economist have to ignore a closely related dogma of folk-psychological introspectionism, according to which such choice rests on, *by logical incorporation rather than causation*, assessments of the relative "felt intensities" of goal-directed desires? Once it is imagined that people phenomenally *experience* their preferences as ordered, it is then peculiar to suppose that they experience them as *merely* ordered. Hume, by contrasting example, clearly thought that we infer our preference orderings *from* our phenomenal awareness of differing levels of "vivacity" in our passions for outcomes. In maintaining this doctrine, Hume speaks for folk-psychological common sense. Robbins never addresses this problem at all, thus apparently not noticing that the "everyday" psychological knowledge to which he crucially appeals is, both conceptually and historically, quite odd if it is read as compatible with strict ordinalism. Nevertheless, Robbins does endorse ordinalism, sometimes quite vehemently by comparison with his generally preferred rhetorical tone.[26] This attitude, I will now argue, borders on philosophical schizophrenia.

Strictly, ordinalism is the thesis that utility functions should be defined only by reference to properties preserved under monotonically increasing transformations. Diminishing marginal utility is not such a property—which is just why the mainstream economists of the 1930s were so pleased to see its apparent elimination by Hicks and Allen (1934). Their replacement property, diminishing marginal substitutability, guarantees convexity of demand curves by supposing that agents will exchange less of any commodity x for another commodity y as their stock of x increases,[27] but makes no reference to any sensationalistic or other causal psychological basis for this fact; that is, it is behavioral. Now, as Mandler (1999, pp. 85–96) argues, in assessing the strength of possible motivations for ordinalism we need to distinguish between the diminishing marginal utility principle as Jevons had understood it and the weaker property Mandler calls "psychological concavity." The former is the thesis that agents are introspectively aware of the *rates* at which the marginal utilities of particular commodities diminish on the margins, whereas psychological concavity denotes the property of *mere* awareness *that* marginal utility diminishes. Mandler operationalizes psychological concavity as follows: "At any point x, the set of psychologically accurate utility representations of preference on any line intersecting x is nonempty and consists of all of the concave utility representations of the agent's preferences on that line. In other words, agents experience diminishing marginal utility in all directions but no further nonordinal psychological reactions; on any line, any concave function representing the agent's preferences is psychologically accurate" (ibid., p. 87). This extensional specification of the property permits assessment of its formal relationship to traditional diminishing marginal utility. Mandler shows that the set of utility-function transformations respecting Jevonsian diminishing marginal utility is a proper subset of those respecting psychological concavity, so the latter is a weaker assumption. However, psychological concavity is still not strictly ordinal.

Though Robbins's classical positivist epistemology gives him no valid basis for rejecting even the stronger nonordinal property, it should practically *compel* him to endorse psychological concavity. He is, after all, committed to the claim that introspection tells us about a great deal more than mere sensory qualia: we are aware of the fact of ordering our preferences. To then rule out, as Robbins does, the suggestion that we are also aware of purely *qualitative* diminishing marginal utility is completely ad hoc. Robbins should therefore prefer psychological concavity as a principle to diminishing marginal substitutability, which seems at first glance to have only behaviorist assumptions—manifestations of the "queer cult"—in its comparative favor.

Historically, there is no puzzle here: Robbins shows no awareness of Mandler's distinction and surely simply didn't think of it. But this just invites the question "Why not?" since the distinction is almost exactly parallel to Robbins's *leading* distinction between mere awareness of order in preferences and awareness of cardinal properties of orderings. The text offers no clue; and in any case we are interested here in actual logical relations, not in Robbins's intellectual biography per se. It is time to do some philosophy.

Let us approach the question this way. For a strict ordinalist, what arguments can be offered in favor of Hicks and Allen's preferred property of diminishing marginal substitutability? Most microeconomics textbooks still endorse it, and many imply that its basis is empirical; it thereby becomes an object of fond regard for those methodologists who pay rhetorical service to Popperian or Lakatosian falsificationism about economics. However, this in turn makes it grist for the mill of philosophical critics of economics such as Hausman (1992) and Rosenberg

(1992), who observe that counterinstances to diminishing marginal substitutability raised by complementary goods[28] are invariably treated, without justification, as limiting instances rather than refuting ones. However, the argument for diminishing marginal substitutability that was actually standard in the 1930s, before Popperian themes had become popular among economists, defended it on logical rather than empirical grounds. This argument goes as follows: if marginal utility on some good is allowed to rise (without limit) then nothing in the model of the rational agent rules out *monomaniac consumption*, that is, maximization of utility through consumption of only that good. But this is taken to be a reductio ad absurdum. Never mind for now whether this is a *good* argument; the point is that it defends concavity in just the way that acyclicity of preferences is typically defended, that is, as an aspect of the definition of economic rationality. As we saw above, Robbins cannot avoid logical (as opposed to empirical) commitment to acyclicity, try though he does to dodge the point. And, in a section of his *Essay* where he is not yet directly focused on topics related to rationality or ordinalism—his philosophical guard, perhaps, thus being down—Robbins explicitly invokes the logical argument for diminishing marginal substitutability.

It is not difficult to construct all this in a way that is charitable to Robbins. If concavity is a necessary aspect of economic rationality, just like acyclicity, then diminishing marginal substitutability is a better assumption for assuring it than Jevonsian diminishing marginal utility simply because the former is more general and epistemologically modest. Diminishing marginal substitutability does not have this advantage, however, *relative to Robbins's own psychological Kantianism*, over psychological concavity. That is to say, psychological concavity requires no additional or more specific empirical assumptions than Robbins had already endorsed for other reasons. Psychological concavity is clearly the property Robbins should have preferred had it occurred to him, and had philosophical consistency been his trumping consideration. However, it did not occur to him because, in the final analysis, his commitment to the generality and axiomatic structure— the systematicity—of a proper scientific theory trumps the special (psychological) Kantianism he shares with classical positivism.

This mirrors what happened to positivism in general. Giving priority to systematicity over philosophical psychology primes Robbins's epistemology of economics for a slippery slope into behaviorism, paralleling the three-decade progress in general epistemology from

Kantian positivism toward Quine, *if* behaviorist foundations for economics can preserve or increase systematic generality. I will be arguing, throughout the chapters to come, that they can. (Thus, for me, the slippery slope is a welcome water slide to somewhere cool.) This, in a nutshell, is why Robbins's definition of the scope of economics—minus the word "human"—and his basis for the separateness thesis will survive through all the twists and turns in the arguments to come.

First, however, we must follow the actual development of orthodox economic methodology one step further, through its historical shift into avowed behaviorism in the 1940s. This will then be the basis for the hybrid view I will call the "Robbins–Samuelson argument pattern" (RASP), which I will spend the rest of the book elaborating and defending by appeal to contemporary cognitive science.

Samuelson and Behaviorism

My treatment of Samuelson's revealed preference theory (RPT) as a *historical* entry will involve no significant departures from orthodox commentary; but there are some philosophical points to add. As carefully demonstrated by Wong (1978), Samuelson was philosophically naïve even by comparison with the usual standard among economic theorists. Over the course of his career, he offered at least three "fundamental," but mutually inconsistent, justifications for regarding RPT as the preferable systematic foundation for consumer theory. The details of these adventures don't merit attention here; the philosophical labels for his position that Samuelson explicitly tried on, "operationalism" and "descriptivism," cannot be reconstructed as serious contenders in any general epistemology of science. He was fond of stating grand justificatory principles in elegant little ex cathedra flourishes, which is a matter of rhetorical taste that offends some and charms others, but in either case invites long efforts at interpretive pedantry—caustic and destructive from the irritated, earnest and heroic from the admiring. My own working principle here is that to wheel out the full war machine of philosophical ordnance on analysis of Samuelson's *declared* philosophical allegiances would show poor judgment in fitting technology to use.

This being said, for a reader with a certain metaphysical aesthetic, one that enjoys the contemplation of smooth and austere ontological constructions from which all "vestigial growths" (Quine's phrase) have been removed, Samuelson's *Foundations of Economic Analysis* (published in 1947 but largely composed in the late 1930s) has many sections of beauty. The aesthetic underlying this judgment is not quite the conventional mathematician's one. Samuelson's formal proofs may or may not be thought elegant, but these are gathered outside of his main text into appendices, and I am in any case not a competent judge of the finer gradations of mathematical elegance. The relevant aesthetic here is instead the engineer's: what Samuelson builds is a *machine*. What exactly this machine *produces* for behavioral science is, however, far from obvious;[29] there is a lot of work ahead before we will be able to say.

The aesthetic reflection, however, is not a side issue, but is integrally connected with the nature of economics in the generations after Hicks and Robbins. In the leading works of all the neoclassical theorists from Jevons and Walras through Hicks, there is a philosophical tension. On the one hand, they seek gains in systematicity through increasingly rigorous analysis. On the other hand, none of them ever lose sight of the worldly object of their inquiries, so that they constantly interpret their objects of analysis, as they go along, by reference to a folk ontology of economic relations continuous with that found in Smith, Ricardo, and Marx: value and wealth, producers and consumers, profits and losses, labor and leisure. (One way of glossing the core thesis defended by Mirowski [1989] is that this tension is fundamental and irresolvable in would-be scientific economics, and that neoclassicism largely is a forlorn attempt to dodge it.) The beauty of Samuelson's work, where it arises, lies in clear stands on what trumps what, as the features of a perfectly abstract and almost purely formal "economy" are finally allowed complete triumph over the ontology of daily human interests.[30] (This same aesthetic is what offends Dupré, and excites Mirowski's postmodernist suspicions about theorists' psychological motivations. I would reject any claim, however, that it is necessarily misanthropic to appreciate conceptions that slough off mundane concerns. Economic *activity* had better feed people, but this doesn't strictly imply anything about the logical character of economic *theory*.)

Since this point will be important later, let me give one example. By the conclusion of his fourth chapter on production functions, Samuelson has defined production equilibrium for a single firm as the point at which the ratio of marginal physical productivity to marginal cost is maximized, the marginal productivity of the last unit of expenditure being equal in every use. This is of course supposed to be an analysis of profit maximization, which provides the terminological link between the mathematical structure and conventional conceptions of economic *behavior*. But this link is to be constrained *exactly*. That is, we are discouraged from smuggling into our interpretation of the analysis anything related to folk associations with the concept of profit that are generated by curiosity over why some firms in empirical economies are profitable and others are not. This, the driving concern of all the classical economists, is now waved aside as a distraction. At this stage of the construction we have no agents and no markets, so no basis for understanding "profits" by some top-down analysis of departures from perfect competition through entry barriers. Samuelson instead defines "pure competition" from the perspective of the one firm as meaning "that the demand curve for any one firm is infinitely elastic, that his sales cannot effect prices" (1947, p. 82). In this condition there is one natural limiting case where at equilibrium demand curves shift toward zero revenue and minimization of marginal cost is equivalent to minimization of average cost. This, Samuelson says, is what "free entry" might mean at this stage. And then we are told: "It is quite clear that in the real world net revenue is not zero for all firms, nor is it tending towards zero. This is true under pure competition as well as impure competition. *It is clear that this residium must be 'due' to something, and it may be labeled by any name we please (rent to institutional advantage, etc.)*" (ibid., p. 87). I have italicized the last sentence for the sake of my point with this example. It could readily be taken out of context to suggest extreme neoinstitutionalism, or even to please a Marxist. Taken in the first way, it would make Samuelson look very hip by reference to currently popular conversations. But in Samuelson's actual context these spins would be egregiously gratuitous. What is going on is just that profits, in the folk sense, are being swept into the same basket of "vestigial growths" on pure analysis as institutional rents—distortions on a clear view of the fundamental economic machine, a pure generator of some selected maximization profiles, at work.[31]

I will leave to Mirowski—and I don't intend this dismissively—speculations about the psychological, social, and historical contexts that can encourage somebody to admire utterly abstract machines that might not be able to actually do anything. What does directly concern me here are the logical sources of such intellectual activity. Let us therefore begin by just saying that Samuelson was certainly a positivist, but in a broader and less historically specific sense than Robbins. As twentieth-century positivism developed after the 1920s, its set of foundational commitments grew steadily more diffuse and open to variations of emphasis and purpose. Samuelson's positivism is of this loose, and progressively loosening, type. If there is just one deep linear trend in the history of positivism, however, it is the steady abandonment of its original Kantian foundations, until by the late 1950s we can flip from the views of the later Carnap into Quine's pragmatic behaviorism by the adoption of just a few famous Quinean slogans.[32] There is no trace of Kant in Samuelson. His generic positivism consists solely in the conjunction of two things: an absolute commitment to axiomatic systematicity as the highest objective in theory construction, and the belief that to prime a theory for verification by deriving measurable empirical consequences from its axioms is the essence of building a scientific theory. Postpositivist philosophy of science has greatly weakened these commitments in various ways, but its mainstream has not altogether abandoned them.[33] Samuelson's positivism is thus less interesting than Robbins's version, because it contains little of what made (early) positivism a distinctive philosophical position. Indeed, it is instructive to call Samuelson a positivist at all only for one reason, the reason that marks his muddled philosophical utterances as representative of their time: he never evinces the slightest interest in ontological questions of the sort that motivate scientific realists. Generic positivism perished along with the death of that attitude; this is one of the main respects in which Samuelson was a positivist and most of us are not.

Samuelson opens the *Foundations* by saying "The existence of analogies between central features of various theories implies the existence of a general theory which underlies the particular theories and unifies them with respect to those central features" (1947, p. 3). It is the purpose of his work, he then declares, "to work out [the] implications" of this "fundamental principle" for "theoretical and applied economics." He notes that economists have "always" been aware of "striking formal similarities" in the equations they used to describe production, consumer behavior, international trade, public finance, business cycles, and income analysis, but then identifies his own novel insight as consisting in the claim that there are "formally identical *meaningful* theorems in these fields, each derived by an essentially analogous method" (ibid.). "Meaningful" here means "operationalizable and empirically verifiable." The aim of the *Foundations* is to elucidate this method and logically unify these theorems.

Based on what is *missing* from his opening philosophical animadversions, Samuelson evidently felt no need to specify at the outset that the achievement of his ambition as applied to consumer theory required the complete elimination of introspectionist assumptions from economic theory. Perhaps a 1947 reader was supposed to approve of this just because she knew that behaviorism was then the established truth in psychology. But a reader who was a theoretical economist could in any case be counted on to share the commitment as a consequence of her knowledge of decades of accumulated details in formal analysis within her discipline. As discussed earlier in this chapter, the development of indifference curve analysis through the work of Edgeworth, Fisher, Pareto, and Hicks had enabled substantive utility to be eliminated from the foundations of economic-agency (consumer) theory, but in a way that left the need for a justification of the convexity of demand awkwardly exposed. However, indifference itself seems to require psychological interpretation if it is to do empirical work.[34] An agent who first chooses a over b and then b over a, without any changes in prices or income, might be indifferent between them or might be irrational for all that any nonpsychological evidence can determine. Indifference therefore seems to be no more satisfactory as a primitive concept than utility itself; and in the absence of such a primitive, which can be used without implicit recourse to strong psychological assumptions, the separateness thesis is hard to sustain.

Considerations going beyond, and more specific than, interest in the separateness thesis also (perhaps mainly) motivated dissatisfaction with Hicksian indifference-curve analysis as foundational. As Blaug (1980) emphasizes, such analysis permits no independent measurements of the income and substitution effects on demand, a distinction nevertheless crucial to the analysis of Hicks and Allen (1934). Indifference treated as primitive is thus inadequate from the perspectives of both systematicity and operationalization: it is unsystematic because it treats diminishing marginal substitution as an axiom when it ought to be a theorem, and nonoperational because it can't be used to empirically distinguish its key relational variables, income and taste.[35]

Jumping straight to the chase, then, Samuelson's RPT is supposed to achieve both systematicity and operationalization by making preference, interpreted simply as choice, its primitive. Even this standard formulation threatens to be misleading, since both "preference" and "choice" are folk-psychological terms. An economically consistent agent is said to prefer a over b if, given a fixed income and set of marginal prices, she consumes a marginal unit of a rather than a marginal unit of b. No Robbinsian reliance on deliberation or calculation is called for in understanding what "choice" means. Instead, it is rendered into a purely technical concept useful for classifying such behavior as can be structured by reference to a particular set of mathematical functions.

Pedagogical practice varies with respect to compact statements of RPT. For facility of future reference, I will explicitly run through one such statement, which will give us all the concepts we'll subsequently need. The definitional fussing to come is intended only to fix conceptual reference; so no challenge is here intended to readers who prefer alternative formulations. But one technical note for economists and mathematicians is in order here if I'm not to risk confusing them. By "RPT" I want to refer to the entire package of Samuelsonian theoretical commitments, not just to what is formally necessary for the axiomatization of "choice as revealed preference." For the latter, one needs only (i) a theory defining "preference" and (ii) axioms relating "preference" to "choice"; or, (ii) plus (iii) axioms defining "choice" in terms of behavioral "revelation." Samuelson takes "RPT" to refer to (ii) plus (iii), and then adds as a corollary that with this apparatus he can avoid reference to "preference" understood psychologically. By contrast, the formulation I will give below is the union of (i), (ii), and (iii), which formally identifies "preference" and "choice."[36] I'm not yet going to argue for that identification; I first just want to state it clearly.

So: preference is first made suitable for axiomatic service by logically reducing it to a binary relation. That is, everything we want to be able to say using the concept is to be obtained recursively by taking the relation $a \succsim b$ as primitive: a is "strictly preferred" to b, $a > b$, when $a \succsim b$ and not $b \succsim a$; and a and b are related by "indifference," $a \sim b$, when $a \succsim b$ and $b \succsim a$. Any properties defined exclusively in terms of this relation are guaranteed to be (at most) ordinal (Sen 1969; Mandler 1999, p. 81). Next, we impose some restrictions on the relation (hereafter following Kreps 1990b, pp. 19ff.) by confining our attention to sets $X \in \{X\}$ with two properties. First, *asymmetry*: there is no pair $x, y \in X$ such that $x > y$ and $y > x$. Second, *negative transitivity*: for any $x, y, z \in X$, if $x > y$ then either $x > z$ or $z > y$ or both. The conjunction of these properties implies four more: (i) *irreflexivity*: for no x is $x > x$; (ii) *transitivity*: if $x > y$ and $y > z$ then $x > z$; (iii) *acyclicity*: if for some finite integer n $x_1 > x_2, \ldots, x_{n-1} > x_n$ then $x_n \neq x_1$; and (iv) *completeness of weak preference*: for every pair x, y either not $x > y$ or not $y > x$ or both. We now define "choice" in terms of the preference relation thus restricted. Given a preference relation $>$ on a set of objects X and a finite, nonempty subset A of X, the set of acceptable alternatives from A

according to $>$ is defined as $c(A; >) = \{x \in A$: there is no $y \in A$ such that $y > x\}$. That is: nothing counts as chosen unless there is nothing else in the set of available alternatives that is preferred to it. Again, then, this is choice defined strictly in terms of a *restriction*. It is compatible with the existence of sets of acceptable alternatives that have more than one member. The restriction formally implies that given two sets A, B if both x, $y \in A$, B and $x \in c(A; >)$ and $y \in c(B; >)$, then $x \in c(B; >)$ and $y \in c(A; >)$.

Kreps (1990b, p. 26) at this stage follows many commentators in worrying that if choice is thus defined in terms of the preference relation we have got things back to front from the perspective of empirical description. It is true, of course, that unless we are introspectionists we cannot imagine verifiably observing preference relations and then inferring consistency in behavior on the basis of them. Kreps (ibid.) therefore goes on to define a primitive *choice function* as follows:

A choice function on X is a function c whose domain is the set of all non-empty subsets of X, whose range is the set of all subsets of X, and that satisfies $c(A) \subseteq A$ for all $A \subseteq X$.

Now, if two restrictions are imposed on the choice function c, namely, (i) *nonempty valuation*: for all A, $c(A) \neq \emptyset$ and (ii) *Houthakker's axiom of revealed preference*: if x, $y \in A$, B and $x \in c(A)$ and $y \in c(B)$ then $x \in c(B)$ and $y \in c(A)$, then our analytic framework is formally closed. That is, choice and preference are consistently defined in terms of each other in both directions: treating $\geq$, satisfying asymmetry and negative transitivity, as primitive is equivalent to taking c, satisfying nonempty valuation and Houthakker's axiom of revealed preference, as primitive.

I just noted that Kreps motivates this analytic closure by reference to empirical operationalizability. This is appropriate in the context. The point of Samuelson's procedure and all subsequent refinements of it, after all, is to operationalize every concept wanted in economics —including, implicitly, agency—by reference to something both observable and nonpsychological. Choice is therefore simultaneously interpreted as referring to a type of behavior with independent reference conditions *and* as restricted by its interdefinability in terms of the restricted preference relation $\geq$. This then opens space for questions such as the following: does it make sense to speak of "choice" from infinite sets? If we think it should, then the axiomatic framework is thus far incomplete. If instead we choose to say that there can be such "behavior" but that it doesn't count as "choice," then what justifies this restriction—methodological pragmatism or facts about some aspect of empirical reality? And if the answer refers to empirical reality, is the aspect in question a *psychological* aspect (threatening the separateness thesis), or some special feature of agency distinguished by its peculiarly *economic* context? A related philosophical question that has received more attention (noted by Kreps [1990b, pp. 26–27], and extensively discussed by Broome, e.g., 1990, 1991) is whether we can or should try to allow instances of choice that are sensitive to changes in time and frames of alternatives. This is a question about the individuation of allowable objects in the set X: is an umbrella through time such an object, or are umbrellas when it's raining and when it's not raining two such objects, or is "an umbrella when it's raining and I have my car" different from "an umbrella when it's raining and I don't have my car"? There has been much discussion of this issue in the literature on foundations of rational decision theory, but here my reason for mentioning it is different: I wish merely to note that RPT as motivated by Samuelson is ambiguous on whether the question is, in the first place, an empirical one or a logical one. If we treat it (and the previous philosophical puzzle) as empirical, then answering it in a way that doesn't threaten the separateness thesis will be a challenge, since we'll be inclined to try by doing experiments aimed at determining whether people act as if umbrellas-with-cars were different sorts of objects from umbrellas-without-cars. If, on the other hand, we treat the question as strictly a logical one about our axiomatic framework itself, then it remains to say what, if anything, RPT has to do descriptively with any real empirical agents.

This is one of the main questions of this whole book. Where a set of alternatives obeys the restrictions described above, we can transform it by a uniquely specifiable strictly ordinal function. The logical equivalence of revealed preference and strict ordinality under its economic interpretation was achieved by Houthakker (1950), who recognized that utility functions must be integrable (Mirowski 1989, p. 364). Then, if the set $A \subseteq X$ from which choice is made is convex and compact, we can select the highest-numbered member of the numerical representation of the choice set by a process of maximization. This brings consumer theory within the ambit of Samuelson's unifying strategy that, as noted above, was to model a complete "economy" as a computer of a small set of maximization functions. We are entitled to interpret maximization as optimization only if we can justify a specifically *economic* interpretation of these mathematics. Of course, an economic interpretation was the ultimate point of the whole exercise; but, as Mirowski (1989, pp. 369–372) discusses, it is not forthcoming from Samuelson or from those who have subsequently engaged in interpretation of RPT. As Mirowski points out, imposing the condition that utility functions be integrable, while mathematically essential, amounts to insisting that utility levels associated with commodity-allocation states are path independent. Mirowski summarizes his interpretation of this as follows: "The integrability conditions insist that your preferences are not at all affected or influenced by what goes on around you, and especially not by the process by which you attain your commodities. It dictates that your preferences are purely time-symmetric. It demands that any change in your preferences inexorably alters your identity. Were neoclassical economists to openly admit the meaning of the indispensable integrability conditions, it would be tantamount to an admission that they refuse to entertain the overwhelming evidence that utility is not conserved in everyday experience" (ibid., p. 371).

Mirowski's list of the formal implications of integrability is certainly right. However, the reading of the significance of this in his final sentence above presupposes something I will dispute (slowly, over the course of the whole book), namely, that for RPT to have a persuasive empirical interpretation "utility" has to correspond directly to something constructible out of folk-psychological categories and concepts. But Mirowski is also correct in asserting that in Samuelson's own work the issue is both central and underacknowledged.[37] For Samuelson, interpreting the selection of members of numerical representations of choice sets as a model of optimization, on both the production and consumption sides, was supposed to be the primitive step of economic interpretation from which all the rest of such interpretation could and should then be constructed. He therefore initially resisted the habit of referring to the numerical representations on the consumption side as "utility functions." Had this preference stuck then, as many commentators have pointed out, subsequent confusions about the relationships between early neoclassical consumer theory and RPT would likely have been much reduced. However, the inertial pressures of disciplinary culture overwhelmed Samuelson's attempt at linguistic legislation. An agent whose behavior could be described by a well-ordered preference relation (subject to various further caveats that need not detain us; see Kreps 1990b, pp. 30–37) was and is described as "maximizing utility." However, given how we have arrived at utility functions of this sort, there should be no remaining temptation to think that they measure internal psychological states or processes in people. They merely index the activities of the class of systems for which RPT is intended as a model. The question of which, if any, real systems are accurately modeled by RPT is empirically open at this point.

Although the historical Samuelson builds a purely abstract economic *system*, he cannot quite be consistently shoehorned into this position of formalistic neutrality over the relationship between the model of economic *agency* defined through RPT and real systems. Without question, he thought that RPT models cognitively competent individual people under at least some systematically important circumstances. This was crucial to his generic verificationism. *If* choice in the purely mathematical sense of RPT is taken to model some class of actual behavioral "choices" (on some account or other of what a behavioral choice is), then, Samuelson supposed, the question of whether a given agent's behavior conforms to RPT can be directly empirically verified by observation of sequences of that agent's behavior (modeled in a demand function; Samuelson 1947, pp. 107–116). This confidence was naïve, and it was not rewarded in practice. Wallis and Friedman (1942) had *already* provided the basic diagnosis as to why it was not likely to be. Economic agency is defined by reference to consistency; but people, as biological-psychological-cultural entities, surely change, systematically and substantially, according to any realistic model of them. Verification of an RPT model in a particular case, however, would require a run of observations over time sufficient for statistical significance. Given this, one would need some operationalization of "preference" independent of observed choice in order to control for preference shifts during the period of observation; but this is precisely what the antipsychologistic motivation of the RPT model, locked in by the integrability conditions, forbids. This basis for skepticism was well justified by later experience. Houthakker (1961) himself expressed disappointment with attempts to justify RPT models of individual people empirically, as did Luce (1959). Matters were hardly made easier by the fact that Samuelson's philosophical impatience, as discussed earlier, makes it difficult to determine from his work just what the boundary conditions on RPT's applicability to real people are supposed to be. Are people plausibly modeled by RPT *in general*? Or just in markets where price signals are unambiguous? If the latter, can we distinguish unambiguous from ambiguous price signals without some reference to what constitutes ambiguity and salience given human biology and psychology? Finally, the logical ambiguities discussed above concerning timing, framing, and the individuation of objects in choice sets have to be settled in some nonarbitrary way before one can even design a satisfactory empirical test of the model's applicability to a particular case.

As noted earlier, Samuelson's attempts at official philosophical self-description blunder against his lack of familiarity with the actual philosophy of science literature. But the label that accurately captures his working assumptions in the chapters of the *Foundations* on consumer theory (1947; see especially pp. 97–98)[38] is Quinean behaviorism. On this view—which Quine (1991), toward the end of his life, explicitly assimilated into Paul Churchland's wider eliminativist view—mentalistic concepts such as "choice" and "preference" have no real psychological referents at all. Objects move about in a physical world. Some classes of them do so in patterns generated by historical processes of selection that lead them to (temporarily) produce homeostatic reactions that combat entropy in particular dimensions of their environments. This we call "behavior."[39] The job of science, according to Quine, is to identify (nonunique) functions that enable projectible patterns of motion to be inductively projected by actual observers. Given this assumption, one can go on to say that if the behavioral motions or some subclass of them are constrained (in extension) by the class of functions distinguished by RPT—and are not more efficiently described by some other class of functions generated by weaker constraints—then RPT has scientifically significant empirical models (again, unless dynamics are added, only in extension). These might or might not approximately conform to the class of real motions neoclassical economists had intended to make generalizations about, but this would be an empirical matter. Such a Quinean stance would not in itself answer epistemological questions about *how* to empirically isolate the relevant class of motions. But the defense of a pragmatic solution to underdetermination problems in relations between theories and observations was Quine's great epistemological project, so a Quinean defender of RPT would at least be promising to meet the skeptical challenges to its empirical verification head-on, rather than appearing to dodge them.

Whenever Samuelson discusses the empirical meaning and significance of RPT in the *Foundations* he does so in a way consistent with this Quinean behaviorism-cum-eliminativism. It is irrelevant how consumers deliberate, or whether they deliberate at all; the equilibrating pressures of the systems in which they are embedded may drive them to move about in ways consistent with description by the class of demand functions constrained by the maximization conditions of RPT.

The entire empirical significance of ascribing preferences or choices to agents is therefore strictly behavioral, in just Quine's sense of "behavior." Samuelson, to my knowledge, never cites Quine's work. It is in fact not surprising that a Quinean-style defense of RPT did not occur to Samuelson. I earlier justified calling him a generic late positivist. It is typical in histories of analytic philosophy for Quine to be regarded as a (leading) *post*positivist, despite the fact that his views differ from those of the later Carnap by little besides emphasis. The justification for this is that Quine takes *ontological* questions seriously and frames epistemological problems partly in terms of ontological (along with logical) assumptions. As I said earlier, though, the best reason for calling Samuelson a positivist is that his philosophical reflections, such as they are, never move outside of the closed circle of the purely epistemological. Samuelson maintains just that we do not *need to* advert to psychological or motivational states of consumers to model and predict their behavior. It is a portentous shift to say, with Quine, that eschewing reference to beliefs and desires (except as a dramatic idiom) in science is justified by our having concluded, on general ontological grounds, that there are no such things.

John Davis (2003) has recently made a closely related point from a different analytical perspective. Davis notes that once economic theory abandons, with Samuelson, an introspectionist basis for the individuation and reidentification of agents over time, it ceases to be clear how, given its subjectivism about value, it retains any basis for consistently distinguishing individuals in the first place. All that are left as analytical units are utility functions, cut loose from folk entities like "agents over time." Samuelson, not flirting with ontological issues at all, simply doesn't address this issue. However, I certainly will be doing so, at length, in later chapters. A major outcome I promised back in chapter 1, when we encountered Mirowski's speculations about where economic theory is going, is that we'll see how to eliminate individualism from economic theory proper without eliminating agents or even individual selves from our wider ontology (as Mirowski mistakenly thinks Dennett and Binmore must do).

I thus won't, in the end, resort to an eliminativist defense of RPT in the way Quine might. However, a more broadly Quinean standpoint *will* crucially inform the thesis I will defend. As Davis observes, if the ontology of mainstream economics is to be defended, somebody has to provide a new concept of *what an economic agent is*.[40] I will be doing just that, and showing how Dennett's philosophy of cognitive and behavioral explanation, with its associated theory of the self, lets us avoid requiring serious revisions to RPT. Given that this is coming, I want for now to avoid imposing any particular empirical interpretation on RPT, but to treat it strictly as a closed piece of analysis, a system of tautologies with no prespecified empirical interpretation. That RPT constrains a class of behavioral responses *in principle*, whether people or anything else actually behave that way, is after all not to be doubted. That is, regardless of whether somebody thinks that Samuelson's constrained behavioral descriptions deserve the name "demand functions" as intended ways of talking about actual economies, there is nothing wrong with his *math* in concluding that RPT indeed constrains them. (Let me just note for the moment that this attitude is neither completely peculiar to me, nor absent from some important contemporary applications of economic analysis. Binmore [1994, 1998], for example, adopts it in his massive inquiry into the relationship between norms of justice and interpersonal welfare comparisons.) What is doubted, most directly by Hausman (2000), is whether the constraints are tight enough to permit useful identification with empirical phenomena that constitute a plausible domain for an economic science.

As noted earlier, "RPT" is sometimes used to refer narrowly to Samuelson's specific axiomatization (or to that of Samuelson-cum-Houthakker). I will henceforth not restrict the term to this narrow sense, even if I continue to identify it with a position regarded as "Samuelsonian," because this is not how contemporary students of economics typically encounter RPT. Perfection of generality and elegance was achieved by Debreu (1959); and it was in this axiomatization that RPT became the standard textbook model of the economic agent, skeptical objections to its empirical significance notwithstanding.[41] This was mainly because, in light of RPT's contextualization within Arrow and Debreu's system of general equilibrium, RPT can be thought to inherit *indirect* empirical significance through econometric testing procedures. To paraphrase Mandler (1999, p. 82), from Debreu's work forward to call an agent a "utility maximizer" is officially not to ascribe any internal motivational properties, but is merely an abbreviated way of saying that some (one hopes, specified) range of its behavior is describable and predictable by means of a function over binary relations respecting asymmetry and negative transitivity.

The body of microeconomic consumer theory since Debreu can be divided, for present purposes, into two piles. First, a great deal of work has consisted in purely formal investigation of the mathematical space defined by the ordinal utility function, in which further restrictions are added to the binary relation so as to generate a kit of sharper tools for flexibility in special applications. (See Chung 1994 for a technical survey.) Second, and more important for our coming discussion, in the half century since the birth of RPT economists have become increasingly interested in how economic agents behave in environments of imperfect or incomplete information, especially in nonparametric circumstances where such maximization requires strategic interaction. This requires widening, rather than just refining, the class of economically interesting choice functions, since if agents can be presented with choices defined over lotteries rather than just "sure things," then their behavior can reveal information that goes beyond what is captured by a strictly ordinal utility function. Since 1944 von Neumann and Morgenstern had made available an axiomatized concept of *expected utility* by which agents optimize over what they *could* get (rather than just over what is lying there on the table, so to speak), and the resulting "von Neumann–Morgenstern (VNM) utility" has lately come to be what "utility" usually means when economists are modeling individual people directly (as opposed to representative consumers drawn from standard markets at or near competitive equilibrium).

The original VNM utility function was applied only to choices over objectively measured lotteries, but the explosion of game-theoretic applications from the 1970s onward relies more often on the incorporation of subjective probability theory (Savage 1954) into the VNM framework. Since this requires reference to ways in which agents idiosyncratically represent the expected values of lotteries, and implicitly ascribes causal significance to differences among these representations, pulling subjective probability inside the axiomatic system is a philosophically portentous step. VNM utility functions in the *absence* of subjective probabilities can still be constructed from revealed preferences without reference to beliefs. What their existence therefore shows, philosophically, is that insistence on strict ordinalism had been an unnecessarily strong weapon against psychological cardinalism; put another way, there is a kind of cardinalism that is not necessarily psychological, and von Neumann and Morgenstern found it.[42] The possibility of constructing a VNM utility function does not imply interpersonal comparisons of the sort that Hicks and Robbins had rejected. Agents bargaining in games can infer relative preference intensities on scales idiosyncratic to each agent from each agent's behavior; but they need not base these inferences on any introspective information, and the scales are not intercomparable. However, introduction of subjective probabilities drags concepts of belief directly into utility representation, so at that point the Quinean defense of an RPT interpretation of preference and choice suggested above ceases to be available.

In his outstanding (and philosophically alert) 1972 economics textbook, William Baumol explains a standard axiomatization of VNM utility, and then, as a consequence, feels the need to briefly revisit the controversies of the 1930s in order to assure students that no slide back to psychological cardinalism is implied (pp. 547–548). Economics students of 1972 likely had no idea what this discussion was supposed to protect them from or why, but at least a Quinean philosopher picking up the textbook would have been comforted. However, at that very moment the ground was shifting decisively in the philosophy of mind. With the rise of functionalism, "beliefs" were returning to center stage in that discipline. Given that economists had reasons of their own, as we just saw, for talking about beliefs again, could a note like Baumol's still have seemed appropriate in a textbook of just a few years later? We have now caught up to the contemporary problem space. Since subjective probability is the core concept of normative decision theory, philosophical epistemologists and microeconomists again found themselves talking the same language; and now philosophers of psychology who again believed in beliefs (without trying to reduce them to brain states) could join the conversation too.

I will argue in the chapters to come that most of this conversation has been confused, because (among other things): no *specific* theory of subjective probability estimation belongs among the *foundations* of microeconomic theory; the relationship between normative decision theory and positive economics has likewise been misunderstood; and beliefs and desires, though there are such things, are not what most parties to the conversation have taken them to be.

A Separate Science of *What*?

In the preceding historical discussion of the separateness thesis, I devoted some energy to the question of whether, and in which senses, Robbins and Samuelson were positivists. Why? Who, aside from an intellectual historian with a librarian's passion for sorting thinkers into constructed boxes, cares? In this final section of the chapter, aimed at pulling its strands together and pausing for breath before another round of slogging, I'll explain why I've bothered with this "ism"-ism.

I suggested at various points above that from one perspective—the one that will matter here—what most significantly divides twentieth-century positivists from the postpositivist philosophy of science in which my discussion will be framed are different attitudes toward the relationship between epistemology and ontology. As I have emphasized, positivism changed dramatically over the course of its evolution. It started as, essentially, Kantian epistemology minus Kant's belief in the cogency of supernaturally grounded faith in necessity, but with the resources of modern logic at hand to furnish a supposedly metaphysically innocent account of necessity (as analyticity within conventional frames) instead. By the end of its development, it looked more like Humean epistemology, but one still so leery of metaphysics that it found Hume's own radical naturalism too bold. Quine's embrace of naturalism was, in this respect, just the next logical step as positivists morphed from Kant to Hume. However, along with that move Quine's work made a decisive break by allowing that the question of "what there is" should be addressed by the philosophy of science alongside questions about how to justify what we say and what experiments we perform. Never mind that Quine's own ontological inclinations were more nominalist than realist, and thereby still tightly tethered to late positivism; from Quine forward, and thanks especially to what Hilary Putnam (1975) did with Quine's starting point, philosophers of science again took it as one of their prime ambitions to unify the scientific worldview not just by reference to methods of inquiry, but to what kinds of causes and systems and things the world is made of.

It is unsurprising that this question, specifically as applied to economics, was allowed to slip from view by positivist economists. Davis (2003, p. 14) opens his recent book on the concept of the individual in economics by saying "I hope . . . to refocus attention on a key question too often neglected in economics: what is economics *about*?" I could say precisely the same thing about my own efforts here. To a philosophically innocent student of science, it might seem a bit amazing that a whole discipline could forget to keep track of what it's supposed to be investigating, but this is precisely what the positivist emphasis on epistemology to the exclusion of ontology encouraged across the board. Thus we can now ask, as a perfectly serious question: is there a real domain of application for economic theory along at least one of its recent trajectories of development?

My reason for spending so much close textual time with Robbins in this chapter is that he was the last major figure to systematically interrogate the question of economics' domain, just as the issue was about to go into decades of deep freeze. As a (Kantian) positivist, Robbins both asked and answered his question inside a peculiar frame of assumptions, in which the domain of the discipline had to be grounded in the *phenomenal* (that is, what's within the realm of the mentally conceptualized) rather than the *noumenal* (out in the actual, objective, world). The task of defending a modified version of Robbins's definition without resorting to introspectionist foundations still lies ahead of me here.

However, although I reject positivist phenomenalism (and reductionism), there are aspects of positivist philosophy of science that are independent of this, and are worth trying to preserve. One of these is explicit concern for the unity of science. Another is a (nonfanatical) measure of verificationism: if a putative hypothesis doesn't seem to hinge in any way on a physical intervention somebody could make in the world to explore its consequences, it is hard to see why the hypothesis in question should be taken seriously. These themes, less distinctive of positivism than its early Kantian commitments, rose to the fore in the philosophy of science precisely as positivism started to blur and fissure in its drift back toward Hume. We have seen in this chapter how Robbins offered a definition of economics as a separate, nonpsychological science, and defended his definition by appeal to Kantian-positivist epistemology. That epistemology included, fundamentally, the idea that science proceeds from phenomenal data, and that direct (as opposed to inferential) access to that data is introspective. But by the time Robbins wrote his *Essay* positivist philosophers were already far ahead of him in moving away from their Kantian starting point. Samuelson's RPT, first stated just three years after the second edition of Robbins's *Essay*, rests on the assumption that verificationism and behaviorism are the twin pillars of sound epistemology. However, if Robbins's definition of economics can be cut loose from his introspectionist basis for it, there is no a priori reason why it might not accommodate Samuelson's formalization of an economic system[43]—except that, as argued above, Robbins's restriction to *human* behavior must be dropped unless other animals generally fail to exhibit behavior rationalizable as minimally locally consistent, which seems to be the exact opposite of the ethological facts.

Thus, if one was a generic late positivist of the familiar sort—like Samuelson—a version of the separateness thesis that fused RPT onto Robbins's definition might seem nicely adequate. We begin with systems that are motivated by goal states: behavioral systems. They face scarcity: given the resources of energy available to them, their budget constraints, they can't satisfy all their goals at once. Is it, then, from the point of view of their intentions, always an exogenously determined *accident* which goals are satisfied to what extent, or do they effect *trade-offs* by some systematic process or processes? If there are systems in nature whose behavior can be nonredundantly predicted and explained through comparing *available* trade-offs in search of the *best* (most efficient) trade-offs, then some Samuelsonian systems describe real patterns, and the science of these systems constitutes "economics" as approximately defined by Robbins.

Or so I will contend.

A loose "Robbins–Samuelson" conception like this is, plausibly, thought to be right by many contemporary economists, whatever confused buzz of noises they make when trying to take recent behavioral-experimental evidence seriously. It captures, after all, what they still generally say in undergraduate textbooks when they're trying to simplify matters for students. Admissions that people are satisficers rather than optimizers, and have systematically inconsistent preferences that seem to be psychologically real states consulted during episodes of parametric and strategic choice, seem to be taken by most economists as complications to a "Robbins–Samuelson" core disciplinary anchor. I join the most radical critics of orthodox economic theory in regarding this as untenable: if the proper domain of economics is the behavior of individual people as they evaluate their subjective well-being by consulting inconsistent preferences in muddled ignorance of probability theory—the picture promoted by the critics these days—then a Robbins–Samuelson conception of separateness is utterly refuted: economics collapses into whatever psychology, sociology, and biology can agree on. But I part from the critics of orthodox economics in asserting that the proper domain of the discipline is *not* the choice behavior of individual people; and then a (suitably interpreted) Robbins–Samuelson conception of that domain and its (carefully qualified) separateness is exactly what I mean to defend.

Mirowski and Dupré, along with Davis (2003), all notice, in their different ways, that economics has been steadily moving in the direction of being about systems rather than about people or even about individual agents. They also notice that if this movement is to be explicitly steered by some self-conscious theory, rather than being left to mere drift, then it is in the wider sciences of behavior, cognition, and information processing that we should naturally look for a driver. However, all are to differing degrees alarmed that if such a driver is successfully found, we will forfeit our good old human selves in an intellectual scientistic distopia. Dupré's response, by far the least sophisticated of the three, is to scorn the possibility of systematizing economics and other behavior, while simultaneously wagging his finger and telling us that trying to do so is wicked. Davis, along with Lawson (1997) and many others, hopes that critical social theory, developed in more systematic directions than have thus far been seen, will carry economic theory in a more humanistic direction. Mirowski's reaction is the most interesting. He welcomes the possible construction of a truly powerful and elegant economics of information-processing systems in which individual agents are not taken as atomic elements; but then hopes that, precisely for this reason, economists will have their bungling hands removed from the delicate business of theorizing the self, leaving this in the more trustworthy care of others—historians? anthropologists? poets?—not corrupted by positivistic scientism.

An intellectual blind spot that Dupré and Mirowski have in common with Davis, Lawson, and many others is an uncritical assumption that if a view can be associated with positivism then there is something automatically wrong with it—it must be naive at best, probably, at worst, harkening after some nasty impulse to grandiosity and dominance over nature. I work here from the opposite attitude. In all sorts of ways, the great positivists—Carnap, Reichenbach, Schlick—exemplified the best and most worthy ambitions of philosophy. In a social-political environment encouraging suicidal and mass homicidal indulgence of contempt for reason, they emphasized and worked to bring into clear view the austere but sweet possibility of *understanding* the world whole. This was to be attempted from a perspective of deliberate emotional restraint in which treating anything—nations, classes, ethnic communities, or, indeed, precious but mysteriously conceived selves—as sites of sacredness to be protected from science is recognized as providing cover for everything atavistic and dangerous in human nature. Their philosophical work, in its subtlety and rigorously self-critical avoidance of dogmatism, fully lived up to the seriousness and importance of their ethical attitude.

Here is an image of recent intellectual history that is extremely wide-spread just now. Several decades ago, positivism was thankfully routed by an aggrieved community of social scientists, historians, and human-ist philosophers. Unfortunately, a gang of the positivists' natural associates who should have surrendered with them, neoclassical econ-omists, hung on in a redoubt that they preserved for years through relentless obtuseness. But gradually, inevitably, the isolated fastness crumbled. Now all can see that neoclassicism has followed positivism into the dustbin of history; and the victorious humanist forces survey the broken ranks pondering whether, and if so on what terms, we should put up with any systematic economics at all.

This image deserves contestation. Positivism and neoclassicism involved significant mistakes, to be sure. Continuing the trope, they tried to hold some patches of territory they were ill advised to want. But the flags still fly from some positions that institutionally resisted the campaign against scientism. One flutters in evolutionary behavioral science; another is waved by game theorists. Let us get back to work and see if we can build a sturdy bridgehead between them.

4   Philosophical Issues in Revealed Preference and Utility Analysis

New Zeitgeists for Old

At various points, while he develops economic analysis as the calculation of extremum positions in the operations of an abstract economic machine, Samuelson cautions against hasty empirical interpretation of this machine. "There is the danger," he warns, "that unwarranted teleological or normative welfare significance will be attributed to the position of equilibrium so defined. To avoid misunderstanding, it is well to emphasize that the conversion of a problem whose economic context does not suggest any human, purposive maximizing behavior into a maximum problem is to be regarded as merely a technical device for the purpose of quickly developing the properties of that equilibrium position" (Samuelson 1947, p. 53). This affirms the attitude I announced I would take toward RPT at the end of the previous chapter. Of course, it leaves us wondering why interest in economic phenomena should have anything at all to do with the solutions to maximizing problems. We will not have a fully satisfactory answer to this question on our hands until the end of this book. For now, let us just note how far Samuelson pushes initial methodological agnosticism about the connection between maximization as an analytical technique and optimizing behavior as an empirical phenomenon: before he begins his chapter called "theory of maximizing *behavior*" (my italics), he advises us not to assume that it will imply that consumers "behave rationally in any normative sense" (ibid., p. 22). A present-day reader should find this remarkable, especially as none of Samuelson's later occasional remarks about the relationship between his machine and actual behavior shed much consistent light on how he saw this relationship.

It was the task of the previous chapter to explain (in logical, as opposed to Mirowski's historical, terms)[1] how economics had evolved to the point where Samuelson's 1947 audience was not baffled by this. We, however, are not members of that audience.

Many contemporary economists, I think, suppose that work subsequent to Samuelson's, swiftly reviewed in the penultimate section of the last chapter, has made grudging, though incomplete, progress in putting real people back into microeconomics. Ever since decision theory and variable beliefs about probabilities and attitudes to risk were included in its foundations after the 1950s, its agents have at least been allowed to calculate (occasionally in real time) and to have some subjective properties, even if these don't look very typically human. The present prevailing feeling is that, thanks to the growing maturity of experimental behavioral economics, a new wave of progress in this direction is now upon us: as experimental evidence piles up and converges, we will at last achieve true seriousness about the behavior of actual people in economic situations. (Camerer 2003b is the new bible for those who emphasize this stance. Kagel and Roth 1995 is the broader but less up-to-date survey.)

In contraposition to this confidence, we find Davis's (2003) argument that recognition of neoclassicism's inadequate concept of individual agency has mainly encouraged abandonment, rather than enrichment, of the concept. Mirowski of course makes the same diagnosis. In the next chapter, I will provide further reasons, more closely situated in the technical details of recent game theory, for believing that they are correct about this. First, though, I want to point out a different sense in which the behavioral-experimental movement, in its often wide-eyed empiricism, encourages historical and philosophical innocence. It is not at all obvious what theoretical resources the new experimental empiricists have available for describing the situations in which they place their subjects as "economic" in either Robbins's or Samuelson's senses. The subjects are no longer to be presupposed as necessarily maximizing anything, or as necessarily competing with one another, or as necessarily rational in any particular sense at all. The scenarios chosen for them by experimental designers can thus be economic in only the folk sense: these are the sorts of scenarios—trying to earn cash prizes by making choices in institutionally rule-governed settings—we traditionally associate with exchange, material consumption, and moneymaking. Aristotle might thus be smiling in his grave. Furthermore, to the extent that this trajectory of thinking is uncritically regarded as wholly progressive, the attitude of Samuelson as just reviewed will increasingly come to seem insane. Can that really be plausible?

Supposing that it is parallels the widely held view of positivism in general that was criticized in the previous chapter. It will not do to treat either positivism or neoclassicism as kinds of intellectual delusion, like racism. Robbins, for example, was more, not less, philosophically sophisticated than most of the contemporary experimental methodologists, wrong though he was in various crucial assumptions. Let us see what we can learn from him and his contemporaries, while knowing what we do now that they didn't, instead of imagining that their positivism was just a crippling handicap.

The immediate task of this chapter is to present the reasons that have led most philosophers of economics and commentators on economic metatheory to regard the Samuelsonian conception as obsolete. These reasons may be sorted into two broad classes.[2] First, some logical arguments, championed most notably by Amartya Sen, have convinced many people that RPT is inadequate on a priori grounds. Second, the accumulating body of experimental work with human subjects has shown that most people systematically fail to be rational in the sense presupposed by regarding them as economic agents, either in some generic sense assumed by neoclassicism, or in a more specific sense taken to be required by the synthesis of RPT and expected utility theory. Of course, if the a priori arguments were decisively persuasive, then the arguments derived from empirical studies would have to be logically redundant. However, the reluctance of scientists to be decisively persuaded by purely philosophical considerations is well founded. Quine (1953), in his famous attack on the distinction between analytic and synthetic statements, reminds us that even axioms of mathematical theories can have their basis of relevance to science undermined by empirical surprises that provoke radical revisions in our conceptual schemes. As Dennett has often put the point, the history of philosophy offers a humbling run of cases in which supposed insights into necessity ("The shortest distance between two points in space *has to be* a Euclidean straight line"; "Continents can't *possibly* move since there's nothing for them to move *through*"; "Nothing as complex as a vertebrate eye could *possibly* evolve through naturally selected increments") have simply turned out to be failures of imagination.

Here is the perspective I will assume here on the relationship between philosophical and empirically motivated arguments. Primarily conceptual arguments are unreliable guides to empirical facts. Such arguments must rely for their force on intuitions; but intuitions are (biologically and/or culturally) evolved devices for helping people form expectations in particular environments and with respect to salient and important objects and events in those environments, classified for practical purposes. It is thus no surprise that intuitions systematically mislead us if we rely on them when seeking general truths holding over nonparochially selected samples of reality. However, conceptual arguments do play crucial roles in helping us to *diagnose* and *domesticate for use* the bodies of empirical measurements that we gather. One of the uses for which facts need to be domesticated is systematization within some conceptual framework or other. Though these frameworks always stand ready for revision, they are not just psychological or journalistic epiphenomena riding alongside and above "real" science; they are the platforms from which hypotheses are formulated and experiments are designed.

In light of this general epistemological stance, my order of procedure in surveying the basis for the troubled standing of neoclassicism and RPT will be as follows. In this chapter, I will concentrate on the more abstract philosophical arguments against the Samuelsonian approach, since widespread endorsement of the conclusions of these arguments have contributed to the way in which the experimental evidence has been interpreted. I will first show that Sen's purely logical attack on RPT simply fails, relying on intuitions about the nature of human thought that will not survive serious scrutiny from the perspective of cognitive science. It will then be argued, however, that the best-known current *defense* of the usefulness of RPT—namely, Gary Becker's— shares important aspects of the very intuitions that drive Sen's criticism. The adequacy of Becker's strategy will thus be doubted. This criticism will fix the philosophical background against which the literature on behavioral evidence will be surveyed and evaluated in the next chapter. However, the fact that I consider philosophical objections before empirical ones should not be taken to imply that I consider the former more important. Quite the contrary: if the philosophical and empirical considerations pointed in rival directions, our rational first hypothesis would be that there was something wrong with the philosophical arguments.

I do not think I am going out on a limb of sweeping overgeneralization or illegitimate attribution of bad faith in saying that many people who call themselves humanists believe that neoclassicism, especially under its behaviorist interpretation, is inadequate partly because they don't *want* it to be adequate. In particular, they don't like the way in which it seems to ask us to think of people as cogs in machines. We have of course already encountered Mirowski assuming this and Dupré shouting it, but we needn't resort just to citations from philosophers or enfants terribles among economists to capture the disdain with which many people express themselves about mechanistic economics. I will instead quote two leading pillars of the economic establishment itself. First, Ronald Coase:

The preoccupation of economists with the logic of choice ... has ... had serious adverse effects on economics itself. One result of this divorce of the theory from its subject matter is that the entities whose decisions economists are engaged in analyzing have not been made the subject of study, and in consequence lack any substance. The consumer is not a human being but a consistent set of preferences. The firm to an economist ". . . is effectively defined as a cost curve and a demand curve. . . ." Exchange takes place without any specification of its institutional setting. We have consumers without humanity, firms without organization, and even exchange without markets. (1988, p. 3)

Although I will of course be dissenting from the normative spin here, Coase's description of Samuelson's framework is, as we have seen, accurate. Buchanan criticizes the Debreu consolidation of contemporary neoclassicism even less indirectly:

Its flaw lies in its conversion of individual choice behavior from a social-institutional context to a physical-computational one ... But surely this is nonsensical social science, and the institutionalist critics have been broadly on target in some of their attacks. (1979, p. 29)

Two anticipatory remarks are motivated by these quotations. First, they express sentiments that are shared by both humanist critics of behaviorist economics and by the new empirical and institutional economists. It is because both groups of skeptics endorse remarks like those just cited that their positions are usually taken to be complimentary. Furthermore, as I will argue, this zone of generic agreement is based on a shared ontological assumption—that people are prototypical agents—that I will question. However—this is the second point of anticipation—the positive direction in which the experimentalist-institutionalist campaign is ultimately leading is the precise opposite of the destination imagined by the humanists. Mirowski, along with Davis (2003), recognizes this, unlike most prevailing accounts. In the next chapter I will provide further detailed reasons for agreeing with Mirowski's contention that humanists and new experimentalists have nothing in common but a shared enemy, their caricature of neoclassicism.

Is RPT Hopeless? Sen on the Psychology of Utility Functions

There is a long march ahead before we get to all this, however. The first steps lead through the details of the humanists' logical attack on RPT. The critic who has by far the best credentials for stating their case has been Amartya Sen. On the basis of some classic papers, especially Sen 1971, he must be regarded as among the seminal systematizers of RPT itself, so his authoritative understanding of its technical structure is incontrovertible. And since he is among the world's leading authorities on poverty and its alleviation, when he asserts that neoclassicism in general, and RPT in particular, have contributed to the ineffectiveness of much social welfare policy, especially in the third world, we are ethically obligated to pay attention to his criticisms. (The reader is advised, however, that I will have nothing to say about applied or policy issues until the next volume of this study.)

Sen begins his most general survey of neoclassicism's dehumanizing aspects with a remark that could hardly be more directly relevant to the problem space opened by the discussion of my previous chapter: "There is something quite extraordinary in the fact that economics has evolved . . . [to characterize] . . . human motivation in such spectacularly narrow terms. One reason why this is extraordinary is that economics is supposed to be concerned with real people" (1987, p. 1). In the context of the ontological innocence that constitutes the working framework here, we must ask which authority told "economics" what it was "supposed to be" concerned with; and then we must ask exactly what "concerned with" might best mean here. The second of these questions was the subject of the previous chapter. Aristotle, as we saw, assumed that economics (in his sense of it) was *directly about* human material satisfaction and security, and that it should interest us just because, and to the extent that, these things are important to real people. Smith, Ricardo, and Marx, and also Jevons and Marshall, thought likewise. But by the time the philosophy of neoclassicism finds mature expression in Robbins's *Essay*, the attitude has decisively changed. Robbins's grounds for including the phrase *"human* behavior" in his definition of economics is at no point motivated by references to welfare; as we saw, it is driven by the role Robbins assigns to articulated introspective consciousness in the epistemology of economics as a positive science. And then when that role falls away, as in Samuelson's work, people recede so far out of view that we face a long *project* in figuring out how and where to work them back into the picture. Are Samuelson and (to a lesser extent) Robbins guilty of a philosophical and/or moral error, consisting in ignoring some prime directive (issued by Aristotle?) on what economics is "supposed to" be about?

In asking this rhetorical question, I am not assuming that someone other than me holds the burden of argument here. The view that Aristotle, Smith, and so on, are right is surely more natural than the opposite view, as Dan Hausman (personal correspondence) has reminded me. For now, I just want to ask the reader, in the spirit of philosophical inquiry, to let the question stand open. I will return explicitly to my reasons for taking the less natural position at the close of the book, in chapter 9.

Experience suggests to me that many people who endorse Sen's negative view of RPT and neoclassical utility theory have not thought very carefully about the conceptual basis of his arguments, but think that he must be agreed with because policy advice based on neoclassical theory often seems narrow, inhumane, and disconnected from legitimate human interests, just as he alleges. It is then assumed that the inhumane policy advice must reflect or stem from the inhumanity of the underlying theory. In one sense, this reasoning is sound. It is very doubtful that most large-scale human suffering is *just* an economic phenomenon, in the sense of economics relevant to economic *science*. If someone therefore arrives at policy advice on the basis of nothing more than economic analysis, that advice is liable to neglect important considerations, which I will for now (but just for now) stuff inside the black boxes of "psychology" and "culture." At the very least, mere scientific interest in the operations of economic machines does not by itself imply concern over whether poverty alleviation should be prioritized over other policy goals (as I believe it should). However, it is a simple logical error to believe simultaneously that social morality cannot be based on economic analysis alone *and* that if economic analysis alone produces insensitive social morality there must be something wrong with the method of analysis. I believe that Sen's conceptual arguments are often given special indulgence on the basis of this error.

Sen's normative and technical criticisms of postwar neoclassicism are linked by him through his contention that it illegitimately reifies the concepts of "utility" and "well-being." He contends that these are different concepts that, though often empirically correlated, are typically *not* both maximized by the same policies (1999). This conclusion, although I also regard it as unsound, depends on views about the metaphysics of agency that are independent of Sen's criticisms of the logic of RPT. I will postpone this issue, which is a central one for my general project, in order to concentrate first on Sen's contention that neoclassicism as interpreted through RPT is *by and in itself* a flawed analytical apparatus.

Sen has, over the years, deployed a battery of arguments against RPT, some technical and some more intuitive. All of them, however, cluster under one master claim: that we cannot understand typical human behavior unless we recognize that much of it is caused or guided or conditioned by factors "external to" preference (Dowding 2002). Description of a few of Sen's examples is the best way to illustrate the intended point. In Sen 1973 we are told that if we infer nontuistic preferences from cooperative behavior in one-shot prisoner's dilemmas (PDs) we may be misled, because the cooperative response may be a function of the person's obeying culturally inherited moral norms that are external to her personal utility function. Similarly, suppose that a person at a social dinner table chooses an apple from a basket containing two apples and an orange, but on an otherwise identical occasion chooses the orange from a basket containing two oranges and an apple (Sen 1977). Here, strict application of RPT might seem to compel us to convict the person of irrationality (violating the negative transitivity axiom), which conflicts with an intuition that there is nothing irrational in being influenced by a social norm demanding that one should not selfishly restrict others' options by taking the last of anything on a communal platter. Again, the social norm is supposed to be an example of a motivating force external to the person's utility function. Finally, consider a person who chooses to eat nothing on one occasion because of a religious commitment to fasting, but on another (otherwise identical) occasion struggles heroically to obtain some food despite her poverty. Once again, the religious norm is held to be external to her choice function as modeled by RPT.

Examples in this family of cases are supposed to challenge the adequacy of RPT in two ways. First, if there are regular empirical motivations for human action independent of, and not capturable by, RPT, then RPT will be *descriptively* incomplete as an apparatus for predicting and explaining actual human behavioral patterns. Second, if RPT is taken as the basis for a *normative* theory of rational agency, then it will force us to regard the altruistic PD player, the gracious social diner and the pious faster, as irrational; but this is supposed by Sen to conflict with intuitions about a broader and more human conception of rationality, by comparison with which RPT offers a "pinched" and inhuman evaluative standard. These two intended notions of inadequacy are of course related: our normative standards are partly a function of what daily experience and common sense show to be descriptively characteristic of people.

Sen's use of these examples depends on the assumption that choice functions and utility functions capture only narrowly personal preferences that hold independently of social and other contexts. This assumption, as Sen recognizes, need not involve what in chapter 3 I called "sensationalistic hedonism"; individuals might maximize their self-interest by reference to something other than properties of personal sensations. However, saying this lands us straight back in the problem space that Jevons encountered when he tried to be a psychologistic utilitarian but not a hedonist, and resorted to an entirely ad hoc distinction between higher and lower wants. Moral and social commitments can always, trivially, be interpreted self-referentially: Nelson Mandela, we might say, was personally better off by his own lights in a world where apartheid persisted and he went to jail for decades than in a world where apartheid persisted and he acquiesced in it as a township lawyer. This of course doesn't imply that Mandela liked prison, but merely that he disliked imprisonment less than he disliked acquiescence in apartheid. Of course, this preference structure requires explanation by reference to his concern for the welfare of others; but unless we are interpreting utility hedonically, why and by reference to what systematic properties should satisfaction derived from an increase in justice be distinguished from satisfaction derived from an increase in the quality of one's food? Why, in other words, should utility not be interpreted in Bentham's "wide and expansive" sense? The standard answer, noted previously, is that doing so makes the claim that people act so as to maximize their utility a tautology. I will confront this worry directly later in the chapter.

Inspired by the tautology objection, Sen (1987) promotes a concept of "agency," which he defines as a person's "ability to form goals, commitments, etc." (p. 40), as something that typically motivates human behavior independently of—and sometimes in opposition to—utility maximization. If one is bothered by the tautology problem then, logically, what one is committed to is finding empirical grounds for belief in a second (or third, or nth) motivating factor that contrasts with utility maximization at the psychological level; and this is what Sen's "agency" is supposed to be. However, one has not made progress here if there is no independent evidence for the proposed nonutilitarian motivator, if it is posited just in response to worrying about the tautology objection. Sen says remarkably little that might help us to see *why* agency, in particular, is not an aspect of utility unless we presume an hedonic interpretation of the latter. He admits that enhancement of agency may contribute to enhancement of "individual well-being," but says that "the point at issue is not the plausibility of their *independence*, but the sustainability and relevance of the *distinction*" (ibid., p. 43). Agreed. So what *is* supposed to ground the distinction? Sen's immediately proffered instance is essentially my Nelson Mandela case above: "For example, if one fights hard for the independence of one's country, and when that independence is achieved one happens to feel happier, the main achievement is that of independence, of which the happiness at that achievement is only one consequence" (ibid., pp. 43–44). It is obvious that the interpretation of "happiness" here has to be hedonic in order for the example to have any intuitive appeal. Of course, it is because the folk concept of happiness *is* hedonic, and utility is then interpreted by reference to it, that Sen's intuition pump is widely persuasive.

An introspectionist account of preference such as Robbins's perhaps has resources for recovering Sen's distinction in nonhedonic terms, so long as psychological facts cooperate. Maybe, for example, Mandela is aware of having ordered preferences as between lamb curry and steak, but not as between social justice and the comforts of personal freedom—or as between social justice and lamb curry. As we will discuss in chapter 6, however, cognitive science undermines hope of giving any systematic empirical sense to this sort of claim. But, in any case, Sen's distinction and his critical use of it begs the question against the best available contemporary defense of RPT; or so I will spend the rest of this section arguing.

Consider, first, Sen's prisoner's dilemma example.[3] If the two-person PD (one-shot or iterated) is held to model the actual behavioral and strategic situation of a pair of agents, then what is being asserted is that, *given everything that matters to them*, each agent prefers (i) the outcome in which she defects and the other cooperates to (ii) the outcome in which both cooperate, prefers mutual cooperation to (iii) mutual defection, and prefers mutual defection to (iv) the outcome in which she cooperates and the other defects. If for any reason, whether related to prevailing social norms or moral commitments or narrowly self-interested reflection, one agent's behavior deviates from this preference ordering over outcomes, then it is simply an empirical error to model their situation as a PD; they are playing some other game. This reasoning is among the most straightforward possible applications of RPT. It is the players' actual behavioral record, from which their rankings of outcomes is inferred, that (along with their information, in the case of extensive-form games) determines the structure of their game. This example also helps to illustrate that the issue has nothing to do with the *contents* of the specific preferences or the extent to which they are tuistic. Suppose that a badly designed aid allocation scheme incentivizes Mother Theresa to request all the money for the children of Calcutta and Mother Juanita to request all of it for the children of Sao Paulo, under circumstances where more children could be fed if both requested a fifty–fifty split. Or, indeed, suppose instead that the two benefactors are led into the mirror image of this fix partly because hyper-Kantian commitments induce them to symmetrically defer to one another's local obligations (i.e., Mother Theresa opts to send all the food to Mother Juanita for distribution while Mother Juanita does the opposite). In that case, the empirical situation is that of a PD, though presumably no one will be inclined to accuse either saint of narrow selfishness.[4]

In game theory, as in applications of other technologies that use RPT, the purpose of the machinery is to tell us what happens when patterns of behavior instantiate some particular strategic vector, payoff matrix, and distribution of information—for example, a PD—that we're empirically motivated to regard as a correct model of a target situation. The motivational history that produced this vector in a given case is irrelevant to which game is instantiated, or to the location of its equilibrium or equilibria. As Binmore (1994, pp. 95–256) emphasizes at length, if, in the case of any putative PD, there is any available story that would rationalize cooperation by either player, then it follows as a matter of logic that the modeler has assigned at least one of them the wrong utility function (or has mistakenly assumed perfect information, or has failed to detect a commitment action) and so made a mistake in taking their game as an instance of the (one-shot) PD. Perhaps she has not observed enough of their behavior to have inferred an accurate model of the agents they instantiate. The game theorist's solution algorithms, in themselves, are not empirical hypotheses about *anything*. Applications of them will be only as good, for purposes of either normative strategic advice or empirical explanation, as the empirical model of the players constructed from the intentional stance is accurate. It is a much-cited fact from the experimental economics literature that when people are brought into laboratories and set into situations contrived to induce PDs, substantial numbers cooperate. What follows from this, *by proper use of RPT, not in discredit of it*, is that the experimental setup has failed to induce a PD after all. The players' behavior indicates that their preferences have been misrepresented[5] in the specification of their game as a PD. A game is a mathematical representation of a situation, and the operation of solving a game is an exercise in deductive reasoning. Like any deductive argument, it adds no new empirical information not already contained in the premises. However, it can be of explanatory value in revealing structural relations among facts that we otherwise might not have noticed.

Of course, the premises must model empirical facts about the agents (among other things). Sen's criticism of RPT combines the correct claim that motivations *should* be endogenized within our models of agents, insofar as these are relevant to the agents' behavior, with the claim that RPT inherently lacks the resources to do this. The second claim admits of two interpretations. If it is intended as meaning that RPT can't endogenize motivations *in general*, then, as we'll see later, it's just false. If instead the idea is that it's particularly difficult, for empirical reasons, to endogenize the motivations of *people* in economic models based on RPT, then it raises a number of interesting and substantive issues. Indeed, it points to precisely the question with which I opened this chapter: what, if anything, is the relationship between utility functions—and their causally relevant manifestation in strategies—and actual people? Sen's critique takes for granted that economic agents, identified by reference to some sort of goal achievement under scarcity, should be identical to actual people, psychologically characterized; and then it makes the easy case that RPT fails to *build in* this assumed equivalence. This amounts to assuming, rather than arguing for, the strongest possible denial of any sort of separateness thesis: to follow Sen here is to implicitly assume that economics *is* a branch of (social) psychology. It thus simply amounts to a brute denial of Samuelson's analytical starting point; hence my charge of question begging against Sen.

In chapters 6, 7, and 8 I will be arguing that not only should we *not* assume that economic agents are identical to actual people, but that the efficacy of economic analysis *requires* the assumption that economic agency is never even straightforwardly *coextensive with* personhood. (Let me say straight out: this is the central thesis of this book; critics take note.) My key foundational assumption for microeconomics will thus turn out to be the precise opposite of Sen's. However, before I begin the lengthy process of building the positive case for this thesis, more description of the basis for Sen's skepticism about RPT and about the strictly internal problems with his preferred alternative approach needs to be given. My own coming account of economic agency should be partly motivated by understanding the background of contrasting views in which I advance it.

Sen's basic strategy depends on assuming internalism about beliefs and other propositional attitudes, when this is exactly the issue at stake. It is worth examining his reasoning in detail, because diagnosing the mistake involved will expose some specific features of internalist assumptions as they play out in economics. My discussion here owes a debt to Dowding (2002), who both nicely synopsizes Sen's generic argument, and locates the pressure point against it in its internalist presuppositions. To my knowledge, Dowding's paper has up to now been unique in the literature in recognizing a connection between internalism in the philosophy of mind and the debates about the foundations of economics motivated by Sen's work.[6]

Suppose, representing one of Sen's favorite examples as noted above, that we start with a set X over which the $>$ relation holds, a subset x, $y \subseteq A$ of X in which, for agent i, we have observed $x >_i y$, and another subset y, $z \subseteq A'$ of X in which we have observed $y >_i z$. Then we can conclude by RPT that in the *unobserved* case where i chooses from $A \cup A'$, $x >_i z$ holds, and x will be chosen. But now suppose that A is a basket of fruit in which y is the largest piece. Suppose that A' is another basket in which x is the largest piece. Finally, suppose that i behaves according to a social rule mandating "never take the largest piece of food from a communal basket," and i is in company. Given this rule "external to" the choice function $c(A \cup A'; >_i)$, and the social circumstance also "external to" $c(A \cup A'; >_i)$, our application of RPT will yield the wrong prediction: i will choose x in A, and y in A', but will be free to choose y in $A \cup A'$. But this violates asymmetry. Since the "external" rule describes the behavioral dispositions of many actual people, and since it is just silly to call these people irrational, RPT is neither generally descriptively true of actual people, nor does it pick out a normatively appropriate set of rationality conditions. This is Sen's generic argument.

As I have said, I will not be holding that RPT *directly* describes the "choice dynamics" of actual people. However, I *will* be holding that RPT is descriptively relevant to behavioral science, and that it captures a scientifically important concept of "economic rationality."

Furthermore, for reasons to be explored in chapter 6, I won't want this claim to depend in any way on either normative or descriptive individualism. Sen's argument thus needs to be blocked, in a way that does not require the outlandish claim that economic agents do not or should not observe norms of social politeness (and so forth).

As Dowding demonstrates, Sen's whole case here turns on confusions about the nature of the reference classes over which utility functions and choice functions are constructed. Sen's argument requires that $x \in A = x \in A'$ and $y \in A = y \in A'$ because x and y denote the same pieces of fruit—say, an apple for x and an orange for y—in each case. But then the argument assumes that i does not hold preferences over pieces of fruit determined only by reference to their properties of "appleness" and "orangeness." She also cares about at least one of the relational properties that each can have or lack, namely, whether one of them is the largest piece in a particular basket in a particular social context. This is of course a perfectly plausible and understandable psychological profile, which is part of the reason we can't regard i as irrational under the imagined circumstances. But then, if RPT is to pronounce i's sequence of choices as implying irrationality, this must be because RPT bans the use of certain kinds of relational properties in individuating objects of preference. However, RPT, as just the system of axioms sketched in the previous chapter, is absolutely silent about what values can be taken by the variables in its range. There is thus no justification *internal* to RPT for Sen's assumption that objects of preference must be individuated independently of the considerations he calls external, such as social norms. On the contrary, as Dowding points out (2002, p. 271), an assumption to the effect that i is the same economic agent across both hypothetical choice situations—that is, that her behavior is described by the function $c(A \cup A'; >_i)$—*entails* that either $x \in A \neq x \in A'$ or $y \in A \neq y \in A'$ or both. By simply assuming that something entailed by RPT does not hold of the psychological description of his imaginary case, Sen thus trivially guarantees that RPT cannot describe it. Again, what is at stake here, just for the moment, is not the question of whether RPT *does* accurately describe any causal dynamics in i's psychology. The issue raised by Sen's argument is more general: do the family of relations axiomatized by RPT have anything possibly to do with notions of rational choice that could be made relevant, descriptively or evaluatively, directly or indirectly, to economic behavior?

Since Sen's assumption that $x \in A = x \in A'$ and $y \in A = y \in A'$ is not entailed by the formal logic of RPT, it must amount to a philosophical rejection of the behaviorist identification of preference and choice involved in Samuelson's intended interpretation of RPT. One wishes, therefore, that Sen provided some nonnormative justification, or even some descriptive account, of the philosophical psychology he takes for granted in this and other cases. Unfortunately, as far as I can tell, nowhere in his voluminous writings does he do either. What is likely presupposed by many of Sen's readers, if not necessarily by Sen himself, is roughly the internalist picture of representational meaning inherited from folk psychology. That is, the agent has psychologically real, causally active, representations of objects, which she privately sorts into equivalence classes for purposes of reference. She uses these referential equivalence classes in, among other things, formulating private (but, of course, often reportable) preference relations. The choice function that the economist constructs in a particular application of RPT is to be defined over these represented equivalence classes. Put another way, a utility function describes psychologically real motivational structures of individuals, causally active representations of preference with determinate semantic content, that cannot vary *just* with external context. Therefore, anything that influences the agent's behavior independently of the properties tracked in formation of the represented equivalence classes is "external to" preference-as-choice. Or, at least, so we'll briefly imagine for the sake of argument clarification, on our way to shaking loose what Sen might *actually* have in mind.

As we saw in the previous chapter, since Samuelson was a behaviorist of the crude, prefunctionalist variety, it would have been more consistent for *him* to have followed Quine in urging the elimination of preference (in the folk-psychological sense) from economic theory, rather than its identification with choice. However, I of course am not going to be defending RPT while strapping the millstone of *crude* behaviorism around its neck. From a perspective of initial neutrality in the philosophy of mind, it is an open question whether the empirical correlates of the family of relations defined by the axioms of RPT will turn out to be "in the minds of" subjects—an internalist interpretation—or only ascribed to subjects for the purpose of describing regularities in their behavior—an intentional-stance functionalist interpretation. Going the second way would obviously block Sen's assumption, since then the analyst is welcome to individuate objects of preference by reference to any properties *he* can detect, whether these properties are or aren't "mentally represented" by the agent (on whatever story is told about "mental representation"), so long as there's *some* nonmysterious causal relation between the informational distinctions coded in the individuation scheme and the agent's behavior. These properties can then include the kinds of relational properties Sen calls "external." Of course, this will leave us needing a nonmagical account of *how* purely externally ascribed representations can be relevant to the causation and explanation of behavior, but this is a project to which all philosophical externalists have been committed in general anyway, and which will be among the principal subjects of chapters 6 through 8.

Daniel Hausman (personal communication) interprets Sen's argument in a way that makes the above reasoning directly relevant to it. "Behaviorist economists," says Hausman, "not Sen, will in fact take the objects of choice to be simply "an apple" or "an orange." Those who are willing to start with subjective preference have the resources to distinguish taking an apple when doing so leaves others with a choice from taking an apple when doing so does not. This is not an objection to any of the axioms . . . of RPT in [the] generalized sense. It is an objection to starting with choice and with a crude behaviorist individuation of the objects of choice." Intentional-stance functionalism, however, escapes this objection straightforwardly. If an agent chooses the apple in the first sort of case and not in the second, then all the available behavioral evidence will lead the intentional-stance functionalist to apply triangulated propositional-attitude ascriptions that individuate his objects of preference as, inter alia, "apples whose selection leaves others with choices" and "apples whose selection forecloses others' choices." Recall from chapter 2 that there are *two* ways of not being an internalist, and crude behaviorism—which, following four decades of philosophical psychology since Watson, had better be reformulated as eliminativism if it is to be taken seriously—is only one of them.

One might here try to follow Davis (2003) in constructing an argument on Sen's behalf that doesn't depend on internalism about agents' *representations* of their preferences. This would indeed be fairer to Sen, since he almost certainly doesn't intend us to regard attention to *all* relational, nonphenomenal properties as implying "external" influences on preference; the preference-ordering-representing mechanism presumably *can* have "oldest-fruit-in-the-basket" in its domain of objects. So what *is* the relevant difference supposed to be? On Davis's account, it is related to sovereignty with respect to *control over* the equivalence classes for preference formation. Someone who maintains an internalist thesis about *some* aspects of behavioral causation might think that the agent gets to decide, all by herself, whether oldest-apple-in-the basket is a relevant kind of object for preference, but might then maintain that society (at least partly) determines which properties a socialized agent must keep track of and guide behavior by reference to. Perhaps, Davis argues, this distinction has a real correlate at some level relevant to the *psychological* explanation of behavior. Intentional-stance functionalism denies this distinction (as Davis recognizes). According to it, we individuate objects, *in general*, into reference classes for purposes of behavioral control by taking the intentional stance toward ourselves, and we do this by modeling the intentional stance as taken toward us by others. Intentional preference classes are thus *in general* (partly) under social control. So even if preference classes do depend in some way on "mentally represented" reference classes, these won't turn out to be independent of what Sen regards as external factors. One side of his fundamental distinction between utility and agency, at least insofar as the distinction is supposed to emerge from his criticisms of RPT (as opposed to his metaethical reflections), is thus empty.

This conclusion might look like the best possible news for the critic of RPT, since the side of Sen's distinction that's been emptied by the path of argument we've pursued is the "utility" side. "Agency," given noneliminativist externalism, infects *all* preference-class individuation. However, now remember that the motivation for Sen's distinction in the first place was the tautology worry. This worry (if it really is something to worry about) has only been successfully addressed if both sides of Sen's distinction have some empirically (and behaviorally) relevant content. What the preceding argument shows is that Sen is, at best, playing a shell game with respect to the tautology issue. If we play it with him, we are led to say that nobody ever behaves so as to maximize their utility—a goal that now has no empirically relevant meaning—but we have no basis for *not* saying that they try to maximize whatever they take the optimal conditions for their agency to be. Now, intentional-stance functionalism, although it is not crude behaviorism that can't find relational properties, *is* a form of behaviorism. That is, it identifies agents' intentions with their behavior, as characterized by intentions. The intentional-stance functionalist will thus have to face up to the tautology objection regardless of whether intentional behavior is characterized in agency language or utility language. For her, Sen's "external factors" argument has changed nothing of substance.

If the concept of "whatever an agent takes its well-being to be" is not understood following the intentional-stance functionalist's approach, but then is also not interpreted in the phenomenalist fashion of Robbins—which Sen certainly does not intend—then all that seems to be left is the old Aristotelian conception. It is thus no surprise that Sen's position on the normative relevance of economics to policy slides all the way back to Aristotle's. Like Aristotle, he denies what in chapter 3 was called "metaphysical subjectivism," since he thinks that what a person *takes to be* her well-being may not actually *be* her well-being. Also with Aristotle, he believes that some minimum threshold of material well-being is necessary for genuine well-being. The economist's job according to Sen is thus to uncover the best techniques for bringing this minimum threshold into universal (or, at least, wider) reach, while the watchful eyes of ethicists, sociologists, and anthropologists, who collectively embody normative and descriptive expertise about genuine well-being, aim to ensure that the economist's schemes don't accidentally (or deliberately) undermine its noneconomic aspects. But insofar as the economist aims to *describe* people's choices and behavior, Sen has given us no reason to abandon the psychological subjectivism that is at the root of his worries about tautology. After all, on the folk model of the role of representations in behavior that Sen's narrower critique of RPT has to assume to be valid, if an agent is wrong about what she takes her well-being to consist in, then we can't explain her behavior, including her preference reports, by reference to the actual conditions that would promote her well-being, of which by hypothesis she's ignorant. We encountered the combination of psychological subjectivism and metaphysical objectivism in the previous chapter. Where the relationship between economics and psychology is concerned, Sen returns us, it seems, exactly to the semi-Aristotelianism of Jevons and Marshall.

Though I think that metaphysical subjectivism is true, it is not among the tasks of this book to defend it.[7] What matters here is that, since Sen has offered no new arguments against metaphysical subjectivism—he just asserts its denial—and since his argument against Samuelsonian economics begs the question against both the eliminativist and the intentional-stance functionalist, he has given no one a fresh reason to return to Aristotelianism or semi-Aristotelianism. The sense in which he has warmed the climate for the neo-Aristotelianism of the new experimentalists and institutionalists is thus purely polemical, and not philosophically justifiable.

While this conclusion might disappoint the experimentalist, institutionalist neo-Aristotelians, it is hardly the end of the world for them. After all, they generally suppose that their approach is mainly grounded not in philosophy—moral or logical—but in cognitive and evolutionary science. Given the epistemological attitude toward the relationship between philosophical arguments and empirical investigation that I endorsed earlier, such a stance by experimentalists would be fully justified. But perhaps if Sen hasn't in fact prepared the ground for them, they can instead come to his rescue.[8] We will later see reasons for doubting this, for thinking indeed that Mirowski is right to believe that experimentally motivated semi-Aristotelianism ends up in the worst possible world from the humanists' point of view. For now, however, I have established just this much: I have defeated any contention to the effect that, since Sen has refuted RPT, we need, a priori, a new framework from psychology and/or philosophy to replace it. Since Sen has not logically refuted RPT, it remains, at this stage of inquiry, one candidate for the formal representation of whatever it is that empirical behavioral science turns out to be telling us.

But does it really? I have just concluded that Sen's proposed alternative to RPT—his "agency" conception—fails to address his own most basic worry about RPT, namely, the tautology problem. But this obviously doesn't license our just ignoring or dismissing the tautology objection where RPT is concerned; the fact that *Sen* hasn't made any progress with respect to it doesn't excuse everybody else from having to try. As we saw in the previous chapter, the tautology concern has played a major role in economic metatheory right from the dawn of neoclassicism. It inspired Jevons to retreat to semi-Aristotelianism against his own subjectivist, Benthamite heritage, and this in turn delayed the full technical maturity of consumer theory for sixty years. Sen, as we just saw, essentially retraces Jevons's path exactly. Even Samuelson (1972, p. 255) took for granted that he had to beware of it. Finally, I noted at several points in the proceeding argument that the intentional-stance functionalist, who *must* identify preferences with patterns in choice, faces the tautology objection with particular urgency. Now, the tautology concern is not empirically generated; it is an instance of an a priori, philosophically motivated problem if anything is. Therefore, before settling finally into the domain of cognitive and behavioral science—where, so to speak, the real action is to be found—let us try to shake loose the venerable bugbear of the tautology issue, and see what genuine constraints, if any, our *way* of shaking it loose imposes on empirical inquiry.

Two Cheers for Tautologies

As we saw in chapter 3, in Samuelsonian economics a utility function, whether ordinal or VNM, is simply a ranking of variables. Nothing in the axioms of RPT restricts the values of these variables. If RPT is to describe some aspects of behavior, the individuation of objects of preference will have to respect, as noted previously, an informational efficacy constraint. That is, though preferences need not be individuated by propositional-attitude ascriptions that correspond in their content to internally accessible descriptions, this can't be promoted into license to individuate them by reference to information that can't causally influence behavior at all. But this restricts our interpretations of behavioral facts far more loosely than a constraint of Robbins's introspectionist kind might; after all, human nervous systems are highly complex processors, embedded in informationally dense environments, so their mere potential informational sensitivity is gigantic. Thus, for *any* behavioral pattern, it will almost always be possible to construct a utility function that describes it without anomalies. Given no restrictions on what kind of causal or dynamic process utility maximization is, to say of an agent that she maximizes utility is thus to convey no empirical information at all.

The exact formulation of the last sentence is important. Economists—and, as we'll see in chapter 6, some philosophers—often *define* agency in terms of goal-directed behavior, which in turn implies commitment to at least some minimal conception of rationality. If goal-directed behavior is generally modeled by application of RPT, it must then obviously be tautological to say that an *agent* maximizes utility. "Agent" is here being used as a technical term, defined by reference to RPT, so an Aristotelian or semi-Aristotelian who consents to talk within the frame of the definitional convention will have to regard *this* tautology as philosophically innocent. However, it would be bizarre to similarly try to define "person" as a technical term. People are empirical kinds of some sort—whether they're organisms or abstract selves or organisms-with-morally-significant-identities, or whatever. Therefore, to say that a *person* maximizes utility cannot be a pure tautology, a literal truth-by-definition. The low information yield associated with the claim derives instead from the fact that the "utility" part of "utility maximization" is exceptionally empirically modest, because "utility," interpreted by way of RPT, simply denotes whatever is maximized. "People maximize utility" is equivalent to saying "people maximize something."

Again, this isn't *literally* a tautology. Perhaps, given some plausible conception or other of people, people don't maximize anything. However, our unrestricted freedom to instantiate "something" however we please still yields *practical* informational emptiness. We know, a priori, that we can always find something such that a person's behavior will be *consistent* with her maximizing it, even if "maximization" denotes no causally real or empirically informative process. To dramatize this, suppose that someone wanted to model rocks as agents (in the technical sense). Rock "behavior" is accurately described by the claim that rocks maximize closeness-to-the-center-of-the-earth, subject to constraints on how much energy they can marshal to penetrate surfaces. (In economese, we thereby indicate their "budget constraint.") But if it's easy to model rocks as agents, then this shows that it's *too* easy to model people as agents for this to be telling us anything informative about people.

This uncomplicated reasoning lies behind the logical speed with which tautology objections have been taken to be devastating in the history of metaeconomics. Jevons, as we saw in the previous chapter, gets from the tautology worry to semi-Aristotelianism in one sentence. Sen (1987) uses the tautology objection to dismiss the purely technical construal of people-as-agents in a footnote.[9] The behavioral economist Richard Thaler (1992, p. 2) briskly endorses it by simply saying "A theory is indeed not testable if no possible set of data could refute it. (In fact, it is not really a theory; more like a definition.)" Instant surrender in the face of tautology objections just looks like common sense.

What is obviously correct is that if all an economist equipped with RPT could tell us is that people maximize utility, this economist would be scientifically useless. (Could he be useful in some other sense? Perhaps he could sing the claim nicely.) However, Thaler's use of the word "theory" in the passage quoted above conceals an ambiguity. Within the broad empire of the sciences, "theory" is used in a number of different senses. Theory sometimes means "a logically linked set of empirical hypotheses." This is the sense intended by Thaler, and in this sense the bare claim that people maximize utility is indeed not an informative theory. However, what mathematicians and logicians mean by "theories" are sets of axioms that fix definitions and relations. On this understanding, RPT is in itself a theory, though not a theory of any sort of *behavior*. The mathematician's conception of theory has in turn influenced usage in those sciences, like physics and economics, that rely heavily on applications of mathematics. The result is yet a third meaning for "theory": in physics, theory typically denotes a particular set of field equations that parameterizes the responses of some prespecified class of measurable variable coefficients of a system or set of systems to some other class of coefficients. In this sense of the concept of "theory," RPT could be *part* of a theory of some phenomenon if it fixed the identification of some measurable coefficients and relations in such a way that the measurements in question served an epistemically worthy purpose, typically prediction or explanation or both.

In terms of this schematic organization of the "theory" concept it is easy to be clear about the possible scientific status of RPT. It is obviously not a theory in sense 1. It equally obviously *is* a theory in sense 2, but then it is just a theory of mathematics rather than of anything empirical. Furthermore, it is not an *interesting* theory of mathematics because it is not mainly motivated by concerns internal to the fruitful organization of mathematical reality; mathematicians do not carve their investigative domain in such a way that the set of functions $c(X; >_i)$ denotes an interesting object that can't be more parsimoniously captured from a more general set of definitions.

The philosopher Alex Rosenberg has argued (1992) that neoclassical economic theory (in general) is respectable as theory because it's respectable in sense 2. However, the last consideration in the previous paragraph suggests that this move damns the significance of neoclassical theory with very faint praise. If economists are actually mathematicians, as Rosenberg proposes, then they are eccentric mathematicians obsessed with a peculiar class of functions, and their organization into a separate discipline has no plausible justification. However, it is obvious that economic theorists should be motivated to study their favorite functions not by mathematical interests per se, but by their conviction that use of these functions permits isolation and measurement of coefficients and relations that have systematically fruitful empirical significance. (As implied at the beginning of the present chapter, this is what Samuelson assumes about his apparatus without remotely adequate philosophical care over what the assumption means in practical terms, a point emphasized vigorously by

Mirowski [1989, pp. 358–386]. That's why we're having to work so hard here.) RPT is thus supposed to be *part* of a theory in the third sense of "theory" above.

This brings us directly back to the point where we left the amalgamation of Robbins and Samuelson in the final section of chapter 3. To show that RPT is useful we must find some real structures that are usefully measured—where "usefully" means nonredundantly relevant to explanation and prediction—using coefficients and relations defined by its axioms. Although RPT, if interpreted as a theory in sense 1, is tautologous, it could nevertheless contribute to our empirical information just in case there could turn out, as a matter of contingent empirical fact, to be no such real structures.

Is this criterion for empirical significance satisfied? In answering this question, attention to the nonredundancy requirement discussed in chapter 2 is crucial. Consider "rock behavior" again. We can usefully approximate the truth about what rocks do using Newtonian physics (and we can best explain and predict what they do using relativistic physics). As many commentators (e.g., Mirowski 1989; Rosenberg 1983) have pointed out, the epistemological and ontological background to neoclassical economics has much in common with the metaphysics of classical physics. Classical physics uses theories (in sense 3) that are just like RPT in that they work by allowing us to solve for extremum values in systems of differential equations. It is because RPT, prior to its independently motivated identification with some particular phenomena for interpretation by means of it, is relatively general as an axiomatization of maximization that we could use it to say some true things about rocks. However, as a way of modeling rock behavior RPT fails the nonredundancy requirement. Neither of the axioms of RPT, let alone the two restrictions on the choice function, is necessary to account for rock motion given a decent theory of mechanics. But one can't explain or predict the dynamics of economic systems by means of physics, nor even (or so I will eventually contend, in volume 2 of this study) by applying the union of psychology, ethology, and sociology.

The nonredundancy requirement will be understood in terms of the information-theoretic account of existence given in chapter 2. Recall that one of the motivations for that account is that it allows us to make sense, in a realist way, of patterns that don't reduce to physical patterns, including intentionality and agency. That is, it allows us to endorse intentional-stance functionalism without sliding into instrumentalism. All this does no more than fix a context for argument. We still need to see reasons to be convinced that, as a matter of fact, intentionality and agency *are* real patterns. This argument will be given in chapter 8. Thus we won't be in a position to be satisfied that RPT, when linked to intentional-stance functionalism, is a useful sense-3 theory until then. There is, however, more to be said now in direct answer to the tautology objection than just the promise that RPT can be defended as the axiomatic component of a nonredundant sense-3 theory.

Binmore (1994, pp. 95, 99, 104–110) is unusually forthright in stating that all of microeconomic theory—specifically presented by him as the union of RPT and game theory—is a system of tautologies that are useful, indeed, "wonderful." He makes explicit that he is thinking of the system as a theory in the mathematician's sense 2, rendering the claim technically watertight. However, he then goes further, trying to put the theory in the best possible company by claiming that Darwin's "principle of the survival of the fittest" is a wonderful tautology of the same type. This is a refreshingly brash reaction to the popularity of equally fast tautology objections, but it is too careless. The philosopher of science Philip Kitcher (1982, pp. 55–60) has considered the tautology objection as raised against Darwin—in this case by creationists—less brusquely, and his treatment merits attention here because it invokes general philosophical considerations that apply equally well to microeconomic theory.

The tautology objection to Darwin begins by attributing to him a "principle" of natural selection, according to which those genes that are most fit are selected for continued survival. Relative fitness is then claimed to be defined as relative expected probability of survival. A bit of seductive but sloppy substitution of nearly equivalent phrases can then render the principle as: those genes most likely to survive are selected for survival. This *almost* looks like a literal tautology. (We must say "almost" because expected survival and actual survival are not the same thing.) As Kitcher easily shows, there are several aspects of this reasoning, as the creationists offer it, that simply rest on special (and willful) misunderstandings of the content of Darwin's work. However, the fact that Binmore, who thoroughly understands Darwin, celebrates his "tautology," suggests that one can construct an empirically uninformative "principle of natural selection," without having to indulge the creationists' scientific and logical muddles. He is right about this. Natural selection is not a process operated by anything external to itself. Therefore, Mother Nature—just, of course, another name for natural selection—cannot entertain any standards of preference independent of what is actually selected. The *analyst* can entertain such standards, by considering what *might* have been selected in nearby possible worlds (thus deriving the distinction between expected and actual fitness). But, as Fodor (1996) has some fun arguing, this implicitly involves treating the environmental variables that are shifted in going to the possible worlds as if their values in the actual world are independent of the inputs to what we take to be the function computed by natural selection. That is, we act as if we already had a general specification of that function that is independent of the contingent history of actual evolution. But this is the very sort of function that the move to possible worlds is supposed to justify. Thus the possible worlds move, if not based on observations of actual variations in response to selection pressures, can repeat the error of forgetting that the computation performed by natural selection just *is* the history of life, incorporating all of its actual contingencies because there's no operator of the computation to distinguish accidents from regularities. Put another way: it takes a good deal of care to formulate an algorithm computed by natural selection that generalizes beyond the actual set of inputs that the historical process on earth has happened to receive.[10] Many descriptions of natural selection in the history of biology would not pass this test, and so indeed render it, by itself, as tautologous in explanations of who went extinct and who didn't.

As Kitcher argues, however, the "principle" of natural selection that the creationists and Binmore alike attribute to Darwin is a straw man. It implicitly invokes the idea that scientific research programs—theories in sense 1 above—are systems of *propositions*. If Darwinian theory is a system of propositions, then we can ask of each such proposition whether it is empirically informative or not. The "principle" of natural selection can, without undue violence to textbook accounts of evolutionary theory, be interpreted, in the way I did above, as a proposition that is not empirically informative; and then a tautology objection can be trotted out. It doesn't occur to the foolish creationists that theories-as-sets-of-propositions can include axioms—that is, that theories in sense 1 can rely on theories in sense 3—and so Binmore is able to kick them around by celebrating the usefulness of Darwin's "principle," interpreted as an axiom.

However, it is a mistake—one often made by philosophers of science, who confuse textbook accounts of scientific theories, what *they* study, with the actual subject matter of science—to identify research programs with systems of propositions. As any postmodernist would agree, and as Hacking (1983) has emphasized, science doesn't make its progress mainly by achievement of *arguments* (however useful its "rational reconstruction" in that way might be for philosophical purposes). Rather, science convinces by performing successful interventions in the causal nexus that demonstrate institutionally accumulated know-how. We believe successful physicists because we see that they know what to do with particle accelerators (and so on). We believe successful economists, if there are any, because we see that they know how to build game-theoretic mechanisms and implement the incentive structures those models identify as efficacious in determining outcomes. (For example, they design public telcom auctions intended to increase government revenue by a factor of x; and then they set up the auction and the extra revenue is indeed forthcoming.) Entirely abstract "principles," like that of "natural selection," are thus important to *describing* science and its history, but much less so to justifying a conviction that a given research program, such as the Darwinian one, has come to grips with independent reality.

Kitcher's response to the tautology objection as invoked against Darwin is based on this clearer understanding of the relationship between research programs and propositional descriptions of them. Darwin, like all great scientists, was the discoverer of a *problem-solving strategy*.[11] His strategy works (very roughly) as follows: explain a widespread trait in a population by asking why the trait in question would have had a competitive advantage over other possible traits that could have arisen, where "possible" is defined by reference to actual historical (environmental, genetic, and morphological) constraints. This problem-solving strategy has been among the most fruitful—perhaps the most unambiguously fruitful—in the entire history of science. The strategy describes something scientists *do*; it is neither an axiomatic nor a hypothetical proposition, the sort of thing that might or might not be tautologous. Nowhere in Darwin's writings—nor, as Kitcher documents, even in the subsequent textbooks in evolutionary theory—does one find something explicitly called a "principle of natural selection," so we are not *required* to search for *any* particular propositional content to file under such a principle. *If* we are convinced a priori that scientific theories are sets of propositions, *then* the "principle" as Binmore defends it is a plausible reconstruction of what both Darwin and the textbooks actually say. But this follows one of the positivists' errors in putting the logical cart in front of the behavioral horse.

Let me be clear that Kitcher's answer is not just a matter of rhetorical topic switching, whereby focus on what scientists believe is shuffled off the stage in favor of attention to what they do, but where they nevertheless must believe *something*, and some of those things might be tautologies. Logically, the principle attributed to Darwin by the tautology mongers functions, relative to the theory, not as a proposition licensing derivations but as a *name* for what Kitcher calls an "argument pattern." Argument patterns aren't sets of statements trying to declare empirical truths directly. Rather, they're procedural tools scientists use in motivating experimental interventions. Kitcher's account of argument patterns is developed with sufficient rigor (see his 1989, pp. 432–448) that it could be operationalized and implemented in a computer program. Thagard (1992) actually has so implemented something structurally akin to Kitcher's argument patterns. This of course guarantees that some elements of the implementation must be axioms, since one cannot have a programmable algorithm without them. To the extent that theories are conceptualized as problem-solving strategies, therefore, they must be theories in sense 3. (Let us also note that both Kitcher's and Thagard's systems have *explanation* of phenomena as their primary intended normative output, with predictive utility as a derivative norm. This will be important to my later discussion of Milton Friedman's economic methodology.) Kitcher exemplifies application of the argument-pattern concept by constructing the argument patterns for three large-scale scientific theories: classical genetics, Darwinian selection theory, and Dalton's theory of the chemical bond. Thagard offers many more explicit examples.[12]

Let us now apply Kitcher's approach, at its schematic level, directly to the tautology objection as it is raised against neoclassical utility theory in general (or against RPT specifically). There need be no empirically empty "principle" of microeconomics that says "People act so as to maximize their utility." Of course, textbooks sometimes do say just this. But to the extent that economists are serious about wanting to shake off the problematic aspects of their positivist legacy they should stop saying this, or at least accompany the claim with suitable caveats about its status. RPT is the set of axioms to which reference is made in the following formulation of a *Robbins–Samuelson problem-solving strategy* that *begins* as follows:

Suppose you want to explain and/or predict what happens when the members of a group of one or more goal-directed systems, in causal interaction wherever the group is larger than one, pursue ends that cannot all be satisfied given available common resources that have alternative uses. In that case, use as much evidence as you should (according to pragmatically governed but scientifically rigorous standards) gather about their behavior to represent the schedule of ends pursued by each system as a (ordinal or VNM, depending on the intended application and purpose of the solution) utility function, defined as per axioms that admit of solution by simultaneously maximizing each utility function for a given allocation of resource constraints.

Obviously, this is only a first step in the problem-solving strategy. It as yet makes no ontological claims about the existence, nonexistence, or identity of actually successful maximizers. (Thus it incorporates no presumption in favor of Judd's revenge as the way to do economics.) Articulating and defending such claims is a task that still lies ahead of us. What we have so far, however, states RPT's role in an economic science understood, approximately following Robbins, as the study of responses to scarcity by intentional systems. It treats RPT as what it is: the axiomatic component of a theory in sense 3, or, less abstractly, as a tool put to use in application of a problem-solving strategy. The first sort of thing is simply the textbook-style propositional expression of the second sort of thing. There is no basis for invoking any sort of a priori "tautology objection," whether fast or careful, against it in either sense. RPT could turn out to be useless for empirical science if there are no real structures it helps us to isolate and measure; or the opposite could turn out to be true. Continuing our inquiry, we shall see.

Mature Neoclassicism: Gary Becker's Program

Given the last claim, and many hints that have accumulated over the past chapter and a half, the reader should not be surprised when I now say this: the mistake at the root of Aristotelian and semi-Aristotelian criticisms of neoclassicism has been an uncritical assumption that economic theory must fail unless the real systems it *directly* isolates and measures are people and/or ensembles of them. A central task for the rest of this book is to pull the rug out from under this assumption.

This will sound like a lot of work to move one rug. Does the need for such an investment of labor not itself suggest that the rug is where it belongs? At the risk of working the metaphor to death, the alternative possibility, the one I favor, is that there is a great deal of heavy furniture on top of it that has to be shifted. The furniture in question is made of unsound metaphysics that partly drives the uncritical assumption directly, and partly drives it indirectly by encouraging unsound philosophical psychology. In the remainder of this chapter and the next, I'll be going after both.

My criticism of Sen should make clear how important the uncritical assumption is and has been to the persuasiveness of Aristotelianism and semi-Aristotelianism. The core of the humanist rejection of neoclassicism is the belief that people who acted like, and exclusively like, economic agents would be morally and pragmatically dubious specimens of their kind—"rational fools" (Sen 1977). The judgment is of course significantly normative, but it is based on factual considerations. *If* the usefulness of RPT depended on the idea that people maximize "internal" utility, thus entailing that they either do not or should not respond to social incentives, then either this usefulness depends on a false empirical (sense-1) theory, or on a normative theory to the effect that narrow selfishness is normatively (ethically or pragmatically or both) good. There is of course an immense literature on the second issue, but it is not the concern of this book.[13] Let me therefore just say this much about it here: for reasons best explored by Binmore (1994, 1998), (i) most people are rationally justified in actively ganging up on people whose utility functions are those of Sen's rational fool, (ii) rational fools will seldom be able to conceal their identities from others for long, and so (iii) rational fools will generally do a poor job of maximizing their utility. Rational fools should thus be pitied while being punished; and this is at least as good an operationalization of the concept of a "fool" as any. There is no reason whatsoever for a neoclassical economist to reject any of claims (i)–(iii), regardless of how many have done so from other motivations; so neoclassical theory does not recommend selfishness, regardless of what some economic journalists and popularizers might sometimes say.

That said, then, let us restrict attention to the empirical, as opposed to the normative, claim on which views like Sen's depend. A hopeless way of trying to resist Sen's skepticism about RPT consists in attempting to show that, appearances to the contrary, most people *are* rational fools. However, it is very widely believed, at least in popular circles, that neoclassical economics is in trouble unless this is the case. It may be that many economists once shared this view. Paradoxically, many recent animadversions on the subject by economists begin by saying that they will set out to refute the view—that is, that people are rational fools—held by most economists! This really *does* indicate something peculiar about economics, because I can think of no comparably widespread parallel phenomenon from another discipline. It is explicable, though. Most economists (including university-based economists) make their living as practical consultants, not as theorists. The consequences for practical cost-benefit analyses of issues in the philosophy of economics as a science are, for reasons to be discussed in the next volume, negligible; and the main consumers of cost-benefit analyses know this as well as the practitioners. Most economists therefore pay no significant professional costs for simply endorsing the popular view. But they also pay low costs if they pay lip service to the rubbishing of the popular view by their own theoretical mavens. This makes them look like psychologically sensible people who go along with an obvious simplification just to be practical. That's just the sort of person you'd want for a consultant, no? Thus we have the following sociological situation. Most economists professionally act as though they assume that people are rational fools. Simultaneously, they will agree if probed that people are *not* rational fools, or so the experts say, and that they will be happy to pass this on to their students and clients as soon as someone comes up with a description of what people are instead that isn't too complicated, or too committed to an implausible altruism, or doesn't demand a formal education in philosophy to be understood. That is the main goal of this volume (though I'm not sure how well it can succeed in being uncomplicated).

In the meantime, I of course join the majority of contemporary expert commentators on metaeconomic theory in agreeing that the usefulness of RPT does not depend on the thesis that people maximize narrowly selfish utility. However, I must now distinguish between two quite different bases on which this can be thought true. There is an approach very popular among more conservative economic methodologists that might seem natural in light of my just-concluded rejection of the tautology objection. It is not the approach I will take however. An important rung on the ladder I am climbing will consist in describing both the approach and my reasons for declining recourse to it.

A common strategy for saving neoclassical theory from the empirical rational-fools objection consists in *directly* exploiting the open-endedness of the arguments that can be taken by utility functions. The strategy's most famous and influential user—in working detail as opposed to just philosophical invocation—is Gary Becker. Becker's own work has inspired a substantial industry, usefully surveyed in

Tommasi and Ierulli (1995), that manufactures the following sorts of products. First, take some arena of widespread human behavior that doesn't appear, prima facie, to involve maximizing the quantifiable return on investment of a scarce resource. Examples from the literature include racial or ethnic discrimination, child rearing, romantic courtship, addiction, listening to music, and religious worship. Gather a persuasively large enough—and, ideally, not counterintuitive—set of data on the behavior in question. Then, find an object of possible preference such that *if* this preference is being optimized within an hypothesized general utility function, then the behavior in question would be rationalized given that utility function. Find a plausible, quantifiable, and measurable proxy for the hypothesized object of preference. Finally, ideally, test independent evidence that the proxy variable in question really is widely maximized. Less ideally, but more frequently, conclude by *speculating* that the proxy is widely maximized and invite social psychologists to attempt the relevant empirical studies.

I will describe one such (very well-known) example, the literature based on Becker's (1981) classic work on modern human fertility and child-rearing behavior.[14] First, people are presumed to (typically) want children. Sometimes they are hypothesized to do so for the sake of being supported later in life, while in other applications they are simply thought to have exogenously determined preferences for offspring wired into their utility functions by biological and/or cultural evolution. (Note this exemplification of the theory's openness, contra Sen, to having objects of preference referenced *either* "internally" or "externally"; this is why Becker's agents need not be presumed to be rational fools.) The preference for children is not (normally) a preference for simply bearing them, but for producing some number of economically successful adult people. Rearing children has ineliminable costs and risks. In general, lowering the risk that a given child will die before adulthood, or be unsuccessful as an adult, requires increased parental expenditure on food, health care, education, and other things. If the parent's goal is to maximize the probability that some child-rearing investment will pay off, she has two general strategies available to her. She can either spread her portfolio by bearing many children and investing relatively little in each one, maximizing *quantity* of children, or she can bear fewer children—perhaps, in the limit, just one—and buy it a superior environment. The opportunity costs of these respective strategies will not, typically, just be paid in cash. A mother choosing the quantity-maximizing strategy may have to surrender the possibility of a professional career. This opportunity cost will be irrelevant in a society that blocks access to careers for women. Thus, to the extent that social norms in a given society evolve to allow women opportunities for professional careers, economic reasoning predicts that more women in this society will choose the quality-maximizing strategy. Therefore, so long as women have some control over family-planning strategies—which, given access to careers, is bound to develop if it isn't antecedently present—we should see average family sizes decline, and average per-child expenditure on child-rearing costs rise faster than average household income, as women gain personal autonomy, up to some threshold where most people have found their optimal quality-quantity mix for their particular, variable, attitude to risk.

Dupré (2001, pp. 132–136) has expressed his distaste for this particular reasoning exercise with slightly savage relish. I in no way endorse his attitude.[15] The distinction between the two general strategies with respect to child rearing is well substantiated, quite independently of Becker's work, in ethology and population ecology. Biologists call maximization-of-offspring-quantity "r strategy," and maximization-of-offspring-quality "K strategy." That the distinction marks a real difference is verifiable by the best sort of empirical fruitfulness test: it underwrites predictions of two measurably distinct poles in growth rates of young organisms. (r-strategy offspring grow very quickly, minimizing the window in which nothing but the availability of their numerous brethren protects them from predators. K-strategy offspring grow slowly, since investment in quality needs to exploit open developmental processes if there is to be any scope for leveraging the capital.) Given the ubiquitous nature of the economic pressures that lead evolutionary processes to find these strategies again and again, it would be surprising if cultural-evolutionary processes operating on human behavior did not stumble on them too. The correlation between women's increasing access to nonmenial occupations in many societies, and declining family size, and increasing per-child expenditure on child welfare, is extremely robust and well documented on all continents for the modern period. Finally, the fact that few people conceptualize their own family-planning choices in the terms described by Becker's theory should not in itself trouble us unless we are introspectionists about choice behavior; people surely, typically, have access to all the generic information about lifestyle options and approximate opportunity costs that Becker's model would demand, and so it respects the informational efficacy constraint. These considerations do not, of course, show that the model is right; but they are sufficient to deflect purely armchair skepticism of the sort ventured by Dupré. The worries I will raise for the Becker approach as a general defense of neo-classicism will neither be a priori nor directed at the empirical plausibility of special applications. Rather, they will be motivated by empirically driven concerns that people are not the sorts of systems that are capable, *in isolation*, of maximizing anything very complex over medium-run temporal frames except under special, case-specific circumstances. (r and K strategies, I suggest, can be stable because the behavior they mandate in short-run frames reinforces itself: if you start off pursuing an r-strategy, the resulting experience of seeing lots of offspring die will discourage growth of any disposition to perceive later offspring as sound investment sites. This exemplifies a general property of those Becker-style hypotheses that can be *successful* on my view: each one requires a special account of the medium-to-long-run stabilizers of the strategies predicted by the hypothesis in question.)

Before I turn to these concerns, however, I wish to draw attention to the fact that the Becker approach exemplifies one of the key themes of neoclassicism as discussed in the previous chapter. The work of Becker and his followers emphasizes as vividly as possible neoclassicism's break with the Aristotelian's exclusive focus on material consumption and money-priced opportunity cost. When economists modeling family-planning behavior search for proxies that have prices in money markets, this can be justified on purely pragmatic grounds. The fundamental currency in which a prospective parent faces opportunity costs is very plausibly *time,* and her primary maximand may be use of her time in such a way that she can narrate her own biography in a way she can ethically affirm. But the working economist will sensibly wish to avoid quantitative estimates of these things that would necessarily be ad hoc. This gestures at the very point of a proxy. A particular proxy may be well or poorly motivated, and is always subject to potential criticism as a sound proxy. But to the extent that the subjects of the explanation live in societies that price time in money with approximately clear and readable signals, the economist's use of money prices as proxies does *not* imply commitment to a belief that the "deep" market structures of social interaction are "essentially" material or commercial. What was implicit in marginalism before Jevons backed away from it because of his worry about tautology, but was restored to emphasis by Robbins and Samuelson, becomes working reality in Becker's approach. I will therefore take him and his followers to be the exemplary instances of neoclassical economic scientists. I will henceforth refer to a working theoretical approach that takes this aspect of Becker's approach on board as "mature neoclassicism."

The most fundamental ontological assumption underlying Becker's applications of the neoclassical problem-solving strategy is that *people*—for example, the sorts of things that can be prospective parents of other people—are *economic agents*. This means that, for people, hierarchies of maximands exist, which can be stacked for application of an axiomatic decision theory, such that their behavior will be found to respect the axioms of RPT. I will refer to any philosophy of economics that incorporates this assumption as "anthropocentric neoclassicism" (which can, then, be either "immature" [Jevons] or "mature" [Becker]). Since I am thus categorizing the main neoclassical theorists I have discussed along two orthogonal axes, the matrix in table 4.1 will be useful for keeping the conceptual books. I will claim that anthropocentric neoclassicism is false, that is, that whole people are not economic agents. The rest of the book will be spent arguing for this claim and exploring its implications.

First, however, a red herring, something many critics suppose to be an objection to mature anthropocentric neoclassicism but isn't, must be disposed of. The assumption that whole people are economic agents does *not* require that people be *hyper*rational, that is, be either capable of or inclined to correctly respect, in their behavior, every possible calculation relevant to the maximization of their ascribed utility functions. As will be discussed in chapter 5, the absence of empirical justification for hyperrationality raises significant epistemological problems in economic theory, especially as regards its relationship to rational decision theory.[16] But here my point is *ontological*: recognizing that utility should fold in *all* potential objects of preference ("maturity") does not entail the assumption that any real agents *are* hyperrational, so taking people as the models of economic agency in mature anthropocentrism need not assume that people are hyperrational. As Stein (1996) argues in

Table 4.1
Neoclassicism

	Jevons/Marshall	Robbins	Samuelson	Becker
Semi-Aristotelian ("immature")?	Yes	No	No	No
Anthropocentric?	Yes	Yes	No	Yes

detail, mature anthropocentric neoclassicism can help itself to the sort of competence–performance distinction made familiar by Chomsky in linguistics. That is, it can accommodate itself to some failures of maximization-within-budget-constraints by recognizing that all agents, including people if they are agents, are physical systems that cannot operate without friction and sensitivity to stochastic disruption. In any case, it must recognize, following Simon (1978 and elsewhere) that calculation itself has an opportunity cost in finite temporal and other resources, so maximizing but finite agents will ignore some in-principle available information, and some logical consequences of information they have processed. It has often been worried that, given RPT's behavioral foundations, the economist could never distinguish between (i) successful maximization given use of all available and relevant information, but of utility functions that incorporate concern for others, (ii) failures of maximization due to performance errors, and (iii) successful maximization in light of "bounded" rationality (i.e., information-gathering and processing costs). This epistemological problem may indeed be severe in many special applications, but it doesn't vitiate the ontology of mature neoclassicism unless it's insoluble *in principle*. It isn't. Those who press the worry as an in-principle roadblock to the application of mature neoclassicism forget that a robust utility function should be an interpretation of *lots* of behavioral evidence, and that the genuine (as opposed to purely formal) possibility of multiple utility-function interpretations of large data streams falls exponentially with the addition of data, as long as data are sampled widely from across densely and independently partitioned spaces. Quinean underdetermination of theory by evidence is not a special problem for the mature neoclassicist unless it is a special problem for all behaviorists. I will consider that question in chapter 8.

The deeper pressure I mean to apply against mature anthropocentric neoclassicism is based on its commitment to the idea that a given biological person must be a *single* agent across her whole temporal biography. Davis (2003) rightly emphasizes this as the central philosophical problem that arises in connection with Becker's approach. Davis argues that on any conception of economic agency, there must be some principled grounds for individuating agents and for reidentifying individuals as the *same* individuals through processes of change. Note that this requirement need not build in an assumption that the individuation criteria in question must be biological, that is, that the individuals in question must be whole biological people. Indeed, Davis points out, dropping the anthropocentric assumption should be a natural move for neoclassicism once utility is depsychologized. There are some phenomena—notably, addiction, and rising appreciation of music and other art over time, in apparent violation of diminishing marginal substitution—that seem to make it simply obvious that people's preferences can change. In that case, if agents are identified with utility functions, then the biography of a typical person can't be the biography of a single (diachronic) economic agent. Unlike me, Davis finds this conclusion unacceptable. I will come back to this (fundamental) disagreement later. For now, I want to keep the focus on the issue as it applies to Becker.

Becker has made heroic efforts to model processes that naturally seem to involve preference revision as, instead, responses to changes in prices and information against backgrounds of stable preferences. (See Stigler and Becker 1977; and, for a concise critical response, Goodin 1990.) This is, indeed, the essence of his approach, which is to model *all* intentional human behavior in terms of maximization by people of their own human capital. The fundamental problem they each face is to allocate their resources—especially their time—so as to realize later investment potentials from earlier allocations. Thus, in one of the classic applications, a typical person's consumption of music increases as they become more knowledgeable about it—in prima facie violation of psychological concavity—because increasing proportions of their later consumption amount to returns on the investment constituted by their earlier consumption. Becker's accounts are of course formally valid—blocking vulnerability to logical error is, after all, the point of being rigorously mathematical—and the fact that they do not capture the *phenomenology* of addiction or musical enjoyment would only constitute a serious objection given introspectionist assumptions. The question of whether they actually do justice to the empirical behavioral facts is much more complicated (see Skog 1999), but fortunately can be bypassed here. The reason the question can be bypassed, I will maintain, is that the enterprise is inadequately motivated to begin with. Understanding why this is so touches directly on the core logic of my whole strategy in this book, so here is a good moment at which to slow down and consolidate.

At the end of the previous chapter I agreed, in effect, to take Samuelson's generic late-positivist philosophy more literally than he did. That is, I have treated RPT just as a set of axioms, leaving completely open the question of which phenomena, if any, the axioms describe. Simultaneously, I am following Robbins in taking economics to be about relationships between given ends, means, and opportunity costs (scarcity). There are "economic agents," in the technical sense relevant to neoclassicism, just in case there *is* a class of entities that "really" have ends and "really" face opportunity costs. Mature neoclassicism provides the right problem-solving strategy for understanding the behavior of such possible entities if and only if RPT adequately organizes the concepts in terms of which we measure their dynamics and responses. At this point, the question of whether there are any such entities remains entirely unsettled. I have emphasized at numerous junctures that this attitude is the opposite of the founding Aristotelian assumption, which is that economics must be about the acquisitive behavior distinctive to individual *people*. Now, in this dialectical context, to the extent that we find a particular hypothesis depending on the Aristotelian assumption—and nothing else—we must treat it as unmotivated. This does not, of course, mean that the hypothesis in question could not come to *be* motivated from inside the path of investigation taken here. This is indeed a key kind of question throughout, since the issue of how much of folk economics will be recovered by a scientific economics (if there is one) was the first one broached at the beginning of the book.

Davis takes the anthropocentric principle for granted. That is, he thinks that neoclassicism is automatically shown to be in trouble by the fact that its development through Samuelson leads in the direction of severing the analytical relationship between people and utility functions. In this context, Becker's enterprise constitutes for Davis a sound recommitment to anthropocentrism. Unfortunately, Davis argues, neoclassicism lacks the independent theory of agent individuation and reidentification that Becker's approach requires. Davis therefore goes off in pursuit of resources from outside economics to rescue the anthropocentric individual—and because, like Mirowski, he's sure that cognitive science threatens the self, that isn't the territory in which he hopes to find these resources.

As will be clear from the previous chapter, I agree with Davis that Becker's anthropocentrism is ad hoc in the wider context of neoclassicism. Indeed, I maintain, nothing motivates Becker's efforts to model *biological people* as having unchanging preferences except the Aristotelian assumption that whole people are the prototypical instances of agency. Unlike Davis, I have no inclination to rescue this assumption. Of course, as a matter of logic, an *economic agent* must have stable preferences; otherwise RPT does not apply to it. But the question of whether biological people are economic agents has emerged as our central one for the moment. Various hypotheses about the nature of the conceptual relationship between people and agents make prima facie sense. Perhaps whole people approximate economic agency when they go shopping with money, but not in general. Perhaps, for any given short run of time—the span in which her preferences *do* remain stable—a nonschizophrenic person approximates or realizes an economic agent. Perhaps—a thesis that has attracted many writers—nobody approximates an economic agent *by themselves,* but *ensembles* of people in interaction with one another approximate *ensembles* of interacting agents. These are among the principal hypotheses we will consider in later chapters. But there is one hypothesis that seems to have nothing going for it *besides* the raw Aristotelian assumption plus Becker's demonstrated virtuosity in consistently mathematically extending it: a (normal, nonschizophrenic) biological person's natural biography maps one-to-one onto the trajectory of a single economic agent.

When I was ten years old I spent countless hours designing historically meticulous board game simulations of battles and whole wars.[17] By the time I was sixteen, the idea of any more such time investment was out of the question. Now, a follower of Becker could try to rationalize this by finding some master outcome I was trying to maximize all along, and which, between ten and sixteen, I learned was poorly served by war game design. If we choose to call this hypothetical master goal "happiness," then it is (by previous argument) just another name for "utility." Very well; tautology worries, as we have seen, don't defeat this move by themselves, if the resort to the master goal better explains and predicts my behavior than the alternative hypothesis that I wasn't the same economic agent at sixteen as I was at ten. This last sentence is not intended as a rhetorical intuition pump: it raises a perfectly serious empirical question, which can't be answered without trying both approaches and comparing in detail the informational consequences. (Again, with stress: it begs all the questions here to try to decide which approach makes sense by starting from some intuition about what it's like to be a person.) The deeper question I am trying to get at here is the following. Given how different, in general, my behavioral patterns at sixteen were from what they were at ten, what other than the Aristotelian assumption could inspire anyone to attempt the very hard work of shoehorning both sets of behavior into the scope of one utility function? (Of course, this hard work would be a cinch compared with the further work to which one would then be committed, namely, also getting my behavioral patterns at twenty-five, and forty, and—I hope—seventy gathered in too.)

Such a large critical literature on time consistency has accumulated, all taking the Aristotelian assumption for granted, that it is hard to pose the last question and have it taken with the full philosophical innocence I am asking for. Here is the reason for this. Inquiring into the grounds of the Aristotelian assumption involves nothing less than asking why we seek to model natural human lives as single projects aimed at achieving (some) consistent goals. That this comes naturally to (at least) western people is among our deepest cultural heritages; perhaps it is even a universal, biological, human heritage, at least in part. I will come back to these possibilities in chapter 7. However, it certainly does not follow from anything in the logical or conceptual foundations of neoclassical economics (just as Davis recognizes and emphasizes).

Becker would maintain that when I currently consume more of the difficult late music of John Coltrane than I did ten years ago, I am still expressing a preference I had then. I am now reaping the fruits of an investment I made earlier when I listened to less Coltrane and more hard bop. I am not, at this point, claiming that this hypothesis is false or silly or explanatorily useless (as, for example, Dupré does). I am merely claiming that the motivation for it rests on a truism of folk psychology, according to which a typical person's natural biography is the unfolding of a single, coherent teleology. But the task of the current project is to interrogate the foundations of economics from the perspective of cognitive science, not folk psychology. In this context, although we must regard neoclassicism as committed to the idea that some phenomena or other are explained by use of a framework that requires stable and consistent preferences *somewhere*, we cannot allow the enterprise to precommit to the idea that the phenomena in question are natural human biographies.

I will mount a direct argument from cognitive science against the assumption that whole people should be taken as prototypical agents, in general, in chapter 6. For now, my aim is just to locate the role and basis of the assumption in recent economics. In the next chapter, we examine empirical evidence suggesting that whole people can't be modeled as neoclassical economic agents. It will follow from this that if whole people are prototypical agents, then neoclassical economic agents aren't prototypical agents. In that case, the neoclassical theory of the agent couldn't be a successful *analysis* of agency. And since, as

I've argued, the neoclassical theory of the agent isn't motivated as an *empirical* theory of anything, there would then be nothing useful left for the neoclassical theory of agency to be about. This is why the question of what sort of agent is constituted by a whole person—as a biological, social, and psychological entity—is central to the ontology of economics. But this (empirical) question isn't a question for economists; it's a question for cognitive scientists.

Or so I contend. Davis, like Dupré and (implicitly) Mirowski, thinks otherwise. My campaign against their view won't be finished until the end of the book. But there is a point to be made against it from within the domain of the current discussion, that is, from within the philosophy of economic methodology. Davis (2003, p. 76) identifies Dennett's supposed instrumentalism with Milton Friedman's advocacy of the idea that, in economic modeling, the truth of assumptions doesn't matter. This, I'll explain, is an error. Furthermore, it's a revealing one, because its basis is closely related to the attitude that leads Davis, and my two foils, to privilege the anthropocentric assumption.

The single most influential contribution (in terms of its actual influence on economists) in the history of economic methodology is Milton Friedman's "Methodology of Positive Economics" (1953). According to the standard interpretation of Friedman's essay, it advocates a philosophy of instrumentalism, that is, an epistemology according to which all that matters in the evaluation of an economic (or other scientific) theory is its usefulness as an instrument of prediction; the question of its descriptive truth or falsity is irrelevant. Many economists find this view congenial to mature anthropocentric neoclassicism because it allows them to treat the thesis that people's preferences don't change as nonempirical; it's simply a measurement convention, a false but useful assumption, as Friedman himself would put it.

Recall from chapter 2 that Dennett has often been taken to be an instrumentalist about propositional-attitude states because, according to his intentional-stance functionalism, they are "merely" ascribed to agents by interpreters. As I pointed out there, this "merely" has no force in the context of Dennett's wider philosophy. As will be described in detail in chapter 7, according to Dennett human selves create themselves by taking the intentional stance; and selves are, for Dennett, fully real empirical phenomena. Furthermore, human organisms are biologically and culturally programmed to take the intentional stance, and the developmental processes executed according to this programming are also fully real empirical phenomena. The whole point of Dennett's metaphysic of patterns, and of its extension into the information-theoretic account of existence sketched in chapter 2, is to deny mereology without denying the primacy of physics, and to thereby explain how "virtual" entities like selves can be real in a physical world—that is, can be something other than either epiphenomena subject to being reduced away[18] or instrumentalistic useful fictions. Dennett is simply not an instrumentalist about minds or agents; he is a realist about them.

Friedman's philosophical assumptions are, as we will see in a moment, very different from Dennett's. However, as Mäki (1986, 1992) shows, Friedman's own text and argument are not consistent with the standard reading of *him* as an instrumentalist either.[19] Friedman in fact argues that the aim of a good economic theory is to capture the essential structure of the empirical relations it describes, which it does by isolating *fundamental* causal vectors through pretenses to the effect that no other forces or relations operate. These pretenses are Friedman's "false assumptions." Now, as Mäki points out, this is the opposite of instrumentalism: it's a quite strong *realism*, taking for granted that there are fundamental, relatively invariant causal patterns out there for us to try to isolate by removing noise. Friedman is not an instrumentalist in the philosopher's sense, that is, in doubting that it is possible for scientific theories to *be* true. Nor is he an instrumentalist in yet another sense, the sense in which Dennett is sometimes wrongly thought to be an instrumentalist: he does not maintain that a theory can be adequate ("useful") even if its primary objects are fictitious entities. He is instead an instrumentalist in a purely methodological sense: he doesn't think that practicing economists should worry directly about the correspondence of their models to reality as they go about their daily business of constructing them. (This surely explains the popularity of the essay among economists. Friedman's view doesn't actually require them to believe any wild metaphysical theses, but allows them to freely decide how much empirical detail their models are responsible for capturing. It's a methodological blank check. We should all like to get some of those.)

This combination of ontological realism and methodological instrumentalism, which Mäki calls "the Friedmanian mixture," will strike most philosophers of science as profoundly strange. (It isn't often that *philosophers* are boggled at epistemological possibilities exemplified by outsiders.) Mäki therefore owes Friedman a charitable diagnosis of the eccentricity, and he finds it by putting his finger on a fundamental point that divides Davis and myself in our responses to Becker, and that separates me from my two foils. Friedman defends his methodological instrumentalism largely by means of examples from classical physics, where isolating idealizations like Galileo's frictionless planes are standard fare. What's good enough for physicists is, of course, supposed to be surely good enough for economists too. But then here is the problem. Friedman has no consistent view about the philosophy *of physics*. He vacillates between realism and genuine, philosophical, instrumentalism about the unobservable objects of physical theory. That is, at various points in his essay he suggests that perhaps these objects are the real, essential furniture of the physical world, and at other points that perhaps, as the philosophical instrumentalist believes, they're just fictions that facilitate prediction. However, Friedman presupposes *realism* about the *commonsense* objects of economics (consumers and firms and so on). Thus when an economist assumes, for example, that a firm is a profit maximizer, she is not imagined to be taking an instrumentalist attitude to the question of whether there *are* firms, in the way that the physicist might (conceivably) take an instrumentalist attitude to whether there are gluons (or in the way that Dennett is wrongly thought to take an instrumentalist attitude to whether there are beliefs). She simply grants that firms don't *literally* maximize profits, and this is the sense in which she is supposed to admit that her assumption is "false." This is not philosophical instrumentalism; it is analogous to the physicist who is a *realist* about gluons modeling them sometimes as particles and sometimes as waves, when they are in fact neither (and the physicist knows it).

This interpretation of Friedman is charitable to him because it demands only the recognition that he is not doing metaphysics; if he's just doing a very practical sort of economic methodology he need not go all the way back to base camp and invent a whole philosophy of science for the purpose. Mäki has effectively explained why philosophers and economists consistently talk past each other when they discuss Friedman; philosophers imagine that economists are trying to endorse philosophical instrumentalism when they aren't, and economists imagine that philosophers, in rejecting Friedman's view, are trying to make each economic hypothesis responsible for telling *the whole truth* about phenomena under investigation, which is of course a crazy objective. However, the interest of Mäki's argument in the present context lies in the attention it draws to the distinction between scientific and commonsense realism. Friedman and his audience of economists are seduced by his analogies from physics *because they take the Aristotelian assumption for granted*. People are commonsense objects. Their consumption behavior is a commonsense object. Their aggregation into firms produces a commonsense object. And these commonsense objects are the objects of economics. Friedman and other anthropocentric neoclassical theorists are not trying to promote philosophical instrumentalism about *those*.

Still following Mäki, let us distinguish among four attitudes toward the constitution of reality:

(i) *Minimal commonsense realism* takes the existence of commonsense, observable types of things (objects and events) as given, and is agnostic about the reality of objects (events and/or structures) posited by scientific theories for purposes of prediction and/or explanation.

(ii) *Radical commonsense realism* affirms the existence of commonsense, observable types of things, and *denies* the possibility of having good grounds for believing in the existence of objects just because they're posited by scientific theories for purposes of prediction and/or explanation.

(iii) *Minimal scientific realism* takes the existence of well-justified (significant for purposes of explanation) theoretical posits for granted, and is agnostic about the reality of commonsense, observable types of things.

(iv) *Radical scientific realism* affirms the existence of well-justified theoretical posits and *denies* that "observability to common sense" is a sound basis for belief in a type of thing.

Instrumentalism in the philosophy of science is compatible with positions (i) and (ii) above, but is also compatible with general irrealism or idealism—and with positivism. Friedman *denies* general irrealism; but this is a position that many critics conflate with philosophical instrumentalism, thus rendering a Friedman who directly contradicts himself. Particular, object-by-object, mixes of positions (i) and (iii) are compatible with one another. Friedman, not doing metaphysics at all, sometimes seems comfortable with such mixes, but, implicitly affirming the Aristotelian assumption, insists that economists, qua economists, should act as though they endorse (ii). Generic late positivists of the Samuelson variety *really* endorse (ii), as a philosophical thesis, *and this is why Friedman's account superficially fits nicely with mature anthropocentric neoclassicism* (Becker). Dupré's attack on neoclassicism as linked to evolutionary psychology discussed in chapter 1, also depends on position (ii).

We have now arrived at the answer to our question, posed at the beginning of this chapter, about how Samuelson's position can have come to seem crazy to thoughtful contemporary theorists. Samuelson, as we have seen, was a positivist; but not a very self-conscious one. One of the aspects of positivism I—and Dennett—reject is its commitment to a commonsense ontology. The general basis for my scientific realism was described in chapter 2. (The position I favor is [iv] above, though for my arguments in this book, position [iii] is strong enough. A reader wondering why I go all the way out to [iv] should consult Ross et al. forthcoming.) This is that the human commonsense ontology is a nonsystematic set of evolved responses to pressures on our specific biological and cultural needs and purposes. Most of the truths about the universe are irrelevant to these needs and purposes, so it would be mysterious—a fact deeply in need of explanation—if our parochial schemes for carving up reality made a close match with ontological principles intended to be objective. Now, positivists weren't commonsense *realists*. Because they regarded an internal sensory manifold as the only possible general object of objective study, and particular "sense data" as the only ultimately reliable sources of evidence, they were agnostic about the reality of the external world, on either a commonsense or a scientific interpretation (Schlick 1933/1979). This was precisely the Kantian aspect in early positivism, still very much present, as we saw, in Robbins's methodological work. As mentioned previously, it gradually withered inside the larger positivist view. When it died, its corpse contaminated the whole position, because without incorrigible sense data none of strict verificationism, subjectivism about meaning, or the rigid analytic–synthetic distinction could be made to work. Carnap himself, seeing this, provided the essential arguments against positivism that were later made famous by Quine. Samuelson was still a positivist just when, behind his back as it were, the structure was falling apart. Having no basis for any ontological opinions at all, he is left with no possible justification for his formalism except that it enables him to produce some existence proofs (which is a form of justification of no possible ontological significance, as Mirowski rightly objects). As I argued, a more philosophically self-conscious Samuelson could have followed Quine into eliminativism; but in 1948, even Quine hadn't gone there yet.

These days, nobody is a positivist and almost everybody is a realist of one sort or the other.[20] The commonsense realist will interpret Samuelson as trying to talk about commonsense people and firms but wholly failing to say anything plausible about them. For the reasons just explained, this interpretation does not do any serious violence to Samuelson's texts. Indeed, historically speaking, it's correct. But I come to rationally reconstruct Samuelson, not to join in burying him. As a scientific realist I need not presume that the objects of basic reference in economic theory are commonsense people or firms—though I will be obligated to say something about how to reinterpret these concepts in light of the story I do ultimately tell about the objects of economics.

Among authors whose arguments have featured in this chapter, Dupré, Davis, Friedman, Becker, and Sen are all commonsense realists. (Mirowski keeps his ontological inclinations hidden. Dennett, despite the way in which intentional-stance functionalism rescues propositional attitudes from eliminativists, is not a commonsense realist—or, at least, must not be if intentional-stance functionalism isn't to collapse into instrumentalism after all, as Dennett agrees it should not (Ross 2000; Dennett 2000). This is why his work can be the basis for an attempted rescue of Samuelson's version of neoclassical economics from *both* humanists and eliminativists.

It should now be clear why I will not align myself with the (mature) anthropocentric version of neoclassicism as a way of defending the scientific relevance of RPT. It relies on the Aristotelian assumption, which is precisely what I don't want to do. Instead, I want to take one aspect of Samuelson's positivism, his devotion to the unification of theory and structure through axiomatization, seriously, while dropping another positivist dogma, namely, the epistemological privileging of commonsense entities over scientific ones. (Note that my truest foil, Dupré, does exactly the opposite—how like a foil!)

We have been working for awhile now in highly abstract philosophical territory, where the air is very thin. Economists and other behavioral scientists are likely to be impatient for a lungful of oxygen. As I have acknowledged at several points, they are justified in this impatience. If the only basis for skepticism about Becker's approach to the defense of neoclassicism were a metaphysical attitude, then a working scientist would be ill advised to pay much attention to it. The point of a metaphysical attitude, as I said earlier, is to provide a standpoint for diagnosis and conceptual domestication of data that cause discomfort given *other* metaphysical attitudes. In the next chapter, we thus turn to the accumulating pile of empirical data that puts great pressure indeed on the Aristotelian assumption that people are economic agents.

Experimental Economics, Evolutionary Game Theory, and the Eliminativist Option

People in Economic Laboratories

The grave of poor old Robbins can't be a still place these days. His philosophy of economics, as we saw, rests on the idea that people's status as economic agents is justified not by empirical observations of their behavior, but by introspection. If this were right, then, full of confidence in the epistemic warrant it would furnish, we could wheel out our best axiomatization of utility maximization and build economic theory from our armchairs. Of course, to make empirical predictions on the basis of this work we'd need some data about production possibilities and the scarcity of resources. But this is economic data in the conventional sense. What we don't need to do, according to Robbins, is investigate human behavior. Thus the strongest possible separateness thesis with respect to economics' relationship to psychology (and to sociology) is supposedly justified by Robbins's philosophy.

To the majority of economic theorists (as opposed to consulting practitioners) these days, Robbins's picture is saturated in sepia. As early as the 1930s, economists began to take seriously Samuelson's claim to have produced a testable apparatus for determining utility functions by going into labs with live test subjects and measuring them. In chapter 3, I mentioned Wallis and Friedman's (1942) early pessimism about the possibility of using RPT to measure actual utility functions, because too few variables could be held constant or otherwise controlled for long enough to get significant data sets. What I did not then mention was that this skepticism was not aimed directly at Samuelson's work, but at an attempt by Thurstone (1931) to infer utility functions from subjects' behavior in a laboratory.[1] Thurstone had been optimistic about the prospects for operationalizing RPT in experimental conditions. Wallis and Friedman questioned this optimism, but not

RPT itself. In striking this attitude they undermined the crude verifi-cationist motivations for RPT periodically floated by Samuelson and others, and so saw themselves as needing some other kind of philosophical justification for it. Friedman's idiosyncratic version of "instrumentalism," discussed in the previous chapter, is perhaps best understood as an attempt to plug this perceived gap opened by his own earlier coauthored critique.

Broadly speaking, economists over the subsequent years divided into two camps in their response to Wallis and Friedman's skepticism about experimental testing of economic theory. Some, certainly, em-braced it as justifying the conclusion implicitly urged by Robbins, namely, that the axioms of economics derive their authority from arm-chair common sense, and that purely mathematical work to extend them fully inherits this authority as long as the math is sound. The economist who invokes this attitude in defense of pure feats of math-ematical analysis, sternly uninterested in the confusing flux of behav-ioral data, has of course become a stereotype, gently satirized in jokes[2] and excoriated by "practical" critics such as Paul Ormerod (1994). Rosenberg's (1992) backhanded defense of economics as a branch of mathematics, discussed earlier, seeks to promote the stereotypical atti-tude into a full-blown epistemology. However, all of this noise should not lead us to conclude that the stereotype is entirely justified, for the simple reason that the level of actual work in experimental behavioral economics has multiplied exponentially with every passing decade since the 1940s, and its literature is now gigantic. Economists have come to take it increasingly seriously, the best possible evidence for this being the award of the 2002 Nobel Prize to two pioneers of the enter-prise, Daniel Kahneman and Vernon Smith. It is especially noteworthy, in light of the present approach to this issue by way of reference to the separateness thesis, that Kahneman is officially a psychologist and Smith an economist.

The reflections on the three senses of "theory" in chapter 4 can help us in diagnosing why the attitude supposedly encouraged by Wallis and Friedman has not been revealed to be the true preference of the discipline, despite the absence of very much felt need to specifically answer their critique. RPT, the subject of their discussion, is, as we have seen, all by itself and prior to its application an utterly abstract and general (sense-2) theory. Sense-2 theories can indeed not be made subject to empirical test. They can become involved in experimentation only through incorporation into sense-3 theories. This, as Roth (1995, pp. 6–7) notes, is exactly what happened with RPT following its enrichment by von Neumann–Morgenstern (VNM) utility theory and subjective probability theory after the 1940s, as discussed in chapter 3. That theory, the union of three pieces of foundational apparatus, is explicitly offered as an account of actual human decision-making functions. Thus it obviously violates the separateness thesis, is obviously not a pure sense-2 theory, and is equally obviously subject to empirical application and testing with groups of human subjects. Equally obviously, however, such application does not test RPT by itself—or, as a philosopher of science would say, "directly" test it, as opposed to testing the union of it and some auxiliary hypotheses.

Since RPT's truth as a theory of mathematics is not in dispute, all that is at stake for it in experimental work is the question of its usefulness in contributing to sense-3 theories of economics. In examining how well it has fared against this question, I thus need to review the experimental literature in a way that distinguishes that part of it that mainly puts pressure on the auxiliary assumptions—especially expected utility theory (EUT) as an account of human decision making—from that which more directly undermines the idea that economic behavior is based on stable and well-ordered preferences, since that is all RPT itself requires to be potentially useful with some set or other of auxiliary hypotheses. Since I will endorse the emerging consensus that EUT as a theory of decision fails to *generally* describe human behavior, my review can follow the standard accounts and need initially support no original claims. What will be most important for later purposes will be my separation of EUT from the *foundations* of economic theory— alluding to roughly the positivist's sense of "foundations"—in RPT and the representation of scarcity.

Since the literature from psychology and experimental economics that has been jointly recognized in Kahneman's and Smith's Nobel Prize is now huge, my review of it must be brusque in the extreme. My main task is less to describe its results per se than to organize it into piles useful for the discussion to follow. Readers interested in the many fascinating details past which I must rudely stomp are referred to Thaler (1992), Kagel and Roth (1995), Rabin (1998), and Camerer (2003b). Noneconomists may occasionally get lost in the quick detailed inferences I'll make as I go, but should plough on regardless, because all relevant philosophical morals will be consolidated explicitly. The point of the section, again, is just to build a filing system, to logically isolate from one another the different general ways in which cognitive science can tell us positive things about what economics should consistently be about. Thus I'll repeatedly be signposting empirical issues for later attention when we've brought some cognitive science on board. The details on the road map are less important, for now, than gathering a sense of the map's general topology—a sense of what, most generally, is at stake over and above the many fine points.

I'll file the accumulated work in experimental economics into three sets. To help keep the books straight, a signpost system will be provided in headings as we go. "Work sets" refer to cumulative sequences of experimental investigations. "Issue sets" refer to the files into which I am sorting the open empirical questions.

Judgment Heuristics (Work Set 1; Issue Set 1)

The first work set, contributed mainly by psychologists, tests the hypothesis that individual people use information to make judgments about likelihood and probability that accord with the norms of sound inductive and statistical reasoning. This hypothesis can in turn be broken into two issue sets, both of which have been experimentally investigated.

First, economic models have often assumed that agents gather all information they physically (or even logically) could, and draw all logically valid inferences from it. As Herbert Simon pointed out as early as 1947, it is seldom rational for a real agent to do this, since gathering information and computing inferences use scarce resources, so these activities should be confined within bounds determined by points in decision problems at which further investments in them yield diminishing marginal returns in whatever (say, expected utility) is being maximized. These boundary points will vary from problem to problem. Determining where they are, problem by problem, is itself a search problem; so an optimally designed but finite agent in a nonstationary world will use heuristics, general rules of thumb for information gathering, retrieval, and processing, that will cause her to get some decisions wrong, but will maximize her expected success rate across her set of expected environments. (For example: when choosing an agent to perform a contract, one might follow a policy of always getting three estimates, regardless of how many potential contractors are out there for any given job. This would not be an ideal procedure if the importance of optimizing the cost-benefit trade-off on a particular job were overwhelming as against all other projects taken together; but this condition is seldom, if ever, actually satisfied. It's thus efficient to just apply the simple, general rule.)

One can ask three related questions about heuristics: (i) what are the ideal heuristics for any rational agent, given facts about computability, a utility function for the agent, and a specification of a set of environments? (ii) what are the ideal heuristics for people, given their actual computational capacities, utility functions, and environments? and (iii) which heuristics, in general, have actually been produced in people by processes of biological and cultural evolution?

Question (i) is itself ambiguous. If it seeks a single bundle of master heuristics whose use would solve all optimization problems that might ever come along, then it's a question that only a philosopher would pose, in the purest of metaphysical moods. As a problem intended to be relevant to implementation, it is, as Mirowski emphasizes, quixotic. Alternatively, question (i) may be taken as indicating an unreachable limit that an implementation program might seek to asymptotically approach. The research program in economics that Mirowski labels "Judd's revenge," as briefly described in chapter 1, is best thought of this way. On this program, one essentially keeps endowing agents with more and more information and computational speed, as new econometric techniques offer new ideas as to what "more information" might specifically consist in. Though Gödel tells us that such agents—and their analysts—can never reach a point where they know they've achieved an ultimate set of guaranteed maximizing principles, perhaps they'd at least be able to suppose they were on a methodological road to getting better and better forever. Mirowski is also right in saying that much work in cognitive science and artificial intelligence has been aimed at question (i) in the nonquixotic sense. Furthermore, before the late 1970s a good deal of this muddled it with questions (ii) and (iii) because of overconfidence in the cross-environmental power of simple algorithms, and/or underestimation of the complexity of interacting decision problems.[3] In those economic applications where this is recognized and attention is therefore directed to computational issues instead of just to econometric ones, one gets the basis for Mirowski's second program, "Lewis redux." Neither of these programs will lay emphasis on experimental work. Though they might perform road tests of the technologies they recommend, both are essentially engineering rather than behavioral approaches.

Lately, however, some researchers on the borderlands between economics and psychology have self-consciously intended the more modest question (iii). (See, for a leading sample, Gigerenzer, Todd, and the ABC Research Group 1999.) Much of this work has been relatively optimistic about the extent to which general, evolved human heuristics are good approximations to optimality given people's actual information-processing abilities, their evolutionary history, the generic utility functions built into them by natural selection, and the costs of various sorts of information as stored in the natural environment. This opens interesting research questions about the normative evaluation of our heuristics in constructed environments—if they evolved for use in "found" ones—and about the extent to which economic models continue to be consistent and empirically useful once they incorporate these real heuristics in place of omniscience assumptions or ideal-person heuristics.

Natural Statistical Competence (Work Set 1; Issue Set 2)

Mention of the new work on behavioral heuristics brings us to the second issue concerning the empirical rationality of judgments. Notice that, because of their multidimensional relativity (i.e., to computational capacities, utility functions, and environments), good heuristics need not necessarily mimic sound principles for statistical inference. And, indeed, the experimental evidence suggests overwhelmingly that normal human judgment deviates from these principles in a number of systematic ways. People tend to apply domain-specific heuristics in novel domains where they apply poorly and lead to errors; over-estimate low-frequency events and underestimate high-frequency ones; ignore base rates in probability estimations even where coming to know these involves no additional search costs; overweight new evidence that confirms existing beliefs, especially beliefs they like; and, heroically ignore consequences of Bayes's rule, which they have trouble applying even when they've explicitly learned it. (See the main sources cited above, and the paper trails following from them; and see Stein 1996 for a careful philosophical analysis of the implications of these data.) In summary, experimental work on individual judgment has shown that folk statistical induction and scientific statistical induction come significantly apart. As Mirowski might put it, people aren't natural econometricians. Experimental work can show in precisely which ways and extents people and econometricians differ.

In principle, this fact need not threaten the empirical adequacy of RPT, conjoined with EUT, as an account of human economic behavior.

If we knew which heuristics people actually use in decision problems, we could plug these into our theory in place of the standard normative account of statistical inference that identifies accuracy-maximizing procedures. Two problems arise for this idea, one technical and one more radical. The technical problem is that judgment and choice interact dynamically through updating of risk estimates as behavior proceeds. As a result, when people fail to behave in accordance with optimal statistical rationality, or optimal statistical rationality relativized to human information-processing capacities, evidence will often fail to disambiguate between departures from sound judgment and failure to optimize *given* sound judgment. I call this problem "technical" for two reasons. First, the literature is full of ingenious experimental designs that isolate judgment errors from violations of parametric or strategic optimization; what is often epistemologically impossible in the field can be achieved in the lab if one is clever enough. This is the very point of experimentation. Theorists, especially philosophers, should be wary of announcing indeterminacies just because they can't imagine a procedure for sorting them out. Second, if we really did have a full theory of human heuristics, this would hopefully include a quantitative model of the tendency for these heuristics to be ignored or misapplied; and then, given enough data points on human behavior in a problem case, statistical regressions could be used to find residuals identifying optimization failures.

However, this leads us up to the "radical" problem about which I will have much more to say later. To introduce it now: the task of developing a full theory of human heuristics is one for cognitive science, not economics. To correctly identify a heuristic, asking people what they think they're doing and why is an inherently unreliable method. One needs to know, instead, what actual objective function governs people's behavior as a result of their natural and causal histories. I say objective function rather than functions because behaviors, in complex systems like people, are not modularized with respect to ontologies of tasks. That is, a given bit of human behavior is often to be explained by a reference to several birds it kills with one stone. Perhaps I puff on a cigar because it delivers some desired nicotine, and makes pausing to think cause less anxiety through interruption of activity levels, and tastes nice, and pleasantly reminds me of my hero, Churchill, and so on. Which problem am I solving by puffing? It looks dangerously like the behavior contributes to solving a general problem of living.

What is worrying me here is not holism per se. It should be possible to run experiments in which, sometimes, the cigar is made to taste worse and at other times Churchill associations are suppressed by neuroelectrical intervention, and so forth, to isolate the respective influences of contributing motivations. Rather, the problem—or so I will arguing over the chapters to come—is that the very project of identifying whole human behaviors as expressions of heuristics presupposes that whole humans manifest enough unity of control to think that inferring backwards from their problems to characteristics of their behaviors-as-solutions will capture the relevant explanatory variables. We have encountered this assumption before: it is the idea that human lives have stable teleologies, the motivation for Becker's mature anthropocentric neoclassicism. I will argue that sometimes whole people are appropriate units of teleological analysis, but that they generally are not; and we won't be able to justify any general theory of human heuristics if we have no principled way of decomposing motivation below the whole-person level. We will need the right sorts of models from cognitive science to do this. But the mere fact that it has to be done suggests that we will not be able to disambiguate empirical characteristics of judgment from characteristics of optimizing strategy just by performing experiments on behaviors of subjects in labs.

This problem duly noted for later reference, let us resume our sorting of the literature.

Testing EUT against Rivals (Work Set 2; Issue Set 1)

In the second file we can put studies that seek to compare actual human decision making with idealized models of agent deliberation (whether or not they succeed in isolating this from use of judgment heuristics). Here is the arena of empirical study that has usually been taken to cast the most direct doubt on the identification of people with classical and neoclassical economic agents. It is robustly demonstrable that people "overcontribute" to public goods, relative to an assumption that all they "should" care about are their own personal returns from provision; that their choices are made relative to reference points that favor status quo endowment distributions over identical, but hypothetical, distributions; that they are strongly averse to choices requiring resolution of ambiguity, and will flee from them to nonambiguous problems even when expected returns from the latter are lower; that their decisions are heavily influenced by "moods";[4] and, most famously, that they will pay significant costs to both respect and enforce prevailing social norms.

The findings listed above can be interpreted by reference to a large battery of direct evidence that EUT does not accurately characterize human decision making in general (Camerer 1995, pp. 619–657). In his 1995 survey, Camerer therefore sorts various sequences of experiments on expected-utility anomalies into accumulating comparative tests among proposed alternatives to EUT, especially Kahneman and Tversky's (1979) prospect theory. According to this theory, people "edit" decision problems, to introduce reference points and psychological decision weights on outcomes measured against a riskless value function over gains and losses, before solving them. EUT, prospect theory, and various other models that borrow, delete, or merge different formal aspects of them, are all models of maximization, and can all be made compatible with RPT through suitable additional restrictions on the construction of utility functions from behavioral patterns. Insofar as Camerer comes to any general conclusion from his review, it can be summarized thus: none of the fully specified models of empirical human decision making provides an unequivocally best account of a plurality of current data, so no one can be said to win the competition in general, across all types of circumstance; and this most certainly includes the initial incumbent and subsequent default model, EUT (Camerer 1995, pp. 638–639).

This should not come as much surprise to philosophers of science. None of the leading alternatives or modifications to EUT-based decision theory were originally motivated by wider theoretical considerations independent of the data they sought to parsimoniously summarize. EUT itself might be thought to be the exception, because its conceptual origins lie not in studies of behavior but in ideal-agent theory. Trivially, however, this is not an independent motivation for EUT *as* a model of real human decision making, absent an implausible theory about what people are and how their behavioral dispositions historically arose and how they adapt under evolutionary pressure. It does not insult the project of formally modeling behavioral evidence on decision making to describe it as "Ptolemaic science." It is Ptolemaic in that it resembles what astronomers before Kepler mainly did, that is, elaborate an established model of planetary and stellar motions by adding, deleting, and combining hypothetical elements (e.g, epicycles and equants) necessary to simultaneously account for a continuously growing stack of observations. Calling some activity Ptolemaic appears insulting only because we know, inductively, that it must sooner or later reach a point of diminishing returns, where the effort required to further improve careful models can no longer be justified by gains in representational parsimony, and in the case of astronomy we know that by the time of Kepler that point had been passed. However, before we can have any serious hope of adequately theorizing an interesting set of phenomena we need some systematic way of summarizing our data, so Ptolemaic phases in the progress of research projects are unavoidable and, when done carefully, productive.[5] When we evaluate competing Ptolemaic models at a given time, however, we should remember that none are likely to be univocally best across all the data. Epistemological stakes rise only when some entrant in the competition looks outside the data being modeled for some principle that might unify it within our larger scientific picture and so produce a new kind of reason for preferring it. (This is a way of reaffirming the Kitcherian epistemological point from the previous chapter.) None of the models reviewed by Camerer is such an entrant *in general* (though, as we'll see in chapter 8, both EUT and the matching rule discussed below are pulling away from the Ptlolemaic pack across some principled classes of problems). Taken together, all the models, including EUT, help us to capture some interesting but still relatively isolated observations about behavioral tendencies. They are helpful folders for filing our data.

Since I have said that the empirical usefulness of RPT isn't directly tested in work set 1, does my last comment not amount just to saying that we should keep using it for practical purposes, along with the various combinations of auxiliary hypotheses represented by EUT, prospect theory, and so on, while we wait hopefully for a paradigm shift? That would be a very bland and disappointing thing to say. Happily, I need not say it, for two reasons. First, there *is* a promising source for independent motivation of auxiliary hypotheses, and that is cognitive science. (Isn't experimental behavioral economics and the associated work in psychology already part of cognitive science? Yes, sure; let me say, then, cognitive science that includes behavioral neuroscience and complex-system theory, i.e., cognitive science that goes beyond modeling of input-output functions.) That is what the rest of this book is about. Second, there are two phenomena revealed in the laboratory that do put pressure on RPT's fundamental commitment to *consistency* in behavior: preference reversals and apparent inconsistencies in intertemporal choice.

Preference Reversals and Time Inconsistencies (Work Set 2, Issue Set 2)

I will summarize the history of work on preference reversal following Thaler (1992), Camerer (1995), and a philosophical discussion by Guala (2000). First, classic experiments by Lichtenstein and Slovic (1971, 1973) and Grether and Plott (1979) showed that people systematically choose gambles involving high probabilities of winning relatively small cash rewards (H bets) over gambles involving lower probabilities of winning higher amounts (L bets) when the expected values are about the same, but that they then demand higher prices for selling the L ($L) bet to what they will accept for the H bet ($H). As long as we think we have reliable grounds for thinking we've constructed an environment in which cash rewards are sound proxies for utility—something for which standard control procedures in elicitation of bids have been devised (see below)—then this phenomenon looks like it indicates intransitivity of preference, since the data are summarized by $H ~ H > L ~ $L > $H. Various other studies described by Camerer (1995) and Rabin (1998) detect similar patterns in a range of choice problems, many of which are relatively resistant to learning.

A good deal of the experimental work that followed the original experiments in the 1970s was aimed at distinguishing between genuine preference reversal and violations of EUT. Two standard elicitation devices used in the early preference-reversal experiments were the Becker–DeGoot–Marshack (BDM) mechanism, for controlling for uncertainty effects associated with lotteries, and the random lottery selection (RLS) procedure, designed to control for effects of subjects' changes in initial endowments when experimental protocols require them to play sequences of lotteries (see Camerer 1995). The general adequacy of BDM and RLS to soundly isolate proxies for utility depends on the independence axiom of EUT, which says that if A > B, then A × probability (x) > B × probability (x). However, several "Ptolemaic" alternatives to standard EUT, such as Machina's (1982) "generalized expected utility analysis," Chew and MacRimmon's (1979) "alpha utility" theory, and Quiggin's (1982) and Yaari's (1987) "expected utility theory with rank-dependent probabilities" drop the independence axiom (Guala 2000). Thus Karni and Safra (1987) argued that the preference-reversal phenomena were artifacts of the assumption of EUT and the resulting reliance on the BDM and RLS procedures. However, work by Cox and Epstein (1988) and, especially, Tversky,

Slovic, and Kahneman (1990) effectively refuted this hypothesis by replicating the basic test conditions in circumstances where only ordinal, rather than VNM, rankings were relevant. As Camerer (1995) points out, Karni and Safra's hypothesis can be criticized as slightly baroque in the first place, since it requires that people violate the independence axiom while respecting the so-called reduction principle of EUT, according to which preferences should be consistent between multistage lotteries (lotteries over chances to play further lotteries) and straightforward (single-stage) lotteries with the same expected payoffs. This idea seems distinctly ad hoc. In any case, Starmer and Sugden (1991) provide direct evidence that people violate the reduction principle in the relevant sorts of circumstances.

Shifting the explanation of preference reversal away from failure of EUT does not force the conclusion that choices cycle. Of course, nothing could literally force this conclusion if we feel entirely free to construct exotic preference maps without limit. However, once we have fixed the identity of the agents to whom preferences are ascribed, then we are entitled to reject RPT as useless if application of it only describes observed cases (as it will trivially) and fails to support any counterfactuals. All parties to the literature under discussion assume that a useful theory of choice must allow identification of people, at least for as long as these (short) experiments last, with agents in the domain of the theory. But this still allows for another interpretation of the data, one explicitly promoted by, and consistent with, the experiments of Tversky, Slovic, and Kahneman (1990). Suppose that, instead of hypothesizing the intransitive preference pattern described earlier, we find that subjects confronted with pairwise choices between gambles and their selling prices prefer $L to L (overpricing L) and H to $H (underpricing H). This predicts the reversal data, and lends itself to a diagnosis in terms of representational heuristics. The specific heuristic promoted by Thaler (1992, pp. 84–89), derived from Slovic, Griffin, and Tversky (1990), is identified by the "compatibility" or "matching" hypothesis. According to this idea, people attach greater weight to aspects of choice-eliciting stimuli that match those picked out in the selected response modality, presumably because processing of matching cases involves less computational work than processing of nonmatching cases. This is supposed by Slovic et al. to be a general feature of human information processing (found also, for example, in sensory perception), and Thaler applies it to the case of preference reversal on lottery choice and pricing as follows:

Because the cash equivalence of a bet is expressed in dollars, compatibility implies that the payoffs, which are expressed in the same units, will be weighted more heavily in pricing bets than in choosing between bets. Furthermore, since the payoffs of L bets are much larger than the payoffs of H bets, the major consequence of a compatibility bias is the overpricing of the L bet. The compatibility hypothesis, therefore, explains the major source of preference reversal, namely the overpricing of the low-probability high-payoff bets. (1992, p. 87)

If matching is indeed a general propensity of human computation, then its application to preference reversals looks like a breakthrough beyond the Ptolemaic, since wider results from cognitive science are partly motivating it.

This might seem to be direct good news for the empirical usefulness of RPT in application to people, since it gives us a way out of concluding that people's "real" psychological preferences are acyclical: behavior just manifests cycles from time to time because of a particular way of implementing bounded rationality. However, there are reasons, both empirical and conceptual, for not settling into complacency on this basis. On the empirical front, Loomes, Starmer, and Sugden (1991) and Loomes and Taylor (1992) found that subjects displayed almost as much tendency to reversal when subjects were prevented from revealing earlier overpricing as when they weren't. These data are equivocal, and in tension with some other more recent experiments; but it cannot be said that Thaler's interpretation above is the end of the story (Camerer 1995, pp. 660–665). On the conceptual front, the motivation that makes attribution of preference reversals to matching behavior seem non-Ptolemaic to many interpretations in the literature rests on a particular computational model of mind. That is, we are invited to suppose by Slovic et al. that there are facts of the matter about whether and how data are matched, as a distinct processing step during computation, to motivate the idea that matching reduces processing effort. Though we will shortly encounter an alternative non-Ptolemaic basis for matching hypotheses, this basis will not rest on a classical computational model of the mind. Finally, a defense of the empirical relevance of RPT would be Pyrrhic if it consisted merely in showing that we can still construe *some* behavioral function in terms of maximization if we *insist* on doing so. To the extent that minimization of processing effort is doing most of the explanatory work in explaining the function in question, economic reasoning brings little to the table, by comparison with evolutionary psychology, in identifying

projectible patterns in behavior. That is, if people's preferences reverse
with respect to the objects with which they compete with other people,
and that's the end of the matter so far as the traditional domain of
economics is concerned, then the fact that this could be rationalized
by reference to energy savings from use of evolved heuristics would
provide no substantive comfort to a defender of a separate economic
science.

It is for this reason that the logic of money-pump arguments is
important to the justification of RPT. The classical money-pump argument works as follows. Suppose that an agent prefers (in the behavioral sense) bundle a to bundle b, b to c and c to a. Then another agent
with acyclical preferences could offer her a sequence of trades in which
she first surrenders her stock of c for some marginal gain in her stock
of b, then surrenders her stock of b for some marginal gain in her stock
of a, then finally surrenders her stock of a for some marginal gain in
her stock of c. If the agent is to be genuinely true to the revelation of
preferences $c > a > b > c$ then there must exist a quantity of c she could
be offered in the final trade such that the total utility of her final
endowment is smaller than the stock she started with. Thus by a series
of such sequences the agent could be drained of all but an infinitesi-
mal proportion of her initial asset stock. Therefore, it is supposed in the
typical application of this logic, if agents with acyclical (and otherwise
consistent) preferences can exist or evolve, market selection will favor
them over agents with cyclical preferences and the latter will go extinct.
This could mean either that they perish as entities, if they cannot adjust
their behavior, or that the underlying biological or psychological entities are induced to become different economic agents by changing their
preferences.

We must be very careful in saying just what this sort of argument
can and can't be used to justify. It has often been wheeled out as a normative argument for agent, or even human, consistency in choice. This
use is quite beyond its resources. Such a prescriptive-normative view
of the money pump requires an assumption that maximization of the
long-run stock of tradable assets must trump all other values as a
matter of rationality, a premise that is ludicrous. More subtly, money-
pump arguments have been used to justify descriptive claims that in
actual markets—perhaps including the grand market of the natural-
selection tournament—actual agents at equilibrium will behave in
ways that respect acyclicity because the cyclical entities will have been
driven out. This conclusion is also much too strong, since it requires

either perfect market stability or a level of foresight by the pump operators that is Platonic rather than Darwinian. Finally, and most respectably, money-pump arguments have been taken to show that acyclicity is a necessary condition if an agent is to choose and maintain a policy she can rationally expect to be conducive to survival.[6] This is often thought to justify using acyclicity as an axiom in deriving other conditions on rational consistency—so, for example, in selecting sets of auxiliary assumptions to go with RPT. However, Cubitt and Sugden (2001) rigorously show that invulnerability to money pumps in itself implies nothing of significance for stronger theories of rational maximization, and that what it must be conjoined with to do so—the presence of omnicapacities to detect and realize any and all possible gains from trade—is a property that selection processes in finite worlds cannot build.

Given, then, that money-pump arguments have proven inadequate for almost all their intended purposes, have they any hope of saving RPT's usefulness if the experimental evidence convinces us that people choose intransitively, and if, as behaviorists or intentional-stance functionalists, we are unprepared to try to save the day by putting "hidden" transitive structures into the recesses of their heads? The key point is, once again, to remember how little we are so far asking of RPT. We are hoping only that it will, as a sense-2 theory, have some role to play in application to something. For now, though, we are engrossed in explaining why empirical evidence suggests that it won't find its vindication by directly modeling the behavior of individual people. Later, we will discover some behaviorally relevant dynamics to which it applies, and I'll use a variation of the money-pump argument to support that application. However, standard money-pump arguments, even the subtle ones, cannot shield the claim that people are economic agents from the demonstrable fact that they reverse their preferences. Rescuing the former thesis would require a Robbinsian move to push economic agency, and possible knowledge of it, back into the inner reaches of a psyche that then systematically fumbles its behavioral expression. This is flatly inconsistent with intentional-stance functionalism. Therefore, unless we are sure that intentional-stance functionalism is false, we can't try to vindicate neoclassicism this way.

I think that the data on preference reversals, especially when interpreted in the light of my abstract philosophical criticism of Becker in the previous section, are sufficient to justify skepticism about anthropocentric neoclassicism. However, I'll now review a second empirical phenomenon that casts still deeper doubt on it, and that will play a larger motivating role in the positive alternative for which I'll be arguing. The phenomenon in question is time inconsistency of preference.

If a normal human life is a single consistent teleology, in the way that mature anthropocentric neoclassicism presupposes, then people ought to care about maximization of utility over their whole lifetimes, rather than about maximization relative to shifting temporal reference points. Of course, the passage of time implies uncertainty, and a lifetime maximizer would be expected to take this into account. So I "should" prefer ten dollars today to ten dollars tomorrow, because I "should" discount the later gain by the probability that I'll be hit by a bus in the meantime (and the probability of price inflation, and the probability that my favorite goods will later be unavailable, etc.). Since I could be more or less risk averse, the curve drawn through measures of the utility I associate with identical goods could decline more or less steeply. Furthermore, different curves could describe preferences over different bundles (as long as I'm not in a perfect market, where such differences would have to be arbitraged away). But if what I'm maximizing is the utility I get over my whole lifetime, each curve ought to decline exponentially: no two curves referring to the same bundle should cross depending on whether I assess the expected utility of the bundle from one temporal reference point or another. However, masses of laboratory and field data show that this is not how people behave. (See Ainslie 1992; Thaler 1992, pp. 92–106; Camerer 1995, pp. 649–651; Rabin 1998, pp. 38–41. The phenomenon was first proposed and modeled by Strotz [1956].)

Deciding today whether to mark a pile of undergraduate essays or watch a baseball game, I procrastinate, despite knowing that by doing so I put out of reach some even more fun possibility that might come up for tomorrow (when there's another equally attractive ball game on if the better option doesn't arise). So far, this is consistent with exponential discounting; if the world might end tonight, with a tiny but nonzero probability, then there's some level of risk aversion at which I'd rather leave the essays unmarked. However, if I bind myself against procrastination by buying a ticket for tomorrow's game, where in the absence of the awful task I wouldn't have done so, then I've violated intemporal preference consistency. (The psychology of self-binding has been explored in detail by Elster [1979, 2000].) Even more vividly, had I been in a position to choose last week whether to procrastinate today,

I'd have chosen not to. In this case, my discount curve drawn from the reference point of last week obviously crosses the curve drawn from the perspective of today. I discount (at least with respect to this choice set) hyperbolically rather than exponentially. (A standard discount function is called exponential because it calculates future value by application of a linear power function to the present value. By contrast, a hyperbolic function produces a bowed curve, in which rewards at short and long delays are valued in a relationship modeled by an exponential function, but bundles of utility at intermediate delays are valued less and so slide off the curve [Ainslie 2001, pp. 30–31].)

The phenomenon of hyperbolic discounting expresses itself ubiquitously in human behavior. People become addicted to various things, but they also take steps to put out of reach the objects that will tempt them to maintain addiction. They avoid buying rich desserts because they know that if they do they'll eat them when they would rather not. They buy cheaper but energy-inefficient appliances even though they'd more than recoup the saving in a short time by buying more expensive but more efficient units—then regret having done so despite having learned nothing relevantly new in the meantime (Thaler 1992, p. 94).[7] They complain about restaurant portions being too big even when they eat everything they're served and don't consider the marginal price of the extra food to be too high.[8] They save for old age at low rates of interest when they could better maximize lifetime utility by borrowing to finance present consumption or higher long-run returns, even when they aren't credit constrained. Ulysses bound himself to the mast because he knew he'd be unable to resist the song of the sirens when the time came.

These examples are all drawn from casual reflection on everyday experience, or from field studies. Laboratory experiments reveal more subtle, and more precisely isolated, effects. Work with test subjects by Thaler (1981) and Benzion, Rapaport, and Yagil (1989) show that when people choose between present and delayed gains and losses, their discount rates decline with time, but kink at least once; that discount rates decline more sharply for small rewards than for large ones; and that discount rates for gains are much higher than for losses. Since all of these dispositions allow potential arbitrage, they imply dynamic preference reversals. Kirby and Herrnstein (1995) tested this prediction explicitly, and found that subjects indeed reverse their choices from smaller, earlier rewards to larger, later rewards as the delay to both rewards increases. Loewenstein (1988) demonstrates that when people

make trade-offs between sizes of rewards and their proximities to reference points, they demand more than four times as much (on average)
to delay the reward than they'll pay to speed it up by the same amount
of time. Relativization of preferences to temporal reference points is
also illustrated by the fact that people appear to prefer consumption
patterns that rise over time to declining or flat patterns, even when total
expected consumption is identical in the three sorts of cases (Thaler
1992, pp. 101–103).

These are, in my view, the most important phenomena discovered
by behavioral economics. First, for reasons to be discussed in chapter
8, they may be the most general such phenomena, since they might
provide the analytical lever that opens the way to non-Ptolemaically
explaining all the rest of the behavioral "anomalies" unearthed by the
experimental literature. The version of the Ptolemaic "matching law"
discussed above as formulated by Herrnstein (1961)[9] is incorporated
into Ainslie's (1992) theory of the phenomenon (see below), and is
thereby generalized (since matching is compatible with both exponential and hyperbolic discounting). Second, the phenomena strike at the
very heart of mature anthropocentric neoclassicism as I have characterized it. People may often rationalize their actions by implying that
they are assembling their lives as triumphant projects in maximization,
as if the goal is to be able to say on their deathbeds that, given the environmental and genetic accidents that constrained them, they did their
best. Becker and those economists he has inspired show what mathematical manipulations we have to perform to be able to round out such
stories in full analytic detail, and that is an impressive technical accomplishment. However, the behavioral facts systematically belie the
individual and cultural rationalizations. The preference for rising consumption patterns is especially evocative in this regard; people are less
concerned with making their welfare best than with being able to think,
at least from perspectives in time not too close to the expected end,[10]
that their welfare will get better.

The implications of this go well beyond technical difficulties in
applying RPT directly to individual people. My analytical approach so
far in this book allows neoclassicists to reserve "economic agent" as a
technical concept, and so holds open the possibility that RPT is the right
device for axiomatizing that concept. However, once that move is made
then acceptance of the data on time inconsistency of preference means
that push must come to shove somewhere; in particular, it implies that
individual people, as continuing biological and/or narrative entities,

are not single, persisting economic agents. This amounts to the flat denial of anthropocentric neoclassicism.

In reaching this conclusion, I am following a path explored by others who have reflected on these data. Most explicit and far-reaching in his analysis has been the psychiatrist George Ainslie (1992, 2001). Ainslie argues that we best capture the dynamics of economic behavior by modeling whole individual people as communities of economic agents whose cohabitation forces them into bargaining and coordination games, as well as social dilemmas, with one another. The Calvin and Hobbes cartoon reproduced in figure 5.1 brilliantly captures the idea. In earlier installments of the story line, Calvin at 6:30 P.M. has come up with a plan for avoiding his homework: he'll use his time machine to travel forward to 8:30 and collect it from his future self. He thereby transfers his identification from his enduring self to his temporally immediate one—just like a real, normal person, according to the data just reviewed. In the cartoon scenario, three things are funny about this. One is the sheer enormity of the discount slope involved: 6:30 Calvin sets out to ruthlessly exploit a self that's just two hours in the future. The second is that when 6:30 Calvin goes to 8:30 he makes havoc of the self-partitioning conditions he started with. It's hard enough figuring out who 8:30 Calvin is at 6:30, but this really is a real-life problem for all of us. However, who on earth is 6:30 Calvin when he goes to 8:30? We can immediately see that this must iterate into a Zeno-style paradox that dooms the whole scheme. However, Zeno paradoxes rest on logical errors, in this case inherited from the magical time-traveling device. Calvin's funniest problem is the third one: he's fallen into a one-person tragedy of the commons in which all temporal Calvins

Figure 5.1
Calvin and Hobbes. © 1992 Bill Waterson. Reprinted with permission of UNIVERSAL PRESS SYNDICATE. All rights reserved.

must suffer losses as each logically possible temporal Calvin seeks another on whom to free ride.[11] As with all richly clever gags, this one works because its author has put his finger on a situationally shocking but logically accurate feature of reality: people are politically complex societies of temporally located selves.

In Ainslie's (2001) model, people are deconstructed into communities of bargaining interests, in which the subunits face conflict because they have different utility functions, but must cooperate because "they are all locked up in a room together" (p. 43). The subunits cannot allow themselves to fall back into a Hobbesian state of nature, because if they do the revealed preferences of the whole community (i.e., the person) will become radically cyclical and it will be money-pumped by the whole environment; that is, the community will be continuously expanding effort to undo today what it did yesterday. However, the device of appointing an internal Hobbesian tyrant is unavailable to it as a result of neurological-informational complexities, which I will discuss in the chapters to come. Therefore, its behavior is guided by the kinds of coalition dynamics familiar from the public-choice literature on democratic legislatures (see Stratmann 1997). That is, as we will see in more detail in chapter 8, from the economic perspective the main thing going on in a mammalian brain is *logrolling*. Just as in the U.S. Congress, the logrolling is stabilized, rather than constantly productive of cycles, because the most threatening competitor to a short-term interest is typically another short-term interest, and similarly for long-term interests; short-term and long-term interests are thus incentivized to form coalitions with one another.

This picture will, at the present point in its explication, seem irreducibly metaphorical. What can it really mean to think of abstract interests as literally analogous to agents in a network of political control dynamics? Where are these agents? How do they causally work? Answering these questions—taking Ainslie's hypothesis out of the domain of pure metaphor, and systematically relocating basic agency at the subpersonal level—will be a primary task of the chapters to come. I have described Ainslie's model as non-Ptolemaic. This is because, as we will see, it is given support by developments across a broad front in cognitive and behavioral science. It does much more than summarize the data accumulated by experimental economists; it motivates, from evidence independent of economic theory, a direct, general insight into what both microeconomics and macroeconomics are actually about.

Davis (2003) argues that the decomposition of the individual economic agent into a community has been implicit in neoclassicism from its deepest intellectual origins in the work of Hume. As soon as Hume turned the self into a mere bundle of perceptions, the core of the self was under threat. The Kantian concept of the transcendental ego was an attempt to pull it back together. As we saw in the previous chapter, this Kantian proposal is still exercising influence on neoclassicism in the first half of the last century through the work of Robbins. The consultation of the inner table of ordered preferences that is supposed to ground our confidence in microeconomic theory for Robbins clearly involves properties of the Kantian unity; something like the transcendental ego must be thought to be studying itself. However, as we have also seen, and as Davis (2003) documents by tracing a slightly different but complementary historical path, "the centre did not hold"—quite literally. The positivists turned into Humeans. In the Samuelsonian framework there is nothing with which to identify economic agents except their utility functions. But if these must be relativized to finely distinguished temporal frames *in the general and normal case*, then the individual economic agent has automatically been sundered. Thomas Schelling (1978, 1980, 1984) may have been the first prominent economist to draw the explicit conclusion and to begin theoretical exploration of its possibilities. As both Davis and Mirowski also notice, and as we will discuss at length in the next three chapters, work in cognitive science over the past twenty-five years has carried us in this same direction.

The conclusion that Davis (2003) draws from the sundering of the individual is that something has gone wrong. He is of course correct that economists who go on promoting methodological individualism in this context are, if their allegiances are broadly neoclassical, flirting with schizophrenia. But, then, all sciences experience such episodes during the lags in conceptual transformation, and their diagnosis is just what philosophical therapy is for. Davis himself seems torn on the matter: he is concerned to salvage a place for the individual, but is certainly no fan of traditional neoclassical individualism. In the end (pp. 130–166) he's content to identify an ongoing tension awaiting further resolution—but cognitive science is identified as part of the problem, not part of the solution. Mirowski, by subtle contrast, is always careful to say that it is a place for the *self*, rather than the individual, he is concerned to see preserved. At this point, that distinction may seem subtle to the point of being scholastic. However, in the next chapter I'll be

showing how cognitive science and economic theory can *jointly* be used
to theorize the distinction and put it to real work. Selves will turn out
to be both cognitively and economically important. However, we won't
be putting either the pre-Humean or the Kantian individual back
together; quite the opposite.

For the moment, however, let us stay closer to the immediate technologies of current economic analysis. It should be obvious that, among
these technologies, the one most suited to the description and explanation of logrolling dynamics is game theory. This is, explicitly, our
mathematical tool for studying what happens when sets of utility functions interact in environments of socially scarce resources. Games may
be either static, played in circumstances where governing environmental parameters are independent of the outcomes of the games, or,
where these parameters themselves evolve in interaction with the
games, dynamic and evolutionary (see Weibull 1995; Gintis 2000). More
will be said about this shortly. But to round off the themes of this
chapter, what we must focus on first is a prior issue, namely, the interpretations of agency and intentionality that is most naturally compatible with game-theoretic reasoning.

I said early in the chapter that the hostility to mature neoclassicism
shared by humanists of Sen's variety and experimental-behavioral
economists obscures the fact that the positive theses to which their
respective philosophical presuppositions incline are as different as
could be imagined. The humanist, recall, objects to mature neoclassicism's demotion of the free human agent to the status of a vector
product of external causal outputs. As I will now argue, however,
emphasis on the experimental and field data I have just reviewed leads
theorists in the direction opposite from, and most repulsive to, the
enlightenment ontology of the humanist. This direction is eliminativism, the thesis that there is no intentionality, no mind, no agency in
Sen's humanistic sense, at all. This is the prospect that is noticed by
Mirowski, and associated by him with Dennett's dangerous idea (see
chapter 1). It is also the prospect resisted by Davis (2003), which leads
him to turn away from both cognitive science and neoclassicism and
to look to the work of Sen for a variety of economics that can take
agency seriously.

I have announced, without yet showing why, that cognitive science
will not support the humanist approach. However, I aim also to show
that eliminativism is an overreaction, a radical extrapolation that runs
well past those empirical data that the humanist fails to take seriously

enough. The middle ground I will defend will turn out to be best held by performing restorative surgery on the stodgy old figure derided by humanists and eliminativists alike, neoclassicism.

Before I begin this restoration project, I must first explain why the new experimentalist-behaviorist wave is being theorized in an eliminativist way. And even before that, one loose end from the present section remains to be tied. I said earlier that for purposes of conceptual organization the experimental-behavioral economics literature would be sorted into three files. The first file (work set 1) holds work that compares human informational judgments with those derived from more traditional normative-epistemological frameworks. As we saw, this is empirically important cognitive science, but it directs our critical attention to various auxiliary hypotheses of contemporary economics, especially expected utility theory, rather than to the ontological core of neoclassicism. The second pile of empirical literature (work set 2), which has just been reviewed, studies the processes that ground actual human choice. As we have seen, the principal upshot of this work is the rejection of anthropocentric neoclassicism's core claim, the identification of human biographies with trajectories of neoclassical agency. The third pile must be mentioned here for the sake of completeness, pending a proper review and discussion at its logical moment in the second volume of this study.

Rationality in Aggregated Markets (Work Set 3)

A popular move by which some theorists have tried to save neoclassicism from experimentally motivated skepticism has been to argue that aggregation of people in markets washes out their individual departures from the patterns of agency, so that although neoclassicism fails to accurately describe them in isolation, its models of markets made of agents are empirically isomorphic to the behavior of markets made of people. (Friedman must implicitly believe something like this, though he doesn't say so. The view is often cited by economic methodologists as being common, but it appears to rest on a folk argument, since attempts to find a rigorous formulation of it come up empty. Recent discussions of what empirical facts would have to hold, very generally, for the claim to be true are Dowding forthcoming and Ross and Bennett 2001.) I will be offering a new variation on this argument, using dynamic systems theory and multiple agent models from cognitive science, in volume 2, and its philosophical motivations will be introduced in chapter 8 of this volume when I discuss the relationship between Ainslie's "picoeconomics" and the classical domain of micro-economics. Now, for the sake of closure in the description of the experimental literature, let us just note one easy route to the aggregation defense that that literature has blocked. Experimental economists have done a great deal of work with markets simulated in laboratories (see Sunder 1995; Thaler 1992, chapters 7–13; the approach was pioneered over many years by Nobel laureate Vernon Smith). The evidence from this work strongly suggests that effects of the two phenomena most devastating for anthropocentric neoclassicism, preference reversal and intertemporal inconsistency, do not necessarily wash out in markets. This does not appear to just be a function of the fact that laboratory markets are small and ephemeral; there is evidence that the point holds good for the largest and most important markets in the actual macro-economy. Thus, for example, Constantinides (1988) argues that the equity premium puzzle (persistent overvaluation of stocks relative to bonds) may be explained by the fact that people prefer rising con-sumption levels. Thaler (1992, pp. 119–120) argues that the domestic savings market in the developed world collectively bypasses an oppor-tunity to exploit arbitrage opportunities created by differences between the values of life insurance policies and bond rates for essentially the same reason. And so on. Though I will later be promoting an aggrega-tion defense of neoclassicism, these field data, and the market experi-ments that support their interpretation, will preclude any attempt to try to rescue *anthropocentric* neoclassicism in this fashion.

The Road from Behavioral Economics to Eliminativism

The position in the philosophy of mind and cognitive science known as "eliminative materialism" (Churchland 1979, 1981), introduced in chapter 2, is the ultimate nightmare hypothesis for the traditional humanist. According to eliminativists, folk psychology is wrong not only with respect to the causal dynamics it imagines as guiding and explaining human behavior (a point with which I, and virtually all cognitive scientists, agree). It is also mistaken with respect to its *fundamental* ontological framework. Beliefs and desires have no direct isomorphs individuable in the ontology of neuroscience. However, nonreflex behavior must be neuronally caused. Therefore, the elimina-tivist argues, the interaction of beliefs and desires cannot be the causal basis of behavior. The patterns of inference and argument we describe by means of the concept of rationality are built from normative relations among beliefs and desires. Therefore, if beliefs and desires are not elements in the causal etiology of behavior, rationality patterns should have no ultimate role to play in a mature science of cognition. Indeed, if minds don't reduce as just identical to brains—the old idea driven to the margins of philosophical opinion by the functionalist arguments of the 1970s—then all that is left for putative "minds" to be is the arenas of reasoning, as opposed to mere causing. But if reference to reasons should disappear from cognitive and behavioral science, then "real" arenas for reasoning become empty. "Minds" might then continue to be useful points of reference for sloppy, everyday getting along—in the same way that most people continue to talk about the sun rising even when they know it's our horizon that's doing the relative moving—but, in fact, there are no minds. Just as some of our ancestors talked about social properties of inconvenient groups of women by reference to "witches," so we rationalize our behavior through loose fantasies about minds and mental causation. But there aren't, really, any witches (and never were), and there aren't, really, any minds or mental causation.

The humanist's eyes are presumably big now. As I noted in chapter 2, the eliminativist hypothesis is apt to look deranged on first encounter, and its leading historical promoter, Paul Churchland, has for some time been working to shed the term so as not to confound his substantive scientific proposals with social noise induced by gratuitous shock (see Churchland 1995). I don't have space, in this book on other subjects, to reproduce Churchland's patient efforts at defending the bare conceivability of his proposal; a reader—perhaps an economist—gasping in amazement is referred to Churchland (1988, pp. 43–49). Let me therefore say just this much before going on. The eliminativist hypothesis has been extremely productive even if, as I in fact think, it goes too far. Folk psychology *does* systematically misunderstand the dynamics of mental processing and its relationships to behavior and to the environment. So when I eventually give comfort, as I will, to people who want to go on believing that minds and reasons are scientifically significant, this will not amount to a defense of folk psychology. The debate over eliminativism has forced questions about how we should adjust our intuitive picture of mind to accommodate cognitive science into vivid and immensely useful relief. My purpose in this section is to show how these questions are, finally, emerging into the domain of debate in economic theory. This will in turn indicate to humanists—

aside from Mirowski and Davis, who have figured it out—what is at stake in my argument with them about anthropocentric economics. In particular, when they resort to experimental-behavioral evidence to support their attack on neoclassicism, they might do well to ask whether their enemy's enemy is really their friend, or is in fact a more dangerous enemy.

When the main arguments for eliminativism were formulated in the 1970s and 1980s, their proponents did not imagine that their efforts would induce those they persuaded to stop using mentalistic concepts then and there. The most influential sources, Churchland (1979) and (1981) were not intended as practical manifestos, but as defenses of a prediction based on an epistemological and metaphysical critique of the foundations of folk psychology. Depending on the speed at which progress was made in the behavioral sciences, Churchland argued, the impossibility of integrating the mentalistic framework within the wider scientific perspective would make itself increasingly evident, to the point where scientists would gradually stop using it altogether. That is, scientists would be persuaded by their own experience more than by philosophical argument, and the scientific work in which such persuasion was manifest would then furnish the decisive evidence for the eliminativist metaphysical thesis. This way of diagnosing the hypothetical situation rested on the central epistemological premise of naturalism, according to which consensual scientific practice is the basic source of evidence in philosophy of science. (I of course endorse this premise very strongly.)

Churchland's original eliminativist hypothesis was thus essentially a prediction. That is, he provided grounds for thinking that, as a matter of fact, the actual behavioral sciences would gradually come to find less and less of a role for the concepts built around normative rationality in their explanatory and predictive activities, until a day would come when reference to minds and reasons in scientific discourse would sound quaint and archaic, after the fashion of phlogiston, vital forces, and Oedipal complexes. However philosophers might sometimes express themselves, the goal of science is not really to construct an ontological catalog from which things called "beliefs" could turn out to be present or absent, but to furnish theoretical perspectives from which the real patterns in nature can best be tracked. As Churchland has always emphasized, the explanatory patterns in which mentalistic states figure are those that seek to account for behavior by citing networks of propositional-attitude states related to one another by underlying assumptions (of varying strength) about epistemic rationality. The genuine (presently interesting) issue between eliminativists and noneliminativists thus centers around the following question: is it worthwhile activity to use and try to explain real patterns organized around the idea of "rational action"? Does such activity advance our understanding of life, behavior, and thought, or does it mainly obstruct that understanding?

We have just reviewed the gathering pile of evidence from experimental-behavioral economics suggesting that people do not respect the canons of either epistemic (judgment-related) or practical (choice-related) rationality in their behavior. This all by itself must obviously give some comfort to an eliminativist. However, it need not much trouble the humanist, since he has never wanted his people to be rational in the sense of RPT and EUT anyway. Rather, he wants them to be rational in roughly Aristotle's sense, as freely choosing, with their share of perceptual and processing errors and natural biases, from among conflicting plans and courses of action in the light of pruden-tial and moral reasons. The experimental-behavioral economics litera-ture does not seem, at first glance, to threaten this image; on the contrary, the mathematically muddled but intensely social creatures it seems to reveal look endearingly like Aristotle's (or Mark Twain's). Ultimately, however, this loose image based on empirical work requires integration into some definite theoretical framework or other if it is to be a basis for a revamped economic science. Because the body of evi-dence has grown so large and compelling, much attention is now being devoted to such explicit theorizing. My task in this section is to simply show that the relevant theoretical integration is drifting in an elimina-tivist direction, and to explain why. The reasons, as we will see, go much deeper than the mere fact that real people don't seem to be very good at consistently maximizing utility functions.

I will begin with some quotations from game theorists that have an eliminativist ring to them. First, consider what Binmore has to say about the relationship between Adam Smith's "moral sentiments" (i.e., social-emotional state types) and evolved norms for coordinating empathetic preferences as emphasized in Binmore's interpretation of evolutionary game theory:

Personally, I think it unlikely that Adam Smith's moral sentiments—anger, con-tempt, disgust, envy, greed, shame and guilt—all have genuine physiological referents. Under certain circumstances, our bodies pump chemicals into our bloodstream. We then invent myths in seeking to explain to ourselves what we are experiencing. Such myths typically do not separate the train of events that caused the experience from the experience itself. (Binmore 1994, p. 183, note 5)

This certainly sounds like eliminativism about nonpropositional mental content. However, Binmore (ibid., p. 193) explicitly calls a halt to this direction before reaching eliminativism about propositional attitudes—as noted in chapter 1, he stands on the Dennettian ground to which we're ultimately traveling. But here is Gintis (2000) on the significance of propositional mental content to the evolutionary game theorist:

If you have previously studied game theory, you will no doubt have noticed that our treatment of Bayesian updating in games with private information has not relied at all on the concept of "beliefs." This is not an oversight but rather a natural side-effect of our evolutionary perspective. Classical game theory takes the decision processes of the *rational actor* as central, whereas evolutionary game theory takes the *behavior* of corporeal actors as central. . . . Beliefs in such a framework are the *explicandum*, not the *explicans*—a shorthand way of expressing a behavioral regularity rather than the source of the regularity. There is absolutely no need to introduce the concept of beliefs into the general theory of games with private information. (Gintis 2000, p. 289)

This is not yet a statement of full-on ontological eliminativism. Gintis's claim is about propositional attitudes, but in a restricted technical context: he is not explicitly rejecting beliefs in general, but only a special use to which some game theorists (e.g., Kreps 1990a,b) have put them (to be discussed below). At least, that is all we can officially hold Gintis to here without further interpretation. He hints at a broader agenda in the paragraph following the one quoted above when he says "the 'belief' concept invites all sorts of philosophical nonsense of the type parodied in the Spinoza quote at the head of the chapter." The quote in question from Spinoza is "The philosophers kick up the dust and then complain that they cannot see."

Evolutionary game theory, when it is being pressed into service as a tool for modeling behavior in general, posits foundations for the observed ranges of behavioral patterns in populations that are essentially economic in Robbins's sense. That is, following Darwin, what drives changes in strategy profiles as games evolve is the existence of alternative and competing means for acquiring scarce resources. As we have seen, this conception is logically independent of the question as to whether beliefs are *causal* engines of behavior; Robbins took them to be, but Samuelson and Friedman are agnostic on the matter and resolutely regard it as none of the economist's business. However, once our purpose shifts to accounting for *general* psychological (as opposed to economic-behavioral) dispositions, partly by recourse to economic logic, neither Robbins's nor Friedman's way of maintaining the separateness thesis remain available. Now we are forced to ask how and where (in networks of causal relations) competitive pressures driven by scarcity enter into the sculpting of behavioral tendencies.

Recent proposals for answering this question—and not just from eliminativists—have tended against traditional stories that get scarcity pressures into the causal networks by making them objects of causally active propositional attitudes. The philosopher Phillip Pettit (1993, 2001), for example maintains that economic agents are only "virtual," their so-called beliefs (*qua* the virtual beliefs of such virtual agents) being, in fact, just counterfactual limitations on what they would to do in ranges of nearby possible worlds. That is, we explain why stockbrokers do not persistently buy high and sell low by reference to forces that *would* impinge to correct such behavior if it were displayed. This approach, however, echoes the traditional money-pump argument as discussed in the previous section, and is less a way of answering the causal question than of bypassing it. Note, however, that it is broadly Samuelsonian in character, preserving a role for a concept of rationality without invoking causally active beliefs.

Recent emphases on the *dynamics* of economic patterns, however, seem to have more radical implications. Thus, for example, Satz and Ferejohn (1994) argue that consumer theory is empirically adequate as a description of behavior only where agents do not think for themselves, but instead find the responses traditionally associated with rational economic action cued by evolved environmental structures. Here, intentional patterns are not being reinterpreted in nonmicrocausal ways, as in Pettit's proposal, but seem to be dispensed with altogether, as posits that actually impede economic understanding. This suggestion is becoming increasingly common. Rosenberg (1983, 1992) has long expressed skepticism about microeconomics *because* it seems to take propositional attitudes seriously; and so back in 1983 he speculated that behavioral, evolutionary, and/or dynamic systems (called "thermodynamic" by Rosenberg, writing before current terminology was widely established) approaches, which aim to get by without them, might offer a way for economists to save their discipline from skepticism grounded in behavioral evidence. The importance for Rosenberg of putting an eliminativist spin on these possibilities could not be more explicit: "If there is anything in the laws of supply and demand, in the possibility of stable or unique partial or general equilibria, at least some of these [systems-theoretic] approaches are designed to capture it without burdening themselves by commitments to the causal force of preference and expectation. . ." (Rosenberg 1983, p. 313, note 15). Similarly, Sugden (2001, p. 120) argues that there is a tension between "appealing to the axioms of expected utility theory" and "rejecting rationality at the level of beliefs" about which evolutionary game theorists have been too quietistic; and he clearly hopes that the tension will be resolved by pushing the eliminativist intuition all the way.

I should make clear that although Rosenberg, and others whose views are directly embedded in debates among philosophers, deliberately intends eliminativism, I am not suggesting that Gintis or Sugden do. Indeed, Gintis can sometimes be found explicitly pulling up short of it. For example, in a recent publication (2003, p. 161), after repeating his oft-made claim that economists using evolutionary game theory need no rationality postulate (see below), he says: "Evolutionary game theory cannot repair all the problems of classical game theory, because evolutionary game theory only applies when a large population engages in a particular strategic setting for many periods. . . . We still need a theory of isolated encounters among 'rational' agents (i.e., agents who maximize an objective function subject to constraints." Not being philosophers, neither Gintis nor Sugden is playing the "ism" contest. So when I (eventually, in chapter 8) go on to resist their route to eliminativism (partly through criticism of things Sugden says), I am not combating *them*, in the way philosophers routinely joust with each other ad hominem. Gintis and Sugden say more things suggestive of eliminativism than not, and a philosophical commentator, whose job is to push across-the-board consistency, will drive them further in that direction. Perhaps, in the quote just given, Gintis signals awareness that he stands to be so pushed by putting scare quotes around "rationality."

Just to complete the point that current discussions around economic modeling are traveling roads on which philosophers have been walking for a few decades, I might note that Colman reacts to an eliminativist interpretation of evolutionary game theory offered by Sigmund (2003) (see below), by repeating the very first, and very naïve, rebuttal that some philosophers tried against Churchland in the 1970s. "Does Sigmund expect his readers to be persuaded that rationality is dead?" Colman asks incredulously. "If he rejects rationality in all its forms, then he can hardly claim that his own opinions are rationally based, and there is consequently no obvious reason why we should be persuaded by them. By his own account, his comments must have arisen from a mindless evolutionary process unrelated to truth. This view cannot be taken seriously, and it is debatable . . . whether it is even possible for Sigmund to believe it" (Colman 2003b, p. 183).

Against this argument, Churchland's vivid demonstration that it begs the question stands:

> If eliminativism is true then [persuasiveness] must have some different source. To insist on the "old" source is to insist on the validity of the very framework at issue. . . . Consider the medieval theory that being biologically *alive* is a matter of being ensouled by an immaterial *vital spirit*. And consider the following response to someone who has expressed disbelief in that theory: "My learned friend has stated that there is no such thing as vital spirit. But this statement is incoherent. For if it is true, then my friend does not have vital spirit, and must therefore be *dead*. But if he is dead then his statement is just a string of noises, devoid of meaning or truth. Evidently, the assumption that antivitalism is true entails that it cannot be true! Q.E.D." (1988, p. 48)

We must distinguish between two different kinds of arguments for eliminativist economics found in the sources surveyed above. Rosenberg's view is that the very concepts of belief and desire are parasitic on that of rationality, so to the extent that people turn out to generally behave arationally, propositional-attitude frameworks will be inappropriate for accurately describing them. Since this argument, as germane to the content of economic theory, presupposes that economics must directly describe people, I will postpone discussion of it to chapter 8, after my sketch of a nonanthropocentric economics has been fleshed out. The argument for eliminativistic economics I want to sketch here— the one implicit in Gintis and Sugden—relies on some additional premises. First, it supposes that the specific ways in which people are arational are products of evolutionary dynamics. Second, it appeals to the fact that evolutionary game theory is the appropriate technology for explaining the development and maintenance of the arational strategies we find in use. Notice that since evolutionary game theory is, like the more traditional tools of economic theory, an abstract explanatory engine, to the extent that it can furnish generalizations about competitive dynamics under scarcity, its conclusions may be thought to have wider scope than the specifically human; it might instead promise a new general account of the phenomena picked out by my reformulation of Robbins's definition of economics. In this context, an eliminativist theory would apply to the objects of economics *whatever they are*, and the psychological phenomena observed in the laboratories of the experimentalists would thereby be explained, as special human cases, by economics, rather than the other way around (i.e., by psychology explaining specially economic behavior). It thus encourages the sort of economic imperialism dreaded by Dupré.

Gintis and Sugden explicitly see avoidance of the belief concept as being implied by the accelerating shift in economic theory from classical to evolutionary game theory. The players in classical games are our familiar neoclassical agents, who choose and can in principle revise their own strategies, and so it is natural to think of such choices as derived from beliefs about which strategies are best replies to strategies of others. By contrast, the players in evolutionary games are the strategies themselves; if there are agents involved at all in evolutionary games, then they are simply passive vehicles for these strategies, coming to play their brief hands and then dying off to be replaced by others who inherit their dispositions with modifications induced by mutation and, at the population level, by selection. Insofar, then, as propositional-attitude psychology is intended as a theory of active (broadly rational) *choice*, the kinds of process it purports to be about simply drop from view in evolutionary game theory. The mechanism that "picks" evolutionary strategies, that is, dynamics of selection, does not appear to most theorists to be a suitable candidate for ascriptions of beliefs or desires, and this may be thought conceptually equivalent to saying that no choices are exercised anywhere in the picture, nor any rational action undertaken. This is the basic intuition behind the growing eschewal of reference to rationality and propositional attitudes by evolutionary game theorists. Karl Sigmund (2003), who has perhaps contributed more to the formal development of evolutionary game theory than any other single person, states its eliminativist agenda in terms Churchland could envy for forthrightness: "In applications to real-life situations (as opposed to philosophical puzzles), game theory can do just as well without the postulate of rationality, and Occam's razor demands, therefore, to get rid of it. That it held out for so long is mostly due to historical contingency" (p. 176).

There is, however, a deeper sense in which evolutionary game theorists are motivated to be suspicious of reference to propositional attitudes in their models, and this is the exact sense intended by Gintis in the remarks of his quoted earlier. Sketching this reasoning here will accomplish two tasks in the context of my project. First, it will efficiently perform the pedagogical function of bringing the noneconomist reader up to date from the historical narrative I left off with the appearance of VNM utility at the end of chapter 3. Second, and more to the argumentative point, it will show why, when I seek to preserve a role for RPT in my positive account to come—and thereby justify taking that account as continuous with neoclassicism—this must not mean RPT "stapled to" EUT, as an empirical theory of decision, at the foundational level.

The main tradition in classical game theory (and the tradition in which philosophers tend to take the greatest professional interest) sees that theory as providing an explanatory, and typically normative, theory of strategic *reasoning*. It therefore constitutes a problem for classical theorists that, in many games, not all Nash equilibria (NE) look equally plausible as the solutions on which strategically rational players would converge. Consider the strategic-form game in figure 5.2 (taken from Kreps 1990b, p. 403). This game has two NE: s1-t1 and s2-t2. If player I is playing s1 then player II can do no better than t1, and vice versa; and similarly for the s2-t2 pair. If NE is our only solution concept for games, then we shall be forced to say that either of these outcomes is equally persuasive as a solution. However, if game theory is regarded as an explanatory and/or normative theory of strategic reasoning, this seems to be leaving something out: surely rational players would converge on s1-t1, where both do better?[12] This illustrates the fact that NE often fails to predict intuitively sensible solutions because, if applied alone, it refuses to allow players to use principles of equilibrium selection that should be favored by expected-utility maximizers.

Consider another example from Kreps (1990b, p. 397), in figure 5.3. Here, no strategy *strictly* dominates another; that is, there is no strategy for either player such that that player is better off using the strategy in question regardless of what the other does. However, player I's top row, s1, *weakly* dominates s2, since I does at least as well using s1 as s2 for any reply by player II, and on one reply by II (t2), I does better.

		II	
		t1	t2
I	s1	10,10	0,0
	s2	0,0	1,1

Figure 5.2
Strategic-form game. (From Kreps 1990b, p. 403.)

II

	t1	t2
s1	10,0	5,2
s2	10,1	2,0

I

Figure 5.3
From Kreps 1990b, p. 397.

II

	t1	t2
s1	10,0	5,2
s2	10,11	2,0

I

Figure 5.4

So should not expected-utility-maximizing players (and the analyst) delete the weakly dominated row s2? When they do so, column t1 is then strictly dominated, and the NE s1-t2 is selected as the unique solution. However, as Kreps goes on to show using this example, the idea that weakly dominated strategies should be deleted just like strict ones has odd consequences.

Suppose we change the payoffs of the game just a bit, as shown in figure 5.4. Here, s2 is still weakly dominated as before; but of our two NE, s2-t1 is now the most attractive for both players; so why should the analyst eliminate its possibility? The argument *for* eliminating weakly dominated strategies is that player I may be nervous, fearing that player II is not completely *sure* to be rational (or that player II fears that player I isn't completely rational, or that player II fears that player I fears that player II isn't completely rational, and so on, ad infinitum) and so might play t2 with some positive probability. If the possibility of departures from rationality is taken seriously, then we have an argument for eliminating weakly dominated strategies: player I thereby insures herself against her worst outcome, s2-t2. Of course, she pays a cost for this insurance, reducing her expected payoff from 10 to 5. On the other hand, we might imagine that the players could communicate before playing the game and agree to play correlated strategies so as to coordinate on s2-t1, thereby removing some, most, or all of the uncertainty that encourages elimination of the weakly dominated row s1, and eliminating s1-t2 as a viable NE instead.

This set of examples illustrates the "refinement program" in classical game theory, wherein theorists try to satisfy demands of propositional rationality by seeking logically stronger solution concepts than NE, concepts that eliminate from consideration NE that foresighted players would find less attractive. In the case just discussed, elimination of weakly dominated strategies is one possible refinement, since it refines away the NE s2-t1, and correlation is another possibility, since it refines away the other NE, s1-t2, instead. So which refinement is more appropriate as a solution concept? People who think of game theory as an explanatory and/or normative theory of strategic rationality have generated a substantial literature in which the merits and drawbacks of a large variety of possible refinements are debated. Kreps (1990a,b) expresses deep disquiet about the absence of any stable metaprinciples for preferring any one refinement to another. The problem here is that in the context of classical games, successful expected-utility maximization by agents depends on players not only being behaviorally rational, but also on their sharing a common and complete model of what rationality is.[13] Philosophers familiar with the endless scope for argumentation on this question in epistemology are not likely to be optimistic on the agents' behalf.

The best way of showing that philosophical worries are indeed justified here is to press straight ahead until we hit actual rocks. Classical game theorists have done just this, by means of the particular refinement idea that Gintis has in mind when he bans reference to "beliefs" in the passage quoted from him earlier. The refinements we have considered so far *could* all be given purely behavioral interpretations; but this is precisely why we can't find principles for preferring one to another as a generally applicable solution concept.[14] The refinement concept known as "equilibrium in beliefs," or "sequential equilibrium," casts away behaviorist scruples in a direct assault on the stability problem. Again following Kreps (1990b), I will illustrate it by reference to the three-player imperfect-information game known as "Selten's horse," shown in figure 5.5. This is a sequential-move game in which player III's action nodes, 3 and 4, lie inside a single *information set*; this can be interpreted as meaning that when III moves, she doesn't know the history of the game, that is, doesn't know whether I played L, or I played R and then II played l_2. One of the NE of this game is Lr_2l_3.[15] This is because if player I plays L, then player II, playing

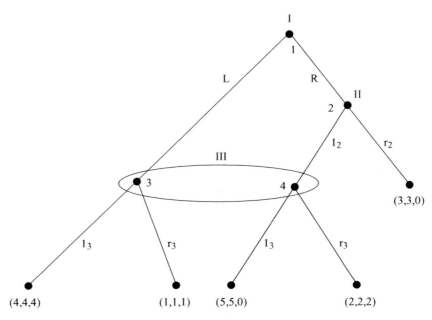

Figure 5.5
Three-player imperfect-information game.

r_2, has no incentive to change strategies because her only node of action, 2, is off the path of play. But this NE seems to be purely technical; it makes little sense as a solution. This reveals itself if we consider the related game in which III's nodes are in separate information sets. In that case, l_2 and l_3 could never occur together in one solution, since III would be directly failing to maximize.[16] Whenever she *does* get a move, player II should play l_2. But if player II is playing l_2 then player I should switch to R. In that case player III should switch to r_3, sending player II back to r_2. And here's a new, "sensible," NE: Rr_2r_3. This NE is sensible in exactly the same way that a so-called subgame perfect (SPE) outcome in a perfect-information game is more sensible than other non-SPE NE: no player is committed to doing something at a noninitial node that she wouldn't want to do if it were the initial node of a new game. However, since this is *not* a perfect information game, we have to look "inside" the players' computational dynamics to see if there is any possible process by which they might be able to find it.[17]

Kreps's notion of a sequential equilibrium (SE), a special case of an "equilibrium in beliefs," is a refinement designed for such cases. Notice what player III here is wondering about as he selects his strategy. "Given that I get a move," he asks himself, "was my action node reached from node 1 or from node 2?" What, in other words, are the conditional probabilities that III is at node 3 or 4 given that he has a move? Now, if conditional probabilities are what III wonders about, then what players I and II must make conjectures about when they select *their* strategies are III's *beliefs* about these conditional probabilities. In that case, player I must conjecture about II's beliefs about III's beliefs, and III's beliefs about II's beliefs, and so on. The relevant beliefs here are not merely strategic, as before, since they are not just about what players will *do* given a set of payoffs and game structures, but about what they think makes sense given some understanding or other of conditional probability. (This is why SE, unlike the refinements considered previously, is not amenable to behaviorist interpretation.) What beliefs about conditional probability is it reasonable for players to expect from each other? The normative theorist might recommend whatever the best mathematicians have discovered about the subject. At the other end of the scale, Gintis or Sugden might insist on imposing only habits that a process of natural or cultural selection can build into its products. Perhaps some actual or possible creatures might observe habits that respect Bayes's rule, as the minimal true generalization about conditional probability that an agent could know if it knows any such generalizations at all. Adding more sophisticated knowledge about conditional probability amounts to refining the concept of equilibrium-in-belief, in the further spirit of solution-concept refinement in general.

Here, we will restrict our attention to the least refined equilibrium-in-belief concept, that obtained when we require players to reason in accordance with Bayes's rule, that is, $pr(F/E) = [pr(E/F) \times pr(F)] / pr(E)$. Kreps's SE concept then requires that players not hold beliefs inconsistent with this equality. A SE has two parts (as informally defined in Kreps 1990b): (i) a strategy profile § for each player, as in any equilibrium concept, and (ii) a *system of beliefs* µ for each player. µ assigns to each information set h a probability distribution over the nodes x in h, with the interpretation that these are the beliefs of player $i(h)$ about where in his information set he is, given that information set h has been reached. Then a SE is a profile of strategies § and a system of beliefs μ consistent with Bayes's rule, such that starting from every information set h in the tree player $i(h)$ plays optimally from then on, given that what he believes to have transpired previously is given by $\mu(h)$ and what will transpire at subsequent moves is given by §.

We can demonstrate the concept by applying it to Selten's horse. Consider again the uninteresting NE Lr_2l_3. Suppose that player III assigns pr(1) to her belief that if she gets a move she is at node 3. Then player II, given a consistent $\mu(II)$, must believe that III will play l_3, in which case her only SE strategy is l_2. So although Lr_2l_3 is a NE, it is not a SE.

What exactly, is this telling us about the game? It says that if each player knows and uses Bayes's rule, and has no more esoteric knowledge of conditional probability, and knows that his opponents are likewise partly educated and that they know this about him and about each other, and that all know that all will correctly compute and use all that they know, then the SE analysis above will predict the observed outcome of play. This is a nifty bit of logic; but is it useful as anything else?

The answer of Sugden, Gintis, and company is "No." Following criticisms pioneered a decade ago by Binmore (1992), they take a dim view of much of the refinement activity, and our last example should help to indicate why. The job of an intended contribution to descriptive behavioral theory is to predict outcomes given some distribution of strategic dispositions, and some distribution of expectations about the strategic dispositions of others, that have been shaped by institutional processes and/or evolutionary selection. On this view, which equilibria are viable in a game is determined by the underlying dynamics that equipped players with dispositions *prior to* the commencement of any particular instance of a game. The strategic natures of players are thereby treated as sets of exogenous inputs to particular games among particular agents. This discourages inclinations to seek *general* refinements of the equilibrium concept itself, at least insofar as these involve the modeling of more sophisticated expressions of rationality over and above merely consistent maximization of utility (reinterpreted as fitness if our models are intended to be evolutionary). This naturally shades, by quick inference, into doubt that the goal of seeking a *general* theory of strategic rationality makes sense as a project. Institutions and evolutionary processes build many environments, and what counts as sound strategy in one environment may not be favored in another.

Only a very special environment and selection history could endow players with the rarified computational dispositions that we used in generating the analysis of Selten's horse above. But now suppose that selection was an optimizer. That is, suppose that it generated *ideally* rational game players? Then we would predict the outcomes of natural games by pursuing the "ultimate refinement," that is, the equilibrium concept that assumed that players compute in accordance with all true mathematical facts. Of course, this is a preposterous approach for a naturalist, turning game theory into the study of Platonic objects.[18] But—and here is the crucial point in the argument—no general assignment of beliefs and dispositions to act on beliefs that falls short of the ultimate refinement seems nonarbitrary, as our comparison of the games in the second and third matrices above might be taken to show. As Young (1998) shows in detail, we can use models of evolutionary learning to find comparative stability levels of solutions, and then we can get around the arbitrariness objection by finding the belief sets that are consistent with these. But the last step in this reasoning *presupposes* that we want to end up with models of the players as (boundedly) rational agents; it doesn't motivate our wanting to do so in the first place. But this is just what's at issue here. This is why Gintis, when explaining why he believes that "game theory is a universal language for the unification of the behavioral sciences" (2000, p. xxiii) says that "it is better to drop the term 'rational' altogether" (ibid., p. xxvi).

Now, this really does imply eliminativism,[19] since it renders all particular conceptions of rationality otiose for explanatory purposes. To model a situation using evolutionary game theory (EGT), pack into the specification of its start state and dynamics whatever you can find out about the initial dispositions of players, the conditions on replication of these dispositions (which fixes learning capacities and rates), the distributions of initial dispositions among the population, and correlational coefficients (if any). The dynamics of the game will then do the rest of the work. This approach holds the promise of unifying the behavioral sciences precisely *because* it is so general. If either social norms or computational capacities are going to evolve, and be causally relevant in the game, they will emerge as—and be strictly reducible to—changes in some of the parameters just listed; so nothing that might be significant for explanation, according to any special philosophy of behavioral science, seems to be left out. Patterns individuated by reference to rationality will be eliminated, either by reduction or by the discovery of more robust cross-classifications in terms of the evolutionary-game-theoretic parameters.

The list of inputs to an EGT model given above includes "initial dispositions of players." "Dispositions" is almost always a weasel word in metaphysics. Could these dispositions not be best interpreted as (externalistically understood) beliefs and desires? Yes, perhaps. But what should matter to antieliminativists is whether such states play any irreducible role in the analyses. And the answer is that, according to Sugden, Gintis, and so forth, they don't. A theorist might want to model a particular token of an interaction between some agents as a static game in the classical fashion. Doing this, she would include in her model some parameters that look just like classical beliefs; and perhaps she'd call them "beliefs." But if asked to justify the content of these beliefs, she would, if she were sympathetic to the evolutionary-foundational story, not produce anything like a sequential-equilibrium analysis. Instead, she'd derive the beliefs as encodings of a dynamic attractor in the phase space of the evolutionary game that gave rise to the agents in her static one. The parameters identified with belief contents thus don't do any causal work of their own in generating the outcome of even the static game; they're just notational conveniences that arise when the dynamic causal backdrop is put inside a black box for practical reasons. This is exactly the sort of reasoning that, I pointed out in chapter 3, Samuelson might profitably have adopted to build a Quinean defense of the empirical relevance of RPT.

What we've generated here in working up to the eliminativist conclusion is an expression of a set of problems that should seem very familiar to philosophers of mind. If propositional-attitude states are taken as descriptions of intrinsic representational states of organisms, whose characters in particular instances have specific implications for real-time computational processes, then we could aim to empirically determine their content independently of strictly behavioral evidence. But if, instead, we are persuaded by the arguments for externalism about propositional content discussed in chapter 2, then the very abstractness of game theory turns into a problem when we try to use it to characterize behavior. NE alone is too blunt a solution concept to generate detailed predictions, but any given refinement appears arbitrary if imposed as a general theory. Neurologically complex agents clearly do compute information, and such processing is equally clearly relevant to their strategic and other behavior. But if the objects over which these computations occur do not map neatly onto proposititional-attitude states, then trying to derive the patterns in their behavior top-down, from some normative theory of rationality or other, seems to have the logic of theory construction backwards.

This is exactly the point urged by Sugden (2001). I will close this section, and the chapter, with some discussion of his reflections on its larger implications for economic theory, since his contestable reading of these nicely defines our problem space for the remaining chapters. Sugden begins by noting that abandonment by economists of commitment to individual rationality—that is, eliminativism—*ought* to appear as "a momentous theoretical revolution, a shattering of hard cores, a dispatch of sacred cows to the abattoir" (2001, pp. 113–114) in light of the history of economics. He then notes the oddity of the fact that most leading-edge game theorists seem to have recently embraced evolutionary-eliminativist thinking without an evident struggle. In sharp contrast to the Kuhnian image of a paradigm shift, the revolution has been "bloodless." This observation motivates the main conclusion of Sugden's essay, which is that "the evolutionary turn is not the fundamental change that it purports to be" (ibid., p. 114). This is not intended as any affirmation of conservative reassurance. Sugden argues that the hard core of neoclassical economics should indeed be shattered, but that economists are thus far not taking the implications of eliminativism truly seriously. For although, he complains, economists may be surrendering the idea that agents manifest their rationality by means of internal processing in accord with private knowledge of norms of rationality, they persist in supposing that what is fundamental about economic behavior is the maximization of utility. This, he objects, is an a priori assumption rather than an empirical discovery, and it is just the same old a priori assumption that has always sat at the core of neoclassicism. Sugden's favored, more radical, eliminativism aims to sweep away not only procedural, psychological rationality, but utility and maximization too. This really would be an all-consuming abattoir, a true furnace of revolution.

I will be agreeing with Sugden's observation about the state of theory here, but differing with him on its evaluation. This is because, in chapter 8, I will be defending a noneliminativist interpretation of the arguments and facts that have been reviewed in this chapter. There, my dispute will be with a number of Sugden's assumptions about evolutionary explanation in general. I will thus postpone discussion of these for now. But, in keeping with the themes of *this* chapter, and nicely setting up the segue into the next one, I will note some subtle differences between the way Sugden reads the history of neoclassicism and the way that I have done.

Let me first quote Sugden's summary of the dominant modeling framework in EGT, one that will feature significantly in my later discussion. This is the *replicator dynamics*.[20]

In biology, the *relative fitness* of a phenotype is measured by the expected number of descendants in the next generation of an individual with that phenotype, as a proportion of the expected number of descendants of the phenotype with the highest number of expected descendants. In a sufficiently simplified biological model, in which reproduction is asexual and the properties of each parent's phenotype are perfectly replicated in its offspring, the expected rate of growth of the proportion of the population that has any given phenotype is directly proportional to the relative fitness of that phenotype. If "expected utility" is substituted for "expected number of descendants," and if it is assumed that higher values of expected utility lead to increases in the frequency of the associated behavior in something like the same way that higher expected numbers of descendants lead to increases in the frequency of the parental genotype, we arrive at the economic version of replicator dynamics. (2001, p. 119)

Sugden is right to note that the devil in these details lies in unpacking the "something like the same way," and this will preoccupy us in chapter 8. However, Sugden more immediately objects that "these strategies for retaining expected utility theory within evolutionary game theory are opportunistic. In classical game theory, the assumption that utility functions exist is grounded in a theory of rational choice. . . . But *evolutionary* game theory cannot make the same appeal" (ibid.).

The discussion of the past two chapters must lead us to dispute Sugden's premise here. As we saw, though classical game theoretic models often *do* incorporate expected utility maximization over subjective utility in the sense of Savage, the VNM utility functions that game theory needs—cardinal but not uniquely determinate up to linear transformation—can be interpreted behavioristically. This is as much of expected utility as has to be mapped onto expected fitness in economic applications of the replicator dynamics. Now, is it true that the claim that behavioristic VNM utility functions "exist" must rest on a theory of rational *choice*? Obviously, VNM utility functions over objective probabilities "exist" as mathematical objects. What Sugden clearly means to doubt is that such functions "exist" in a *psychologically* operational sense. This can in turn be given either an internalist or an externalist reading.

On the first reading, the thesis would be that processes modeled by some theory of rational choice are realized, step by step, in some inboard computational mechanism in people. On the second reading, the claim would merely be that patterns of behavior are isomorphic to input-output relations captured by some extensional choice function. (To be nonmysterious, this isomorphism would have to be explained by some account respecting what I called the "core internalist constraint," that is, would have to be buttressed by an empirically supported model of physical information flow through a system; but some of the flow might couple the mind with the environment and lodge parts of the processing outboard; see Clark 1997; Juarrero 1999.) As we have seen, there seems little historical or logical basis for thinking that neoclassical theory is or has ever been *committed* to the ontological priority of choice on the internalist reading. Bentham was agnostic about whether preference weightings—his "intensities"—have measurable psychological reality. The modern, Hicksian, utility function was given its philosophical interpretation by Robbins, who postulated as real psychological objects only raw, introspectible orderings but held psychological choice dynamics to be none of the economist's business. And Samuelson would have saved himself much critical grief had he been aware of, and followed, a Quinean eliminativist line. If Sugden intends the internalist reading of his premise, then, his proper target is really EUT, and he could join me in regarding the implications of contemporary behavioral and cognitive science for neoclassicism and RPT as being open. On this interpretation, Sugden's argument is not really with neoclassicism but with *nonbehavioristic* neoclassicism of the post-Samuelson variety.

If, on the other hand, Sugden's premise is interpreted externalistically, then it need not imply a foreshortened understanding of the history of economic theory, since Samuelson is obviously committed to the external, empirical applicability of a consistent choice function if RPT is to be descriptively relevant to economic behavior; and, as we saw, Robbins's attempt to rhetorically wriggle out of such a commitment fails. So Sugden then really *would* be arguing fundamentally with neoclassicism as I am reconstructing it. However, the belief that an *externalist* choice function is descriptively useful as a modeling device is perfectly compatible with the idea that individual people aren't procedurally rational, which is all the evolutionary turn, on Sugden's eliminativist spin, entails. For all the evidence and argument we have reviewed so far, and the justified premises available to Sugden, that question also remains open. Since I will defend an externalist understanding of choice, I can recruit Sugden's argument to my case against *anthropocentric* neoclassicism, but it will have no force against Samuelsonian neoclassicism if we turn out to still require some explanatory work from the concept of (external) rationality. In chapter 8 we'll see why we do.

Sugden's core complaint is that economists who have embraced EGT cling to utility functions for purely a priori reasons: their newfound enthusiasm for EGT isn't based on empirical considerations but on the fact that it gives them a way of continuing to model utility maximization while avoiding the philosophical embarrassments associated with the refinement program. But the thrust of my immediately preceding remarks is that Sugden's presupposition that utility-maximization models are descriptively empty is equally *a priori*. (His implication of bad faith also requires his claim that the embrace of EGT by economists is driven just by disenchantment with the refinement program, and not by empirically inspired, good, bloody, and Kuhnian, arguments over interpretations of the experimental-behavioral evidence. This would certainly be news to Gintis; and he's the one who's written the most institutionally important EGT manifesto [2000].) The issue can be settled only by considering some empirically motivated, plausible models of the information-processing dynamics involved in the management of scarcity and then *finding out* whether the functions most useful for modeling them are or aren't like those promoted in neoclassicism. Sugden, as an eliminativist, doubts that these dynamics will locate maximization at the level of the individual. As we'll see in the next chapter, we don't have to be eliminativists, but just conscientious students of cognitive science, to agree with him about this. But this would be devastating news for neoclassicism only if we must cling to the hoariest of all dogmas associated with the standard stereotype of neoclassicism, methodological individualism, as licensing what I've been calling "anthropocentrism." If there's one sacred cow that belongs in the abattoir, methodological individualism is it. I'll argue that when that is dispatched, the rest of neoclassicism can comfortably stay on four legs.

The action from here, then, proceeds as follows. Individualism is now to be led to the block. Contemporary cognitive science will be its executioner. We will then face the question of what neoclassicism shorn of its influence looks like. Among the options that will be seen to collapse with it are both Robbinsian introspectionism and mature anthropocentric neoclassicism. Both RPT and the possibility of interpreting it as relevant to an economics fitting my revision of Robbins's definition will remain unscathed. Eliminativism will be shown to threaten both, but reasons will be given for doubting that the eliminativist hypothesis is actually compatible with the kinds of evolutionary explanations presupposed in applications of EGT. This will then leave us with an answer to the question of whether we can and should construct an interpretation of economic science that respects the separateness thesis, but nevertheless takes the new behavioral-experimental evidence seriously. The answer will be positive.

Individualism,
Consciousness, and
Agency

From Sound Pedagogy to Unsound Metaphysics

All of the positions on the philosophical foundations of economics that
have been critically reviewed so far—from Aristotle's, through Jevons's
semi-Aristotelianism, Robbins's introspectionism, postwar mature
anthropocentric neoclassicism, anti-neoclassical humanism, and even
eliminativism—share the common assumption that adult, cognitively
competent people are the prototypical agents. Eliminativists doubt
that there are, actually, any agents. But their particular version of the
anti-neoclassical attitude depends on the assumption that agency as
economists have invoked it is *conceptually* intended as a model of
personhood, which then fails empirically. Hence my inclusion of them
in the list, odd though this may seem at first glance. Samuelsonian
behaviorism does *not* feature on the list, because although Samuelson
himself no doubt shared the assumption, the austere logical reconstruction of his official position that I have adopted is ontologically
uncommitted altogether where either agency or personhood are
concerned.

In the previous chapter I presented both conceptual and empirical
reasons for questioning the identification of economic agents with
people. The arguments I have given to this point, however, undermine
the various philosophical alternatives to different extents. Mature
anthropocentric neoclassicism and Aristotelian anti-neoclassical humanism both take the assumption more or less for granted, as a piece of
common sense. This leaves these positions vulnerable to a logically
weak level of skepticism: they get into trouble as soon as it is merely
established that the identification of people with prototypical agents is
not *obviously* justified. Mature anthropocentric neoclassicism is in an
especially tight corner, because its commitment to the manifest image

of common sense is not even consistent; while common sense surely does identify prototypical agency with personhood, it equally clearly does not suppose of natural persons that their preferences never change over the course of their lives. Aristotelian humanist views, however, could still be rescued if Robbinsian introspectionist foundations for the thesis that persons are agents could be successfully defended. I have said on a few occasions that cognitive science casts doubt on this possibility, but I have yet to show why this is so. The experimental-behaviorist literature reviewed in chapter 5 only threatens the introspectionist if her thesis that persons are agents is given a mature neoclassical interpretation, but this is just what the Aristotelian humanist denies. As for eliminativism, I have thus far presented no argument to undermine it at all. Eliminativism is simply the *denial* of the humanist position from the perspective of the *same* conceptual understanding of agency. My aim is to dissolve this conflict, rather than grant victory to either of these sides, by rejecting the common conceptual understanding. I have not yet started to do that, however. All I have done so far is renarrate the philosophical history of economics in a way that squeezes mature anthropocentric neoclassicism between a rock and a hard place, leaving both Aristotelian humanism and eliminativism relatively unscathed.

The goal of this chapter is to directly undermine Aristotelian humanism by challenging individualism, introspectionism, and the thesis that people should be viewed as prototypical agents, even on the modest Aristotelian interpretation of agency that makes fewer demands than elaborated postwar neoclassicism. The three targets will all be shelled from one artillery placement: an interlocked set of theses on the metaphysics of personhood and agency inspired by contemporary cognitive science, and by philosophical interpretations of that science that derive directly or indirectly from the work of Dennett. Little in this chapter will surprise one of my foils, Mirowski. That Dennett's philosophical theses threaten humanism on the three fronts assailed here is, after all, just what he regards as dangerous about it, especially when it teams up with neoclassicism. The surprise for him will come in the next chapter, when despite the denial of all Aristotelian themes, the self will be preserved precisely by enriching intentional-stance functionalism with resources from game theory. My other foil, Dupré, will want to have his shields up at every point in this chapter.

One final note of orientation is in order before we get to work. The discussion in chapter 3 began with the posing of questions about the basis for the separateness thesis concerning the relationship between economics and psychology. The perspective taken there was that the separateness thesis should seem prima facie surprising. It should now seem especially dubious in light of the recent turn toward behavioral foundations in economics. As I have said several times, I will ultimately defend a new basis for separateness not found in any previous literature, let alone in canonical neoclassical sources. In light of this, my naturalist attitude to the philosophy of science makes me sensitive to a potential charge that I am *redefining* economics from a purely abstract and conceptual point of view. This is not allowed by the rules in force here. Philosophy is to be led by scientific practice, not the other way around. Hence my concern to anchor my account in the actual history of economic theory, to build a reinterpretation of the foundations of that theory that does not have to demand any radical, across-the-board discontinuity or sudden paradigm shift. There is a delicate tension here, because at the same time it should be clear that I mean to take the new experimental-behavioral evidence very seriously; achieving continuity will not mean agreeing with Jevons or saving his tradition by way of Becker's conservative bullet biting on preference stability.

One crucial fact that cannot be ignored—must, indeed, be explained, as philosophers of economics such as Rosenberg (1992) and Hausman (1992) have explicitly recognized—is that the working methodology of microeconomics, and its associated basic pedagogy, has shown much greater stability than have its high-level theoretical commitments. (In his essay discussed in the previous chapter, Sugden [2001] emphasizes the same point, and deplores it.) New textbooks such as those of Gintis (2000) and Bowles (2003) aim with forthright Kuhnian rhetoric to close this gap. But the gap has been undeniably persistent, and equally clearly more stubborn than what we seem to see in other disciplines. This leads to suspicion that either economic practice, or economic theory, are intellectual *games*, in the pejorative sense: on the first interpretation, theory is something practitioners need not really take seriously, while on the second interpretation the practice is a con job, unmasked by theorists, that economists will willfully pursue until policymakers wake up and stop paying them for it. My hypothesis, however, of a deep philosophical assumption about personhood and agency that hasn't been adequately questioned by *any* theoretical school in economics may be the key that enables us to hold on to continuity while going forward, and that accounts for the apparent faddishness of theory relative to practice without implying bad faith anywhere.

Let us thus retreat for a few moments from the dazzling new landscapes we considered with the eliminativists at the end of the previous chapter, to the duller and more familiar world of Economics 101, where Jevons could still feel at home. Undergraduate economics, like most technical subjects, is usually taught from a standard template, a small set of canonical textbooks very similar to one another, that varies with time but not place. For many decades—indeed, through what is still the major part of the discipline's history since 1870—the template for teaching microeconomics began by directing students' attention to Robinson Crusoe, alone on his island.[1] Robinson will allocate a certain proportion of his time to harvesting fruit for himself, another proportion to entertaining himself by rambling about the island, and another proportion to sleeping. These allocations will reveal his marginal preferences among labor and leisure. Suppose, then, that he decides to devote some of his time to making a fishing rod. He might first stash away some extra fruit to tide him over while he whittles, thus sacrificing some present leisure for the sake of an enhanced consumption-and-leisure basket later. Thus we have capital investment, and an opportunity for the rational Robinson to apply some neoclassical analysis in deciding how much time to spend harvesting the stockpile of fruit. Note that, so far, all of this is strictly uncommitted to any particular psychological or philosophical interpretation. It assumes only that Robinson's behavioral patterns are related to goals that are *his* in some sense or other, and that he faces scarcity in that all of the goals can't be maximized simultaneously.

There are good reasons why this pedagogy appealed to the early neoclassicists. First, it vividly isolates scarcity—in this case, of time—as the fundamental and distinctively economic condition, just as Robbins's definition emphasizes. Second, it helps to combat the Aristotelian fixation on money and commercial relations as the subject matter of economics by showing that the concept of capital analytically precedes that of the market. It is for both of these reasons that it is important that Robinson is alone: money makes no sense outside of a society of transactors, but both scarcity and capital do. Finally, and relatedly, an ideological purpose is served (but should not be exaggerated into justifying, all by itself, full-blown antisocialism): Robinson faces an economic problem, as an irremediable fact, for reasons that have no possible relation to social exploitation, and which he cannot will away by political action. If he wants to become wealthier (i.e., better and more interestingly fed, and capable of spending more time playing on the beach or lying in the shade) then he has to forego some present consumption of something.

The textbook story goes on to introduce Friday after this point, so that the teacher can explain neoclassical theories of exchange. Typically one will bring third or fourth or nth parties into the population as the topics to be studied become more complicated. This pedagogical procedure, of beginning with one person and then building an economic society by progressively adding individuals, each of whom arrives with a fully formed utility function, *need* not be motivated by metaphysical atomism; its building-block structure in serving day-to-day teaching objectives is sufficient to explain its roaring success as a meme complex. However, there is no doubt that it has been seductive in seeming to be *evidence* for atomism among people disposed, for either metaphysical or political reasons, to that picture. But this is just pure confusion. The story is consistent with atomism but is no evidence for it in any sense at all.

Many people have learned economics through Robinson Crusoe without being thereby led to deny, as Margaret Thatcher famously (and hilariously) did, that there is such a thing as society. However, it is harder to resist a subtler mistake, based on reasoning as follows. Something important, from a strictly economic point of view, clearly happens when Friday appears on the island; new kinds of economic variables and calculations—of the velocity of the circulation of money, for example—enter the graphs and equations that make no sense in his absence. But Robinson's utility function (by assumption) hasn't changed, and Friday's was likewise supposed to be already in place before he laid eyes on his new companion. So then what if both parties' *psychologies* are changed by their socialization, as seems highly plausible? In that case, given the claim that their utility functions have not altered, the socially sensitive psychological properties must be external to (privately determined) utility.

To appreciate why I am calling this mistake subtle, notice that it can go on to feed any member of the standard set of philosophies of economics (Marxism excepted). That it fits the neoclassical picture is obvious; it is designed to. Sen's anti-neoclassical humanist likewise accepts it (conceptually, at least) in going on to assemble internal utility and external social influences as distinct components of a vector of behavioral causation. Radical interpreters of the experimental-behavioral evidence can express *their* view by arguing that the causal weight of the internal component tends toward zero as the external influences are factored in; and this amounts to eliminativism about agency if one goes on identifying Robinson the economic agent with Robinson the solitary biological person. Where policy is concerned, both humanists and eliminativists can (though of course they might not) derive recommendations ideologically compatible with the Marxist's, by virtue of their stress on the importance of the external vector component; whereas neoclassical theorists who have given more weight to the internal component have ended up in both the socialist (e.g., Bergson) and libertarian (e.g., Becker and Friedman) camps. The very fact that one can reach so many different and incompatible theoretical destinations without having to abandon Robinson Crusoe pedagogy helps to shield the philosophical view it incorporates from isolation and criticism.

Marxist and radical feminist economists and philosophers of economics *have* consistently seen this point. This is, indeed a crucial part of what *makes* somebody a Marxist and/or a radical feminist if they're philosophically sophisticated about it. Of course, these perspectives are driven mainly by normative theses, and I will not be following them there. Let me note, however, that if part of my project here were to defend the normative political philosophy I happen to favor, liberalism, then in doing so I would *not* invoke any premises that depended on Robinson Crusoe pedagogy.

To be clear: the crass mistake encouraged by Robinson Crusoe pedagogy is to imagine that there really *are* pre-Friday Robinson Crusoes. (Margaret Thatcher's amazing idea depends on two crass mistakes, the second one being that the essence of *all* people is their "inner Robinson Crusoe." This is just the logical twin of the equally simplistic Marxist notion that the essences of all people are their ideologically constructed roles in material—Aristotelian—production relations.) What I am calling the subtle mistake is the belief that the conceivability of a totally socially alienated holder of preferences—a lone agent—bears some conceptual relationship to any aspect of an actual person, *and that this partly justifies the separateness thesis.* As noted above, Marxists (and radical feminists) are right in resisting this inference (which, typically, is usually a conceptual slide rather than an argument).

If the Thatcherite is somebody who relies on this slide to derive the claim that social relations are (or should be) unimportant to behavior, then few theoretical economists have been so silly. Recently, the "new institutionalists" (see North 1990; Ben-Nur and Putterman 1998; Bowles 2003; and the exploding associated literature) have recognized that such relations are in fact overwhelmingly dominant influences on human behavior, and experimental work has supported their insight. But if one goes down this road without reconceptualizing the relationship between economic agents and people, as opposed to just embedding its application in a model of society, the result is likely to be either Aristotelian humanism—decomposing the causation of behavior into internal and external vector components—or eliminativism—thinking that the empirical causal weight of the internal component is zero. *Because* the mistake is *not* crass or ideologically self-serving, and because in its eliminativist version it comports with some exciting new developments in wider behavioral science, it can lead to a rejection of the separateness thesis. That is, one can thereby suppose that after decades in the doldrums caused by isolation from behavioral science as encouraged by the separateness doctrine, economics is catching right up to its cognate disciplines. Indeed, it is just (properly) merging into them, as part of a seamless behavioral science that will have no space at all for either methodological individualism or a rationalistic conception of solipsistic utility maximization. But, the thinking proceeds, the maximization achieved in the Samuelsonian machine is supposed to be built out of the maximizing activities of the individual people that are its ultimately constituent cogs. So the Samuelsonian conception of economics is utterly wrong.

I certainly endorse the aspirations of economists to be contributors to a unified behavioral science. However, I want to resist the idea that unification requires, or is even well served by, the absence of seams. The sound basis for the separateness thesis is indeed not to be found where either Jevons or Robbins looked for it. However, the common mistake of the currently leading schools of thought in fundamental economic metatheory lies in their doubting the ontology encouraged by Robinson Crusoe pedagogy purely as an *empirical* hypothesis, when it in fact rests on a conceptual error. Working scientists might suppose that this charge, so flattering to the importance of philosophy, must, even if made persuasive, amount to trifling scholasticism, or to fussy intellectual history at best. The thesis is philosophical, to be sure. But I will argue that missing it threatens to undermine scientific economics altogether, and to carry us all the way back to the Aristotelianism from which Jevons and Walras and company began to set us at liberty, and of which a rigorously updated Samuelsonian conception truly makes us free.

It may help to orient philosophers and cognitive scientists if I now mention a well-known analogue to my charge, one to which I will later return for more substantive, nonanalogical purposes. Dennett (1991b) argues that neuroscientists and cognitive psychologists interested in the brain have, at least until the time of his book, treated Cartesian mind–body dualism as an *empirical* mistake instead of as *conceptually* hopeless, and that this had undermined their prospects of thinking usefully about, or appropriately trying to model and investigate, consciousness. In particular, it led them to imagine that consciousness could be the special function of some sort of organ sited at a particular place in the brain. On this view, Descartes's error was just the empirically bad guess that this organ wasn't made of physical stuff. However, as Dennett argues, the idea that consciousness is the function of an organ at all is conceptually muddled and misleading, and any hope of an adequate scientific account of consciousness requires that this be recognized. It is by means of this sort of insight, I claim, that philosophy can be truly helpful to science; and it is this sort of insight I am trying to urge on our understanding of the relationships between economics and psychology.

Individualism, Lockean Introspection, and Contemporary Models of Mind

Limited, purely methodological individualism might just refer to the virtues of Robinson Crusoe pedagogy as discussed above. That is, it is perhaps easier to think clearly about the foundational concepts of scarcity, capital, and marginal utility if you don't first complicate them with exchange (or with social norms). There can be no objection to this sort of methodological individualism as long as one takes steps to remind oneself that, some extreme autistics or psychopaths aside (perhaps), there are actually no such things as human preference profiles that are independent of social norms. More substantive theses of the kind that lead down the road to mistakes like Sen's must rest on one or another version of ontological and/or normative individualism. Substantive individualism can be analyzed into three distinct theses that have reinforced each other or, worse, sometimes been run together as indissoluble, during the history of economic (and wider philosophical) thought:

(1) *Social atomism.* All properties of social groups are decomposable into properties, some intrinsic and some relational, assignable to specific individuals constitutive of the groups in question.

(2) *Microeconomic individualism.* Individual utility functions range over only those objects that an individual could in principle evaluate in the absence of social relations.

(3) *Normative individualism.* All objects claimed to be socially valuable must find the justification for this value, if it can be found at all, in what is valued by one or more whole biological people.

According to Blaug (1980, p. 49), the phrase "methodological individualism" was first coined by Schumpeter[2] in the context of the latter's attempt to sharply separate thesis (3) from (1). Blaug blames Popper for muddying the water Schumpeter sought to clear, but this responsibility could no doubt be widely distributed.[3] It should in any case be obvious that (1) and (3) are entirely distinct claims, indeed barely logically related, since (1) is a descriptive claim about the properties of social groups and (3) is a normative claim about the properties of what people value. Indeed, I suggest that but for the implicit presence of thesis (2), (1) and (3) would have been much more difficult to confuse than has in fact been the case. Of course, (3) does not follow from (2) any more than it does from (1); but at least (2), unlike (1), has something explicitly to do with value. And since I have just argued that it is the additive construction of economies from individual people in Robinson Crusoe pedagogy that, abetted by the background assumption of (1), gave rise to (2), (2) forms the main historical-conceptual bridge between (1) and (3). Indeed, the normative, policy-relevant thesis of Sen's that leads so many people to casually accept his fallacious argument against RPT is precisely the "discovery" that (2) erroneously links (1) and (3).

As a political liberal[4] I am well disposed to thesis (3). However, as noted above, a sound defense of it—which is no part of the topic of this book—cannot be derived from an argument involving (1) or (2), since both of these theses are false. Denial of (1) requires a metaphysical argument against reductionism (but which does not involve magical emergentism). Such an argument can be either general or specific to social sciences; general arguments should be preferred as both more powerful and more secure. There are many such arguments, including a few sound ones, available in the philosophical literature; the one to which I am party is given in Ross 2000, Ross and Spurrett 2004a, and

Ross et al. forthcoming, and is the basis for the nonreductionist theory of existence stated in chapter 2. The argument will be summarized in outline form here. The only adequate basis for any metaphysical thesis—including, therefore, thesis (1)—must be induction over general trends in the progress of science. Although I do not suppose that special sciences must reduce to physics, if (1) were to have any hope of being true, it would have to at least be the case that the most plausible ontological interpretation of contemporary physics is atomistic. However, it is not.

Batterman (2000) argues that most theoretical (as opposed to purely manipulative) activity in physics consists in the search for what physicists call *universalities*. By this they do not mean, as a philosopher likely would, metaphysical principles necessarily holding everywhere, but physical facts that allow them to extract "just those features of systems, viewed macroscopically, which are stable under perturbations of their microscopic details" (p. 129). John Collier and coauthors have discussed the nature of the properties that hold perturbation-resistant systems together—the properties that result in what they call *cohesion* (Collier 1986, 1988; Collier and Muller 1998; Collier and Hooker 1999). Cohesion is the unity relation for a dynamical system (Collier 2002), and this in turn is the basis for regarding something as an entity. It then is a question of physical fact, not an a priori metaphysical principle, whether an object's cohesion relations reduce. When, in a given case, they don't, then the object in question is nonreducible. Such cases are ubiquitous in quantum physics. As Ladyman (2004) notes, "Entangled states of joint systems are just those that violate the principle that the joint state of the whole should supervene on the states of the parts, and as is well known, Bell's theorem tells us there is no consistent way of attributing states to the parts from which the properties of the joint system can be recovered (without action at a distance)." Wallace (2004) makes clear that this is not just a characteristic of exotic quantum objects:

Even a particular object like a table cannot really be regarded as a simple composite of non-overlapping microscopic parts. It's a tempting idea, to be sure: an extended body is just the mereological sum of its top and bottom halves, so why not subdivide indefinitely until we get to the microconstituents? But a solid object is a cloud of vastly many overlapping electron and nucleon wavefunctions: it's not clear even what is *meant* by which electron is in which spatial subregion of the object. . . . Furthermore, even the paradigmatically "physical" properties of the object are defined not in terms of the microconstituents, but dispositionally—even the mass (!) of a solid object can't really be defined as the sum of the masses of its atomic constituents. That algorithm gets the answer nearly right in most cases—but a helium nucleus weighs about 1% less than its constituents (that's why fusion works); a neutron star weighs about 10% less (Arnett 1996) than its constituents (that's why supernovas work). Our actual definition of mass is dispositional: something has mass m if it behaves thus-and-so on the scales, or creates such-and-such a gravitational field. It's not definitional that mass is additive; it's a physical law, and only an approximate one at that.

Modern metaphysical atomism reflects the fact that *physical* atomism was, for a long time, a productive working principle in physics. However, physicists have been progressively retreating from it as a serious ontological hypothesis since Newton. As the citations above indicate, it certainly does not comport naturally with current physical theory.

If metaphysical atomism fails in physics—and in chemistry and biochemistry (see chapter 2)—then, as Kincaid (1997) argues at length, it is surely an extraordinary idea to imagine it holding over the networks of relations among complex systems like people. I will not try to summarize here the extensive arguments against social atomism that have been the products of an enormous literature in the philosophy of social science. Even most economists these days, however traditional some of them might be in clinging to *methodological* individualism, do not deny that, as a result of the evolution of cultural norms that feed back into the dynamics of self-formation and create attractor basins in dynamic spaces that constrain and guide the behavior of individuals (and, therefore, interpretations of individual preference), there are irreducible social facts (Gilbert 1989). I will henceforth just assume that social atomism is flatly false. When I turn, in the next chapter, to the positive theory of the self, then the denial of social atomism will take a more interesting form (since merely claiming that a very strong reductionist claim isn't true says nothing about what is true).

Thesis (ii) above, economic individualism, is historically closely related to metaphysical and social atomism, but doesn't follow from it without a number of further, and tendentious, premises. Davis (2003, chapters 2 and 3) provides a compact but accurate philosophical survey of the relevant history. Classical economic individualism finds its deep roots in the early modern metaphysical psychology of Descartes and Locke, which amounted to an effort to run as strong a form of general atomism as has ever been essayed into the domain of the mental. These roots constitute an associationistic influence more than they do any clear paradigmatic argument; when science in general, and especially physics, were presumed to succeed on the basis of atomism, it was largely taken for granted as a working principle for any scientific economics. The fact that macroeconomics arrived so late onto the scene after years of refinement in microeconomics made it easy to ignore, for years, the fact that the assumed atomism was almost entirely inexplicit. This became more difficult when economists after Keynes had to confront questions about the relationship between macroeconomics and microeconomics. If metaphysical tradition suggested that the former ought to find its foundations in the latter, as it did, then some *explicit* formulation of the microeconomic individual needed to be accorded ontological priority, in some clear sense or other. By then the Samuelsonian formalization of the economic agent, usually supplemented by EUT as an account of that agent's maximization capacities, was available. Thus the new classical macroeconomics of Lucas (see Hoover 1988 for a philosophical and methodological study) could launch its program for applying microeconomic theory to macroeconomic phenomena by developing models of the maximizing behavior of an infinitely lived representative agent of the Samuelsonian type. However, as Davis (2003), following many others, notes, the kind of individualism promoted by this enterprise is purely methodological. Requiring as it does the assumption that all individuals whose dispositions are aggregated into those of the representative agents are identical can hardly be a basis for being theoretically explicit about what it is that determines the economically relevant *boundaries* between individuals.

Of course, the purely synchronic identity conditions on individuals are clear enough in any formalism that rests on RPT, with or without EUT: individuals are the numerically distinct objects of which utility functions are predicated. But, as I emphasized in my discussion of the absence of ontological commitment in Samuelson, this has no connection with any psychological, biological, or social phenomena at all until a nonformal interpretation of the relevant sort of "individual" is provided—and this is exactly what's at issue.

As Davis also discusses, however, even if the history of philosophy yields few arguments from metaphysical atomism to economic individualism proportionate in centrality and clarity to the importance of the association, the early modern philosophers certainly didn't fail to ask plenty of questions about what their presumed atomistic individuals had to be like in order to appear as plausible models of people.

Descartes launched the grand tradition by "gazing inward" and finding "clear and distinct ideas" whose only connection with anything external was via the roundabout guarantees of a benign deity; but it was Locke who theorized the modern atomic individual in its full richness. All of its distinguishing properties are inward and imminent: an individual "finds herself" directly in the registration of subjective perception—that is, introspection. As Davis discusses at length, this conception at once raises the issue of *reidentification*. If the individual is picked out by present, ostensive introspection, then on what basis can an individual be identified as *the same* individual at two or more separated points in time? Davis (2003, p. 50) accurately summarizes the Lockean answer as follows:

1. It is by our consciousness that we are selves to ourselves.

2. We remember or are conscious of ourselves being in our memories of the past.

3. The consciousness we have of ourselves in the present in our current experiences is the same consciousness we have of ourselves in the past.

4. Therefore, we are the same individuals in the present as we were in the past.

It is difficult to contest Charles Taylor's (1989) claim that this encapsulates the almost-universal picture of the self, consciousness, and the basis of the former in the latter, which constitutes the modern, Western metaphysics of personhood. This claim is tested, and confirmed, in freshman philosophy and psychology classes all over the Western world every September (February in the southern hemisphere): first-year students intuitively recognize it, and reason by means of it, on first encounter. So of course it has informed disciplines that rely on an ontological account of the self but haven't built one for themselves—such as economics.

The most sophisticated and critical extension of the self as a transcendental ground for unity in the history of Western philosophy is that of Kant. As Brook (1994) shows in detail, Kant's account is especially relevant in the present context because it is a direct response to the absence of an adequate basis for unity of consciousness in Locke's theory of mind, an absence that had been spotted by Hume. It thus isn't surprising that the most explicit and self-confident reliance on introspection we find from a major economic methodologist comes from the one who blended Kantianism and empiricism, that is, Robbins. Now, although I argued in chapter 3 that Robbins had imbibed a reasonably sophisticated epistemology that came indirectly from Kant, I can find no evidence that he either studied or inherited Kant's elaborate theory of the self, which was of much less interest to the early positivists. (Indeed, positivism had, throughout its history, Locke's problem in spades.) What can at least be said, however, is that if one wanted to construct a basis for economic individualism from some explicit psychological hypothesis found in an important economist, then working from Robbins's starting point would be the best bet. That is, if one were an introspectionist about utility, one could then advance an empirical thesis—and it would have to be empirical—to the effect that introspection of ordered preferences discovers them to range only over in-principle solipsistic desires. We have already seen that one can't get all the way from this starting point to Sen's criticism of RPT without invoking a strange theory of psychological reference. However, perhaps one could use it to at least get as far as an ontological justification for methodological individualism by way of methodological solipsism (see chapter 2). Now, we saw in chapter 3 that Robbins's own arguments fail to establish the economic psychology he wants for the sake of his denial of interpersonal comparisons of utility. That is, they license nothing stronger than Mandler's property of psychological concavity, which doesn't hold any promise as a possible premise for economic individualism. (They would be compatible, of course. What I mean is that after one derived or assumed psychological concavity, 100 percent of the work required to restrict the scope of the utility function would still remain to be done.)

So much for defensive parrying. I now want to defend a stronger claim, namely, that introspectionism in general is a hopeless thesis. The pendulum in philosophy of mind has at various times and for various reasons supported this verdict (and then swung back against it), but I will here ground it in reflections on contemporary cognitive science. Two accounts are specifically endorsed: Lyons (1986) puts the inadequacies of introspectionism as a psychological hypothesis into careful historical context, while Dennett (1987, 1991b) demolishes it in all its possible varieties.

Lyons's target is slightly more specific than Dennett's. That is, Lyons argues against the coherence of the idea that there could be anything like a faculty of inward perception. This thesis that Lyons disputes was the one embraced and elaborated by theoretical, as opposed to just folk, introspectionism in psychology in the days before behaviorism. This was known as "faculty introspectionism," and was supposed to be scientific because it was partly based on pseudoexperiments[5] intended to isolate the operations of the "faculty of introspection." This is probably what Robbins, who read some of the psychology of his time, had in mind in the passage I quoted in which he dismisses behaviorism. The value of hypothesizing a dedicated introspective faculty lies in the extent to which, in suggesting something like an organ, with a possibly distinctive modality of presentation, this gives clear content to the idea that introspection is a form of inner perception.

Unfortunately, the putative output of the introspective faculty lacked precisely the property that made perception the first and leading topic of systematic study in early psychology, namely, the existence of intersubjectively stable stimuli with which to compare it. To make matters worse, there was no physically accessible and independently demarcated transduction apparatus that could be studied from an engineering perspective. In the context of early, Kantian, positivism, there was a tension built into faculty introspectionism from the outset: the distinction between the noumenal and the phenomenal that lay at the heart of Kant's balancing act between realism and empiricism was not straightforwardly applicable to it. The positivists, tipping strongly toward the empiricist and phenomenal strains in Kant, but trying to eliminate the transcendental element, had no choice but to stress the importance of intersubjective access to data in their philosophy of science. This almost automatically gave faculty introspectionism the status of a pseudoscience.

At the same time, positivists could not be skeptics about phenomenal consciousness, since this was needed as the site of their famous "sense data," the ultimate epistemological anchors for all meaningful theoretical claims, according to them. They thus needed, for the sake of their epistemology, to believe in processes that were not obviously amenable to study by the lights of that very epistemology. The resulting ambivalence about consciousness in the philosophy of mind of the 1930s is reflected in Robbins's strange combination of the denial of the possibility of interpersonal comparisons of utility, on the one hand, and realism about introspectively available ordinal-utility judgments, on the other. To embrace behaviorism as an ontological thesis, as Quine eventually did, was to substantially abandon positivism. An unstable halfway stop on the way to this outcome, typified by Ryle, was to endorse a merely *methodological* behaviorism. This was, of course, exactly where Samuelson tried to settle. Like many views that compromise on relentless philosophical consistency, methodological behaviorism has attractions for common sense. Only the most extreme, and genuinely implausible, versions of behaviorism deny that people (and other animals) process information about some of their internal states, and that this information influences their behavior. (Such extreme behaviorism has never really been taken seriously in psychology; see Lyons 1986, chapter 2.)

The problem, however, is that agnosticism about facultative introspection strands this commonsense conviction from any systematic connection to the rest of one's science. Hypothesized introspectively accessed information is interestingly different from other information only in the presence of background suppositions to the effect that there is something called consciousness that plays a special role in both guiding (some) behavior, and in establishing the identity conditions of a person, and that introspective awareness is the distinct mode of awareness characteristic of this sort of consciousness. (Note that the role of such consciousness in fixing personal identity is especially important to microeconomic individualism, since this is what might give some preferences—the consciously accessible ones—suggested by or manifest in an agent's behavior special normative priority over others.) It is evidence for the importance of the urge to systematicity in science that philosophical instability of this sort is seldom tolerated for long, however appealing the temptations of "common sense" might be.

In the case at hand, there are only two options for resolving the instability. One must either surrender *all* commitment to verificationism, that is, to the idea that intersubjective access to data is a requirement for scientific objectivity, or one must find a way of studying internal information processing without relying on facultative introspectionism to do so. It is not a great simplification to say that Dennett's philosophical career has been the leading implementation of the second option. Note carefully that this option does not require an a priori denial that there *is* such a thing as facultative introspection that could be empirically discovered; it merely requires eschewing introspection as a direct source of evidence. This puts the finger exactly on the point of substantial difference between Robbins and Samuelson as economic methodologists.

As the history of empirical cognitive science has worked out, no empirical evidence for facultative introspection has been forthcoming. As we will see in a moment, this is not retrospectively surprising. Skepticism about introspection as a distinctive kind of process does not entail skepticism about consciousness. But this is partly because, whereas the concept of introspection is a relatively clear one, the concept of consciousness is anything but. Often by "consciousness" the folk just mean "awareness" (of the world, including, as above, some aspects of their internal states). Dennett agrees that there is certainly plenty of that around in the animal kingdom. On other occasions, the folk mean by "conscious content" whatever it is that is stable in their descriptions (to others and to themselves) of their own characters, that is, the cluster of properties that people use to construct and maintain "selves." As should by now be clear from the past few chapters—and as both Mirowski and Davis recognize—this is the sense in which questions about consciousness are relevant to the foundations of microeconomics. As we will see in the next chapter, Dennett provides a subtle and illuminating theory of what selves are and how they arise, so he doesn't doubt their reality either. What he *does* deny, and what then sometimes gets confused with denial of consciousness, selfhood, or "real" agency,[6] is introspection: that there is any *one* kind of psychological phenomenon or process that could serve as the intended referent for *both parts at once* of the undifferentiated folk-psychological concept of consciousness.

It will be helpful to now schematize the bodies of thought I have discussed in detail in terms of the disjunction between denying introspection (either methodologically or ontologically) and denying consciousness and selfhood (either methodologically or ontologically). This is just the disjunction to which, I claim, Mirowski and Davis pay inadequate regard. Neither Samuelson nor the eliminativist economists discussed in chapter 5 clearly notice the disjunction either; thus their positions should charitably just be regarded as methodological. Samuelson, I argued in chapter 3, should probably have sided with Quine *had* he attended to the disjunction; but, I also argued, in his methodology he didn't, and so when as more philosophically self-conscious analysts we ontologically interpret his methodology, we find him stumbling into the view explicitly maintained by Dennett and Binmore. Where the eliminativist economists are concerned, a parallel interpretative procedure lines them up with Quine. This is summarized in table 6.1. It is time now to remove the positions occupied by Robbins and the humanists as options. The positions occupied by Quine and the eliminativists will stay open until the end of chapter 8.

We talk of "finding" conscious contents in ourselves by "looking inward" with a "mind's eye." These are obviously metaphors, though:

Table 6.1
Targets of denial

	Denies introspection	Denies consciousness and selfhood
Robbins	No	No
Sen (Humanist economists)	No	No
Samuelson	Yes	No*
Dennett	Yes	No
Binmore	Yes	No
Quine	Yes	Yes
Eliminativist economists	Yes	Yes*

* Unwittingly, by implication.

there are no pictures in our brains (it's too dark in there, for one thing), or clangings, or tastes of curry powder. The metaphors must be trying to pick out some analogous structures, which share explanatorily relevant properties with (moving) pictures, and so forth, located in some physical or functional parts of our brains. There is thereby supposed to be a stream of conscious content that plays before us like a film in what Dennett calls the "Cartesian theater." This theater anticipates the coming virtual media made possible by our newest technologies, because its patron can not only see and hear the actors, but can taste, smell, and touch along with them too. One wants to say that she can also introspect with them . . . but then we realize we mustn't say that and the whole story begins to unravel. We have just stumbled over the regress problem, which Dennett makes vivid by asking who is supposed to be watching the film. If consciousness is taken to be (inter alia) the behavioral headquarters that defines the self, then it must be me that watches the film and makes behavioral and other decisions on the basis of what I see. Now we have the worst sort of regress: I am "in" me. And how does the first me, the watcher, work? Is there another, smaller, Cartesian theater in *there*?

This folk picture is self-evidently hopeless. Before I sketch Dennett's positive alternative to it—which will lead us back toward a new, defensible version of behaviorism—let us first note that the purely negative points just summarized are already sufficient to banish the folk concept of introspection. There is virtually no positive content to that concept other than: what a person does when she examines the display in the Cartesian theater. Since there cannot be any such thing as the Cartesian theater, there is therefore no such thing as simple introspection in the crude folk sense.

Is there, then, a less implausible kind of introspection that might be supported by cognitive science? As Lyons demonstrates, the prebehaviorist version of the idea that probably influenced Robbins was not rehabilitated after behaviorism's fall from power. Many models in the days of classical AI blithely posited mental analogues to random-access memory in models of mind based on von Neumann–style computer architectures. However, as Dennett (1991b and elsewhere) points out, these models were almost all silent on the question of who is supposed to receive the information retrieved by such processes. That is, they precisely avoided identifying mental reference to internal content with introspection. An exception is the account of Baars (1988), in which consciousness is analyzed in terms of computational processes that implement self-monitoring. However, here the large philosophical literature on putative phenomenal *qualia*[7] is relevant.

Although I am, like Dennett, skeptical about the explanatory value of supposing that the concept of qualia picks out any theoretically unifiable class of cognitive objects (see Ross 1993a), one thing the qualia debate of the 1990s established is that mere retrieval of internally stored data in computational processing is at best a weak necessary condition, falling far short of sufficiency, for introspective awareness (see Chalmers 1996). Indeed, a key element that divides Dennettian behaviorists from defenders of qualia is the insistence by the latter that qualia are distinguished from other objects of cognition by being amenable to individuation only by reference to qualitative properties that can't be captured in computational representations. What Robbins needs to ground his introspectionist account of economic agency, namely, direct perceptual access to the fact that preferences are ordered, is exactly the sort of thing that current believers in introspection distinguish such processes as *not* being about.

The above debate is in many ways a philosophical by-product of assumptions about the mind built into classes of computational models that are no longer taken very seriously in cognitive science. What, then, of the more plausible models coming from neuroscience? The rapidly developing picture of the way in which brains contribute to mind furnishes no evidence at all for, and much evidence against, any physically or functionally specifiable distinction between the inner (i.e., methodologically solipsistic) registration of information about internal states and registration of information about external states. (See Quartz and Sejnowski 2002 for an accessible and philosophically alert survey.) The brain must of course track various boundary points between the organism and its environment, but these boundaries can be cross-cutting and flexible, and are certainly not distinguished by some general procedure of tagging all processed information with generic "inside" and "outside" markers. I will say more below, in the context of discussing the biological basis for agency, about why evolution would be most unlikely to, indeed probably could not, build brains that implemented any such procedure.

I thus claim that the cognitive and brain sciences, even in those theoretical quarters most hostile to behaviorism (in either Watsonian or Dennettian versions), show no sign of underwriting the kind of introspection necessary to support a Lockean basis for economic individualism. For the benefit of readers who are philosophers, let me emphasize that I am not here asserting that no broadly Kantian understanding of consciousness is compatible with contemporary science. I think this is so, but no arguments given here are nearly sufficient to justify such an assertion. I'm claiming only that the development of cognitive science is making the idea of direct inner perception of facts that might underwrite neoclassical economic individualism look increasingly quaint and far-fetched. I don't think that this claim will be controversial among either cognitive scientists or philosophers of mind.

Having planted this modest flag on ground I don't expect to be contested, I will now add that the case against an introspective basis for economic agency looks especially hopeless from a Dennettian perspective. The reasons for this will be evident as I now go on to develop that perspective for application to economics and its relationship to psychology. My criticism of introspectionism therefore doesn't end with the point I'm claiming to be uncontroversial. However, it gradually passes over into the positive account of consciousness and selfhood that is necessary for showing why we do not confront a disjunction between introspectionism and eliminativism.

Since, as noted, Dennett denies neither the fact of awareness of some internal content, nor the existence of processes that fence off some content as constitutive of a "self," the dissolution of introspection promoted by him and by Lyons must be accompanied by a positive theory of thought and content that can explain both of these things that the folk mistakenly reify under an undifferentiated concept of "consciousness." Dennett's theory of consciousness is called the "multiple-drafts model" (MDM), and it stands in an essential relation of mutual support with intentional-stance functionalism. Indeed, these are two faces of one general theory, since neither part is ultimately plausible without the other.[8] To this I now turn.

The Multiple-Drafts Model of Consciousness

Before I begin describing and then extending Dennett's theory, let me offer a few self-conscious reflections about the weight I'm about to rest on his highly controversial MDM. The way in which MDM and intentional-stance functionalism are stronger than the sum of their parts (see Ross 1994a) is logically similar to the intended relationship between my account of economics and Dennett's philosophy of mind. If the former makes economic theory more internally coherent against pressure from doubts like those of Mirowski and Dupré, this can simultaneously be new *evidence for* the Dennettian theory on which it partly rests, because part of what rationally grounds belief in a theory's truth is its fruitfulness in explaining facts that weren't part of its original brief. This kind of nonvicious circularity in justification is risky, and is often ridiculed by scientific philistines, but it's an indispensable and historically ubiquitous part of scientific justification. (Note also that in what follows I will freely supplement Dennett's own theory with later contributions from others that build on it.)

Brains are massively parallel processors. At any given time, a synaptically large brain, especially the largest kind (ours), is busy computing a staggering quantity of distinct informational transformations. In this respect, brains are like national economies. Decades ago, Hayek (1960) offered his devastating critique of central planning as a basis for economic policy—one subsequently, and overwhelmingly, borne out by experience—when he pointed out that massively parallel information processing can't, as a matter of physics, be controlled through a serial bottleneck if it is supposed to keep up with a dynamically evolving and partly independent set of external control targets. Early AI research rediscovered Hayek's point when it naively took "the person" to be a site of executive control and tried to build such control sites into computers; the result, diagnosed and known as "the frame problem," was a series of models whose successes in narrowly serial tasks that people find hard, like arithmetic, were accompanied by hilariously flat-footed failures in real-time tasks, like avoiding walls, that people find easy thanks to neural parallelism (see Pylyshyn 1987). (Note, contra

Mirowski, that it was this, not crashing against Gödel's incompleteness theorem, that wore away confidence in classical AI.)

The key to stability of response in large brains, as in national economies, lies in getting lots of distributed information processing coordinated *without* having to bring it all together in a command suite for an executive decision. Most information needs to be handled by semiautonomous sites whose isolation from the global tasks faced by the system doesn't matter much, thanks to the existence of filter and alarm systems that call in other resources only when the relatively ignorant functionaries are surprised. This much was grasped even in classical AI. The subtle point requires going one step further and recognizing that, though a possible account of thought can let semiautonomous processes and recursively assembled teams of processes get called in for novel situations, one kind of helper we must *not* try to recruit, on pain of vitiating the whole project, is a president who sits beyond the filter or who listens for the alarms.[9] There cannot be a boss with the capacity to coordinate everyone else, or even with the capacity to decide when everyone else needs coordination; for such a boss must represent the very kind of bottleneck that a successful theory has to discharge.

As everyone who has taught undergraduate economics, or evolutionary theory, or cognitive science, knows all too well, powerful human intuitions cause us to worry that in complex systems without strong executives we must get chaos. However, equally persuasive experience competes with the force of this intuition. Economists understand how prices and rates of supply can remain within stable, relatively predictable bands—far from perfectly reliably, of course, but *astonishingly* often relative to folk expectations—and be more or less coordinated with each other, even when nobody in particular monitors and manages them. Ecologists understand, in general, how ecosystems can approximately maintain equilibria without executives; this is why they stress the danger in our hope that we can manage ecosystems back to grace after we've damaged them. Let us not overstate the point: many subtly but significantly different stories can be told about just what is and isn't understood about these sorts of dynamics. For the moment, we just need the claim that dynamic stability is no longer, in general, mysterious. What is needed, most generally, is some sort of feedback in the system, so that processes that wander too far from equilibrium will either die out through selective pressure or be corrected by some autocatalytic regulative damping. And, of course, this sort of stability need never be absolute: all it's sensible to demand is explanation of stability that lasts long enough to be interesting. No stability need be forever, and presumably no stability can be.

MDM is the hypothesis that, in effect, the brain is a kind of decentralized information market. I imagine that Mirowski would be inclined to read some ideological or tropic faddishness into this, but I don't think the actual intellectual history suggests this. One is driven to something like MDM by the combined pressures of the frame problem and the impossibility of a Cartesian theater. Both imply that there can be no central site in the brain where, as Dennett puts it, "everything comes together." Aspects of complex problems have to be handled in parallel by distributed teams of subagents, and these teams have to be partially encapsulated from each other with respect to their sharing of information. "You" *couldn't* be directly privy to everything going on in your brain—I say directly because, in principle, a neuroscientist could study your brain and then tell you—and, for the same reason, no functional processing in the brain can be sensitive to all other, or even to many other, concurrent functional processes. We mustn't suppose that the multiple drafts of partial solutions to problems being computed in bits of brains functionally partition problems into any neat disaggregation, since even that requires an implausible level of internal bureaucratic organization. The level of abstraction at which a given problem is solved, both at the subsystem levels and at the whole system level, is itself up for grabs. As a result, whole systems sometimes solve their problems at ineffective levels of abstraction. If all I manage to see about my investment problem is that I should try to sell my portfolio for more than I paid for it, I won't make any money except by accident. This, alas, is the normal predicament where that problem is concerned.

According to MDM, the self-as-executive, or as central receiving depot for integrated information, does not occupy any stable site in the neural information-processing architecture. When the ongoing dynamics are probed—because the person is asked a question by an interrogator, or surprised by a novel environmental contingency—*some* information being processed *somewhere* will get privileged ("selected for fame," as Dennett puts it) and interpreted as the current content of consciousness. However, this is itself a product of the very dynamics being probed, coupled with the action of the probe itself. The "content of consciousness" at a given time is not a background fact independent of the subject's behavioral response to the probe. It is not, in particular, a fact about what happens to be going on in some special physical or functional part of the brain. The reported content of consciousness is in every case an *interpretation*, a *judgment*, by a subject of some subset of all the information physically available to it, only some of which will be information about internal states. The judgments in question involve exactly the sort of triangulation among external conditions, proprioperceptive signals, overall behavioral track record, and expectations about what the source of the probe wants, that go on in conversations between people. Reports about the contents of consciousness are thus judgments that result from a subject's taking the intentional stance toward herself.

The idea that consciousness is not an inner state challenges the folk view of the person quite radically. One therefore can't reasonably expect it to be accepted until one has shown how it can handle a range of phenomena. In particular, one must show how it, or any similar story that effectively turns the person into a *process* of dynamic coupling between internal information processing and environmental stimulation, can account for both behavioral and affective stability. (Davis [2003] has his finger on this, and is right to see that neoclassicism shorn of Lockean foundations faces the same challenge.) One might suppose that a raw theory of neural equilibrium dynamics coupled with environmental control parameters could explain the stability of cat behavior, or, if even that is asking too much, cockroach behavior. Cats, or at least maybe cockroaches, don't (we reasonably suppose) have any sense that there *is* a unifying fulcrum, a place where perceptual output, judgment, and behavior all come together.

But people do. If *your* brain (*whose* brain?) processes the thought that the officer writing your traffic ticket has funny ears, *you* get to both notice and register this judgment *and* decide not to integrate it into the rest of your behavior. *You* can treat this as one of many draft models of what could be said or put to other further use, but will not (at least for now) be published. Indeed, *you* even have the power (up to a point) to decide whether to store the draft away for possible later use (in your anecdote of the event), or edit it out so irrevocably that it won't even be subsequently available to *you*.[10] We haven't successfully disposed of the intuitions supporting the folk concept of introspection until we've said who this "you" is, in a way that doesn't turn you into an internal executive. This is why, far from abolishing the self, Dennett's underlying main project has been to explain what the self actually is, which processes give rise to it, and how it indeed stabilizes behavior to the extent that it does.

The account I will give of the foundations of the self emerges from Dennett's, but then expands on and enriches it by linking it back to the Robbins–Samuelson conception of economic explanation that I'm constructing. It thus forms a crucial part of the positive answer to both the eliminativist challenge described in the previous chapter, and to the humanist skepticism that resists neoclassicism and behaviorism because they supposedly threaten the self. However, before I start building this positive thesis in the next chapter, there is still some more negative work to be done in this one.

Not all of the intellectual background to individualism comes from the modern period. Older than either social atomism or economic individualism is a conceptual association between personhood and agency that goes back at least to Aristotle. Now, as argued in Ross 1994a, another aspect of Dennett's challenge to our folk view of ourselves lies in something he himself hasn't explicitly noted, namely, that his accounts of intentionality and consciousness, when put together, sever the tight Aristotelian link between personhood and agency. Driving this wedge as deep as possible is an important part of my project here, because doing so will be the basis on which my account of the relationship between economics and psychology will preserve separateness, and thereby differ significantly from the philosophy of economics encouraged by the standard philosophical gloss on behavioral-experimental literature.

Agency and Personhood: Entirely Distinct Ideas

Agency, like almost all notions central to philosophizing about people, began its career as a folk concept.[11] Folk psychology, and much legal and normative practice based on it, requires a distinction between responsible initiators of states of affairs, and mere unwitting participants in causal chains who happen to be animate or human. When using their concept in philosophical innocence, the folk intend nothing very clear, in general, about what kind of responsibility agents must have. Since most applications of the concept occur in normatively charged circumstances, particular uses typically rely on the wider social context to pick out mixes of epistemic and moral standards against which members of the relevant community are judged, and are expected to expect to be judged.

Since the idea of agency has these roots in overtly normative social dynamics, and has seldom been used in such a way as to make it hostage to the development of any science, including psychology or economics, a humanist (such as Dupré) who might have suffered through my expropriation of "intentionality" and "consciousness" as objects for contestation between eliminativists and Dennettians, will have extra grounds for crying foul when I propose to carry off "agency" for scientific legislation too. We surely make the victory of scientism too easy, it will be objected, if the scientific realist gets to determine *all* the terms of debate, even on terrain where no one imagined that conceptual construction was partly engaged in protoscience. In general, if social contexts usually make particular applications of the concept of agency clear enough for business at hand, why should a philosopher seek to reform it? In doing so, are we not egregiously ignoring Wittgensteinian injunctions against trying to regiment well-functioning language games out of misguided Platonic impulses?

Wittgensteinian objections of this sort are too complacent. I think this is so in general, but I will here confine my attention to the concept at hand. If all we may demand of a well-functioning language game is that the folk participating in it "know how to go on," then perhaps we might not be moved to philosophical intervention in the case of agency. However, the chief reason why the folk feel little pressure to be clearer about what sort of responsibility is entailed by agency, even in circumstances of life and death, is that agency inherits a good deal of *apparent* clarity from its embeddedness in the larger folk theory of mind. If people were machines driven about by internal ghosts, then we could say roughly, but efficiently for everyday purposes, that they exercise their agency whenever their bodies' motions are more or less direct consequences of the interactions of their beliefs and their desires. Insofar as their bodies move as a result of other sorts of causes, no agency is involved. Particular legal and moral codes would then represent, in part, community decisions as to just how unmediated and uncomplicated the relevant causal relations between internal belief-desire complexes and actions have to be for various normative purposes. However, in that case what enables the folk who play language games involving agency to go on is merely a network of false beliefs about their own psychology. As discussed in chapter 2, almost no behavioral scientists these days are internalists, and suppose that people have causally efficacious states in their brains corresponding to isolable beliefs and desires. No one who is persuaded by either intentional-stance functionalism or eliminativism can claim to know how to "go on with" a nonregimented folk concept of agency, unless she thinks that attributions of responsibility are *merely arbitrary* communal rituals, and that it's alright to base moral and legal rewards and sanctions on such things.

As Davis (2003, p. 65) recognizes, we can also motivate some reform of agency through considerations that humanists agree to be philosophically well motivated. One of the more fraught clusters of issues in social scientific methodology centers around the question of which kinds of active units should be modeled as agents. Both social atomists and methodological individualists hold that nothing larger than a whole person can be a proper agent, and that characterizations of larger aggregates—countries, classes, corporations, and so forth—in terms of goals, purposes, beliefs, and desires (even on an externalist, attributionist interpretation of them) are at best risky metaphors. Structuralists of various sorts protest that this amounts to denying that there is a meaningful sphere for social-level explanation at all; but then even they must do implausibly hard philosophical work to legitimate claims that don't seem at all difficult to take as true and informative, such as "Britain wanted to win World War II." This issue smells like a pseudo-problem—that is, something perennially difficult to settle intuitions about, but unreal outside of a self-consciously philosophical context. Most people know how to reason tolerably well with statements that treat groups as agents, in the absence of any attention to metaphysics; and yet when the methodological individualists pose their challenge, it seems to be a stumper. How *could* something like Britain be an agent? This sort of question discomfits historians and sociologists because of the way in which the folk concept of agency derives its coherence from folk psychology. If Britain is an agent, then we are apt to think that we need an ontologically respectable place in which to lodge its beliefs and desires; but there seems to be no such place.

There is a large philosophical literature not driven by scientific realism that is no less shy about regimenting the folk conception of agency. The point of this activity has mainly been to bring coherence to the folk concept by holding it accountable to standards of logic. I am of course not much in sympathy with this project, which might be referred to as the "pure" philosophical enterprise. However, it provides a useful wedge for motivating conceptual reform without directly begging the question against the humanist. I will therefore initially orient the discussion in this section by reference to it, before ultimately discharging its assumptions.

Agency has been among the two or three most central concepts of philosophy throughout its history. Its celebrity status starts with Aristotle, who makes its exercise the logical basis for ethics. From this first moment, agency was also linked tightly to human distinctiveness. Thus, for Aristotle, an agent is roughly defined as a being that can entertain, and take steps to fulfill, "reasonable desires." Since reason is taken by Aristotle to be the defining property of the fully human, it follows for him both that only humans (and, perhaps, divine spirits) can be agents, and that all morally competent humans must be agents. Aristotle makes no self-conscious distinction between moral competence and moral significance, and this led some later philosophers to weaken the logical bond between agency and moral importance. Thus the utilitarians replaced agency with sentience as the essential property in this regard, and contemporary environmentalists typically reserve moral responsibility for agents while distributing moral significance very generously. However, these days utilitarianism is out of fashion and Aristotelianism (of a sort) is in. Due to the present Aristotelian renaissance in several branches of both moral philosophy and action theory, the doctrine of agency as the distinctive locus for distinctively human kinds of responsibility, both causal and moral, is flourishing. The work of Martha Nussbaum (1981, 1994) has been especially influential in this regard, and plays a direct role in the foundations of Sen's distinction, discussed in the previous chapter, between utility-based and agency-based conceptions of well-being.

For present purposes, I will bypass questions about the relation of the agency concept to specific moral theories simply by conceding that moral discourse has no practical point except among agents, whatever, precisely, agents turn out to be. That is, I will grant that if a system's behavioral dispositions can be modified by moral arguments directed to it for its own consumption then it is an agent (in at least some, possibly extended, sense), though the converse is of course not generally true. This leaves the question of what makes something an agent in the first place open. Such pre-ethical, ontological, inquiry into the basis of agency has generally focused on the relationship between agency and personhood, which, as just noted, is rendered into something close to necessary coextensivity by Aristotle and by some contemporary Aristotelians. In strong contrast to this view, I will argue that on the most parsimonious conceptual regimentation consistent with contemporary cognitive and behavioral science an individual cognitively and emotionally competent adult human only approximates agency in an indirect sense, and that although there are organisms that are indeed paradigmatic agents—insects, for example—humans are not instances of such organisms.

Approaching the problem, as agreed, from a social-pragmatic rather than a scientific perspective, let us start by asking: what, in advance of putting an already constructed concept of agency to work in moral practice or theory, do we want the concept *for*? That is, what intuitions about the way the world works is the concept supposed to integrate? The popular conception of an agent, directly descended from Aristotle's, turns it into something like a synonym for "human self," but puts emphasis on the causal effectiveness of such selves. Some candidate agents—countries and corporations, for example—may not be human selves, but if they can coherently be regarded as agents at all, then their agency is expected to be understood and justified by reference to the kind of causal effectiveness associated with such selves. On this understanding humans are of course prototypical agents, by assumption. This by no means renders the concept trivial. On this interpretation, being an agent is an *aspect* of being (typically and competently) human, and the aspect crucial for full-blown ethical and epistemic responsibility.

Consider, for example, the very typical procedure adopted by John Bishop in his 1989 study of the conditions for naturalizing agency (as part of what I have called the "pure" philosophical project). It might superficially appear that Bishop provides an analysis of agency itself, but such an impression would be misleading. Rather, Bishop shows us how to reduce reference to causation-by-agents to certain formulations of more standard event causation, so as to eliminate the otherwise apparent need for special, crypto-Cartesian kinds of causal relations (that is, causal relations of a metaphysical kind that is special to reasoning beings). How is it possible for this task to be attempted without some prior analysis of agency itself? The answer lies in Bishop's Aristotelian assumption about why agency matters. His naturalization project mainly involves answering skeptical arguments to the effect that the natural causal order leaves no room for moral responsibility. Hence he requires a variety of event causation sufficient for justification of assignment of events to agents as causal authors, where the sense of agency involved must be strong enough to support moral as well as epistemic agency. Bishop can therefore derive his relevant distinguishing properties of agency-in-general from whatever is taken to be *necessary* for the exercise of moral agency. But since he certainly does not take agency-in-general to be sufficient for moral agency (as almost no one does), he need never ask what is necessary and/or sufficient for agency-in-general. In this respect, as noted, his approach is typical of work on the metaphysical foundations of moral and epistemic responsibility.

Action theory, as another branch of "pure" philosophical analysis, often takes this foundational picture for granted. It thus proceeds in a way that is largely orthogonal to a large literature in the philosophy of cognitive science in which the concept of agency is taken as a placeholder for whatever helps us to systematically distinguish the class of *behaviors*, motions directed at goals on the contingent initiative of the systems whose goals the goals are, from motions in general.[12] The exchange of presuppositions in these two literatures has usually been mutual. That is, action theorists since the 1980s often assume that cognitive science will furnish accounts of the empirically necessary conditions for agency-in-general, while they work toward sufficient conditions for its more demanding regions of application in science and in moral life. Cognitive scientists, in turn, often imagine that the action theorist's (and the moral metaphysician's) agent lies somewhere in the future developmental trajectory of their own disciplines. However, the standards against which these conceptions of agency are evaluated are fundamentally different. In the one case, agency is whatever is necessary for moral and epistemic responsibility. In the other case, agency is whatever is sufficient for goal-directed behavior. Some contemporary work—that of Dennett, and of many contributors to the now flourishing "naturalized moral psychology" literature (see May, Friedman, and Clark 1996)—is sensitive to the conceptual dialectic here. However, a good deal of other philosophical work, consisting in studies of the syllogistic apparatus necessary and sufficient for practical rationality,[13] *looks as if* it bridges a conceptual gap that it in fact merely finesses.

This tension within the concept of agency has been manifest in philosophical explorations of the significance of AI research since the 1960s. If agency is the capacity to implement practical rationality, then it follows that the class of agents might be wider than that of the human. What has usually been taken to be crucial to issues around this possible growth of the agents' club is the question of the etiology of goals. Thus Searle (1980), trying to argue that the club will not expand, thinks he can do this if he can show that no computer could be the source of its own intentionality, in part because it could not be the source of its own intentions. (See Dennett 1987, chapter 8, for discussion.) By contrast, Dretske (1988) and many others suppose that they *do* need to— and can—win the day for the possibility of nonhuman agency by showing that certain systemic properties, not essentially anchored in biology, can be the basis for autonomous goal generation and modification.

In this debate, Dennett (1987) occupies a lonely position by denying that anything is an *autonomous* goal generator, and for this reason he has not infrequently been accused of denying the possibility of agency. Dennett rejects this imputation, for reasons I regard as sound. I will return to this issue, in a wider context, in the next chapter. My point in referring to it at the present juncture is only to indicate that most contemporary philosophers agree, as the debate shows, that the class of agents and the class of "fully selved" humans are not logically coextensive, thus enabling them to wonder about the extent to which these classes are contingently coextensive. But the majority of participants in the debate think that the right way to pose the question is to ask whether computers could do what humans can in the domain of generating, representing, and justifying relations between their goals and their actions. They thus show themselves to be firmly in the Aristotelian tradition of taking humans to be the prototypical agents, even while they no longer suppose that agents are essentially human.

Many contemporary philosophers, however, are no longer willing to help themselves to a style of reasoning that was historically central to Aristotle's identification. For him, the rationality that was the distinguishing mark of agency was not just instrumental. Aristotle takes certain *kinds* of goals as necessary for agency, and then he makes one of them—the goal of seeking truth—sufficiently abstract that it seems to be beyond the reach of creatures who cannot linguistically metarepresent. This is not an aspect of Aristotle's thought, however, that has enjoyed the renaissance of his ethics. Although there are still plenty of philosophers—and, thanks to Sen, some economists—around who endorse his view that some objects of striving are objectively rationally superior to others, few any longer try to get to this conclusion by the classical route. The putative members of the set of superior objects of pursuit that once seemed to require explicit metarepresentation in order to be pursued are basically Plato's trio: goodness, truth, and beauty. But it was Aristotle himself who began to back away from

Plato's insistence that what is pursued by the rational agent is *the* true or *the* good, as opposed to specific beliefs that are thought to be true and specific forms of action that are thought to be good.

Aristotle's worries here were mostly logical, but the combined influence since then of empiricists and pragmatists and, most important of all, of Darwinian thinking, has added anthropological grounds for this particularism: it simply does not seem to do justice to the facts about human behavior to regard most people's conduct as being a confused or mistaken approximation to that of the Platonic philosopher. As Quine (1969) emphasized, nonhuman animals have the same motivation, whether it is entertained or not, for seeking some true beliefs (though not qua "true" beliefs, of course) as people do, namely, their value to survival. But, furthermore, this value is not absolute in either case. Inferential processes that are likely to lead to false beliefs more often than not may be preferable for animals, including humans, wherever the cost of acting on a false positive is lower than that of not acting on a false negative, or where the computational costs of caring relentlessly about truth are very high, as they often are. Stephen Stich (1990) has pushed this skepticism about the rationality of the pursuit of the classical epistemic virtues to extreme, but not implausible, lengths. The idea that humans set the standard for agency by virtue of having special goals whose rational pursuit is the core of agency is thereby undermined. As we saw in the last chapter, no account of epistemic rationality, neither EUT nor any of its more recently articulated rivals, can at present claim clear support from empirical studies as a *general* account of actual practical reasoning.

Considerations of this sort weaken one metaphysical motivation for the classical conception of agency, but they are unlikely to be decisive. Still taking care not to just legislate away the humanist's worries about scientism, can we nevertheless help to answer the pragmatic question about the ontological point of the agency concept by looking into its uses in science? Behavioral scientists of various sorts have required some practical *work* of the concept of agency, and they have generally not been prepared to make this conceptual role hostage to any particular normative theory of the hierarchy of goods. Economists, especially, have needed agency for purposes very similar to those of analytic action theorists, namely, to ground formal theories of practical rationality. But whereas action theorists have often been content to test their models against intuitions about how a morally and/or epistemically rational *person* would proceed, thereby begging the question as to whether agency and personhood are coextensive concepts, economists have usually preferred to be more cautious in their foundational assumptions. Philosophers (and others) have often tended to mock economists' conception of agency as being, among other things, unresponsive to everyday experience and intuitions about the nature of people (Dupré 2001 being exhibit A), but, again, this begs the present question. In fact, as Davis (2003) recognizes, the attempts by neoclassical economists to work out a specifically *economic* conception of agency for their practical purposes exemplifies my present claim that a body of intuitions about people is not the appropriate standard against which to judge theories of agency.

As we saw in chapter 3, economists began by assuming that people are prototypical agents. Robbins, in making agency depend on an output of introspection that he didn't imagine went on anywhere but in the mind of a person, continues that assumption, and builds it into his definition of economics. However, with Samuelson the assumption has been dropped. A Samuelsonian economic agent, as we saw, is simply any system that observes certain consistency conditions in its behavior, such that it can be interpreted *as if* it is maximizing the value of a function that maps a system of preferences over commodity bundles onto the real numbers. As already discussed, celebrations of this achievement by Samuelson's contemporaries based on either anti-utilitarian or crude behaviorist considerations were confused: the sensationalism historically associated with utilitarianism that was rejected in the 1930s and 1940s was never more than an incidental appendage to utilitarianism, and it isn't true that a behavioral science must abjure all reference to internal mental processing to count as respectable science. However, two defenses of a conception of agency consistent with RPT can be given that are not residues of a redundant philosophical environment.

One of these appeals to money-pump arguments. In chapter 5 I argued that money-pump arguments cannot be used to justify any normative conception of rationality. That is, they don't help us choose among EUT and its rivals in wondering what theory of descriptive epistemic rationality might be stapled to RPT, and they cannot be used as a basis for claiming that people must be rational economic agents. At the moment, however, we are interested in neither of these questions; indeed, we are pursuing grounds for *breaking* the analytic link between economic agency and personhood. In this context, money-pump arguments are useful for highlighting one of the properties that makes economists interested in having an agency concept that is not Aristotelian.

Suppose we define a market in the most general way possible, that is, as an unordered set of sequences of exchanges among a group of consumers whose preference orderings are complete (which I will here interpret as: defined over all possible states of the world distinguished with respect to all and only scarce commodities) but (initially) unrestricted with respect to acyclicity. Then, given at least one member of the group whose exchange behavior reveals no cycles and who always prefers more to less, and given complete information on the part of that consumer (so that she can select the member of the set of sequences of exchanges that maximizes her utility), there will be a point in the actual sequence of exchanges, reachable in a finite number of steps, such that at that point all of the agents whose exchange choices reveal cyclical preferences will have lost all power to influence the market, in that any assets they continue to hold at that point will be at the sufferance of the consistent consumers. Those with cyclical preferences, in other words, disappear from the market *as economic agents*. The use of "agency" in this phrase is not at all idle. If the inconsistent exchangers are subjects of welfare concern in the preference orderings of the consistent, then the existence of the former still influences the state of the world at equilibrium, in the same sense as does the existence of tornados or ocean currents, but they can have no such influence *through the exercise of market agency*. That is, nothing happens directly because they want it to. An adequate theory of the process needs a way of conceptually marking the distinction. Thus a Samuelsonian economist can say that whatever these entities may be (though they are surely still *people*), they are not economic *agents*.

The conclusion of this money-pump argument will not directly predict allocations in typical real markets, since it depends on the satisfaction of conditions that real markets can't have. (It may be indirectly relevant to their prediction as a step in a mathematical induction, however.) Its main interest is philosophical: it helps to illustrate what is supposed to be agentlike about *economic* agents in mature neoclassicism. This is that it is *their* preferences that drive the distributive consequences of responses to scarcity (given initial endowments and human capital). This is the only remaining respect, in the Samuelsonian framework, in which economic agency excludes rocks—and, by implication, people with cyclical preferences.

This ontological point then leads to a consideration that will impress the promoter of scientific unification. If we value that, we will have grounds for wanting a form of economic analysis that we can apply to patterns of exchange in any market whatsoever, regardless of whether the agents that comprise it are people, animals, firms, countries, or computers selling derivatives to each other, and regardless of whether they calculate their goals and strategies themselves. RPT, precisely by giving us a notion of agency that derives the concept from influence over market processes (through restrictions on preference structures) rather than from typical aspects of personhood, furnishes a principle for ontological discrimination that can support the Robbins–Samuelson argument pattern that I started to outline in the middle of chapter 4.

Of course, if intended as an argument against the Aristotelian, this all just begs the question. The Aristotelian will hardly be impressed that people who attach great importance to having a general mathematical theory of markets will appreciate a special and deviant notion of agency. However, what I want to do now is use the reasoning that leads the mature (but nonanthropocentric) neoclassicist to sever agency from personhood as a wedge with which to show how an analogous case can be made with respect to the wider conception of agency intended for use outside of economics.

Notice first that the reasoning that generates the Samuelsonian's conceptual bifurcation between people and economic agents is not *logically* as parochial to economists' special concerns as one might at first think. Essentially, it is driven by the need, in modeling complex goal-directed behavior, to hold *something* constant when systems can both adjust their responses to environments *and* modify through their behavior the very environments against which the goals are set. Since the agent–environment boundary is not empirically stable in any analytically rigorous way—a point lately receiving increasing stress among philosophers of cognitive science, as I will discuss later in this chapter—the economist achieves tractability by changing her agents whenever the distribution of preference sets changes, whether this is because psychological dynamics cause organisms to change their tastes, or, in an evolutionary game-theoretic model, because population dynamics adjust the topology on which maximization is defined, or, in a really complete model, because both processes feed into each other. It is for this reason that economists care about the distinction between economic agents and other sources of causal influence on markets—tornados, currents, and inconsistent exchangers. The former must be modeled as strategic participants in cooperative and noncooperative games, whereas all of the latter are either fixed in game structures, or appear as stochastic perturbation devices ("Mother Nature" in the usual parlance of game theorists). An economist's use of the concept of agency here, although deviant relative to the Aristotelian tradition, is not casual or arbitrary. Rather, it is justified by its emphasis on what is central to many philosophical uses of the concept, namely, the distinction between the self-regulation, through negative feedback, of behavior against goals, and passive receipt of causal tugs and pulls. Happily for economists, who have often been conceptually lonely, this cluster of concerns and motivations, and of tactics for addressing them, is coming increasingly to the fore in cognitive science.

The idea that *servosystematicity*—control of local entropy through sensitivity to negative feedback—is fundamental to the concept of agency has become increasingly emphasized across the cognitive sciences, especially since the rise of models derived from work in artificial life and, in AI, models based on learning through back propagation of error signals. To gesture at some of the relevant literature here: Lloyd (1989) provides an early, philosophically conservative (i.e., representationalist) account of agency in terms of servosystematicity, generalized in Ross and Zawidzki 1994. Godfrey-Smith (1996) launches a similar project in a less restrictive context.

This won't surprise Mirowski, Dupré, or Davis, who expect cyborgs and neoclassicists to end up in antihumanistic cahoots. However, even Bishop (1989), my representative moral metaphysician here from a few paragraphs back—the humanist's friend—appeals crucially to servosystematicity in his final definition of the conditions for natural agency. His theory must, like others aiming to make morality real and causally efficacious but nontranscendental, find a means of recovering in purely causal terms the intuition that some cases of deviant causal links between intentions and actions upset moral responsibility while others do not. Bishop uses some well-known philosophical thought experiments to set up the problem.

Peacocke (1979) has us consider an imaginary neurophysiologist who reads off formed intentions in others by examining their brains and then executes matching actions. Here, our intuitions are supposed to tell us that, as long as the subject doesn't know this is happening and can't take steps to stop it, any resulting mayhem isn't her fault.

The contrasting case is provided by Davidson (1980), who asks us to imagine a malignant climber who fully intends to let go of the rope holding his partner, but whose excitement at the thought causes him to let go before he can act on the intention. Here, though the wicked intention didn't bring about its effect in the standard way, the intention was nevertheless the cause of the dropping by way of a causal path that never left the agent's domain of responsibility, so he is indeed guilty of murder.

Bishop argues that what distinguishes Peacocke's case is that maintenance of the stability of the causal relationship between intention and act is performed by another mind, thereby transferring the locus of responsibility. He must have recourse here to "maintenance of stability" conditions, rather than simple causal responsibility. Otherwise, the two sorts of cases cannot be analytically distinguished, since in both cases a cause intervenes that preempts the *direct* causal efficacy of the intention. But whereas Peacocke's patient would not counterfactually execute his intentions in the absence of the neurophysiologist, Davidson's climber (by hypothesis) does whatever he physically can to preserve the matching relationship between his intentions and actions, and so would have taken steps to drop his partner by more direct means had the indirect ones not arisen.

The capacity to *maintain stability* of causal relations between intentions and consequences thus becomes a necessary condition on agency for Bishop, and is explicitly incorporated into his analysis (1989, pp. 167–172). He does not, like some contemporary philosophers of cognitive science, suggest that servosystematicity is *sufficient* for agency. However, he maintains that what is necessary and sufficient for an exercise of agency in a particular case is the capacity to bring about a content-matched causal relation between an intention and an action in that case where the mental architecture that counterfactually supports the content match is servosystematic. Since "intentionality" is a primitive here, there is no reason why we could not graft into it one of the available accounts of intentionality in terms of the local entropy control cited above. (Nor is any presumption of an internalist theory of intentionality playing an essential role in Bishop's analysis.) Let us ignore for now any doubts we might have about the appropriateness of the causal metaphysics of mind underlying Bishop's analysis; what is significant for present purposes is that even an account driven explicitly by Aristotelian concerns ends by giving pride of place to the idea that agency is fundamentally a matter of the homeostatic maintenance of informational relationships that constitute the basis for systematic and reliable correlations between goals and actions.

As we have seen, the neoclassical economist who is not persuaded by Becker's version of anthropocentrism is motivated to break the coextensivity relationship between human individuality and economic agency because people fail to demonstrate sufficient stability of goal specification over time. Now, it might be thought that this sort of problem is less significant where agency-in-general (i.e., outside the context of special concern with markets) is concerned. Following both Dennett (1991b), and such moral metaphysicians as Charles Taylor (1989) and Bernard Williams (1976), for example, we might think of a typical human biography as instantiating a general project of creating and sustaining a coherent narrative self, and then we might try to analyze agency as the active aspect of the servosystematic maintenance of this project. Now, this is just the sort of analysis of the typical human agent I will advocate in detail in the next chapter, and it is one to which humanists—especially the humanists' humanists, the modern Aristotelians—have been particularly partial. However, since our concern is with the *general* basis of agency, on which its idiosyncratic expression in humans might then be analyzed as a derivative case, the issue for the moment is not whether typical humans are agents in *any* sense, but whether our Aristotelian habit of treating typical people as *prototypical* instances of agency is sound.[14]

I maintain that it is not. There is a strong cross-dimensional analogy between the breakdown of servosystematic constancy over time with respect to economic agency and the breakdown of servosystematic *unity of control at a point in time* with respect to agency in general. Let us use Bishop's account as a point of reference yet again. Bishop clearly assumes, implicitly, that there is a one-to-one relationship between a typical human and a locus of servosystematic control that maintains content matches between intentions and actions. He depends on this assumption to break the logical symmetry between Peacocke's and Davidson's cases of causal deviance in the intention–action relation; responsibility shifts in the Peacocke but not in the Davidson case because in the former, but not in the latter, servosystematic control is preempted by "another central processing unit" (the neurophysiologist's).

Now, I have thus far not been quibbling with Bishop's assumptions about mental metaphysics, because he tries hard throughout his study to leave empirical issues about cognitive architecture inside analytic black boxes. At the point where CPUs are invoked as the loci of fundamental agent differentiation, however, we encounter a loss of philosophical innocence. The idea that human minds might be well described as classical von Neumann architectures with single processing bottlenecks at the level of basic intentional control has already been challenged in this book from three perspectives independent of neoclassical theory: externalism in the philosophy of mind, the theory of behavioral control that makes best sense of experimental data on preference reversals and time inconsistencies in preference, and Dennett's argument for MDM. A constantly growing empirical literature in neuroscience lends it further support (see Damasio 1994 and Quartz and Sejnowski 2002). To the extent that consciousness, and the locus of behavioral control more generally, is distributed in the way suggested by all of these arguments and literature, we may significantly undermine the Aristotelian intuition by way of the following claim: *If prototypical agents are stable servosystematic loci of control of relations between goals and behavioral actions, then cognitively and conatively typical adult humans are not prototypical agents.*

My suggestion here is that the logic of the relationship between economic agency and the prototypicality of the human, on the one hand, and that between agency in general and its prototypical instances, on the other hand, is basically the same. Humanists have no stronger grounds available for resisting it than do anthropocentric neoclassical theorists. It may help to make the point of this suggestion clearer by considering a positive case of agency that satisfies the criteria for prototypicality. A good example of a prototypical economic agent is an insect. As briefly discussed in chapter 3, because the relations between an insect's goals and its behavioral responses are hardwired and sensitive to environmental variations only along finitely specifiable and tightly stereotyped dimensions, insects are ideal subjects of microeconomic study. Once the ethologist has identified an insect's budget constraint and condition-action repertoire, the derivation of its utility-maximization function is a straightforward technical matter. We then have a one-to-one mapping between the biological individual insect and a well-behaved economic agent, and we will never be tempted to explain disappointments in its career of utility maximization as resulting from preference reversal. We can make a precisely analogous set of points with respect to agency in general. The condition-action pairs that govern an insect's behavioral repertoire at a single point in time make a neat LISP stack (but equally implementable in a von Neumann architecture), readily programmed as a hierarchical control structure regardless of the extent to which electrochemical and electromuscular control might be distributed in instantiation. Whereas humans are relatively loosely coordinated coalitions of agents, both over time and at a time, there is just one agent to a typical bug. The colony of agents that constitutes a typical human will emerge under analysis as a complex assembly of buglike homunculi just in the way that Dennett has been urging for three decades. These homunculi, following Dennett, will be the causally simplest systems with respect to which explanation and prediction from the intentional stance is warranted. And these are exactly the prototypical agents.

We must be clear that what makes insects and other "simple minds" (Lloyd 1989) more prototypical cases of agency than whole people is *not* that the former fail to be subject to conflicting goals. A cockroach best satisfies its goal of finding nourishment by leaving its hole in the wall; but this impairs its goal of avoiding predators. The potential for goal competition leads, in insects as in mammals, to competition among distributed loci of behavioral control. The important difference (of degree only, as always in biology) lies in the nature of the architectural mechanisms by which conflicts are resolved. Ritzman (1984) discovered that cockroaches decide whether to fly or run from possible threats based on whether their feet are or are not touching the ground. Toad ganglia provoke tongue firings if and only if moving objects occlude the center, but not the periphery, of fixed, cell-specific receptor fields; and all information about stationary objects is ruthlessly blocked by the mechanism (Ewert 1987). In general, competitions among goals and patterned behavioral responses in simple nervous systems are moderated by various kinds of implementations of synaptic and-gates, arranged in turn into cascades of such gates at the virtual level that would be described from the intentional stance, and explained in each case by a neural-control mechanism coupled with specific environmental-control parameters. (See Maes 1991; Shackleford 1989; and Beer 1990 for a small sample of the many particular architectures that implement this ubiquitous pattern of control in simple minds.) Such gates are bottlenecks. Thus, in modeling these creatures as agents, the analyst can black-box the distributed systems that handle optimal-response searches at the subagent level, and concentrate on the output of the central bottleneck. The function that maps transduced sensory inputs over time to the output pattern of this bottleneck constitutes the simple creature's utility function. Because such systems learn (insofar as they learn) only by augmenting inhibitory and excitatory weights within stacked and-gates, these utility functions are stable: preference reversals are not exhibited in their behavior. This justifies McFarland (1992, p. 197) in modeling insect behavior as the minimization of a simple extremum cost function, from which a Samuelsonian utility function can be constructed by straightforward transformation. Sibly and McFarland (1976) and McFarland and Houston (1981) provide instances of its successful empirical application.

Human subcognitive processing modules probably use similar architectural principles (Amit 1989). However, human *selves* employ a significantly different control structure. In particular, by talking to themselves, and thereby feeding back data structures encoded at the community level in public languages, they continuously disrupt their own program stacks (Dennett 1991b; Clark 1997). The details of this will be described in the languages of both cognitive science and game theory in the next chapter. As a result, as we have seen, biological humans show ubiquitous preference reversal and time inconsistencies if modeled as economic agents. Whole people thus approximate stable agency just to the extent that their narratively constructed selves inherit relative behavioral stability from the network of community pressures on them to do so. To predict and explain their behavior well, therefore, one must model them as (internally complex) nodes in complex dynamic systems, rather than simply as agents.

Data from experimental economics aside, the economic theorist's motivations for severing the conceptual coextensivity of personhood and prototypical agency are not the same as the cognitive scientist's. The latter is persuaded for mainly empirical reasons, whereas for the former the conceptual issue is one that logical positivists would approvingly have called conventional. Let me now, however, add an argument that ought to have some force for a representative of any behavioral science. We have thus far compared people and simpler components of their control structures with respect to the prototypicality of their agency. Let us focus now on the opposite end of the spectrum (arrayed according to the Aristotelian view) with respect to prototypicality of agency. Philosophers of social science have spilled a good deal of ink investigating the extent to which attributions of agency to such structures as countries, classes, and corporations, with which both political journalism and serious history are rife, can or should be taken literally, or merely analogically and metaphorically. Both views have their proponents, but here I am less interested in the outcome of these controversies than in the assumptions under which they go on. Even those social scientists whose group-level functionalism is most unabashed do not take countries to be prototypical agents, or even as literal ones except by extension. Why not?

Almost surely, the answer is that the locus of behavioral control in such entities is too distributed *and* too internally equivocal with respect to goals, to permit confident intentional isolation and ascription except within very wide and interpretation-sensitive parameters. But this is just how things are with people, if Dennett and company are correct. Human behavior is complex, like national behavior but in a way insect behavior is not, precisely because humans and nations pursue varieties of goals arranged in no definitive hierarchy of priorities, in which one and the same mechanism may support both one goal and a second that is in tension with the first at the same time. With both people and countries, we can often make unequivocally true attributions in terms of agency if our specifications are sufficiently general. Thus it can be uncontroversially the case that Britain sought to prevent German victory over her in 1940, or that Al Gore sought to win the U.S. presidential election in 2000. But as we narrow our focus of specificity in attribution, we quickly reach levels of exactness at which we doubt that any facts of the matter, even if they were available to us, could be decisive. Did Britain also want to advance the interests of its allies in 1940? Well, yes and no; some Britons wanted to advance these interests intrinsically, others wanted to do so instrumentally (i.e., insofar as this encouraged German defeat), others preferred and sought not to advance them at all. Mining historical statistics here, although crucial to enriching our descriptive capacities, cannot in principle settle the question, at too tight a level of specificity, of what *Britain* sought in 1940 because "Britain" is just not a straightforward sort of agent; it is a coalition of agents. Similarly with Al Gore. Did he seek to win by morally appropriate means? Or just by any means he could sincerely morally rationalize to himself and others? Or only to others? Again, the point is not that no facts about Gore's biography could not shed light on these questions, just that it is a mistake to think that there must be some deep psychological-historical fact about Gore that, if only we knew it, would conclusively answer them. Like any other typical human, Gore is simply not a sufficiently straightforward or unified agent for that.

All of this needs expansion and elaboration to be convincing, and I will duly be providing that in the next two chapters. I anticipate the claim now in order to make the following point. Most of the philosophical tradition takes humans to be prototypical agents. Simultaneously, it encourages analysis of agents in terms of their capacities to serve as loci of causal intervention that stabilize relationships between networks of goals and patterns of behavior. On this basis, it consistently takes groups of people, however effectively and explicitly organized they might be, as agents only by extension; or, speaking less essentialistically, as nonprototypical agents. *But it is then inconsistent in treating the agency of whole humans as prototypical relative to insects or subhuman homunculi.* The well-rehearsed difficulties in social science related to arguments for and against methodological individualism stem ultimately from equivocation between Aristotelian conceptions of agents as whatever is typically human and more modern conceptions of agents as stabilizing knots of causal reliability. That is, we first see that countries and corporations, and so forth, are often appropriate objects for the intentional stance. This leads us to think that, *qua* agents, these entities must then be similar to our prototypical agents, namely, people, with respect to the properties that causally implement their agency.

So far so good, on my view. But then we fill in our image of the person, *qua* agent, with a picture of an internal input-output processor whose inputs are represented beliefs and desires and whose outputs are actions. Note that what we've plugged in here as our causal model is appropriate enough (as long as we don't think of the input representations as ascription-independent propositional attitudes) as an image of a prototypical agent, according to me. But it is not appropriate as a characterization of people. We've thus used one feature that aggregates have in common with people—instantiating complex narrative selves under the intentional stance—to think we should grant agency to them, and another feature the folk merely *attribute* to people as prototypical agents—guidance by stable central control bottlenecks—to deny agency to aggregates. This looks like a classic Kantian antinomy as long as the false belief about people persists. But once that belief is abandoned, the tension disappears. People approximate agency under the intentional stance, and then insofar as relations among some aggregates require that the intentional stance be taken toward those aggregates, they approximate agency in exactly the same way. Methodological individualism is thus false in general, though traditional arguments against some collective agents will still be sound just to the extent that, for empirical reasons, the intentional stance is misleading or otiose in those cases.[15]

Table 6.2

	Agents	Persons
Nations	By extension	By extension
People	By extension	Prototypical
Insects	Prototypical	Not

Table 6.2 shows the logically *consistent* way of distributing nations, people, and insects across the application spaces of the concepts of agency and personhood that I have been urging. Let me now consider what seems to me the most likely (humanist) objection to this conceptual proposal. (This will do double duty in helping to summarize the logic of the case I have been making.) I have relied on the fact that one of the key things we want a concept of agency to do is facilitate generalizations about the kinds of causal patterns typical where control systems are servosystematic. Causal patterns of this sort are practically definitive of the domain of the behavioral and life sciences (as Schrödinger [1943] first emphasized), and although the study of human behavior is certainly a part of this larger domain, it is hardly typical of it, precisely because people are complex assemblies of servosystematic architectures, and these complexes involve higher-level organizing principles that are special to them. Study of the behavior of groups of people moves still further from the standard biological paradigm, and for the same reason. Therefore, if coordinated groups of people are agents only by analogical extension, then by the same logic people are agents-by-extension when compared to simpler servosystematic units such as insects and people's own cognitive subsystems.

Now, it will be evident that this argument is driven by its emphasis on *agency* as being used to pick out a certain distinctive sort of *causal* structure. Someone in the Aristotelian tradition, however, might object that agency is at least as important for helping us to generalize about certain sorts of normative responsibility (moral and/or epistemic), and that simple servosystems are anything but prototypical in *this* respect. Neither, of course, are corporations or countries; so this counterproposal is fully consistent with traditional intuitions about the logic of the concept.

My answer to this objection is simply that it begs the question. It certainly *diagnoses* the classical intuitions that undergird the traditional concept of agency, and to that extent it explains its standard use. But science just is, among other things, the enterprise of revising our intuitive way of carving reality in light of deeper observation and more self-conscious logical rigor. One of the things (cognitive) science has recently shown us is that our old notions of human "wills" as pointlike causal fulcra are fundamentally false (see Wegner 2002); that, indeed, the very idea of a will as a specific causal engine is not a very helpful idea (except where it is substantially reconceptualized in non-Aristotelian terms, as in Ainslie 2001). The steady and continuing rise of naturalized moral psychology (see, e.g., the papers in May, Friedman, and Clark 1996) as a branch of cognitive science testifies to our recognition that it is our conception of special human responsibility that must be nuanced, deepened, and modified in light of newly understood facts about our mode of causal agency, not the other way around. (Dennett 2003 takes up this project directly.) Now, try substituting an alternative word for "agency" into the last sentence. If none will quite do as well to permit expression of its meaning, then I think the objection is met.

I thus conclude that biological-psychological people are not economic agents, except within limited time horizons, and even then only to whatever approximate extent the need for the intentional stance empirically requires in a given case. The application of economics to people will thus have to follow the same methods, and meet the same ontological and epistemological demands, as the application of economics to countries and corporations. A rigorous version of intentional-stance functionalism will provide the basis for both. All this will be the subject of the next two chapters, and of my next volume.

Note that severing the conceptual coextensivity between whole people and economic agents closes off *one* route to eliminativism. You can't get there by starting from the humanist's conceptual separation between the atomic individual's "inner" utility function and "external" influences on it, and then make an empirical case for setting the causal force of the former asymptotically close to zero, because that approach depends on taking human individuals to be prototypical economic agents. Davis (2003), recognizing that economic agency is problematic as applied to whole people, joins me in resisting the path to eliminativism just mentioned, but he relies on arguments—which he admits to be normative as much as descriptive—for setting the force of the individual-volitional component higher. He thus arrives back at Aristotelian humanism. This should help to make it clear how, in disidentifying personhood and economic agency, I am cutting away the neoclassical target that eliminativists and humanists typically seem to *share* on their respective journeys to their different destination points.

There are other routes to eliminativism that are still open, in particular Sugden's (2002) argument described in chapter 5. Aristotelian humanism will now recede into the background for the next two chapters as eliminativism is faced down. However, in one respect the humanist can look forward to a bit of revenge. Although from the perspective of *economics* people resemble countries, they have peculiarities of their own, as humanists have always emphasized. Principal among these is that people stabilize the games they play with one another by means of constructed *selves* that enable them to approximate agency more closely than countries or corporations can. Eliminativists, as we will see, pay too little attention to this.

The concept of the self I will describe in the next chapter will, of course, be built from the combined resources of intentional-stance functionalism and the MDM. It will thus be very different from the sort of self that humanists such as Sen and Davis rely on. Most important, the materials out of which selves construct themselves will not mainly be inner resources, but triangulations of environmental regularities—in particular, regularities that have to be tracked for the successful playing of games. Before I get to that story, a further aspect of Dennett's theory of the person, worked out in greater detail by others than by Dennett himself, needs to be presented. This aspect is the destabilization—but *careful* destabilization, not just wrecking—of the inner–outer distinction as it applies to complex behavioral systems. This is the subject of the next and last section of this chapter.

Out into the World: Moving the Locus of Control

As mentioned in chapter 2, the work of Dennett's teacher Gilbert Ryle was aimed at discharging "the ghost from the machine"—that is, eliminating the impossible idea of an executive mental pilot residing inside and directing the physical organism. Because Ryle wrote without the benefit of computational models of information processing, he didn't clearly grasp the point that internal representations *per se* need not imply a ghost, as long as there's no central internal *site* of all these representations that replicates the cognitive complexity of the whole system (thus driving the regress discussed earlier). Ryle thus can be, and often has been, read as eliminating the mind in the way that Quine and some of his contemporaries in psychology such as Skinner intended to do.[16] However, this is a misinterpretation. Ryle's thesis was instead that "mind" is a concept invoked to *interpret* relationships among patterns of behavior, the world, and purposes and functions. The mind is thus neither identical with the brain nor "in" the brain; indeed, minds are not physical things at all in the same sense that brains are—but they're not therefore supernatural things. As Dennett once put the point, mind is what brains (in developmental interaction with environments) *do*.

This conception of mind is, of course, functionalist without being internalist. It thus set the specifications for Dennett's later intentional-stance functionalism, in the context of much richer theories of information processing that Dennett incorporates. Functionalism, very generally, frames possible explanations of *how* brains do mind by prior reflection on *why* they do it. Brains, if they are to be more than mere collections of modular or serially connected reflexes—if, that is, they are to control behavior in ways that are not narrowly rigid—face formidable bookkeeping problems. Produced as they are by (natural) selective processes, they are built to try to track patterns of information indicative of goalstates, and of relevant means to these. (That is to say, in light of the argument of the preceding section: they are evolved to try to be economic agents.) This is physically possible only because of redundancy in the informational environment; *this* thing, viewed under *these* circumstances, is "food," as is *that* thing, viewed under *those* circumstances. An information processor that is to be of any use at all has to be able to spot, and control behavior by reference to, relevant differences with respect to the consequences of eating one or the other, and to costs of procuring one or the other, but at the same time must be able to ignore irrelevant differences. Furthermore, it can't (in general) determine which differences are relevant and which irrelevant by explicit computation from first principles, because the marginal increase in computational complexity implied by marginal increases in informational complexity are nonlinearly explosive. All this is just to say that brains must abstract from the full range of objective information that is potentially available at the level of physics.

Anyone who has thought through a tricky computational design problem will recognize that there is a systematic trade-off between flexibility of response and the extent to which the principles of informational abstraction in the control system can be hardwired. My word processing software, to be useful, needs to be able to distinguish my typing of a "p" from my typing of a "q," and it should be insensitive to differences among angles of impact between my fingers and the keys. The engineers who designed the system never had to think at all about this problem, because the physical constraints of the hardware on which the software runs simply block its access to the irrelevant information. (Special steps could be taken to make it available, but these would involve quite difficult design measures, mainly because information about angles of impact would automatically carry along a bunch of *other* information, which would then need to be screened out by new constraints, and so on indefinitely.) This information access and abstraction problem in design is easy because word processors are only supposed to be able to do a very limited and specific range of different things. As many people have noted, everyday computers are a bit like cognitively primitive natural organisms in this respect. Amoebas work well precisely because, given their low complexity, they need only track a few highly abstract distinctions: between organic things and nonorganic things, between smaller things and larger things, and between more and less oxygenated local environments. Far more information than is captured by these binary distinctions is relevant to a given amoeba's prospects for survival, but, thanks to the massive structural redundancies in the world that make natural selection, and therefore life, possible, most of this other information just rides along for free with the general abstractions. The amoeba's control system therefore doesn't need to explicitly track it.

It will be evident that as possible flexibility of response increases, the information access and abstraction problem rises with it. However, the basic trade-off principle is always there; whatever information can be relatively reliably treated as redundant will, in a design produced by efficient selection, be allowed to be captured only implicitly by a disposition to abstraction built right into the working dynamics of the system. One point about paths along increasing gradients of complexity will be especially important later, however, and so should be noted here. This is that, from the point of view of which informational redundancies can be exploited directly at the level of system design, the boundary between external and internal information comes immediately up for grabs once the processor acquires much structure.

As Clark (1997) describes in detail, brains store much of the information they rely on by letting the external environment store it for them. Clark's general term for this is "scaffolding." Human brains (probably because they are parallel rather than serial processors) aren't very good at arithmetical calculation that requires storing and remembering the precise outputs of stages of decomposed tasks (long division, for example). They solve the problem by writing the sequence of outputs on a piece of paper, using a special-purpose visual-display format they learn in school that recomposes the sequence into the overall answer at a glance. Busy people remember what they have to do, and efficiently represent the relative magnitudes of their tasks, by piling associated documents on their desks and floors. Experienced grocery shoppers can hit within a few dollars of their allocated weekly budget—thus better approximating economic agents—by taking the supermarket aisles in the same order each time and checking that their baskets have the familiar-looking load size at the end of each aisle. Crucially, in the case of humans, public languages store vast and complex networks of relationships in their structures, which people can then access by talking to themselves and being talked to. (Important use will be made of language as social scaffolding in the next chapter.)

Scaffolded representation enables the subpersonal units in the brain to coordinate without a central captain, just as Hutchins (1995) shows sailors doing in operating an aircraft carrier. The predesigned or pre-evolved condition-action rules ("stigmergic" procedures) followed by the sailors and incorporated in the division of labor among them store the global relationships among their individual actions so that the individual sailors don't have to (which is essential, since they couldn't—an aircraft carrier is too complicated). Similarly, a brain need not explicitly know that "democracy" is in the same semantic field as "autocracy," or search a large lexical database from first principles, if the similar sounds on the ends of the words cue local pattern associators to make activation of one pattern more likely given activation of the other.

Wherever a state of some part of the processor is reliably correlated with some state of the environment, other parts of the processor have the option of attending only to information about the former. That is, parts of a complex brain will devote themselves to monitoring other parts of the brain, but need not explicitly mark their inputs as coming from outside or inside any fixed boundary recognized in common across the whole system.[17] Here lie the roots of consciousness—not in the search for a central captain but in the need to get by without one.

This point undermines the idea of introspection in a more sophisticated sense than the folk notion that is defeated just by the rejection of Cartesian theaters. One level of subtlety beyond the view that internal representations can be like pictures or smells—a level classical AI reached but then tried to get too much work out of—is the idea that they occur in some abstract internal code. This is compatible with hypothesizing a faculty of introspection responsible for tracking the global internal state, albeit in a medium that only structurally resembles whatever subserves external perception. Many classical AI models have this idea built directly into their architectures. One faculty, or hierarchically organized system of faculties, gathers information about the external world. Another such system consolidates the inner realm. Reason, implemented as general, domain-neutral axioms, then governs behavior by taking input from both. Outside of philosophy and cognitive science, this is probably still the dominant image of mind among the relatively sophisticated. It is the image Robbins presumes in his introspectionist model of access to preference ordering, which, as we've seen, has the resources to make sense of a more-or-less clear distinction between internal and external components of utility. However, our recent reflections suggest that there is in fact no reason why natural selection, or even a human AI engineer trying foresightedly to build a mind, would set things up this way. Indeed, there are overwhelming, entirely general, reasons why it wouldn't work. Such a model fetishizes an internal–external distinction that must cause a profligate waste of opportunities for redundancy exploitation throughout the system, that can only cripple real-time response capacities by running control dynamics through a pointless bottleneck. Nature simply does not, and could not, build systems like that. The frame problem cannot be solved by foresight, let alone by blind selection; it can only be accommodated by automatic exploitation of the stabilities in the world's network of reliable correlations.

I'll conclude this discussion by relating the scaffolding hypothesis to the general network of relationships among distributed control, intentional-stance functionalism, and the MDM. Let us start with an interesting fact. Some echinoderms (brittle-stars) and cubozoan jellyfish have eyes but no brains. Their eyes are connected to nerve nets, but there's nothing that could support the functions of a central cortex, or even a central spinal column (Johnsen 1994; Aizenberg et al. 2001; García-Arrarás et al. 2001). Could that be possible? Well, is it possible that most of the widget sellers in Lower Slobovia might all increase widget prices by three cents on the same day without a central pricing bureau to order or coordinate the idea? Both things are actual. And they have similar explanations.

We will come back to the widget sellers later. For the moment let's reflect on the brittle-stars and jellyfish. It might be objected that one goes too far in calling their light-sensitive receptors, of which each type of animal has an array, eyes. (The scientists cited above are cautious about this, though Conway Morris [2003, pp. 157–158] makes the leap.) We have no basis for believing, after all, that they generate internal images; and perhaps that should be thought essential to something's being considered an eye. But *stop right there*—this is exactly what is at stake between the MDM and internalist models of intentionality and consciousness. The brittle-stars almost certainly do *not* form images. Given the absence of an internal integrating device, what would be the point of their doing so? Biologists don't yet know exactly how the photosensitive responses of the brittle-stars or the jellyfish work, but behavioral photosensitivity there certainly is. So let's imagine some possible details—but based on how some actual robots work (Brooks 2002), to ensure that no magic is being smuggled in anywhere. Each brittle-star arm, let us suppose, responds to changes in light frequency directly. If the center of radiation (either of the light in general or of some particular frequency, depending on how sophisticated we think the receptors are) is shifted away from the middle of the sensor's occlusion point, the arm associated with that sensor moves forward. It encounters no argument from the arms on the other side of the brittle-star's body because their sensors, finding the radiation center shifted toward them, inhibit movement of their associated arms. The forward-moving arms can keep going until the radiation center is shifted their way, at which point they will stop and the formerly still ones will swing into motion. By such simple dynamics the brittle-star will move efficiently toward the light, without needing any central guidance system to integrate information from the sensors. If the system were sensitive to particular frequencies rather than just brightness gradients—as it actually seems to be—it could move toward red parts of things or green parts of things by the same methods. An organism thus does not need a brain even to track abstract packages of information.

Again, if someone wants to deny that the brittle-star photoreceptors are really "eyes" because the integration of the information they gather doesn't happen *inside* the system, then this merely amounts to an assertion of the internalist's intuition that functional ascription should be reserved for instances where an articulated internal construct tracks the function. Of course, noninternalists might still want to invoke a concept of "internal representation" to mark design differences along these lines. Thus, for example, Lloyd (1989) argues that representation arises where and only where a minimal level of internal integration correlates at least two independent informational channels and some behavioral regularity; such an implementation is then defined by him as the basis for a "simple mind." This is useful because it permits us to identify representational error relative to the system's capacities in normal circumstances of sound functioning. The brittle-star can't misperceive a red patch as a green patch because, by hypothesis, it isn't even a simple mind in Lloyd's sense. This doesn't preclude its "malfunctioning," in a different way, in an environment where light sources are cunningly placed so as to, say, cause it to keep turning around in circles. This would be "error" relative to the evolutionary function of its photoreceptor system as a whole, rather than to that of an internal integration mechanism that it doesn't have.

In one of his most important papers, Dennett (1987, chapter 8) argues that however useful a distinction like Lloyd's might be for distinguishing different patterns in the dynamics of behavioral causation,[18] the intentional stance abstracts away from it. If we say, from the intentional stance, that the brittle-star "sees" red patches, or, indeed, that a given brittle-star "believes" there's a red patch in front of it, we should not be interpreted as committing ourselves to the claim that the brittle-star's internal mechanics implement a simple (or complex) mind in Lloyd's sense with respect to color discrimination. We commit ourselves only to the idea that the animal's behavior is reliably differentially sensitive to a systematic informational difference *we* can represent in Lloyd's sense (i.e., between red patches and patches of other colors). This is why and how intentional-stance functionalism is a form of behaviorism that does *not* imply denial that some behavior is influenced by internal representations and some behavior isn't.

Applied to the brittle-star, though, intentional-stance functionalism looks instrumentalistic in exactly the way that Friedman (1953) is urging instrumentalism when he says that an economist might explain leaves unfurling toward the sun by ascribing internal desires to them. This, as we saw, is how Davis (2003) reads Dennett. We can best see why intentional-stance functionalism does *not* imply instrumentalism however, by considering it in light of its use *along with* the MDM account of consciousness—just what none of the critics of the use of the intentional stance in economics do. In the process, we will see why and how intentional-stance functionalism and the MDM constitute one unified theory stronger than the sum of the parts. This will ultimately permit us to build intentional-stance functionalist foundations for economic theory while using the MDM to avoid losing the self in the way Davis and Mirowski fear. Indeed, we'll be going one better: since the MDM will be part of what makes intentional-stance functionalism, rather than eliminativism, essential in microeconomics, we'll get the stronger result that we don't merely not lose the self; we recover it endogenously as an essential part of the account.

Selves and Their Games

Surveying the Wreckage

It's considered bad form—or, at least, it was before postmodernism—
for a novelist to self-consciously announce inflection points in his plot
structure. But this isn't a novel. So let me say: the narrative has reached
a turning point. Almost everything accomplished so far, aside from
identifying the points of potential rapprochement between Robbins's
and Samuelson's foundations for neoclassical theory in chapter 3, has
been negative. Bits of theoretical machinery are now lying about, dis-
assembled, on the floor. It is time to start seeing how, if at all, they can
be put back together to make an orderly machine that actually does
something useful.

Before this starts, a general stock taking is in order. In chapter 3
we followed neoclassicism as it struggled, but repeatedly failed
in quite succeeding, to shake itself loose from the Aristotelian
metaphysical psychology of the first economists. In this story,
Robbins's methodological work is a pivotal and fascinating moment.
On the one hand, the positivistic urge for systematicity leads him to
expose foundational tensions that had been swept under the carpet
by Jevons, Marshall, and others more impatient with philosophy
(or, alternatively, brushed aside by *too much* Kantian self-assurance
in the case of a thinker like von Mises). Furthermore, it is Robbins
who at last shifts the central subject matter of economics away
from the behavior of people and toward an in-principle nonanthropocentric, general phenomenon: responses to scarcity. But, then, the
residual occurrence of the word "human" in Robbins's identification of economic theory's ontological target shows that genuinely
systematic foundations for economics have not yet been found by
him. As we saw, reliance by Robbins on an hypothetical faculty of

introspection to deliver the crucial data about preference structures blocks the way.

On the basis of the work in the last chapter, I'll now regard that basis for blockage as cleared. There is no such thing as introspection, so it is not a potential source of data, crucial or otherwise. Given neoclassicism's other ontological assumptions, this leaves no reason for retaining the restriction to *human* behavior in Robbins's conception of economics. Again, though, this is mainly a negative point, leaving us confronted with a confusion of alternatives.

Samuelson finally completes neoclassicism's escape from Aristotelianism by focusing strictly on the abstract mathematics of maximization among competing ends and the competing means to them, and everything that might be thought special about people disappears from view in his formulation. However, now the cleared ground is left too smooth for obvious purchase on anything empirical. With Samuelson, we barely have agents left in the system; we have merely a necessary condition for formally representing them, namely, that their behavior conform to the axioms of RPT. Unfortunately, we're given no guidance as to which, if any, empirical systems realize these abstract agents. The default Aristotelian expectation that it must be biological-psychological people lingers on even in Samuelson, and prevents him from taking the otherwise obvious step to an eliminativist interpretation. Unsurprisingly, however—as Mirowski and Davis recognize and make salient—the road to the eliminativist interpretation was subsequently found by others.

The main, if still somewhat subtle, upshot of the previous chapter, however, is that there isn't just *one* clear road to eliminativism, or hence to some sophisticated alternative if we find that road problematic, that emerges from the Samuelsonian campaign for ontological austerity. Two main factors complicate the path.

The first of these was the historical development that grafted a partly psychological theory of individual decision making onto RPT's necessary conditions for agency. I say "partly" here because this theory, EUT, was at least as much driven by the concern for formal systematicity that motivated Samuelson as it was by any empirical model of people. The problem was that EUT was casually interpreted—Aristotelianism, like a movie villain, *still* not being dead—as if it were a direct empirical theory of people. This then opened one route to eliminativism. EUT, taken as a hypothesis about people, is open to empirical refutation; and was duly refuted by the experimental work described in chapter 5. No replacement for it as an entirely *general* model of human decision making that can be attached as *part of* a model of abstract economic agency has come forth or looks likely to, despite the fact that prospect theory and other alternatives are useful for various particular applications. (Just to be clear: every particular application of RPT requires use of some theory or other of what is being maximized, since RPT by itself isn't an empirical theory at all.) Hence we get the eliminativist conclusion as described in chapter 5: people are not economic agents *and neither is anything else*. There are (empirically) no such things.

Aristotelian humanism flourishes now as it hasn't since the days of Aristotle himself, largely in reaction to this inference. Becker's heroic attempt to have the whole Samuelsonian cake without surrendering the identification of people with economic agents sharpens the perception of crisis precisely by being relentless and systematic in its logic: when it generates what seems, to most observers, to be a zanily implausible model of personhood, the result is to cast the whole neoclassical tradition into doubt. If economics is supposed to be about people buying and selling things, then it looks as if it was Aristotle, and perhaps his classical successors like Smith and Marx, who were on the right path after all. (And, in macroeconomics, we can back away from the neoclassical road of Lucas and return to developing Keynes's legacy in the direction Keynes himself encouraged.) Smith, on a warmly humanistic reading of his moral philosophy, is enjoying a spectacular renaissance just now. (See Muller 1993; Rothschild 2002; and an exploding supporting literature.) Sen repeatedly and self-consciously traces his philosophical direction to Smith's influence (see Sen 1999, among many places). Even Sugden, perhaps recoiling in some sense from the eliminativism suggested when he discusses evolutionary game theory, has been tending Smith's blooming garden (Sugden 2002). (In this chapter, we'll critically encounter the results of combining Smithian humanism, game theory, and cognitive science in the work of Robert Frank.) As for Marx: his historical determinism and utopianism may now be regarded as mostly embarrassing. But, as I noted in passing in the previous chapter, his contemporary followers in the philosophical foundations of economics—especially in association with feminism—are practically the only theorists who are untouched even by the nihilism that has so far been forthcoming in this book.

The problem with all this humanism is that, as we saw over the previous two chapters, it relies on letting normative considerations trump scientific-behavioral ones, as the latter emerge from cognitive science, completely. Its people are free beings, and with the right focus of will to build the right institutional structures, they shall be much freer yet. Their dynamics—especially their internal dynamics, but, given the previous chapter's assault on the internal–external distinction, their social dynamics too—are totally mysterious and increasingly disunified from the wider context of science. This is strikingly evident in Davis 2003. After spending half a book marching resolutely along a diagnostic path largely compatible with the one I have followed here, he confesses in the second half to having only the sketchiest concept of how to derive a model of the economic individual grounded in empirical evidence, and turns to normative pleading instead. Dupré (2001) goes over to a strident attack on the scientistic case against humanism—to which I will reply in the last chapter of this book—but revels in his "promiscuous" disdain for the very idea of a systematic alternative.

My other foil, Mirowski, is much cagier, thanks to his laudable irony. He alone among the humanists—and he is the least moralistic of them—sketches something systematic for economics to do that is compatible with his concern for the free self but that doesn't depend on assuming that very freedom (in a strongly metaphysical sense of "freedom"). He will thus remain in the wings until the very end of this book.

The previous chapter was intended to undermine the positive case for Aristotelian humanism. In doing so, it also opens what I regard as the more interesting road to eliminativism, which is gained not by *preserving* the conceptual identification of people with economic agents and then doubting that economic rationality competes very well with the other components of the causal vector behind behavior, but by denying the conceptual identification in the first place. It is perceptive of Mirowski, up to a point, to associate Dennett's name with this route to eliminativism, which is a version of much greater ontological force. It consists not in the claim that people—poor things, or noble things, choose your attitude—don't happen to *pull off* economic agency. The bracing form of eliminativism is the philosophical thesis that the very concept of economic agency is incoherent because no behavioral system in a real dynamic world could at once be that unified in its control architecture and *survive*—let alone optimize.

What is perceptive about associating Dennett with this approach to eliminativism is that it recognizes that consistent intentional-stance functionalism implies a radical revision of the ontology of folk psychology—in particular, as we saw in chapter 6, the denial that people are prototypical agents. Yet, as I will argue through this chapter and the next, the destination to which this logic actually carries us is not eliminativism. Dennett's central theses are that the intentional stance is an essential part of systematic behavioral and cognitive science; that intentional systems are really empirically realized, not just theoretical instruments; that using the intentional stance is an exercise in the logic of optimization; and that among the objects the intentional stance reveals in the world are relatively stable selves, with important causal work to do and all the freedom that someone who likes people a lot should want. Having come to the brink of the strongest form of eliminativist economics, I'm now going to turn away, and go down this other path. Humanists are warmly invited to come along and give it a try.[1]

I will build the Dennettian structure in a logical order different from Dennett's own. That is, I will start with his theory of the self, because it follows directly from where we left off in the previous chapter. I'll then add further support for it grounded in *economic* logic. This will in turn facilitate the explanation of how and why there is real natural optimization for economics to be the systematic science of.

Machiavellian Intelligence and the Breakdown of Straightforward Agency

Consider again the brittle-star that sees without a brain. Notice that the complexity of its behavior, which is relatively low as biological systems go, does not *require* that its control system be so radically decentralized. We cannot, in general, assume that reliance on external scaffolding of control through the environment covaries with complexity. Though simpler creatures are ideal instances of economic agents, because their behavioral repertoires can be successfully modeled—practically and in detail, not just theoretically and in principle—by von Neumann, LISP, or production-system architectures, this does not license any inference to the effect that nature should be expected to implement them that way.

Here is one generalization that can cautiously be ventured, however. If a group of organisms is to achieve the benefits of socialization without following the hapladiploid route to the suppression of individuality (i.e., relying entirely on kin selection at the genetic level), then the complexity of the informational demands placed on them must increase. Individuals who aren't near-clones will inherit divergent (biological) utility functions. Social cohesion, however, depends on regular success by populations in solving coordination games (see Brinck and Gärdenfors 2003 for a survey of evidence). These two facts together imply that in social animals with standard genetics, a greater proportion of an individual organism's behavioral challenges will require solutions to radically nonparametric problems than will be the case for their nearest asocial relatives. That is, in social species individuals are under strong pressure to be good at games. This in turn poses special information-processing challenges because, as classical game theorists vividly experienced along the road to the refinement program, easy solutions to control problems available through environmental scaffolding cease to be at all easy when the environment to which the scaffolds must be attached are social environments, in which the parameters relevant to optimization interact dynamically with individual organisms' behavior.

Let me be clear here on what I am *not* claiming. It isn't true that asocial animals face "fewer" nonparametric problems if the level of aggregation at which problems are specified is not fixed. (Scare quotes occur around "fewer" because no genuine metric for quantitative comparison here would make sense.) Tigers, for example, are embedded in complex games with their prey species and their competitors simultaneously. However, a greater proportion of tiger games arise at the population level than is the case for, say, wolves. That is, individual tigers are, to a greater extent than wolves, just instantiations of prevailing tiger strategies in exactly the sense emphasized by Gintis's eliminativist interpretation of evolutionary game-theoretic models. This means that tiger games get played out over longer time frames, in which natural selection can process the necessary information directly. In social animals, by contrast, there will be strong selection pressures favoring (perhaps up to some limiting asymptote, perhaps not) increases in social intelligence at the level of individual organisms. This gives natural selection reason to shift control over to individuals. In turn, this raises the same sorts of problems with bottlenecks that are familiar to economists who model institutional mechanism design.

Carefully qualified, it is not unreasonable to identify social intelligence with intelligence *tout court*, at least if our units of focus are individual organisms. (So: saying that a parrot is "more intelligent" than an ant colony is conceptually sloppy—as is saying the reverse. But it's reasonable to say that a typical parrot is much more intelligent than an individual ant.) One way of operationalizing the idea of intelligence is in terms of the ratio of genuinely available behavioral responses per relevant environmental variable.[2] By that measure—again, restricting our attention to the level of individual organisms—almost all, perhaps even all,[3] of the very intelligent individual organisms are found in the social but not eusocial species: parrots, corvids, canines, rats, raccoons, pigs, cetaceans, elephants (and hyraxes), monkeys, and apes. Though this list is not claimed to be fully inclusive or comprehensive,[4] it is important to note that the relationship between sociality and intelligence is highly convergent. That is, though the species in the club don't share a common ancestor relative to the distribution of common ancestors among birds and mammals as a whole, they also are not just the present phylogenetic limit points in the evolution of a trait that shows incremental increase and normal distribution along most clades (of birds and mammals): the socially intelligent animals form a distinctive club, whose members have a cluster of behavioral traits in common that are not strongly linked with relatedness. In the terms of chapter 2, what I am saying here is: thanks to its convergent character, social intelligence is a real pattern.

I will discuss issues around the justification of adaptationist hypotheses more fully in the next chapter. In advance of that discussion, let me just claim that intelligence is an adaptive response to pressure for social coordination, and move on. (The target concept at the moment is the self, not adaptation.) I noted above that as evolution builds more intelligent individuals, it will encounter limits set by information bottlenecks in their cognitive architectures—unless these can somehow be engineered around. In the conceptual terms established by the argument of the preceding chapter, the engineering challenge can be put thus: the intelligent individual must be rigged up to be *less* like an economic agent than, say, a pigeon or a rhinoceros can be. This immediately raises a special problem, which I will now set about explaining. Selves, I will contend, evolved as its solution.

The fundamental kinds of games that social animals need to solve—indeed, the class whose solution is almost *constitutive* of sociality—are *coordination games*. These may not pose special challenges to cognitive resources when they're *pure*. A pure coordination game, of the sort made famous by Schelling (1960) and Lewis (1969) and exemplified in the collective choice a jurisdiction makes between driving on the left or driving on the right, is one in which equilibria are symmetrical in value. Such games don't, of course, have unique solutions. But communities of socialized individuals can solve them, in the sense of converging on one of the equilibria, using a maximum of environmental scaffolding and a minimum of inboard processing, precisely because it doesn't matter to any individual which solution is chosen. As Skyrms (1996, chapter 5) shows, in a basic replicator dynamics symmetry among pure coordination equilibria will be broken inevitably by raw, and exogenous, historical accident. (Just a few more people driving on the left than on the right, for no strategic reason at all, is sufficient to tip the dynamics into stable convergence.) This demands nothing of individual cognition beyond the capacity to mimic. Although this capacity eludes most the world's creatures, it still falls short of the kind of intelligence that distinguishes the members of the social (nonhapladiploid) club.

The truly challenging coordination games are those in which players differentially rank equilibria, but care more about arriving at *some* mutually beneficial equilibrium with one another, for the sake of maintaining cooperative relationships, than they care about which member among a subset of possible equilibria is chosen. Players in such games are incentivized to, and thus may be selected for the ability to, send signals to one another that are just clear enough to achieve the latter goal, but not so transparent as to cede strategic control of equilibrium selection entirely to others. The point here is that there are ubiquitous trade-offs between cooperation and competition among social animals who play repeated games with one another. On the one hand, there is pressure to successfully coordinate for the achievement of joint projects. (Were there not, sociality couldn't evolve at all.) On the other hand, individuals are incentivized to elicit cooperation without paying for it (in proportionate contributions of energy to joint projects, or in reciprocation) wherever they can do so without expecting social penalties more costly than the gains from cheating.

In some environments this may seldom be possible. Thus Dennett (1991b), expanding on the famous field studies of predator signaling among vervet monkeys by Cheney and Seyfarth (1990; Seyfarth and Cheney 2002), notes that in their open savannah landscape vervets find few opportunities to lie without getting caught, and suggests that this reduces pressure on the evolution of complexity in their signaling system. To the extent that the appropriateness of most signals can be relied on owing to exogenous constraints, convergence to shared conventions on the meanings of vocalizations and other signs approaches the dynamics of pure coordination (Skyrms 1996). But as coordination drifts away from purity, arms races in signaling complexity, and therefore in cognitive capacities, may be triggered. Whether or not Dennett's speculation applies to vervets or other specific animals, the logic underlying his point is important: it is the tensions between pressures for coordination solutions and strategic *exploitation* of coordination that probably drive social animals so reliably up the intelligence gradient. (This is the "Machiavellian intelligence" hypothesis elaborated and explored in Byrne and Whiten 1988 and Whiten and Bryne 1997.)

In the present context, we need to be especially careful with respect to the ontological presuppositions with which we encounter this story. It is tempting, if we begin from the kind of gene-centric reductionism popularized by Dawkins (1976, 1982), but well criticized by Keller (2001) and Oyama (2000), to think of the individuals who race against each other up this gradient as *already* endowed with fixed individual utility functions before the process starts. When this is done, application of the logic becomes fairly straightforward—and has been vigorously spread through Western popular culture over the past few years—but we risk falling into the kind of complacent pan-neoclassicism that rightly raises Mirowski's ironic eyebrow (2002, p. 533), and provokes Dupré to book-length campaigns of mockery. While there of course *is* a perfectly good sense in which genetic evolution builds individual organisms—there really are distinguishable individual tigers—we must fail in a project to find a distinctive function for the self if selves are just extrapolations of distinct genomes. That is, if we *begin* by positing a well-ordered macroeconomy composed of individuals competing in a vast natural marketplace, with selves then emerging as a technology for improved competitiveness, we logically guarantee that the result won't shed any interesting light on the foundational questions about economics itself that constitute our topic here. As we saw in the last chapter, the sort of atomism that builds economic systems by aggregating preformed Robinson Crusoes is just what has carried economic theory down a path to the point where selves no longer have any distinctive work to do. Most of the pop evolutionary psychology literature encourages this by treating selves as excretions of maximizing genetic bundles that, in the prevailing metaphor, "hold them on leashes." Putting the point yet another way: one cannot somehow vindicate the empirical usefulness of neoclassical economic logic to the study of people by presupposing an atomistic neoclassical framework and then building an evolutionary behavioral science on the basis of it. We will then simply get out of our analysis what we put into it. All existing attempts I know of to defend the relevance of neo-classicism by reference to evolutionary psychology are subject to this criticism.

I thus want to do things differently here. Let the first step of our logic be to individuate *biological* organisms in noneconomic terms; that is, not as players of games, but strictly by reference to boundaries across which genetic information can be transferred only by cellular processes. That is, we can delineate some sets of cells as individual organisms by picking out sets in which each member carries common information transmitted through DNA from one or two parents, and is closed to cellularly transmitted information from the DNA of any other organisms.[5] If we so distinguish individual organisms without reference to any economic properties, we can subsequently subject them to economic analysis without introducing circular reasoning into our ontology. Then we want selves to emerge from the social dynamics that can arise when some of these biological individuals become enmeshed in complex (nonpure) coordination games.

The conceptual twist required for this way of understanding matters is novel, and striking in its implications. To the extent that something is a (relatively) simple biological individual its behavior lends itself well to description as an economic agent—that is, its behavior will respect the axioms of RPT under budget constraints that can be independently specified from data gathered by ecologists and field etholo-gists. There is a flourishing literature providing microeconomic accounts of foraging, mate selection, habitat selection and exploration, sexual competition, nepotism, sibling rivalry, navigation, predator avoidance, reciprocal grooming, interspecific mutuality (symbiosis), and other topics in behavioral and cognitive ecology (see Krebs and Davies 1984; Bell 1991; Dugatkin and Reeve 1998; Dukas 1998; Noë, van Hoof, and Hammerstein 2001), that constitutes paradigmatically good science. That is, as a body of work it passes epistemic muster in the straightforward, good old-fashioned way: the accounts in question regularly generate surprising but accurate quantitative predictions of parameters whose values can be specified and measured independently of the theoretical models used to produce them. RPT shines here as what I called, back in chapter 4, a "theory in sense 3." If human behavior conformed anywhere near as well to the predictions of good old-fashioned neoclassical microeconomic models as that of asocial animals repeatedly does, nobody not in the grip of pure ideology would be calling for a new kind of economics.

To make this point vivid, we can refer to some comparative experimental work with people and pigeons on the phenomenon of so-called base-rate neglect. This is a much-observed EUT violation in which subjects ignore or undervalue available background information in favor of situation-specific information. Goodie and Fantino (1995) induced it in a typical way in a group of human subjects confronted with the task of predicting the colors of light flashes for rewards. Hartl and Fantino (1996) then replicated the experiment with pigeons. The birds behaved like good Samuelsonians. We should invite the researchers to deploy their ingenuity on trying to devise a setup that induced the people and the pigeons to compete with one another on the task. If it were possible to find a common currency of reward, perhaps the people would get money-pumped.

If complex sociality is negatively correlated with straightforward economic agency, this should lead us to model some biological individuals, those that got enmeshed in complex coordination games with others, as evolving *away from* such agency. As they develop selves, they become different kinds of individuals, and the coextensivity between them and the biological individuals on which they are historically based breaks down. In the limit, the microeconomic approach with which we logically begin stops applying to them very effectively, and an evolutionary *macroeconomics* is called for—as we will start to see in this book, and will explore more fully in its successor volume.

We have been moving quickly, so some recapitulation is in order. We begin with organisms that are individuated genetically, not economically. It turns out that we can use Samuelsonian microeconomics to build models of these systems as they respond to scarcity in food sources, mating opportunities, and other resources that give us surprising but accurate empirical predictions. This in turn feeds back to provide constraints on the cognitive models of the animals. Here, then, is the relationship between economic theory and cognitive science that was hoped for in the optimistic early days of classical AI. If it worked for people I could have written a very different book—much more technical, and much less complicated in its conceptual logic.

However, increases in nonparametric environmental complexity that arise with sociality put pressure on the power of straightforward economic agency. Problems arise on two dimensions at once. First, there is just the fact, pointed out repeatedly, that nonparametric optimization is exponentially more demanding of computational resources than parametric optimization. But, second, even in an environment where nature had solved the refinement problem for socialized individuals (in some mathematically arbitrary but stable way), each *single* coordination game faced by an agent would be massively complicated. In an informationally dense social network, a coordination strategy I use with individual x in game G_1 will simultaneously be a move in another game G_2 with another individual y and in yet another game G_3 with another individual z; and x, y, and z are likewise embedded in multiple coordination games of their own. For all individuals at once, this situation represents a general equilibrium (GE) problem, with no possible central planner to locate an optimal solution set. (So, pace Mirowski, never mind Gödel's theorem, troubling though that might prove in the limit where one aimed at a *unique* solution to the GE problem. In the networks of games envisaged, there's nothing with an incentive to try to compute *any* solution.) This GE problem for each individual will be informationally intractable unless the strategy sets available to them all are sharply constrained in advance of each specific interaction, and unless many of the relevant constraints are common knowledge. *Some* constraints will be supplied by biology, physics, and shared culture. I can't, in selecting coordination strategies, promise or threaten to fly out the window, and I can't *credibly* threaten to kill myself if you don't pass the salt. However essential these sorts of background constraints might be, however, they can't carry nearly enough of the load to get us to the kinds of refined social equilibria on which human communities manage to converge. If, in any given strategic situation-type S with you it were open to me to do *any* of the things *any* person, or even any person who shares our approximate cultural history, might do in S, reaching equilibrium would still require a computational miracle.

Why did I just introduce the idea of strategic situation types, rather than continue referring to games directly? This is related to the point made above that we can't assume our initial individuation of agents to remain stable as we let socialization feed back into their economic agency profiles. Identifying a scenario as a game presupposes that players' strategy sets have already been constrained by determination of their specific utility functions. But the whole point of the hypothesis of Dennett's that I'm working up to here—which is also the point of denying Robinson Crusoe metaphysics—is that a raw, socially unrefined, biological instance of *H. sapiens* isn't yet a *human self*. If utility functions in games among individuals attach to human selves, then we can't identify a game G among two or more such selves with the preconstrained situation S that they might be modeled as confronting if they were rhinos. What we have to explain is what allows socialized agents to *get from* situation types to particular games.

As theorists, we should feel perplexed. On the one hand, as the biological individuals are drawn into social games they are challenged to become *more* sophisticated economic agents. To get a picturesque image, think of them as encouraged by selection pressures to track the refinement program. As we discussed in chapter 5, this challenge is quixotic. On the other hand, then, the biological individuals must literally break up under the pressure, distributing their behavioral control, evolving into communities of agents, and relying to increasing degrees on external informational scaffolding. At some point, if we continue to insist on modeling them as straightforward economic agents, we will start observing preference reversals and time inconsistencies. We can try, for a while, to save the day with Ptolemaic measures, inventing new models of maximization targets to replace EUT on a case-by-case, custom-fit basis that lets us still apply RPT. But as always with Ptolemaic strategies, the returns on this must diminish. Well before we reach the point at which we're forced to represent each biological individual as a distinct *kind* of economic agent—the limiting point of methodological futility—the empirical value of modeling them this way must vanish.

Well, this is our problem *as modelers* (if we just plod along without revising our conceptual framework). But what might be going on with the systems we're trying to model? One possibility is that the evolution of social complexity just reaches an asymptote as the power of economic agency crashes against limits on real-time computation in brains. In some limiting sense, asymptotes with respect to complexity are inevitable: the speed of light is a barrier, and there is only so much energy in the universe. But selection has some further resources it can turn to that keep the asymptotic limit from being reached at the point where individual nervous systems can't hold agency together by themselves. The evolved social environment can itself be exploited as scaffolding. Selves can evolve. People are the evidence for this.

What Selves Are

Dennett (1991b) invites us to think of selves on the model of characters in novels. Like such characters, they are not the sorts of things that can be directly built by natural selection from chemical materials.

This is why there can be no Cartesian theater: that idea would make sense only if there could be a prebuilt self in place to watch the film and hear the soundtrack, and it would have to be built out of the sole kinds of materials, biochemical ones, that natural selection can work with *in advance of* cultural and social learning. The only cultural stories that have been told about such selves without falling into internal incoherence have been mystical, not scientific, ones. If you want that kind of account, Plato still sells the best one on the market.

A scientific account of the self, however, entails that selves must, like the creations of novelists, be made at least partly by human activity. Many thinkers, coming from different disciplinary perspectives and with varying metaphysical biases in mind, call all types of entities with this property "constructed." This is a sensible label, but it is often intended with a suppressed adjective like "freely" or "arbitrarily" riding along in front of it. Thus humanists, led by their normative emphasis on freedom, are typically partial to finding construction everywhere because they take this to maximize human independence from external constraints. When we speak of "constructions," however, we do well to remember that the extent to which a given construction is optional for a given group of people is a case-by-case empirical matter. Many constructions are near-inevitable but unintended consequences of particular social dynamics, and are not interestingly avoidable. Perhaps they're all metaphysically avoidable in some sense. But who cares? Popular wisdom makes a sound point in associating death and taxes together, because no country is ever going to have a radical libertarian government that abolishes taxes, no matter how hard or well libertarian activists work.

Selves have something else in common with fictional characters: they make excellent points of reference for the generation of expectations in observers of them. Let us consider the fictional characters first. As the lion springs at Jane, we're told that Tarzan has just swung into the tree above her. Were it anyone else but him, the next thing that happens would be utterly astonishing and would require a great deal of prior explanation indeed. But if we've been following this character, we'd be *more* surprised if there were, from him, a shout for the ranger's help, or a gunshot, or weeping, than we are by what we're told happens. This lion is more or less sure to get stopped in midleap and stabbed to death. Tarzan is such a reliable character that, with respect to literary values, he isn't interesting. That he's implausibly strong and athletic isn't his main literary flaw; it's that he's too predictable and simple to be a model of a real person.

A *real* person? Tarzan fits the definition of a real pattern stated back in chapter 2. If you don't track *that* pattern, whether because you just don't bother or because you try to reduce it to recurrent marks on a printed page, you would lose other information. That you would lose information is made evident by the fact that someone else, but not you, would win the money on the quiz show when asked what are, to them, easy questions *about* Tarzan: was he married? Did he (eventually) speak English? There are other easy questions about him that make clear that the information loops through expectations—a sure sign of real patternhood—rather than just memory derived from actual marks on paper. Did Tarzan know how to write computer code? Did he compose bagpipe music? Edgar Rice Burroughs never mentions these things one way or the other, but the answers are obvious. What we mean when we say Tarzan isn't real is that he isn't *autonomous*; he initiates none of his own behavior. This is one perfectly useful and (in context) comprehensible meaning of "not real," but the real–unreal contrast can have other equally good meanings in other contexts. In those contexts, Tarzan is as real as any other real pattern. Let's agree to call him "virtual" when we want to mark the contrast between him and things nature *can* make directly out of chemicals, like the phenome that came to be named "Edgar Rice Burroughs."

The point that fictional characters aren't *arbitrarily* constructed by their authors, and the fact that they serve to stabilize narrative expectations, are closely related. Let us switch our example from one colonial-era fictional hero to a slightly more complicated one. As Conan Doyle wrote the early chapters of his first Sherlock Holmes novel, in each situation into which he put Holmes lots of behavioral possibilities were open. Holmes might, for example, have mocked Watson's episodes of befuddlement by composing naughty limericks about him. However, long before the fourth Holmes novel this strategy was closed off by the fictional biography Conan Doyle had spun for Holmes. "Closed off" here of course denotes no metaphysical or logical impossibility: Conan Doyle was perfectly capable of writing *the words* "then Holmes began 'There was an old doctor from Cork . . .'." The impossibility here is a function of pressures for coherence that come with Conan Doyle's social purpose in being a novelist (and a novelist of modern, rather than postmodern, sensibilities); Holmes can't do this sort of thing and still be Holmes.

So it is, Dennett argues, with real people. When I was six years old it was still possible for me to be many more sorts of people than the person I now *am* in my forties. Again, the constraint here is not that I physically couldn't, like the accountant Mr. Phipps in the Monty Python sketch, announce an intention to become a lion tamer. Rather, it's that if I made such an announcement and really meant it, with all its behavioral implications, I'd undermine the whole complex of expectations about me *as* me that make it possible for me to reach equilibria in the battery of daily coordination games I simultaneously play with the many people in my life, including interactions with erstwhile strangers.

This last point should invoke surprise. How could my biography be relevant to expectations on the part even of people who are previously unacquainted with me? A *beginning* to an answer here is that to play coordination games with others I need to have relatively stable expectations about *myself*. But now the nonexistence of introspection raises a problem. I'm a complex system, with inner causal dynamics very nearly as obscure to my direct observation as they are to yours.[6] Radical unpredictability to others would have to imply radical unpredictability to myself; but this condition, called "loss of self" in popular parlance, is a condition that most people sensibly regard as a catastrophic state of affairs. Relatively stable selves may be contingent historical creations rather than given internal essences, but they are the most precious properties that people develop nevertheless, and are almost universally so regarded.[7] A further element of the answer is that I can't keep the various games I simultaneously play with different people in encapsulated silos; this is why, as I intimated above, a move in a game G_k with the stranger will also represent moves in other games $G_k, \ldots, {}_n$ with more familiar partners.

But how do I pull off this stabilization? Unlike Burroughs's or Conan Doyle's enterprises of narrating their reliable protagonists into being, self-creation looks at first glance like magical bootstrapping. So it would be if I were under only my own observation. However, others are watching me, and building their own narrative biographies of me from the intentional stance, and I know this. Furthermore, the success of projects that require our coordination also require that I not radically disappoint their narrative expectations. It is sensible for people to avoid attempts at coordination with highly unstable selves. Given the massive interdependency among people, this incentivizes everyone to regulate the stability of those around them through dispensation of social rewards and punishments. Blinking at someone in perplexity, as long as that someone interprets the blinking as possibly representative of how others in general might respond, is a *severe* form of punishment; making this so is the main bit of hardwiring that natural selection has to do in evolving a social animal. But why should I take the other's blinking as (often) representative of a more widespread social judgment? Well, simply because their dispositions to find certain sorts of departures from stability alarming are *also* formed under the pressures of the social-intentional judgments that gave rise to *their* selves.[8]

It is a familiar observation in evolutionary game-theoretic models of society that distributed maintenance of norms by everyday acts of reward and sanction is the cement on which all the more explicit infrastructure of laws, corporations, regulations, churches, and organized science rests. The distributed nature of the enforcement is crucial, because it keeps the costs of the rewards and sanctions from getting so high as to demand heroism from the enforcers. Binmore's (1998) analysis of these dynamics is recommended as the most philosophically astute to date. His observation that social stability is maintained by reciprocal relationships of guardianship over radical deviations from predictability, and Dennett's (1991b) claim that people as the authors of their own selves are assisted by multiple coauthors, are thus expressions, at different levels of causal analysis, of the same point.

I may safely presume, dear reader, that you have a self. Who constructed it? Well, not a preformed Cartesian mind you were born with, because there can't be any such thing. Your parents or other everyday guardians in infancy played the main role in getting the process started (McGeer 2001). In games with them, you began as a straightforward economic agent with a consistent utility function that any closely and continuously watching economist could have constructed from your behavior (most of which was a range of different crying productions). However, your parents refused to treat you as the straightforward economic agent you were. This was fortunate for you; as evidence on feral children (Candland 1993) shows, infants not encouraged to become selves don't and subsequently can't. Your parents acted as if you were trying to reach coordination equilibria with them in the sorts of games they'd play with simplified versions of themselves. (They did this instinctively, not deliberately.) You started to turn into a self when your behavior began responding to the fact that you received rewards for consistency *itself* along certain dimensions, and mild sanctions—slight expressions of disappointment—*just* for being an *erratic* player of the coordination games your parents imagined you to be capable of playing. McGeer (2001) refers to this constructive activity of your parents as "sculpting" the person into being. Such sculpting relies essentially on scaffolded learning, the basic information-processing dynamic of the intelligent animal.

Dennett (1991b and elsewhere) has often stressed the salutary point that philosophers ought, wherever possible, to state their conceptual hypotheses as possible empirical experiments. (Real, grant-proposal-type experiments, that is, not ones that require trips to Twin Earth.) Let me thus propose an experiment that would help to refine the above thesis about development into an explicitly game-theoretic one. The child's task in learning to be a player of coordination games would be made easier if the dimensions along which parents rewarded consistency and sanctioned inconsistency were *irrelevant to* the *established* behavioral patterns that regulate satisfaction of the infant's utility function in the first weeks of life, since this avoids confronting the baby with noisy learning problems. Does baby *always* smile when she sees the yellow elephant? Terrific: beam back and point out the behavior excitedly to visitors. Does baby *always* welcome the warm bottle or the blanket? Of course not, and who would have expected she should? This could readily be investigated by means of a series of experiments. Begin by finding an environmental contingency that's reliably but accidentally correlated with a subject baby's receipt of food or hugs. The baby can be counted on to make the association in the standard Skinnerian way, provided the contingency is salient. In one experimental series, don't inform the parents of the experimental variable so that they act naturally. In another experimental series, enlist the parents to manipulate the baby by rewarding extensions of the experimental variable but *without* providing the stimulus—food or hugs—elicited in the associated cases. (That is, reward the extensions one way and the associated base cases the other [usual] way.) I predict that the second group of babies will learn to extend responses in the unassociated cases more slowly than the first; and that both groups will learn the extensions more slowly than either learn to extend responses to environmental features *not* correlated with their feeding circumstances, but which parents encourage. If this prediction were borne out, it would be evidence that babies are taught to play coordination games *for the sake of learning to do so.*

Merely learning to play social coordination games didn't yet endow you with a self. At this point you were a social animal, standing in a similar relationship to the straightforward economic agent as a dog or a baboon does. That is, your behavioral patterns were significantly looped through social scaffolding, so we wouldn't have been able to economically model you so easily as when you were born; to get reasonably fine predictions right, we'd have needed a model of the social dynamics in your household. If those dynamics had changed in some important way—say, you acquired a new sibling—we should have expected to see preference reversals if we'd insisted on modeling you as the same economic agent but hadn't resorted to Beckerian technical feats or Ptolemaic manipulation of whatever theory of cognitive judgment over utility we'd stapled to RPT. On the other hand, any decent economist would have been able to effect the Beckerian transformations or cooked up a phenomena-saving heuristic without too much sweat. The resident economist would have started to really work hard, however, soon after you began to *talk*.

One respect in which Dennett has been unrepresentative of recent thinking on the self is in his giving more emphasis than average to the role of language. (See Clark 2002 for a careful discussion.) He is led to this emphasis by the way in which MDM and the theory of the self are built together. Theorists who share similar views of selfhood but who don't partly get there by way of reflections on consciousness thus don't share his motivations for seeing language as quite so central. Acknowledging, then, that in continuing to follow Dennett here I rest some weight on claims that are far from consensual in the relevant theoretical community, let me continue.

It is useful here to return to the analogy between fictional characters and selves. The constraints that box in Conan Doyle as he builds up Holmes, and which thus make Holmes a real pattern, are *narrative* ones. Just what narrative constraints amount to is a subject that has received a good deal of attention from cognitive scientists, especially those working in schema-theoretic frameworks in AI (Schank and Abelson 1977; Mandler 1984), and from philosophers of history who have sought to better understand historical explanation (e.g., Roberts 1996). While I don't doubt that innate cognitive dispositions place *some* limits on what anyone can judge as narrative coherence, and although a logical model can always be constructed to define the common features and production structure of any given, finite set of narratives, I am doubtful that any account of narrative not itself grounded in a game-theoretic dynamic can be adequate. This is because I expect that what are taken by people to constitute sensible narratives is itself a constantly negotiated product of cultural evolution (Polanyi 1989). For this reason, I will leave the concept of a narrative constraint as an unanalyzed black box here; although I suggest that the notion of game determination I will be explaining shortly might be an important part of the theoretical apparatus needed to pry it open. In any case, let us for now just understand a narrative constraint in the vague operational sense of whatever it is that leads a given group of people to judge some behavioral sequences as ones in which earlier behavioral patterns *explain* others, and other sequences as ones in which explanation must draw on synchronic factors exogenous to behavioral patterns alone. (This is roughly the operationalization from which debates in the philosophy of history start out.) It may be helpful in explicating this idea to note that a given culture's sense of narrative coherence will tend to stand in a mutually implicative relationship with its theory of *insanity*. Thus a good source of evidence relevant to discovering a community's sense of narrative would be the judgments and rationales of its courts in cases where criminal responsibility might be mitigated by standing or temporary madness. Insanity, interpreted as a social kind, consists in permanent or temporary departure from minimal narrative coherence.

Working with this operational notion, we can state Dennett's thesis thus: selves, just like fictional characters, are narrated systems of behavioral dispositions that extend across nontrivial numbers of schematic boundaries (i.e., that imply networks of expectations in multiple types of situations). For Dennett, narrative structure essentially requires language. This derives not from the implicit analysis of narrative itself (which I have just tried to make a bit more explicit), but from the MDM.

As we saw in the last chapter, the paradox of consciousness-as-selfhood arises in that, to understand it, we need a subject who can adopt the intentional stance toward herself as a whole system, and this subject cannot herself be a *part* of the system. The most immediate and vicious sort of circularity thus seems to threaten. To escape it, we need a structure that is ontologically prior to and wider than the system itself, which can serve as an external scaffold for judgments by parts of the system about its own whole. A requirement on this scaffold, if it is to do the job, is that it mustn't be too plastic. That is, it must encode a relatively determinate system of procedural rules. Otherwise, as Wittgenstein's famous "private language argument" emphasizes, we can't understand how the sequences of intentional-stance judgments could find a grip. Public language seems to be the obvious such scaffold available to people, perhaps, as Dennett suggests, *the* scaffold that makes humans so strikingly different in their ecology from other intelligent animals.

"I can't think of anything else" is a worrying premise in an argument, but we can do a bit better than that here. A striking thing we learned from the first generation of AI research is that human capacities proved easiest to model in von Neumann architectures just when they were most discursive in character. Theorem proving, which people can't do at all without lots of specific scaffolding to hand (pens and bits of paper, at the least), is easy to implement in digital computers, whereas tasks that people perform smoothly without having to invoke particular intentional-stance judgments on their occasions, like getting an egg fried, are hard. Trying to implement the latter, and then successfully integrate it into a larger sequence like making a whole breakfast, crashes into the frame problem in a way explicitly discursive tasks don't. The moral seems to be: throw enough explicit rules at a problem and you thereby modularize it. Modularization is the way to lick the frame problem (Fodor 1983, 1987). But then the second-order control of the modularization parameters can't itself be under the direct control of the system, lest we get the Wittgensteinian regress.

Now, chimps can be taught to fry eggs, and it's a moral certainty that we'll soon have robots that can do so, if they aren't already on sale in the Japanese novelty gadget market. Constructing a self is a project of the egg-frying type—that is, not premodularized in advance, like theorem proving—but vastly more daunting to contemplate from the engineering perspective. For it, then, we need: a source of external scaffolding that's strongly articulated, flexible enough to evolve, and beyond the manipulative control of the individual agents that rely on it. Systems of money prices are such structures, but obviously too limited in their range of use to build selves with. Public languages are also the right sort of structure; and although there are also things that can't be done with them—keeping your balance on a surfboard, for example—it's plausible that they're up to the job of *everything* we find in self-construction.

Making the assumption, then, that it's appropriate to lay a good deal of stress on language, let us continue with your logical biography. We left you socialized but yet without a self. A further task on which you and your parents came to coordinate was offering judgments about your behavior within the rules of your parents' public language. You were massively rewarded when your output was situationally appropriate and narratively coherent. Dennett describes the process, in the context of the MDM, as one in which you learned to install the digital software that is a public language on the analog neuroelectrical and neurochemical hardware of your brain. ("Analog" here refers to the fact that your brain is a neural network whose global states are modulated continuously by chemical state changes—with two-way feedback relationships between the two systems making the overall system that much harder to approximate in a digital representation.) Like all software, a natural language tightly constrains processing options; that is the very point of software. *Most* of the information being processed somewhere in your brain couldn't be expressed as an articulated judgment coordinated with your parents' expectations; thus your learning problem was simplified by external pressures, and thus your coordination problem was soluble. Embedded in a chattering community, *you* appeared as the maker of judgments about specific ways in which your whole system responded to its environment *insofar as such judgments could be expressed using the digitizing software.*

Dennett emphasizes a next crucial step. Since talking throws software-encoded information out into the physical environment, you could process your own output as input. You could talk to yourself. The literal wiring of your brain provided the basis for a particularly neat extension of this trick: some of the drafts generated in your complex internal economy could get the attention of processing channels tuned to incoming public language and thereby *become* judgments about the global priorities of the system. These judgments, being cast in the public language, are subject to the general constraints imposed on everything filtered through that software. (If you doubt that these constraints are tight enough to do the work the present theoretical framework is requiring of them, reflect on the fact that violating them without getting *total* breakdown of coherence is a *feat*. Repeatedly accomplishing it made Bob Dylan a hero, and rich.) Once you started talking to yourself you were, willy-nilly, assuming the intentional stance toward yourself. You could even make second-order intentional-stance judgments about the extent to which you were achieving, preserving, and extending your own narrative coherence. Receiving regular critical feedback from a highly motivated (I hope) audience, you could construct a character much more nuanced and interesting than Tarzan. (That you're less predictable than Tarzan is one reason, less obvious than Tarzan's physical skills, that I'd rather have him on hand if I were being attacked by a lion.) With luck, your brain didn't get so well dominated by the control of the scaffolding device that you came to interpret your intentional-stance judgments as being *wholly* external to the system, for here lie the roots of schizophrenia. But, of course, pathological schizophrenia is just a limiting instance of the normal and effective case, and different cultures will draw the limits in different places in different circumstances: one culture's divinely inspired prophet is another's lunatic.

A few years after this initial self-sculpting, you climbed another steep part of the self-learning curve when you and other novice selves you met at school began to play coordination games with one another. This raised deep new challenges for you for two reasons: you hadn't idio-syncratically coordinated with these selves in advance of tricky strate-gic interactions, as you had with your parents, and they wouldn't, like your parents, be highly tolerant of your stumbling attempts to find equilibrium strategies. Social punishment for slow learning was thus more rigorous, and you had to endure frequent embarrassment. (Of course, your small partners did too.) This discipline made you sub-stantially more socially intelligent, quickly. The subsequent history of your learning had punctuated periods of relative stasis and unstable fluctuation, depending partly on accidents of your circumstances, but predictable in places; adding the drive to coordinate with possible mates likely produced one of the steeper moments on your curve. Viewed with a gross analytical grain, however, the overall tendency was for your curve to flatten with time as you discovered a repertoire of strategies you could deploy with passing success in wider sets of cir-cumstances and with less situation-specific information. This stability reinforced itself, for it made you easier for others to coordinate with and so reduced the *ex ante* costs to them of playing games with you.

As usual, however, there were trade-offs. Stabilizing on one reper-toire of general strategic dispositions made others that would be optimal in particular situations harder to find, thus locking you, to some extent that varies from self to self, in a cultural niche. You didn't find it efficient to try to play coordination games with everyone who came along, if there were others about who, given your niche, were much easier to settle on equilibria with. On deep questions of social value, to at least some extent you became an ideologue. But, left or right, religious or agnostic, conventional or bohemian, your particular subtle blend of coordination-game strategic dispositions was unique—partly because people *enjoy* a certain amount of new learning in their games, so didn't reward you for becoming as two-dimensional as Tarzan. With their help as coauthors, you had narrated yourself into being as a character.

This is the Dennettian theory of the origins and ontology of the self. In presenting it, I have run a thread of game-theoretic logic through it that is mostly only implicit in Dennett's original (1991b) account (although in Dennett 2003 the conceptual links with game theory emerge more clearly). Now, in order to bring the ideas more securely within the analytic framework that will take us directly back to the foundations of economics, I want to state the dynamics of self-stabilizing coordination yet more explicitly. As so often in this book, I will do so by contrasting the account with one that tries to achieve a similar integration but handicaps itself by taking Robinson Crusoe economics to be a merely *empirical* mistake instead of a conceptual one. This is Robert Frank's (1988) well-known and influential model of the strategic role of emotional signaling. Frank's theory, I want to show, goes wrong by playing out the implications of *one* basic mistake in both its evolutionary-psychological *and* its economic dimensions. The exercise of criticizing it will thus be a case study in application of the general theoretical perspective I am promoting in this book.

Before launching into this, however, there is some tricky and unusual conceptual logic that needs to be clarified. I have argued that selves aren't straightforward economic agents. They are more like nations than insects. As with nations, if we try to model them as straightforward economic agents we'll find them exhibiting preference reversals, and behavior that represents outcomes of internal logrolling among the multiple drafts jostling for system-level intentional-stance narrative control. There are crucial gaps remaining in this framework. Is there *any* systematic relationship between economic agency and selfhood (aside from the ontogenetic one)? If not, talk of internal logrolling is just metaphorical, and eliminativism about economic agency as descriptively applicable to *people* is correct (even if we've successfully blocked *general* eliminativism with Dennett's help), and microeconomics is only empirically relevant to the study of simple minds (in Lloyd's precise sense).

There is of course a branch of economics that studies aggregated systems facing scarcity collectively: macroeconomics. Whether we have, or can have, a systematic macroeconomics is the subject of the next volume of this study. But now we can see that the logical relationship between microeconomics and macroeconomics, whatever it is, is mirrored in the logical relationship between the study of simple minds and the study of strategic interactions among selves. If selves don't analytically reduce to aggregations of simple minds, as I have argued they don't, then two possibilities for the relationship are open. If eliminativism about economic agency is correct, then the only possible macroeconomics is evolutionary game-theoretic institutional economics, which will have no obvious relationship at all to microeconomics where people are concerned because all the structure relevant to explaining the macroeconomic patterns would lie, irreducibly, at the macro level. Microeconomics, on this outcome, would be useful for studying asocial animals but would have no application to people at all. So far in the account, this outcome is looking rather likely.

But there is another option that is logically possible, if even local eliminativism is not correct and the behavioral stability brought about by selfhood allows us to construct some systematic relationship between selves and economic agents that gives microeconomic analysis some purchase on people after all. If we got that far, we'd then be motivated to look for a possible systematic relationship between the microeconomics of people and the macroeconomics of their social dynamics in the relationship between the ethological study of simple minds and the *cognitive ecology* (Dukas 1998) of their interactions. This is the possibility I will explore in detail in the next volume of this study. First, however, we have to achieve the first of the above ambitions. This will now be done by explicitly elaborating the foundations of selfhood in game-theoretic terms.

Game Determination

To launch this discussion, it is worth repeating, word for word, some remarks from the previous section, *part* of the full meaning of which will be clearer now that the Dennettian model of the self has been presented. (The work in this section will unpack the *rest* of their point.)[9] I said

We can't assume our initial individuation of agents to remain stable as we let socialization feed back into their economic agency profiles. Identifying a scenario as a game presupposes that players' strategy sets have already been constrained by determination of their specific utility functions. But the whole point of [Dennett's hypothesis as just discussed]—which is also the point of denying Robinson Crusoe metaphysics—is that a raw, socially unrefined, biological instance of *H. sapiens* isn't yet a *human self*. If utility functions in games among individuals attach to human selves, then we can't identify a game G among two or more such selves with the preconstrained situation S that they might be modeled as confronting if they were rhinos. What we have to explain is what allows socialized agents to *get from* situation types to particular games.

As argued in the previous chapter (and expanded on in the previous section) a socially unrefined (i.e., newborn infant) biological *H. sapiens* instance, being a straightforward economic agent, *does* have a utility function, inherited from natural selection. But no *selves* are such instances. Let me therefore construct, simply for explicative purposes (since it has no actual empirical models) the concept of a situation-type S that abstracts away from the differences between the game G (as a model of S) faced by two selves and another game G'' (as an alternative model of S) they *would* play if they were straightforward economic agents equipped with the biological *H. sapiens* utility function. S might describe their circumstances as they would strike an otherwise astute observer innocent of both game theory and externalism about the contents of thought. (For example, I think that Hobbes reasons within the analytic modality of S-type characterizations, both when he discusses the state of nature and when he discusses interactions under Leviathan.)[10]

We are not *directly* interested (in this section) in games of type G'', since these are only played by infant (and perhaps severely autistic) *H. sapiens* individuals. (By contrast, G''-type games are the *only* kind played between individual asocial animals like tigers.) Consideration of G'' is (for now) just a conceptual ladder for introducing a third game-type G' that might, for all we know in advance of an empirical study of a particular instance S_i, be the right way to model S_i. G_i' is a game played by two *strangers* to each other who are already distinctive human selves. Its structure is of course determined by their preengagement utility functions. By reference to this game we can state the narrative theory of social self-construction as follows: many engagements involve incremental refinements of the selves of the (non-straightforward) agents who play G_i' so that they become new agents who, still in S_i, will play G_i. Now, strangers, unlike biological *H. sapiens* instances, really do strategically encounter one another, so G'-type games really occur. The idea I will develop in this section is that G'-type games will typically center around coordination over which of a class of games G_i: $G_1, \ldots, G_n$ will be played by the new agents, with new utility functions, that they will jointly agree (by resolving G_i') to become.

I understand the relationship between G_i' and G_l following the general approach of Binmore (1998). When Binmore himself encountered my suggestion, he interpreted my saying that the G-level game is *negotiated* in G_i' to suggest that the *overall* social coordination game is cooperative because it involves a stage of binding preplay negotiation represented as G_i'. This is not what I intend: every game I envisage here can be thought of as noncooperative. That is, if we construct the metagame G_l, G_i' ε $\mathbf{G_i}$, we should impose the requirement that all plausible solutions to G_i must be subgame-perfect Nash equilibria of $\mathbf{G_i}$ (where $\mathbf{G_i}$ is played among the agents featuring in G_l, since the outcomes of $\mathbf{G_i}$ are defined in terms of the utilities of the players of G_l). Cooperative game theory is then relevant by way of the so-called Nash program, according to which we test the robustness of a proposed solution to G_i by making sure it is *also* a solution to $\mathbf{G_i}$. It is true that players of G_i' (if G_i' is to make any sense as a construct) must make promises relevant to the play of G_l without strategic commitment. However, recent work by Skyrms (2002) shows in detail how use of costless signals can be relevant to reaching equilibria in noncooperative dynamic games, even if such signals are strategically irrelevant *at* equilibrium; and that is all that will be needed.[11]

Recall, from remarks of the previous section, the pressures under which G'-type games are played. Because of the dynamics underlying self-narrative, people can't simply *assume* self-predictability; they have to act so as to *make* themselves predictable. They do this so they can play and resolve coordination games with others. (To be predictable to others, they must be predictable to themselves, and vice versa.) Then all of this is compounded by the fact, also noted earlier, that nature doesn't neatly partition games the way analysts do in game theory texts. A person can't keep the various games she simultaneously plays with different people in encapsulated silos, so a move in a game G_i' with the stranger will *also* represent a move in other games $G_k, \ldots, {}_n$ with more familiar partners—because these partners are watching, and will draw information relevant to $G_k, \ldots, {}_n$ from what she does in G_i'.

Both of these points can be expressed by saying that nature doesn't hand people cards telling them which games they're in when. Games have to be *determined* dynamically—and determination processes are themselves games. Nor can we, in the limit, bundle all the games played by a given biological individual into one giant many-person noncooperative game **G!** played by her "core" Robinson Crusoe—an idea implicit in much of the work by political philosophers who use game theory, for example, Gauthier (1986) and Danielson (1992)[12]— because there *are no* core Robinson Crusoes.

It should be obvious that the whole system of logical pressures set up by these dynamics will be computationally intractable to a finite information processor in real time. As I said above, it's a general equilibrium problem, and a nonparametric one at that. Note that in raising this analytic intractability as a puzzle, I do not presume that people *literally* solve it, that is, that they often actually find optimal solutions to their sets of simultaneous games. The familiar phenomenon of the midlife crisis, for example, arises when people regret the formerly open possibilities their self-narratives have closed off, and so try to withdraw some but not all of their investment in their self; but, equally famously, the various pieces of the portfolio are difficult to unbundle, so valued stock is unintentionally thrown away with what's deliberately discarded, and we get the familiar Hollywood scenario of the successful lawyer who begins by acquiring a sports car and ditching his loyal wife for a young girlfriend, then ends up destitute and abandoned by all. However, I take it as a datum that most people achieve tolerable success as satisficers over the problem space. They do this at the cost of increasingly sacrificing flexibility in new game situations. This, happily, trades off against the fact that as their selves become more stable, they can send clearer signals to partners, thereby reducing the incidence of both miscoordination by error in games at the G level, and of inadvertently selecting destructive prisoner's dilemma scenarios from the G' level. This general fact itself helps to explain the prevailing stability of selves in a feedback relationship. It is sensible for people to avoid attempts at coordination with highly unstable selves. Given the massive interdependency among people, this incentivizes everyone to regulate the stability of those around them through dispensation of social rewards and punishments. As described earlier, this is how and why we get selves, as stabilizing devices, in the first place.

So how do people achieve satisfactory performance against what look like impossible computational odds? The answer lies in the fact that their selves can be stable without being rigidly *fixed*. This means that the GE problem doesn't have to be technically "solved" by reference to a stationary set of utility functions. The "satisficing," then, is all *ex post*, and "solution" has to be put in scare quotes. This will be technically disappointing to an economist, and perhaps it's morally disappointing also. But that's life. If, as Binmore (1998) argues, it is possible for the process, at the social level, to find and climb up welfare-enhancing stable equilibrium paths, it is rational for us to each concentrate on playing our corners so as to facilitate location of the paths in question rather than regretting the loss of Kantian moral optima *or* perfect Arrow–Debreu efficiency. More will be said on this in the next volume, when I consider the implications of my account for policy questions.

The basic kinds of strategic actions in coordination games are signaling moves. In a *pure* coordination game no agent has any incentive to conceal any relevant information. However, in a game where agents differentially rank equilibria, but share the desire to reach *some* equilibrium, agents are incentivized to send signals just clear enough to achieve the latter goal, but not so transparent as to cede control of equilibrium selection entirely to others. I will assume that games at both the G' and G levels often have this structure, and these are the sorts my analysis will concern. I am not thereby assuming that *no* pure coordination games or purely competitive games go on at either level—they obviously do. I merely leave them aside because they don't raise the problem of interest here—why are selves strategically useful?—and I have nothing new to say about their analysis.

When studying strategies evolved for use across whole sets of individual games—which is what we're doing when we inquire into the dynamics of a signaling system—we are automatically in the domain of dynamics. Therefore, equilibria of interest must be defined dynamically, rather than in the static way familiar from neoclassical economics or classical game theory. A common equilibrium concept used in evolutionary game theory (EGT), due to Maynard Smith (1982), is that of an *evolutionary stable strategy set* (ESS). This defines an equilibrium as a distribution of strategies in a population that satisfies two properties. The first of these is the Nash equilibrium idea inherited from classical game theory. That is, the distribution must predict expected vectors of strategies in individual interactions such that agents would not be better off, given whatever utility functions define them at the motivated point of analysis, if they switched to another existing strategy. The second property constitutive of an ESS is that the distribution not be *invadable* by some other strategy that can arise naturally in the population, either through its endogenous dynamics or through exogenous mutation.

In any formal application of an EGT model the equilibrium concept in use must be specified more exactly than has been done above. Nor will ESS, however carefully specified, suffice as a *general* solution concept for EGT, because it ignores the possible effects of correlation in strategies (which, as Skyrms 1996 shows, can be dramatic). However, focus on the general conceptual idea underlying ESS draws attention to a question that is of particular interest in coordination games: what counts, in a given context, as "a strategy that can arise naturally"? If we are welcome to consider any logically or physically possible strategy at all, then almost no plausible state of a real empirical system would literally be an ESS equilibrium. Limits on the sets of possible invader strategies to be assumed in any particular application should be based on direct empirical familiarity with the target domain, and mediated by trained judgment arising from that familiarity. However, for purposes of the coming reflections on signaling, a way of understanding the sources of these limits is provided by the idea of game determination itself. What counts as a possible strategy in a G-type signaling game will be constrained most directly by the history of the signaling system that sets up G_i'—that is, by the public language in which the players narrate themselves. Since this is beyond the control of the players, it is stable in the short or medium run from which G_i' and G_I are analyzed. This is of course one of the key themes emphasized by semantic externalists, so it is a premise that will by now be familiar here. We don't have to imagine these constraints as being tighter than everyday experience suggests. I can draw my network of intentional-stance judgments from different semantic resources in describing the same state of affairs S_i to, respectively, the board of directors, my daily coworkers in the marketing division, and my spouse. The important point here for my GE problem is that the stability of expectations governing the three different scenarios hinges on histories of coordination. Similarly, the set of "naturally available strategies" in a game G_i' will be constrained by the history of the long-run evolutionary games that produced our species.[13] Thus I speculate that no human metalinguistic signaling system gives anyone a convention for signaling in a G'-level game that there is a high probability of their changing their sex, something we *would* expect in a population of intelligent social snails if there were such things.[14]

It is not the point of the foregoing remarks to suggest that anyone will, or should try to, develop an explicit metatheory of game-level individuation that could then be wheeled out at the first stage of formally modeling some signaling phenomenon. All I have been up to over the past few paragraphs is offering some conceptual bridges between the domains of empirical behavioral science, on the one hand, and the more austere logical space of game analysis, on the other, so that my subsequent discussion of the relationship between agents and selves need not be entirely metaphorical. As emphasized above, someone setting out to model a particular social negotiation over a choice of signaling frames would and should be guided much more by empirical knowledge of the community in question than by abstract intuitions encoded in a particular formalism. But since the questions pursued here are abstract, philosophical ones, it has been necessary to sketch the general *kinds* of considerations that should enter into model specification. The reader will get a much clearer idea of the logical framework I am suggesting, however, if it is illustrated by application to some actual human communication dynamics. As promised earlier, this will simultaneously illustrate the problems, both for game-theoretic economics and cognitive science, that arise from taking Robinson Crusoe ontologically seriously.

An Example of Game Determination: Emotional Signaling

Much of the traditional literature on emotions in philosophy and psychology, which influences the understanding of that subject in economics, assumes that emotions are *inner states* of people that they can then choose—or choose not to—report (signal) or misreport (strategically or by accident) using conventional digital labels in their public language. Thus, someone might use English to say to someone else "I'm feeling blue today." Frank (1988) generated a new game-theoretic discussion of emotion by arguing that people simultaneously signal emotional states by *non*conventional signs such as facial expressions, posture, and gait, of the kind also found in social animals that lack digital signaling systems (and therefore, by Dennett's hypothesis, lack selves). The strategic significance of this duality of signaling media, according to Frank, lies in the fact that people typically have much finer discretionary control over the first kind of signaling than over the second. This makes feigning at what I have called the G-game level more difficult, since feigners are apt to be detected through mismatches between the conventional and nonconventional signals they send. This is supposed to facilitate successful social coordination by preventing information about emotional states from being rendered useless through susceptibility to strategic manipulation. Threats and promises are useful strategic moves only if agents are committed to following through on them when necessary, and if this commitment is known to other agents. An emotion such as anger can commit an agent to a threat only if the anger might cause her to retaliate even against her calmer, rational judgment. But if people could easily claim to be angry even when they weren't, without strong fear of being found out, then the strategic utility of anger would be systematically undermined by the fact that claims to being angry would not reliably signal commitment after all. Frank gives a symmetric account of those emotional sentiments, such as love and pity, which can sustain promises.

This general hypothesis can be framed in the conceptual space I sketched in the previous section as follows. Strategy availability in signaling games at the G level is *widened* by *restrictions* on the strategy space at the G' level. The restrictions in question derive from the fact that (for Frank) individual agents aren't the players at the G' level; evolutionary strategies are the real players engaged there—since they hardwired the emotional dispositions in the people—and their interests are supposed to hold the strategic flexibility of individual communicators on a helpful leash that lets them reach efficient equilibria in their G-level games that would otherwise be closed off.

Ross and Dumouchel (2004a,b) offer a number of criticisms of this hypothesis. As we will see shortly, it trips over logical objections that have their roots in microeconomic individualism. There are also, however, four empirical shortcomings to the account: (1) It seems only relevant to direct, face-to-face encounters among people. (2) It relies on an implausibly simple cognitive-behavioral dynamics, according to which emotions are exogenous forces that invade people's motivational spaces from outside, after the manner of blows to the head. All systematic study of human behavioral-control mechanisms shows them to be far more dynamic and integrated than this picture allows. (3) The hypothesis relies on a model of the social drivers of evolutionary development as anchored to an implausible extent around PD and assurance problems. (These are the sorts of games in which commitment devices are most important.) As Hampton (1986), Binmore (1994), and others have argued, games of this sort are much less ubiquitous and recurrent in the political life of a social animal than coordination games; but the hypothesis sheds no interesting light on the latter. Frank's theory requires us to believe that natural selection, when designing fundamental behavioral-control architecture, found PDs and assurance games more functionally important to hominid success than stable solutions to coordination games; but such an assumption contradicts all plausible models of how and why sociality evolved in the first place. Finally, (4) as Elster (1999a) objects, Frank selectively emphasizes the advantages emotional commitments can confer in PDs and assurance games, but devotes little attention to the harmful effects of uncontrollable rages and passions that have been the bane of everyone throughout history who has aimed to improve the general human condition.

In the context of the present concern with the relevance of cognitive science to the foundations of economics, it is objection (3) that merits further elaboration. Although Frank presents his hypothesis as a challenge to what he characterizes as a traditional "self-interest" model of agency that he associates with neoclassical economics, on close analysis it fits very naturally and comfortably into the semi-Aristotelian picture, presupposing microeconomic individualism as the conceptual starting point, of Jevons or Sen. (Therefore, as always, it can be grist for the mill of the eliminativist who sets the motivational force of self-interested utility maximization at or near zero.) Frank's agents are rational maximizers of individual utility who control their own strategic behavior by private manipulation of internally calculated options. The extreme strategic freedom this gives them can produce perils of anarchy that justify some limited government. Mother Nature—biological evolution—then helpfully steps in as an external regulator, using exogenous emotional drives to prevent her rational agents from getting entirely out of her control, and from outsmarting themselves by putting their short-term interests ahead of their long-term ones, which more approximately coincide with hers.

There is a deep reason this account sheds little light on signaling dynamics in general, one that echoes the familiar failure of neoclassical economics and anthropology to cohabit constructively: *cultural dynamics are allowed to drop out of the explanatory framework altogether*. Expressing this within the terms of the framework sketched above, G-level games among people are controlled directly by G''-level games among biological individuals. The intermediate dynamics of G'-level games are missing from the picture.

There are some strong affinities between Frank's account of the relationship between emotional and linguistic signaling, on the one hand, and internalistic semantics, on the other hand. Consider the design problem involved in coordinating a group of social organisms around a digital code. Nobody supposes that *biological*-level causation determines whether a given person settles on English or Chinese as her public language. That is, everyone agrees that the English and Chinese lexicons—let us leave aside their grammars—are solutions to cultural coordination problems. Internalists have generally left these problems inside black boxes. Chomsky (2000) justifies this by arguing that what goes on inside this box is, at present, too conceptually obscure to be understood by science at all. Pinker (1994, 1997) hopes that we will open it by explaining the histories of cultures as responses of domain-specific cognitive modules evolved in the Pleistocene era to novel environments encountered by different groups of our ancestors as they migrated about. Now, Frank no more supposes that his theory of emotions as commitment devices is a *complete* theory of the psychology of emotions than Pinker supposes that Chomskian linguistics is a complete theory of language all by itself (i.e., unsupplemented by Pinker's favored version of evolutionary psychology). But insofar as both Frank's and Pinker's accounts leave cultural coordination dynamics inside black boxes, both leave precisely the phenomena that most persuasively motivate semantic externalism—whether about the contents of emotional signals or about communication using digital language—outside their respective scopes.

I will now show how we can have a better understanding of both the cognitive phenomenon Frank aims to analyze—the nature and function of emotion—*and* the logic of game-theoretic dynamics among people, using the theoretical framework I have been developing, by summarizing the alternative account given in Ross and Dumouchel 2004a,b. Since Frank has responded to our challenge, I will return to considering his account in the context of his explicit argument with us.

The most fundamental difference between emotional signaling systems and public-language systems is that the former aim primarily at representation of an analog domain. As Dumouchel (1999) emphasizes, emotional signals are produced as outputs of continuous systems of expression; people do not go about in affectless baseline states that are then periodically modulated by the flashing of emotional phase-shift signs. The continuous dynamics of signaling between agents that goes on through variations in facial expressions, pitch and loudness of voice, posture, physical distance, degree of movement, rate of smiling, extent and duration of eye contact, and so on, settle into local equilibria to the extent that the agents reach implicit agreement on the modality of their standing relationship to one another. Are they allies or adversaries? Very significantly, do they attach value to the maintenance of the relationship modality itself that is or isn't more important to them than the outcomes of particular interactive projects in which they engage? Folk psychology codes this sort of information through a complex gradation of friendship concepts in any given culture, and it has a natural interpretation in the logical framework I have been developing here. People use emotional signaling to reciprocally coordinate their self-narratives. As such, they are determining which specific agents, as individuated by reference to utility functions, will engage in further coordination games at the G level.

This logical structure is obscured to superficial observation by the fact that G'-level and G-level games are of course not played in sequence. As always in the construction of a logical analysis, translation of the phenomena into the terms of a specific logic represents a mapping of actual bookkeeping dynamics in nature onto a more abstract dimensional structure. Resolution of equilibria at the G' level is continuously calibrated by the play of the G-level games that the former dynamics in turn regulate. As Griffiths (1997) discusses at length, empirical work on cross-cultural interpretations of emotions shows that the states and dispositions referred to together as "emotions" display high variation on the input side—that is, with respect to their causal etiologies as regards mechanisms, stimuli, and degrees of cognitive penetration of emotional responses—relative to the degree of *output* variability, that is, cross-cultural disagreement in typing and understanding of emotional responses. This can be glossed in present terms by saying: intentional-stance resources as culturally evolved compress data into restricted sets of possible narratives. This is, then, a manifestation of coordination around restrictions on G-level strategies using G'-level resources.

Let me sketch the general dynamics of this. Two people who share a substantial body of cultural conventions will have at their strategic disposal a range of labels for emotional state types encoded in their public language, which neither controls. A history of G'-level games between them will make available to them a subset of these labels with which they can characterize *salient* moments in their negotiating dynamic. Each time one person labels such a moment and the other does not demur, they will have succeeded in establishing restrictions on their expectations over strategy sets in some immediate run of G-level games. (Note that the games so influenced will often not *just* be coordination games; one agent might be selling the other some real estate. This requires, but isn't exhausted by, coordination success.) These expectations could be represented by the analyst as functions of ordered pairs matching particular assignments of emotional expressions to emotional state types, on the one hand, with assumptions about situationally sensitive incentives, on the other. (E.g., to interpret another's signal I may need to know which emotional modality as well as which incentive structures a behavior is set within. Her staring at me indicates strong interest; but is it love or anger or . . . ?) Each such function compresses the dynamics of a G'-level game, that is, maps a G'-level game structure onto an equilibrium solution. This equilibrium is then input that structures games at the G level, until such time as somebody makes a move that requires renegotiation at the G' level. Each such move is a call for some degree of self-renarration by one or both parties. (In these terms, we might characterize the folk concept of a dysfunctional relationship between two people as follows. If both agents tend to regularly demand G'-level renegotiation in which only the other is asked to renarrate herself, then they will either agree in (temporary) equilibrium on a master-slave relationship, or their G'-level games will often be zero-sum. Neither pattern has much chance of being a long-run stable or welfare-efficient one as soon as other agents enter the picture to complicate the games.)

Interpretation problems confronting signaling in such a system are formidable. This suggests a strategic rationale for the compression of highly variable input etiologies into constricted ranges of conventionalized emotional expressions: combinatorial explosion on the receiving ends of signals would otherwise destroy the informational efficacy of the signaling system. As Greenspan (2000, p. 485) notes in considering the idea that bargainers may cognitively manipulate emotions—conceived as inner states—directly, "at a certain point, calculation would become impossibly difficult, and this yields a further reason for relying on emotions as snap interpersonal evaluations." This challenge to computational load arises equally for (and so is combinatorially compounded by) mapping conventional emotional state types onto observed information about strategic settings, given *their*, external, input variability—surely even greater than the internal neurochemical variability that worries Griffiths—unless emotional outputs are themselves products of conventionalized signaling equilibria evolved at the level of cultures.

On this account, emotional signaling does, just as Frank suggests, derive its strategic usefulness *partly* from the fact that the contents of emotional signals aren't wholly under the discretionary control of senders. The content of an emotional signal is determined by judgments from the intentional stance, and the mappings between particular bodies of evidence and judgments allowed by the coherence criteria that are the very point of the intentional stance in the first place are intersubjectively negotiated. The natural intentional-stance judgments that people make incorporate culturewide patterns in these negotiations. This constitutes the social scaffolding that rescues people from the impossible task of trying to compute game determinations at the G' level simultaneously with their equilibrium strategies at the G level when these are reciprocal functions of each other, and embedded in a general equilibrium dynamics comprised of other games. Note that although this is a general equilibrium *problem*, widespread satisficing with respect to self-maintenance doesn't require computation of a unique general equilibrium *solution*—so doesn't run up against Mirowski-type worries about effectiveness. The intentional-stance judgments (most) people make about emotional signals will remain dynamically stable as long as the G'-level games they constrain determine soluble coordination games, rather than PDs and similar disasters, at the G level, often enough. This isn't *guaranteed*. Under various sorts of pressures to be studied in the second volume of this study, communities *can* fall out of signaling equilibria and break down. The dynamics of game determination relying on general use of the intentional stance merely explain why and how relative social stability is *possible* at all.

This account of the strategic role of emotions handles all of the objections raised above to Frank's theory. It applies to long-distance and extended bargaining because the constraining information provided by conventional emotional tropes, unlike the information contained in facial expressions and body language, travels through multiple media and over wider expanses of time and space. (Of course, more information doesn't hurt, and there is plenty of evidence that bargaining *is* easier in face-to-face settings. This is the standard explanation for the syndrome of "road rage," and for the frequency of "flaming" in chat groups on the Web. People in cars and communicating by keyboard emotionally miscoordinate with higher than usual frequency because they can't exchange visible signal modulators.)[15] It obviously takes better account of the continuous and feedback-modulated nature of emotional experience, since this is one of its central motivating premises. A similar remark can be made about the basic evolutionary function it attributes to emotions; it directly takes assistance in coordination, rather than escape from or avoidance of PDs, as the central problem natural selection had to solve in evolving sociality. In placing less emphasis on pure spontaneity of emotional signals, it has an easier time explaining Elster's objection as pointing to a cost worth paying, rather than one that might equally well balance or exceed the imputed benefits. Finally, it gives cultural evolution at least as powerful a role as biological evolution in explaining the specifics of emotional behavior, and so helps to make sense of the data to which Griffiths calls attention. In general, then, I contend that our account makes better sense of the data about a wider range of emotional judgments than Frank's, while retaining his sound insight that emotions are evolved bargaining aids that facilitate cooperation.

However, Frank (2004) objects that our story fails to account adequately for one datum on emotional life that he takes to be salient. This is that people often express themselves as wondering and worrying about the emotional *sincerity* of those with whom they interact. On Dumouchel's and my account this might seem puzzling. According to it, emotional signals and their interpretations (including self-interpretations) are intentional-stance judgments about the implications of situations, including data furnished by the brain about itself, but also taking account of external factors; they are not *reports* of internal, introspected, phenomena. This seems to make the very idea of sincerity, and hence of sincerity detection, impossible.

This objection is worth careful consideration here, not just because it has to be met if our account of emotions *per se* is to be persuasive, but also because it exactly isolates a general issue at the core of this book: the tension in the foundations of economics between RPT's privileging of behavioral consistency as the essence of agency, and the venerable neoclassical temptation to identify the agent with an inner, maximizing, Robinson Crusoe. It is particularly helpful here that Frank, as an economist, sets his objection in the context of its relevance to a core microeconomic topic, principal-agent problems.

Frank asks us to consider the following standard principal-agent scenario:

You are the owner of a successful local business. After careful study, you conclude that an outlet of your business would thrive in a similar city located 200 miles away. You cannot manage the outlet yourself, and the limitations of external auditing and control mechanisms will prevent you from knowing whether a hired manager has cheated you. If you could hire an honest manager, you could pay him $100,000 (twice the going rate) and still expect a net gain of

$100,000 by opening the outlet. The difficulty is that any manager you hire will face powerful incentives to cheat. By managing dishonestly, he could augment his own return by $40,000, in which case you would lose $100,000 on the venture. In that event, you would have no recourse, since there would be no way to know, much less prove, that your manager had cheated you. Would you open the branch outlet? (2004, pp. 288–289)

Frank confuses the answer he gives to this by explicitly modeling it as a game in which the payoffs represent only the two parties' narrowly self-interested, monetary incentives. If this model accurately describes their agency, then the game has a unique equilibrium: the potential manager's dominant strategy will be to cheat if the outlet is opened, so the owner will choose not to open the outlet. This result is of course Pareto inferior, but Pareto-inferior things happen. Frank seems to think that this is how a typical, neoclassically influenced model will represent the situation. It is thus supposed to count as an objection, both to me and Dumouchel and to neoclassicism, that people overcome principal-agent dilemmas like this fairly often. Frank argues that they do so using a device we can't allow: the manager can promise not to cheat, and emotional signals he can't entirely control—because his biology controls them—will enable the owner to reliably detect his sincerity.

There are two kinds of mistakes going on here: a confused technical application of game theory, and primitive cognitive science. It is central to my purposes here, because it's highly illuminating with respect to the most general thesis of this book, to show how these two mistakes comport with and compound one another.

If neoclassical economics is committed to microeconomic individualism, under Jevons's or Sen's semi-Aristotelian interpretation of that thesis, then perhaps the principal-agent game *has to be* modeled by such an economist in the way Frank models it. But classical game theory is, as discussed in chapter 4, a deductive machine for finding Nash equilibria. Therefore, if *human* principals and agents might be expected to agree to open the outlet, game theory itself convicts neoclassicism of being committed to a false model of people.

I will not here reprise the arguments of chapter 6 against the claim that neoclassical theory is or should be committed to microeconomic individualism. I *do* want to again insist, following Binmore (1994, pp. 173–256), that game theory can sensibly be applied to a situation only *after* the empirically correct model of the players and their information dynamics is inferred from the data. If Frank's principal and agent get their outlet open, then this *shows* that the game he draws for them does not accurately model their preferences. This follows from RPT itself, directly. Thus, precisely by maintaining RPT as one's modeling tool, microeconomic individualism would be rejected. Since Frank doesn't believe that microeconomic individualism provides a good *empirical* account of human behavior—for the same reasons as most behavioral-experimental economists—it might seem he ought to be on the side of me and Dumouchel here.

Frank doesn't argue this way because he feels he has to reject RPT. (He does so by repeating the standard tautology objection. Yes, use of RPT makes equilibrium selection tautologous once the right game-theoretic model of a situation is found. That's why game theory is real mathematics, not empirical science.) He rejects RPT precisely *because* use of it prohibits access to the opaque inner agent whose properties, including sincere correspondence or duplicitous mismatch with verbal announcements about preferences, are supposed to be targets for identification by both her partners in interaction and the economic analyst. Such identification would be hopeless if the possibly duplicitous person could, with relative assurance of success, strategically block access to the inner self; by an application of Grisham's law, wicked coordinators would then drive out the good and all promises (and threats) would be treated as cheap talk. Luckily, Frank contends, Mother Nature, by sending irrepressible signals through the portal of the emotions, gives us independent access to the inner agent.

The logical confusions in this picture force Frank into a raft of further conceptual revisions. Among other things, he needs a new standard of rationality against which the insincere agent will be found wanting. For this new standard he borrows the term "adaptive rationality." An adaptively rational agent is supposed to be one who acts in accordance with preferences that would produce cooperation in one-shot PDs. Thus Frank is committed to the idea of "constrained maximization" (Gauthier 1986), according to which an agent can act *against* what the neoclassical theorist regards as her preferences. Trivially, then, preferences cannot be determined by the application of RPT.

Regardless of what is true about the cognitive dynamics of people, the principles of agent individuation underlying this picture are extremely hard to make sense of. The inner self, in the case of the sincerely honest manager, is not the narrowly self-interested agent. Indeed, in this case there is no narrowly self-interested agent on the scene at all. But the person *might* have a self-interested maximizer lurking within her. So some people have inner Robinson Crusoes at their cores and some don't! Fortunately, if we pay attention to the emotional signals that the inner agent, where she exists, can't help but send, then we can catch her out. Because the proliferation of such agents would wreck our chances for Pareto efficiency, natural selection of emotional signals stands by to rescue us from them.

So natural selection, on Frank's way of thinking, builds myopically ruthless maximizers and then *also* builds devices to make them ineffective. This seems a very roundabout thing for natural selection to do. But, we are told by Frank, the pressures imposed on "nervous systems" by natural selection are "ruthless." "Of course," he says, "the *utility* experienced by dishonest managers might be no greater than that of honest managers, those who are constituted to enjoy a warm glow from behaving honestly. But the central Darwinian feature of the central nervous system is not to make people happy. It is to prompt actions that enhance reproductive fitness. And in the struggle to survive and reproduce, it is material resources, not warm glows, that count" (2004, p. 292). Therefore, "in Darwinian terms, the notion that a person might feel motivated to pass up an opportunity to cheat when there is no possibility of penalty is an anomaly of the first order" (ibid., p. 291).

As a generalization, this is just false. Even in entirely asocial animals, natural selection can build dispositions to seek "glows" that come from aiding, or even sacrificing life and limb for, offspring and relatives. It has been recognized for decades now that kin selection, although insufficient by itself to account for the complex social dispositions found in some birds and mammals, is the platform on which rich sociality can arise. (And of course, given the right genetic circumstances, kin selection alone can build rich social dynamics of other sorts, as in eusocial animals like hapladiplod insects and naked mole rats.) Evolutionary theorists thus generally do not share the amazement Frank attributes to "neoclassical economists" that one-shot PDs and similar dilemmas don't recurrently cripple social coordination and cooperation. Binmore (1998), as a student of Darwin, Dennett, and neoclassical economics all at once, appreciates in rich detail how evolution—by Darwinian steps—can build sociality out of kin selection, and then, given sociality, can build selves as what he calls "sets of coordinated empathetic preferences."[16] He provides an account (pp. 178–228), fully complementary to mine, of the Darwinian and game-theoretic steps by which a lineage of organisms can get from governance just by the logic of kin selection to the evolution and maintenance of more generalized benevolence. Needless to say, at no point in Binmore's story do any agents have to mysteriously act against their preferences, so the tautologies of game theory are not violated. (As a further point against Frank's understanding of evolution, Sober and Wilson [1998] show how even group selection can trump selection of the individuals who would be fittest in the absence of groups, under some circumstances; and their account has not been particularly controversial.)

For all these reasons, Frank's statement that "the higher material payoffs received by dishonest individuals should spell eventual extinction for honest ones" (2004, p. 292) is unmotivated as a generalization. Thus, as Hampton (1986) shows to have been recognized even by Hobbes (using different terms, obviously), one-shot PDs likely played little role in the evolutionary development of human preference dispositions by comparison with coordination games. It thus seems unlikely that natural selection built emotional dispositions to get people "out of" PDs (even if we could somehow make analytic sense of that idea). Something that comes for free with the evolution of sociality, based on dispositions to play G'-level games, is a tendency for PDs and similar efficiency traps to be avoided in the first place.[17] If we want to seek an adaptive account of the ubiquity of emotional signaling in people and other nonhapladiploid social animals, we should be asking about how such signaling might assist coordination. In this section I have suggested an answer to this question, which can be put in two complimentary ways: emotional signaling systems, coordinated by cultural evolution within communities of people, coordinate intentional-stance judgments and the stabilization of selves; they make game determination tractable.

What is left to deal with in Frank's objection is the folk phenomenology he appeals to, according to which we are aware of monitoring others' emotional signals for signs of inner sincerity or its absence. Let us try to sketch the way in which the folk model supposes that information conveyed by emotional signals facilitates cooperation and coordination. We all know that people sometimes make promises they don't intend to keep and threats on which they wouldn't really follow through. Fortunately, most people have special personal bonds with some others. These bonds are experienced by each person emotionally. The emotions in question are publicly manifest in tones of voice, body language, directness of gaze, and various other cues that people can discern and which require some skill and effort to fake. We can therefore do things with people whose emotional expressions are consistent with their bonds with us—such as form business arrangements—that would pose difficult principal-agent problems if attempted with strangers.

I needn't argue with any of this. The account isn't a theory competing with mine and Dumouchel's because it offers absolutely no explanation, and doesn't try to, of why emotions successfully signal anything. For that, one must move outside the folk picture, since folk pictures merely *describe* familiar patterns and their practical implications. The fact that folk pictures aren't built for explanation is typically exposed when they are extended to handle even slightly off-center situations; at that point, the fact that the network of folk assumptions is pure surface description with no underlying theoretical ontology tested for coherence, as in the case of a scientific theory, reveals itself.

Thus suppose you're considering hiring a manager, in the scenario described by Frank, with whom you *don't* have an established personal bond. Suppose you notice that you have a principal-agent problem. Then perhaps the potential manager stares hard into your eyes, seizes your hand in a firm and steady grip, and says with measured (but not too measured) gravity "Honesty with a business associate is more important to me than any amount of money." Now what might the folk suppose? When they *do* theorize about this—as they from time to time do—they might well turn to their description of the situation as it arises with friends. This person, they might say, is sending recognizable emotional signals that constitute a window into his soul. And, look: it's a good soul; his expressions are sincere. Or, alternatively: it's a wicked soul; he's acting. Either way, they know what to do.

At least that's how things might be rationalized post hoc. Fortunately, in this as in most important things, people are generally more sensible in their actions than in their impromptu theoretical confabulations. In real life, most people's behavior would suggest they don't take the idea of inner souls with windows for the insightful too seriously. They instead examine the behavioral track record by seeking letters of reference from disinterested parties, checking credit ratings, and asking the regulars at their pub if anyone's ever done business with this person. Certainly, they might look for indications of shiftiness, hesitation, and unusual efforts in self-presentation when interviewing the potential manager. But there is no need to interpret this as an effort to test for the presence of an inner Robinson Crusoe. Unless a person *usually* lies in his self-predictions to others, a would-be deceiver can't just let his snap, automatic, intentional-stance judgments about himself pour forth. Like someone trying to troubleshoot his computer who isn't expert in its design principles, he'll pause, revise plans, and backtrack because the operation isn't one he can just let roll. What we detect if we pick up and are warned off by such behavior is inconsistency in the whole intentional system, not a property of an inner agent. However, some people, as wise folk know all too well, *do* make careers of generating false intentional-stance judgments about themselves, and *can* smoothly mimic the G'-level strategies of cooperators. This is why the folk know to be sensible about checking references of complete strangers, but can (costlessly) hold onto Cartesian theories of personhood when probed for theoretical explanation. They can interpret their overall behavior as compatible with the idea of peering through windows into souls but there's no logical need for such interpretation. It's fully as compatible with all the behavioral facts, but much less ontologically profligate *and* more directly compatible with direct application of correct game-theoretic logic, to say that what people probe each other for in risky situations is consistency. It is, after all, a folk truism that what's hard about lying is keeping one's whole story, with all its implications, coherent under inspection.

We have the best of scientific reasons for preferring this second interpretation of sincerity-detecting behavior: our most carefully considered metaphysics of mind, in light of all available scientific evidence, tells us that you can't look into a person's soul, just as you can't look into your own, because there *are* no souls to look into. The kind of theoretical construct a soul has to be in the account Frank promotes is a Cartesian theater. But there can't be any such things. Of course, there are internal *brain processes* that are causally relevant to the contents of intentional-stance judgments. Those one can obtain some independent evidence about by watching for unusual pupil dilation, and so forth. However, Ainslie (2001) argues that the basic motivational force *at the level of brain processes* is simply "excitement"; an instance of such excitement becomes some particular conventional emotion only given a Dennettian judgment that is, again, sensitive to external dynamics, including social dynamics.

Just to resolve a kind of residual worry that usually arises when a philosopher or scientist proposes abandonment of a bit of folk ontology: it is no part of my suggestion that everything intended by the concept of sincerity, or implied by the use of the *word*, is a myth. I am not claiming—as Frank misinterprets me and Dumouchel as claiming—that people don't care about sincerity under any theoretical interpretation of that idea. Indeed, the whole Dennettian account of the self on which I'm leaning here stresses how *very* important the establishment, maintenance, control, and monitoring of consistency is in human affairs; and overall behavioral consistency is an *entirely* adequate theoretical interpretation of "sincerity." People don't need to examine souls because they can examine emotional biographies, both their own and others'.

This concludes the exercise of showing, by application to the debate over the role of emotions in bargaining, how the Dennettian theory that separates agency from selfhood conceptually undermines microeconomic individualism, and why it matters that the undermining in question is *conceptual* rather than just empirical. Frank doesn't believe that microeconomic individualism well describes human economic behavior. But because he holds onto a traditional *concept* of the neoclassical agent in one sense—as a narrowly self-interested maximizer—he twists himself into conceptual knots when he tries to capture the observed facts about human microeconomic interaction.

Should this matter much to an economist? After all, if Frank, like Sen (and for similar reasons) predicts roughly the right facts relevant to policy choices—that people will empathize and coordinate relatively well unless their surrounding institutional frameworks give them perverse incentives or their cultural distances interfere with their empathetic capacities—why should the economist need to worry if cognitive and behavioral scientists use a different model of personhood for their purposes? On either account, policy implications seem similar: try to locate and fix the harmful institutions, and set up safeguards against cultural misunderstandings while globalizing people get to know each other better. Meanwhile, won't economic modeling activity be able to proceed smoothly as before?

There is one obvious reason, repeatedly stressed in this book, why an economist might care about using a more philosophically sophisticated model of persons, informed by cognitive science. She might care about the unity of her science with others, despite not wanting to cease to be an economist and turn into a cognitive scientist or an applied philosopher. I have tried to show in this section that adequate cognitive-scientific foundations can't be provided for Frank's model of the person. Similar things have been said about Sen's model. Davis's (2003) frustrations in this respect lead him to reject cognitive-scientific foundations and to resort to normative justifications for models of personhood to be used in economics. (Mirowski, as ever, is amusing here. Recall from chapter 1 that he thinks economists won't ground their theories usefully in cognitive science because they won't be able to understand it.) If one of the things we want from a science, including economics, is *explanation*, then, as Kitcher argues and as I have emphasized, we have to care about scientific unity. Sciences borrow premises from each other. For the sake of explanation, these premises have to be at least approximately true. A science that allows itself to become ontologically stranded is a poorer science for that.

Indeed, this point can be pushed with considerable force. A science will be accepted as institutionally legitimate as long as it gets passing grades (against people's intuitive judgments) on at least one of two tests: the accounts of phenomena generated by its core argument patterns cohere smoothly with the rest of our worldview, or it produces novel and accurate predictions. Thus astrology is wholly rejected because it fails on both counts. Plate-tectonic geology attracts virtually no skepticism because it passes with flying colors on both. Now, if economists are willing to dodge the first test and disregard concern for unity, this implies that they must be prepared to rest all their claims to legitimacy on the second test. Many, persuaded by Milton Friedman's eloquent but sloppy logic, have done just this in their philosophical moments. The result crowds library shelves with popular denunciations of economics as a sham,[18] and more sophisticated jeremiads by philosophers and sociologists whose conclusions are similar even when their tone is more balanced.[19] Even increasing numbers of economists gather stones for throwing at their own house; see Heilbroner and Milberg 1995 and Lawson 1997. I see no reason to mince words about the Heilbroner and Milberg and Lawson books: I think they mainly propagate nonsense.[20] However, it is far from hard to see why they exist, and why more people who understand the subtlety and power of real, day-to-day, professional economic reasoning don't dismiss them as I have just done. Prediction, especially knockdown persuasive quantitative prediction of the sort we get from quantum physics, is immensely hard in the domain of economics. If the whole legitimacy of the discipline is allowed to rest on that, then the edifice must inevitably be plagued by termites.

In fact, it is not my view that economists predict as well as ever if they rely on false conceptual models; Friedman is just wrong about that. Frank's model, for example, would lead us to expect the honest manager to be *hyper*consistent, across vast ranges of bargaining scenarios, because his cooperatively disposed inner Robinson Crusoe maximizes its utility function consistently over its whole range of games. (Put another way: his hypothesized inner "sincerity" property is always standing by, barring another hypothesized event of inner psychological change, for use in generating predictions of what he'll do in new situations.) As I will discuss in detail in the next chapter, actual human behavior in social coordination games is a good deal more complicated than that. The manager who won't cheat in Frank's envisaged scenario, for example, might well free ride in other, only slightly modified, circumstances if he can find a way of rationalizing it to himself and others so it doesn't predict a general policy of free riding and thus undermine his self. Strong institutions should be designed for people as they actually are, and not for people as they appear in instrumentalistic models.

This point has emerged in some recent debates over the applicability of Hollis's (1998) idea of "team utility" (see also Sugden 2000; Colman 2003a). The suggestion is that people conceptualize utility functions for groups of which they are parts, distinct from their individual utility functions, and in certain types of triggering circumstances act so as to maximize the utility of "us" rather than "me." I will deal with this hypothesis extensively on its own terms, as relevant to a cognitive macroeconomics, in my second volume. For now, however, note that the distinction it draws between personal and team utility rests on the contrast between a supposed inner Robinson Crusoe and a socially embedded person, rather than following my approach of regarding the very idea of a person as presupposing social embeddedness. As Camerer (2003c, p. 157) observes, whether one opts for Hollis's and Colman's conceptualization or the one implied by my kind of account makes a predictive difference:

A correlated equilibrium requires a publicly observable variable that players commonly know. If identity is a correlating device, then when it is not commonly known, cooperation will fall apart. For example, suppose members of the A team ("informed As") are informed that they will play other As, but the informed As' partners will not know whether they are playing As or Bs. Some theories of pure empathy or group identification predict that who the other players think they are playing won't matter to the informed As because they just like to help their team-mates. The correlated equilibrium interpretation predicts that cooperation will shrink if informed As know that their partners don't know who they are playing, because As only cooperate with other As *if they can expect cooperation by their partners.*

Camerer's point can be glossed in my terms by saying that informed As play different G-level games with uninformed As than they play with informed As, because different G'-level games have determined the G-level games in the two cases. But notice, ironically, that the team-utility hypothesis, precisely because it projects team dispositions back into a Robinson-Crusoe-utility function, predicts too much social stability across situations. This exactly replicates the logic of my complaint against the predictive consequences of Frank's model of the honest manager.

I have referred several times in this book to the way in which philosophical confusions about the foundations of neoclassicism lead humanist and new-experimentalist critiques to seem to support one another, on their way to diametrically opposed pictures. As David Spurrett (personal correspondence) has pointed out to me, the argument of the present section enables us to isolate a specific instance of this. Heinrich et al. (2001) ran ultimatum, public good, and dictator games in fifteen small-scale societies and found a wide range of behavior, none of which corresponded to what they take the "canonical model" of *Homo economicus* (p. 73) to predict, namely, maximization by each player of monetary reward. However, the "canonical model" makes this prediction only for games of the relevant sort as played by asocial agents. Selves playing the games designed by Heinrich et al. have different utility functions, because they couldn't play so as to maximize monetary rewards without undermining their investments in themselves, unless their societies had institutionalized such activity in specially established settings, such as (some) industrial-society commercial markets. Nothing in the technical foundations of neoclassicism requires Heinrich et al. to assign the payoffs they do to the players of the games they set up. Thus their results do not support the humanist variety of anti-neoclassicism that is often trotted forth as their interpretation.

The argument of this section can be seen to add a further basis for concern by economists with getting the relationship between agency and personhood right. I argued that Frank's conceptual problems make it impossible for him to apply game theory in a technically consistent way. His concept of adaptive rationality has no axiomatization, and until and unless it is given one, it can't be regarded as a proper competitor to economic rationality as defined through RPT. Similarly, Sen's concept of agency fails to admit of formalization. Now, as I discussed in chapter 1, we should not insist on formalization just for its own sake. To the extent that some economists appreciate the use of arcane mathematics because it keeps a gate on their profession, we should remain self-consciously critical about this (psychologically understandable, indeed sensible) motivation. However, as I have argued, a scientific virtue stressed by the positivists that should not be retired with their incorrect theory of meaning or their reductionism is their concern for systematicity. When a microeconomic hypothesis is written in the language of RPT and game theory we can understand *exactly* what it is saying. Frank, and Sen in his recent work, are incapable of saying much that they want to express exactly. We should not *fetishize* systematicity by demanding exactness where it is *impossible*; much of "management science," for example, is a series of embarrassing attempts to express folk-psychological platitudes in spuriously technical terms, when old-fashioned, empirically careful, and strategically wise narrative histories of business decisions would serve all justifiable purposes far better. However, where exactness is possible it should be sought. As I have argued in this section, Frank does not *need* to do violence to the technical foundations of game theory to explain the strategic role of emotions, so we should resist his doing so. Binmore (1998) shows how very far one can get in applications of economic logic to complex behavioral issues while remaining scrupulous about axioms. Where a well-developed formalism can be made to fit, wear it.

Of course, the fact that we can make *a* particular formalism fit some facts doesn't show that we should adopt *that* formalism if there are alternatives available. As Gintis (2000) demonstrates, the economic eliminativists certainly don't lack for clear and rigorous mathematical resources. Evolutionary games, when modeled properly, are real, mathematical games, and my basis for interpreting Gintis as urging eliminativism, whether he self-consciously means to or not, is that in the models he and others favor there seems to be no need for either agents or rationality. In this chapter I have explained how we can use game-theoretic reasoning to understand selves as distinct from the agents with which they are ontogenetically related. I have *not* yet shown that we can't *reduce* the patterns tracked in terms of both agency and selfhood using a more general framework, such as evolutionary game theory, that need make reference only to selection and inheritance of properties without distinguishing any of these properties using concepts of maximization or intentionality. If that is possible, then we could conclude that both microeconomics and Dennettian cognitive-behavioral science have common foundations directly in biology, but that neither draws foundational resources from the other. Note that this picture would preserve unity between microeconomics and other

behavioral sciences—something that is among Gintis's explicit goals—
but by means of reduction. By my definition of pattern existence from
chapter 2, this would imply that rational agency is not a real pattern
because it is informationally redundant. Thus we'd get eliminativism,
the conclusion opposite to the humanist's, and the one glimpsed and
resisted by Mirowski, Dupré, and Davis.

This sets up my task for the next chapter, which is to show how the
dynamics of the evolution of selves make agency irreducible, at least
where humans are concerned, and perhaps in application to all social
animals. When this is accomplished, the explication of the foundations
of microeconomic theory would be complete but for one thing: it will
turn out that, in inversion of the traditional picture, microeconomics
rests on as-yet-underdeveloped *macroeconomic* foundations. That is
why the present account won't reach its full conclusion until the end
of a second volume.

8   Rational Agency and Rational Selfhood

Consolidation

Let us take stock of what's been argued. The following propositions have now been defended:

1. For the sake of maintaining a consistent foothold for systematic applications of the mathematical theories of revealed-preference analysis and game theory, economic agents are to be identified with well-ordered sets of preferences manifest in behavioral patterns.

2. The test of any scheme for individuating such agents is empirical: does application of the scheme, for a given run of cases, generate accurate data prediction of a sufficiently quantitative character to provide confirming evidence for the scheme?

3. Accurate quantitative prediction in animal ethology and ecology, obtained from application of Samuelsonian economics and game theory, justifies our modeling individual asocial animals as economic agents.

4. Robust preference-reversal and time-inconsistency phenomena from experimental economics, along with the philosophical case against introspection as a source of empirical evidence and the explanatory emptiness of mature anthropocentric neoclassicism, combine to justify the conclusion that whole people are not straightforward economic agents.

5. As individual animals become increasingly complex and social, drifting further from straightforward economic agency, stabilization of their behavior and maintenance of their cohesion (Collier 2002) requires increasing reliance on external scaffolding.

6. In people, use of evolved public signaling systems as scaffolding, in the context of pressure to resolve coordination games, results in the narrative construction of selves as behavior-stabilization devices.

7. Selves are maintained by the operation of the reflexive intentional stance.

In light of all this, the main foundational question about microeconomics that remains is: what kind of economics, if any, applies in an empirically justified and productive way to selves (which will be taken as ontologically equivalent to whole people)?

This question is still slightly ambiguous, for it can be parsed in two different ways. First, how does economics apply to people's *internal* dynamics? Second, how does economics apply to interactions *among* people?

The distinction between these questions is closely related, but in a complex way, to the distinction between microeconomics and macroeconomics. The notion that we should systematically need such a distinction in the first place must be motivated by some variety or other of antireductionism; for if mereological reductionism is true then macroeconomics constitutes practical placeholder activity that we pursue for the sake of policy while we wait for a fully mature microeconomics that has figured out how to comprehensively model complexity. In the limit, according to a mereological reductionist, only microeconomics can be ontologically serious science. (I stress the adjective "ontologically" here. Someone could hold that macroeconomics is ontologically legitimated by mereological relationships even if they don't expect anyone to find the relevant *intertheoretic* reduction principles, and thus don't anticipate achievement of a reductionist epistemology.)

In denying mereological reductionism,[1] I deny that there are general philosophical grounds for expecting macroeconomics to collapse into microeconomics, or for thinking that unless it does so macroeconomics is not serious science. This is absolutely not to suggest that substantive questions about the relationship(s) between macroeconomics and microeconomics can or should be decided on general philosophical grounds: development of economic theory and explanatory and modeling practice will determine this. The philosophical considerations merely provide a conceptual blueprint for interpreting the various possibilities that are open.

This will be the subject of my second volume. For the moment, I want to offer just enough anticipation of it to frame the closing issues of this volume in a way that indicates how much we can and can't expect to understand about economic theory by considering microeconomics alone.

Macroeconomics was born in the context of Keynes's *pragmatic* antireductionism. Though Keynes was an astute student of philosophy, he made it utterly clear that his working antireductionism was justified by the urgency of making policy in a crisis (and the urgency of minimizing future policy crises), for which an economics based on a priori atomist assumptions had failed. For this, he is rightly regarded as a hero. However, the philosophical issues in the foundations of economics as a whole that he deferred have never been adequately revisited by the profession. The new classical macroeconomics (see Hoover 1988) was also mainly motivated by policy concerns, but seemed more philosophically significant than it was for the accidental reason that, believing microeconomic analytical techniques to have matured, it couched itself in the language of "microfoundations." The foundations in question were purely technical, and not ontologically serious: nothing in the empirical world corresponds to a representative, infinitely lived agent. (Note that I add no skeptical comment here about atomless measure spaces. In keeping with a running theme in this book, applied to RPT and game theory too: there is no reason to require that mathematical objects—atomless measure spaces or utility functions—correspond to empirical objects. They are modeling tools.)

The argument given so far in this book invites us to inquire into the relationship between macroeconomics and microeconomics as a topic in (nonreductionistic) *ontology*. The seven propositions listed above enable us to identify some remaining questions that need to be asked in order to set up this inquiry.

To the extent that selves can and should be modeled, following the suggestions of Dennett, Ainslie, and many others (Minsky 1985; Kavka 1991; Schelling 1980, 1984), as *communities* of economic agents, then, given the denial of mereology, we might expect that if systematic macroeconomics turns out to be possible, it should apply not only to interactions among people, but to the interactions among agents whose dynamics constitute people. We might, that is, model people as markets. This idea has been mooted before: it is an apt way of describing Schelling's (1980, 1984) suggestions, and, as we will see in a bit more detail below, it is a good interpretation of Ainslie's (2001) and Glimcher's (2003) research programs. Davis (2003, chapter 4) surveys attempts to break up the person into economic agents and then analyze their dynamics like those of any other market—something he, as a humanist, of course resists. But this is clearly an idea much in the air.

The reader might now be hoping and expecting that I'm going to offer a further mixture of technical analysis and philosophy of cognitive science to permit us to pronounce for or against (perhaps modified versions of) these programs, so that we can have the theory of the economic person all cleared up in advance of the foray, in the next volume, into the systematization of relationships among people. Unfortunately, things can't and won't be that neat. The problem is that if the denial of atomism and mereology is to be taken truly seriously, there are two ontological stories we should not, on reflection, expect to be able to tell. First, we won't be able to additively *assemble* multiperson markets out of people. Second, we also won't be able to additively *assemble* people out of internal agents. Indeed, more than the denial of atomism and mereology stands in the way of the second ambition. Led by Dennett, Clark, and other contributors to the foundations of cognitive science, I have doubted the existence of a stable boundary between the interior and exterior of the person. This suggests that the interface between the microeconomic and the macroeconomic won't nicely coincide with the point at which persons—however unlike Robinson Crusoe they might be—are fixed and dressed up to enter interpersonal markets.

Completing the theoretical construction of the economic person thus can't precede investigation of macroeconomics. Microeconomics and macroeconomics are going to be built *into* each other, not worked up as separate modules and then glued together. So the scene at the conclusion of this volume is still going to be a construction site. However, there *is* further work to do first that's still on the traditionally "micro" side of the lot. For the sake of leaving us with some sense of interim resolution, this will at least enable us to complete a main task pursued in the first half of the book, namely, closing off the debates between neoclassicists and others that dominated the philosophy of economics in the age of atomism, and finishing the specification of an economic argument pattern as identified by Robbins and Samuelson between them.

So, back to work.

Selves and Agents 1: Lessons from Neuroeconomics

Straightforward observation of nature tells us that biological individuals don't *have to* play coordination games (beyond low levels required by sexual reproducers and those whose offspring require periods of care) in order to maintain themselves. Indeed, most species of animals are asocial. It is equally obvious that sociality is one strategy that can work, often quite spectacularly. Finding coordination equilibria, as I have stressed, is the *essence* of sociality. Thus the economic agency of some biological individuals itself promotes the evolution of coordination capacities. But the hump in evolutionary design space that must be mounted to reach sociality is evidently steep, since natural selection doesn't generally climb it. What accounts for its steepness, as I indicated in the last chapter, is the work that must be done to prevent socialized individuals from being overwhelmed by complexity. The porousness of the internal–external boundary in social conditions threatens the cohesion of the individual.

It is implicit in the account of the previous chapter that selves serve two functions simultaneously, but I have so far laid more stress on only one of them. I have concentrated on the idea that *H. sapiens* agents who are identified as representative types within ranges of flexibility determined by cultural evolution play G'-level games, in which they stabilize dynamics in bargaining by digitally compressing information, attaching conventional labels to some salient, recurrent elements in their dynamics using resources drawn from a digital public language. This then enables them to play particular G-level games *as* particular agents, well defined by specific utility functions that both bargainers can infer to tolerable levels of determinacy. This in turn permits them to find equilibrium often enough for the satisfaction of typical social goals. I have further suggested, drawing on Dennett's account of the person, that the G-level agents are *brought into being by* their G'-level dynamics, that is, by the judgments they make about themselves using publicly anchored natural-language semantic distinctions they don't individually control. This yields one notion of "function" relevant to the explanation of selves. Note, however, that it corresponds better to the sociologist's conception of function than to the biologist's. We can see how having a self is useful to an already socialized agent. In addition, we can see how being a member of a community of selves might confer competitive advantages over membership in a group of social agents without selves, which could make operative the conditions for efficacy of group selection, as described by Sober and Wilson (1998). But this doesn't functionally explain how natural selection stumbled across dispositions to build selves in the first place.

Note that it wouldn't be a decisive objection to the theory of the self I have given if no such explanation were available. Perhaps selfhood arose as an accidental by-product of digital signaling, which was itself selected for some other reason. Alternatively, perhaps selfhood arose through the operation of the Baldwin effect. That is, perhaps barely self-conscious protoselves captured higher utility in a manner visible to others, and were imitated. Natural selection might then have favored the special genetic properties of the good mimics, setting up a ratchet process in which better and better self-narrating capacities evolved biologically. On this account—which often seems to be Dennett's favorite candidate (see his 1995)—no *original* "disposition to self-narrate" need be *directly* grounded in biology. Selves could just be what you get when cultural evolution goes to work on skilled mimics with digital signaling systems, and biological selection follows along.

This being acknowledged, it is still to an account's advantage, all else being equal, if it *does* suggest a biologically based function—a "proper" function in the sense of Millikan (1984)—for selfhood. The account I gave in chapter 7, I want now to argue, does so. Furthermore, adding this second function for the self accounts parsimoniously for empirical data that otherwise require a separate explanation. I will make this argument by considering and contrasting two views that both motivate an "economics of the internal," those of Glimcher (2003), and Ainslie (1992, 2001) (as already described in chapter 5). The verdict of this argument will indicate why we can't expect to develop complete foundations for microeconomics and macroeconomics as distinct projects and then just glue the results together.

Glimcher (2003) offers a methodological and epistemological manifesto for a research project that has come to be known as neuroeconomics. Montague and Berns (2002) provide a partial survey from a somewhat different perspective. The name of the program is intended to convey its fundamental idea—one I of course share—that economic analysis is a crucial tool for understanding evolved behavioral patterns in animals. Montague and Berns (p. 276) express the relevant conception of "economic" in terms corresponding closely, at the conceptual level, to the perspective defended in this book. That is, they note that mobile animals are confronted with a special class of problems—economic problems—because they (1) confront markets offering assets at prices they don't control, (2) must comparatively value these assets in a common currency, and (3) live in conditions in which both the assets and their resources, as measured in the currency, are scarce. Neuroeconomics takes (1) and (3) as assumed, and seeks to discover the currencies used by brains in valuing goods and services from disparate asset classes (e.g., food, drugs, investments in mates, security from predators, etc.) against one another. Note that this methodology is justified by the philosophy of economics for which I have been arguing. Ordered preference (1) and scarcity (3) are taken as foundational, while the target of maximization (2)—expected utility? minimization of losses? lexicographic maximization within frames?—is treated as the variable whose value must be discovered.

Because I am still engaged in the project of understanding the foundations of economics, I will follow Glimcher's justification of neuroeconomics as a research program, as his first principles don't take the very ones I am defending for granted. He develops the argument for neuroeconomics as a cascade built out of several subarguments. Up to a crucial point, this cascade is similar to the one Dennett (1995) gives in favor of a broadly adaptationist methodology in the behavioral sciences, though with more explicit attention to the details of economic theory. I will say quite a bit more about the importance and justification of adaptationism later in this chapter. First, however, I want to stay focused on the issue of the relationship between selves and subpersonal economic agents. I will do this by identifying what I just called the crucial point of divergence between Glimcher and Dennett, which in turn will take us to Ainslie's quite different conception of subpersonal agency, and thereby to the role of such agency in explaining the biological basis of selfhood.

The first step in Glimcher's cascade consists in showing how carefully and seriously throughout its history neuropsychology has tested Descartes's conceptual scheme, as refined into a proper scientific paradigm by Arthur Sherrington and Ivan Pavlov, for understanding the causal generation of action. Descartes of course resolved such generation into a volitional, nonphysical component and a mechanical, physical component. Sherrington modeled the latter as the operations of networks of reflex arcs whose connections were described by Boolean algebraic relations. Pavlov added the concept of conditioning by stimuli to avoid Cartesian dualism yet retained the fundamental distinction between efferent and afferent pathways. Glimcher reviews the meticulously designed series of experiments in the late twentieth century that empirically refuted this model, showing that efferent and afferent functions cannot be taken as modular. Dennett (1991b) provides a complementary conceptual argument for exactly the same conclusion on his way to motivating the MDM. Just as there is no place in the *whole* organism, as Dennett insists, where representations are

delivered to a Cartesian theater to stimulate action, so there is no physical location in a nervous system, or even in a single neural node, where
sensory input stops and motor output starts.

Glimcher's next argument is methodological, and again echoes
Dennett exactly. If we cannot do neuropsychology from the bottom up,
because the brain doesn't include many or any mechanical reflexes,
then we need a top-down strategy that begins by identifying the tasks
that neural circuits evolved to perform. Glimcher follows the brilliant
and influential AI theorist David Marr (1982) in arguing that we should
link specifications of evolutionary functions to the physical implementation theories we ultimately seek by specifying a computational algorithm for each identified function. How modular a given system is in
functional terms is in each instance an empirical question, though one
that will be underdetermined from evidence at either the neurophysiological level or the evolutionary-theoretical level (what Dennett calls
the "design stance" level; see Ross 2002a) alone; we need to determine
the computational account of the system by working to reflective equilibrium among evidence and inferences at both levels. This perspective
of course involves use of adaptationist reasoning of some sort and to
some extent. Again, I will say more about this later in the present
chapter. Glimcher defends adaptationism by appeal to evidence for
convergence, the widespread tendency of evolution to repeatedly
produce morphologically and behaviorally similar organisms whose
similarity does not result from inheritance (see Conway Morris 2003).
By inference to the best explanation, convergence justifies viewing evolution as often facing and solving functional design problems, although
it is neutral about the relative contributions to these problems made by
limitations on the niches ("ways of making a living") available in the
terrestrial environment, and limitations on the phylogenetic pathways
opened by historical accidents ("canals"). Dennett (1995) argues that
we should expect the former to be dominant the longer our temporal
horizon, but I will postpone this issue for now. (It will be discussed in
the final section of this chapter.)

Functional accounts of organisms implicitly assign utility functions
to them, to be identified with expected fitness. We can avoid practical
underdetermination problems with respect to sorting organisms into
kinds for assignment of utility functions only by motivating particular
phylogenetic trees on the basis of independent—fossil and molecular—
evidence. (This is a domain of lively disputes [Wheeler and Meier
2000], which I will need to bypass.) Functional decompositions of

organisms by means of computational specifications in turn imply assignments of utility functions to *parts* of organisms.

At this point we are of course automatically in the domain of economics. Furthermore, the economics in question must obviously be Samuelsonian, since no one imagines that parts of organisms have utility functions based on internally represented preferences. Glimcher's main argument is that the neuropsychological method should consist in using economic analysis to generate hypotheses that assign maximization problems to functional groups of neurons. These hypotheses may then be tested by monitoring brains (under functional magnetic resonance imaging [fMRI] and other probes) while subject animals perform carefully isolated tasks. Most of the intellectual challenge in such work consists in cleverness at designing experiments that perform the relevant isolations. As with the efforts of experimental economists reviewed in chapter 5, philosophers and other abstract theorists should refrain from armchair skepticism about the limits on such cleverness until they have studied histories of experimental protocols and their justifications. Glimcher provides outstanding reviews of several such histories (2003, chapters 10 and 12). These resist summary because the density of their details—as with the computational implementations of Kitcherian argument patterns discussed in chapter 4—is the source of their power as arguments. The reader is therefore again referred offline here. The basic method can be stated, however. One habituates subjects to associate reward levels with optimal performance in tasks that require groups of neurons to perform anticipatory focus—for example, saccading the eyes across the external manifold in a way that tracks the past frequency distribution of the target on the scene—but then violates the expectations in question. By measuring properties of the response lags as the subjects adjust, the experimenter can distinguish between the monitoring of matched present value and the monitoring of expected utility by the neuronal groups themselves. Such measurements can consist in two sorts of probes: behavioral (e.g., measuring saccades) and neuronal (e.g., measuring activation rates of the isolated neurons). These measurements then can be compared in seeking to confirm or reject particular hypotheses concerning the representation and processing of economic information by neurons.

Glimcher's general case for the efficacy of doing biology by application of Samuelsonian economics relies, like mine, on appeal to the impressive track record of the approach in behavioral and cognitive ethology and ecology. His review (2003, chapter 9) of the surprising, accurate quantitative predictions delivered by microeconomic analysis in these domains is recommended for any reader unfamiliar with this literature.

Of course, Samuelsonian microeconomics cannot be used to generate *quantitative* predictions unless some specific theory of utility is stapled to RPT. But, as in experimental economics generally, the theory in question is itself isolated for independent testing by the sorts of procedures described above—with the advantage here that Becker-style insulation of utility theories by resort to exotic preference hypotheses is blocked by the fact that the evolutionary-functional frameworks in use have already been constrained by the prior phylogenetic analysis.[2]

Here we face an issue with which I have wrestled at several points in this book. Glimcher, like Dennett (1995), argues that we should treat EUT as our null hypothesis, on grounds that when we model natural selection as a designer, we have no motivation for treating it as working within heuristics, since it faces no time constraints. However, because the individuals, organs and functional modules it produces *do* face such constraints, we should not expect to find that *they* maximize expected utility if expected utility is identified with expected fitness. What interests the biologist or the neuropsychologist is how they actually process information. This goal allows the scientist some interpretive slack, to be used pragmatically, in choosing a framework for economic analysis. She can continue to work with EUT throughout her study and aim to discover information-processing dynamics by comparing actual behavior with behavior that would be predicted *if* the systems she studies were expected-utility maximizers. Alternatively, if she has already established some properties of the processing, she may treat a given system as maximizing the value of a function identified by a heuristic she has justified by computational analysis following her initial economic analysis. Either way, of course, she relies on RPT throughout; without it, nothing in the methodology makes sense.

The punch line of Glimcher's main argument comes in his discussion of the significance of work done by him and his collaborators in which monkeys are trained to play inspection games against computers. In an inspection game, one player faces a series of choices either to work for a reward, in which case he is sure to receive it, or to perform another, easier, action ("shirking"), in which case he will receive the reward only if the other player, the inspector, is not monitoring him. Assume that the first player's (the worker's) behavior reveals a utility function bounded on each end as follows: he will work on every occasion if the inspector always monitors, and will shirk on every occasion if the inspector never monitors. The inspector prefers to obtain the highest possible amount of work for the lowest possible monitoring rate, thus deriving profits from her private information. In this game, the only NE for both players are in mixed strategies, since any non-random pattern in one player's strategy that can be detected by the other can be exploited. For any given pair of specific utility functions for the two players meeting the constraints described above, NE is well defined as a pair of mixed strategies in which the worker is indifferent, on each trial, between working and shirking and the inspector is indifferent, on each trial, between monitoring and not monitoring.[3] (See Ross and LaCasse 1995 for a general discussion of inspection games in the context of a revealed-preference interpretation.)

Applying inspection game analyses to pairs or groups of people requires us to have *either* independently justified their utility functions over all variables relevant to their play, in which case we can define NE and then test to see whether they successfully maximize expected utility; *or* to assume that they maximize expected utility, or obey some other rule such as a matching function, and then infer their utility functions from their behavior. Either such procedure can be sensible in different empirical contexts. But epistemological leverage increases greatly if the utility function of the inspector is exogenously determined, as it often is. (Police implementing random roadside inspections to catch drunk drivers, for example, typically have a maximum incidence of drunk driving assigned to them as a target by policy, and an exogenously determined budget. These determine their utility function, given a distribution of preferences and attitudes to risk among the drivers.) In the case of Glimcher's experiments, the inspector was a computer, so its program was entirely under experimental control and its side of the payoff matrix could be known. Proxies for the subjects' expected utility, in this case fruit juice for the monkeys, could be antecedently determined in parametric settings. The computer could be programmed with the economic model of the monkeys, and could search the data on their behavior in game conditions for exploitable patterns, varying its strategy accordingly. With these variables fixed, expected-utility-maximizing NE behavior by the monkeys could be calculated and tested by manipulating the computer's utility function in various runs of the game.

Gödel's theorem being a theorem, Glimcher's monkeys presumably did not instantiate complete models of mathematics in their computations. Nevertheless, their behavior after training tracked NE very robustly, as does the behavior of people playing similar games for monetary prizes (2003, pp. 307–308). Working with trained monkeys, Glimcher and colleagues could perform the experiments of significance here. Working and shirking behaviors for the monkeys had been associated by their training with staring either to the right or to the left on a visual display. In earlier experiments, Platt and Glimcher (1999) had established that, in parametric settings, as juice rewards varied from one block of trials to another, firing rates of each neuron in the parietal cortex that controlled eye movements could be trained to encode the expected utility to the monkey of each possible movement *relative to* the expected utility of the alternative movement. Thus "movements that were worth 0.4 ml of juice were represented twice as strongly [in neural firing probabilities] as movements worth 0.2 ml of juice" (p. 314). Unsurprisingly, when amounts of juice rewarded for each movement were varied from one block of trials to another, firing rates also varied.

Against this backdrop, Glimcher and a colleague (Dorris) sought to investigate the way in which the monkeys' brains implemented the tracking of NE. When the monkeys played the inspection game against the computer, the target associated with shirking could be set at the optimal location, given the prior training, for a specific neuron under study, while the work target would appear at a null location. This permitted Glimcher and Dorris to test the answer to the following question: did the monkeys maintain NE in the game by keeping the firing rate of the neuron constant while the optimal and actual behavior of the monkey as a whole varied? The answer, robustly reflected in the data, was "Yes." Glimcher reasonably interprets these data as suggesting that neural firing rates, at least in this cortical region for this task, encode expected utility in both parametric and nonparametric settings.

Further analysis pushed the hypothesis deeper. When the computer playing the inspector's role was presented with the same sequence of outcomes as its monkey opponent had received on the previous day's play, for each move it was asked to assess the relative expected values of the shirking and working movements available on the next move. Glimcher reports a "positive correlation" (though unfortunately indicating no strength coefficient) between small fluctuations around the stable NE firing rates in the individual neuron and the expected values estimated by the computer trying to track the same NE. Glimcher comments on this finding as follows: "The neurons seemed to be reflecting, on a play-by-play basis, a computation close to the one performed by our computer. . . . [A]t a . . . [relatively] . . . microscopic scale, we were able to use game theory to begin to describe the decision-by-decision computations that the neurons in area LIP were performing" (2003, p. 317). Since the computations seemed to be the same in both parametric and nonparametric tasks, "neurons in area LIP *did* seem to see all of behavior as a single continuum governed by a single set of goal directed rules and computations" (ibid.).

This general hypothesis has begun to be experimentally applied to people, with encouraging preliminary results. Breiter et al. (2001) found correlates of utility tracked by discrete elements of the human reward pathway. Interestingly, in this case the maximization target was predicted by prospect theory, rather than by unrefined application of EUT. Montague and Berns (2002) report the astonishing result that human orbitofrontal cortex responds to changes in the expected utility of monetary rewards—that is, *values* such rewards—in accordance with a functional form that, given distributions of risk-aversion levels in groups of randomly drawn subjects, corresponds to the dominant Black–Scholes model of portfolio option pricing in financial markets. The idea is not, of course, that everyone has replicated Black's and Scholes's analysis. (Nobel prizes for all!) It is that Black and Scholes accurately captured the market data resulting from the valuation principles that brains really implement.

In some obvious respects this research program, if it continues to support impressive empirical results as it is extended further, is good news for the defender of old-fashioned microeconomics as a behavioral science. RPT, classical game theory, and the various models of maximization targets are used directly to establish optima for specific organs or functional modules in specific task settings. We then gather performance data on the organ or module performing the task, using the conceptual vocabulary of economics, and compare these to the optima we have calculated. The difference is used to make inferences about both the computational and causal-dynamical properties of the system, and these inferences can then be empirically tested. This conceptual logic can be iterated at a higher level of analysis. Once one has discovered how an organ or module works, and in precisely which ways it falls short of optimality relative to its own utility function, one can ask how the mechanism or algorithm might be optimal after all, in the sense of implementing a heuristic in the wider context of its integration into an economic agent—the whole organism—who must make trade-offs in light of its range of ecological pressures and budget of resources. This last step would call, essentially, on the tools of general equilibrium analysis (with the whole organism treated as analogous to a macroeconomy). The entire postwar neoclassical kit is thus brought to bear, and in just the way its builders envisaged. Glimcher (2003, pp. 334–336) explicitly promotes this as the method of neuroeconomics near the end of his book. It had been anticipated repeatedly by Dennett (see his 1994, though Glimcher does not cite him), as the epistemology of "reverse engineering."

Since I am going to point out some difficulties faced by this happy picture, let me first make clear that I will most emphatically not be impugning its importance. The discoveries about neuronal activity reported by the neuroeconomists are intensely exciting, and they could not have been achieved without the application of Samuelsonian economics. Along with the successes in behavioral ecology and ethology I have joined Glimcher in citing and celebrating, they thus solidly verify the empirical utility of good old-fashioned microeconomics as described in chapter 3 of this book. Berns (2003) states the point in a way that explicitly echoes the conclusion of the argument in Ross 2002c (reiterated in chapter 6) about the subpersonal level as the site of straightforward agency in people. "The interaction of different pools of neurons in the brain," says Berns, "may result in phenotypic behavior that appears to be irrational, but it is possible that the rational agents are the neurons, not the person" (2003, p. 156). "Neuroeconomics" is exactly the apt name for the program for understanding the neural basis of the behavioral response to scarcity.

However, I will now argue that we cannot rest in satisfaction that this picture approaches the full story about the application of economics to behavior. (Glimcher nowhere claims that it might.) The neuroeconomists' discoveries about brains describe rather more than they explain, for a reason that will by now be familiar to a reader of this book. They complicate, as much as they illuminate, the ontological and dynamic relationships between straightforward economic agents and the larger systems in which they are embedded.

Following Marr and the tradition in classical AI that Marr's thought influenced, Glimcher repeatedly invokes modules as the basic engines of behavior. The visuomotor cortex, as a system, is the starring module in Glimcher's discussion. As with modules generally in cognitive science, this one seems to fill a crucial explanatory need because it implements an aspect of monkey intelligence without itself being as complex as the whole monkey. It has a stable and hardwired goal that determines its maximization target when we describe it with a utility function: find a set of firing rates, one for each of its component neurons, such that corrections demanded from elsewhere in the system are minimized. It has the information necessary to make its optimization problem well defined because the component neurons actually encode expected utility. It is relatively encapsulated from the rest of the system, so we can understand how *it* works before trying to integrate it into a functional model of the wider system. (See Cummins 1975, Fodor 1987, and Ross 1993b, chapter 6, for why this is so useful in psychology.) With reference to my argument in chapter 6, and Berns's remark about "rational neurons" quoted a few paragraphs ago, it is thus a straightforward economic agent, just like an insect.

Before Dennett, in his 1991b and thereafter, turned more of his attention to the evolutionary dynamics of selves, he gave more emphasis than he has since to the idea of explaining complex behavior by "the progressive discharge of homunculi." It is worth quoting him (from 1978) at length on this:

> One starts . . . with a specification of a whole person or cognitive organism . . . an intentional system . . .—or some artificial segment of that person's abilities (e.g., chess-playing, answering questions about baseball) and then breaks that largest intentional system into an organization of subsystems, each of which could itself be viewed as an intentional system (with its own specialized beliefs and desires) and hence as formally a homunculus. In fact, homunculus talk is ubiquitous in AI, and almost always illuminating. AI homunculi talk to each other, wrest control from each other, volunteer, sub-contract, supervise, and even kill. . . . Homunculi are *bogeymen* only if they duplicate *entire* the talents they are rung in to explain . . . If one can get a team or committee of *relatively* ignorant, narrow-minded, blind homunculi to produce the intelligent behavior of the whole, this is progress. A flow chart is typically the organizational chart of a committee of homunculi (investigators, librarians, accountants, executives); each box specifies a homunculus by prescribing a function *without saying how it is to be accomplished* (one says, in effect: put a little man in there to do the job). If we then look closer at the individual boxes we see that the function of each is accomplished by subdividing it via another flow chart into still smaller, more stupid, homunculi. Eventually, this nesting of boxes within boxes lands you with homunculi so stupid (all they have to do is remember whether to say yes or no when asked) that they can be, as one says, "replaced by a machine." One *discharges* fancy homunculi from one's scheme by organizing armies of such idiots to do the work. (Dennett 1978, p. 119)

I still think this program is broadly right as a way of explaining what the *brain* contributes to intelligent, complex behavior. So it is the right program for a neuroscientist like Glimcher. However, I speculate that there is a good reason why the strategy of explanation-by-homuncular-discharge receives less emphasis in Dennett's later work. Once we start to understand the self as a product of *social* dynamics, in the way described in the previous chapter, and once we invoke external scaffolding in the environment to account for much of its information processing, it is no longer plausible to think that we can decompose the *self* into buglike economic agents—the soldiers in Dennett's "armies of idiots"—even if we can so decompose the *brain*. The program of homuncular discharge is a basically reductionist program; but by at least the time of his 1991a, Dennett had moved radically away from reductionism about intentionality. Ross 2000 and Ross et al. forthcoming, as invoked back in chapter 2, push his ideas to their logical limit in the antireductionist direction.

Now, do Glimcher's empirical findings about monkey cortex carry us in the direction of reductionistic homuncular discharge or not? They will seem to as long as we emphasize functional modules. However, although Glimcher often gestures at modules in his methodological remarks—especially when locating his foundations in Marr's work—his empirical focus is on individual neurons. Are these the homunculi so stupid that all they have to remember is to keep firing at one rate until an error signal tells them to try an adjustment? Yes, perhaps. But then what system are they decompositions *of*? Note that the utility function relative to which they enable the tracking of NE is the whole monkey's, not theirs. Somehow, the monkey's utility function controls the parameters that determine the specific firing rate at equilibrium for each neuron. Perhaps this control is modulated by modular structures at the level of cortical regions, but if so the work described by Glimcher gives no evidence for this, and even if it did this would just amount to a detail about implementation architecture from the perspective of the concern now being raised. A module buffering the economic relationship between the monkey and the neuron would, just like the neuron itself, be an agent with no autonomy. This is, of course, precisely why neurons and modules, if there are modules, make such nice economic agents. But crucial questions about the dynamics of control in this economy they implement are left unanswered.

The sociality of monkeys is perhaps reflected in the fact that their neural agents coordinate so as to track NE; it would be surprising if natural selection bothered to give asocial animals such capacities.[4] This is part of the reason Glimcher chose monkeys as subjects. (It would be interesting to know what tiger visuomotor neurons do when tiger economic problems are turned nonparametric by an experimenter.) But, if the account of selves given in chapter 7 is correct, it is unlikely that monkeys stabilize their social coordination by narrating selves. To the extent that we can therefore identify the whole-monkey-as-agent with its whole brain, the explanatory questions about control left open by Glimcher's findings don't raise conceptual problems, but just invite study of neural feedback mechanisms. Let neuroscientists by all means get on with this. But Glimcher's closing philosophical reflections on his work suggest one element of naïveté that will cause problems when we try to develop the general model as a hypothesis about humans. Glimcher wonders, naturally enough, about the possible role of consciousness in the setup. "It is," he speculates, "a process, produced by the brain, that generates behavior. . . . It is presumably an evolved mechanism with which our neurobiological hardware achieves behavior" (2003, p. 344).

Whatever exactly Glimcher has in mind by "consciousness" here, it is evidently something he thinks can be produced internally. Since whatever sets the maximization targets for the neurons must be information tracked at the level of the whole monkey, using "consciousness" to denote the awareness of this information isn't unreasonable with respect to some folk usages of the term. As ever, the philosopher should not try to lecture scientists on how to talk. But if "consciousness" just labels the black box by which monkeys coordinate their internal agents, then the problems with explaining human *self-consciousness* that the MDM was partly developed to address have just been bypassed.

Suppose human visuomotor neurons also encode expected utility (either unrefined or, as suggested by the Breiter et al. 2001 results, refined by prospect theory). In that case, this would partly explain how our *brains* contribute whatever they do to our ability to track NE. (We still, of course, have the same unanswered questions about the feedback mechanisms as arise with the monkeys.) But, in the conceptual framework of the last chapter, this would explain only our ability to play games at what I called the G'' level. Recall the point that only pre-socialized infants (and perhaps severely autistic people) play these games. It's no doubt essential that the infants can do so, since this is their wedge into socialization, that is, into the ability to play G' and G-level games. But in figuring out how G''-level games are monitored by brains, we haven't even started to address the cultural game dynamics that provide the functional explanation of selfhood.

Like the evolutionary psychologists—Cosmides, Tooby, Pinker—who try to get too much work in the explanation of human behavior out of strong internal modularity, Glimcher in his philosophical moments still hasn't escaped entirely from Descartes's shadow. In the context of the issues I've canvassed in the foundations of economics, his neuroeconomics is still individualist. In the context of issues in the foundations of cognitive and behavioral science, he hasn't wholly broken free of what Dennett (1991b) calls "Cartesian materialism," because if we try to apply the story about whole monkeys *directly* to whole people, we lose the *virtuality* of the self and are sent looking for it *in* the brain.

"Neuroeconomics" denotes exactly what the label suggests: an economics of brains. Neurons, and perhaps, at one level of organization higher, modules, are its agents. As with applications to the straightforward agents who feature in the cognitive ethology and ecology of asocial animals, it is an ideal site for Samuelsonian microeconomics, loaded and run just as the original manual from the shop instructed. But if we're interested in applying economic theory to people we need something more. Because selves are stabilized by the external pressures of social dynamics—which they reciprocally stabilize—they won't decompose into bugs and macroeconomics (as behavioral science) won't reduce to microeconomics.

We can drive this point home in a context of real behavioral research by turning to a program that is in tune with the Dennettian songsheet all the way: George Ainslie's "picoeconomics."

Selves and Agents 2: Lessons from Picoeconomics

Since taking the intentional stance toward a system is to explain and predict its behavior by reference to its reasons, modeling neurons or modules as maximizing utility functions involves taking the intentional stance toward them. Recall from chapter 2, however, that if intentional-stance functionalism is not to be a form of instrumentalism, then the only "ontologically serious" ascriptions of intentionality are those that capture information that could not otherwise be tracked by any physically possible tracker. (The claim that some such ontologically serious proposals can be justified is the core commitment one makes in denying mereological reductionism.) This is why, if we explain how a system instantiates its intentionality by decomposing its information processing into the operations of Dennett's idiot soldiers, intentionality as *a process* is "discharged" (and thereby explained).

This point motivates a distinction between two quite different senses in which an agent can be analyzed as a community of subagents. In the case of Glimcher's neurons, use of the intentional stance is *epistemologically* nonoptional as a methodology because the whole agent is an ineliminably intentional system; but once one has figured out how the neurons work by use of the method, and can account for their operations in isolation in terms of physical properties, they should not be conceptualized as real intentional systems. (Just to be clear, let me stress: this is not a version of eliminativism because the *methodological* necessity of the intentional stance for studying the neurons derives from the fact of ineliminable intentionality at the level of the larger system. Thus the complete explanation of the neurons' functioning requires recognition of intentionality as a real pattern—but the pattern in question isn't the neurons' *own* intentionality.) Thus this form of agent decomposition explains how an agent implements aspects of its intentionality by reference to nonintentional subsystems.

By contrast, we sometimes analyze irreducibly complex intentional systems by reference to systems whose intentionality is also irreducible. One will get nowhere in studying international politics if countries aren't sometimes recognized as irreducible intentional systems; but almost all of one's generalizations about countries' behavior will come out false if one doesn't also recognize that countries are the products of dynamic relationships among other irreducibly intentional systems (individual people of course, but also networks of shared identity—the Microsoft Corporation, the Canadian federal civil service, the gay community of San Francisco, the Council of Xhosa hereditary chiefs, the Southern Baptist Church, the United States Marine Corps, the fishing communities of western France). To deny mereology in the case of an intentional system is to deny that the intentionality of a system like a country is just the intentionality of all its citizens composed by addition.

Neither of these approaches to intentional-system decomposition is all that controversial in practice (regardless of how tendentious philosophers, in their deliberate methodological naiveté, sometimes make them seem). What has caused a great deal of confused debate, however, is the idea that in the case of any given system we ought to decide to do the decomposition *one way or the other*. In fact, the two approaches are not mutually exclusive. The information flow that makes a system intentional has to be carried in physical signals, so part of understanding a system's intentionality involves studying these signals as transmitted by nonintentional subsystems. If, empirically, the function by which these signals produce the apparent intentionality of the wider system *does* turn out to be an additive function then one will have discovered—*empirically*—that the wider system's intentionality *was* merely apparent. A Martian reverse engineer who figured out what's going on with the automobiles of Earthlings by initially treating them as intentional systems would make this discovery. But with systems that rely on a great deal of feedback between external scaffolding and internal dynamics for behavioral regulation, this will almost never turn out to be the case. To explain the behavior of such systems will partly involve analysis of the dynamics of irreducibly intentional subsystems. It will always, *also*, partly involve *orthogonal* analysis of the dynamics of nonintentional subsystems.

What causes this point to be so often missed is the fact that both kinds of analysis require the intentional stance. That the stance can (and must) be discharged by one kind of analysis leads people to imagine that, for any system, either all aspects of its intentionality are dischargeable or none of them are. This in turn follows from treating intentional-stance functionalism as a form of holism. There is of course a sense—when it is being contrasted with metaphysical atomism—in which intentional-stance functionalism is holistic. But intentional-stance functionalism isn't just, or even mainly, an assertion of holism (whatever an assertion of "just" holism might possibly mean—the philosophy of F. H. Bradley, perhaps?); it is an empirical and conceptual thesis about what intentionality is *and* about how it's implemented in nature.

We can thus distinguish between the complementary activities of "methodological intentional-stance functionalism" (MISF) and "ontological intentional-stance functionalism" (OISF). In an application of MISF, one assumes an intentional-stance description of a system in order to discover something about it at the design-stance, or perhaps ultimately at the physical-stance level. Here, one looks for subsystems with discharge of intentional properties in mind. OISF, by contrast, aims at explaining, still in intentional terms, the dynamics of systems one already has reason for believing to be irreducibly intentional. You need MISF to explain how a given intentional system is possible physically, or how it arose. But not all aspects of an intentional system need be explained by the MISF account, because some of them result from interactions with other intentional systems that the MISF account of either system taken separately can't, and doesn't need to, explain. In the case of ineliminable intentional systems—systems whose intentionality is a real pattern—this is guaranteed. The crucial upshot of the distinction is that, as applied to the very same system, there is no *a priori* reason why a MISF analysis and an OISF analysis should identify isomorphic networks of subsystems. In the case of a system that we have good antecedent reasons to believe is ineliminably intentional, like a person, MISF and OISF *will not* identify isomorphic networks.

This distinction enables us to state the fundamental difference between neuroeconomics and Ainslie's "picoeconomics" as discussed back in chapter 5. The various long-, medium-, and short-term interests modeled by Ainslie as competing for control of the person will not map onto Glimcher's modules (let alone onto individual neurons). These interests are, like the selves their dynamics partly explain, virtual entities—but no less real for that.

It is time to describe more details of Ainslie's model than I did in chapter 5. The model is based on two empirical facts, one from economics and one from cognitive science. The economic fact is that people—and some other animals—display hyperbolic discount curves except in special, socially constructed situations (more on these below). The fact from cognitive science is that before (in the logical, rather than the temporal, sense of "before") a cognitive system can respond selectively to stimuli evaluated with respect to valence—that is, can sculpt its behavior by reference to rewards and punishments—it must have a basis for selecting the stimuli to which it will pay most behavioral attention.[5] If you could pay maximum attention to all the information that would in fact make you rich, you would probably be rich; but for that you'd need to depend on progress in applied AI, and you'd need to monopolize the resulting new technology, because your brain is ill equipped for the job.

Let us see how these two facts combine to drive the model. First, from the mere fact of hyperbolic discounting the postulate of divergent subpersonal interests analytically follows. Long-range interests are valued more highly than medium-range ones. But long-range interests will all be defeated if the (also) valuable short-range interests are maximized. That this is analytic is indicated by the fact that it simply *redescribes* the fact that discount curves are hyperbolic. Back in chapter 5 I called this a "metaphor." I did so then because the MDM had not yet been introduced onto the scene, so we were still imagining that selves and their properties might need to be identified with processing modules to be declared "real." By this point in the argument, however, we know how to take a more sophisticated view. Selves are virtual, and real, and so are their first-order properties. Of course, the interests of the person must be implemented as patterns of synaptic dispositions. But there is no reason to think they should turn out to be modules that will be identified by the neuroeconomist deploying MISF.

But here's a point we do need from the application of MISF. Selves have to be based on information, and information has to be processed and filtered in some particular way or other. If one supposes *in the first place* that attentional motivation is determined by properties of the self, then one has a genuinely vicious regress problem. The *brain*, as opposed to the self, implements differential attention by activity in the nucleus accumbens (Gardner 1997, 1999). It seems to work by stimulating release of dopamine in response to *surprises* with respect to stimuli related to hedonic rewards and punishments, rather than to already calibrated rewards and punishments directly.[6] At least, so Ainslie interprets a range of data;[7] and, for logical reasons, this is the right *kind* of interpretation, since, for the reasons emphasized by MISF, we can't explain assignments of utility functions (to neurons) in neuroeconomics unless we discharge intentional "wanting." (Ainslie later uses this interpretation to explain the attentional urgency of stimuli that are of little consequence in a *person's* utility function, stimuli that are indeed nuisances to personal maximization, such as persistent itches. He also cites evidence that the attentional mechanisms are excited by pain, including pain for which behavioral responses are already in train. Such pains are also [sometimes grievous] nuisances to personal maximization. Thus, as he says, at this level pleasure and pain are not opposites.) This gives short-range interests an immediate advantage over long-range ones, since the attentional mechanisms seem to get "bored" by information that predicts reward once it has become familiar (Hollerman, Trembley, and Schultz 1998; Schultz, Dayan, and Montagve 1997). Neuroeconomics is directly relevant to Ainslie's next reasoning step, which is to note that, in light of these interpretations of the neurophysiological data, the efficacy of rational planning for long-range goals can only be efficacious at all if some neural mechanisms or other respond to incentives encoded in a common currency. Shizgal and Canover (1996) survey some evidence for such mechanisms; and the work of Glimcher, and Montague and

Berns discussed in the previous section is preliminary evidence that the common currency in question is expected utility. Whether this might be expected utility relative to a general, brainwide utility function, or relative to different utility functions associated with different modules, is an empirical question. Montague and Berns (2002) assert the former, but the status of the evidence for it is not obvious to me.

If mechanisms that solicit attention to hedonically relevant and surprising stimuli are inputs to utility calculations distributed through the brain, and if personal-level processing fed back into the neural circuitry is too, then we can see how bargaining between interests at different temporal ranges can be implemented even though the interests don't reduce to cognitive modules. (Exactly analogously, connectionist models of aspects of the brain and mind enable us to see how propositional attitudes can be implemented without reducing either to brain states or to discrete computational states; see Clark 1989.) Interests are virtual real patterns—and so are the bargaining games they play.

Picoeconomics thus relies on some neuroeconomic data to establish its legitimacy, but whereas neuroeconomics only applies MISF, picoeconomics aims at an OISF account. It is thus unsurprising that neuroeconomics has nothing directly to say about selves, while picoeconomics literally *is* the microeconomics of the self. Let us now briefly survey some of the things that picoeconomics has to suggest. This will lead us to supplement the functional account of the self as a social stabilizer given in chapter 7 with a (proper-functional) evolutionary story.

If the dynamics of the self consisted simply in a struggle between short-range and long-range interests, then the relationship between picoeconomics and conventional microeconomics might be relatively uncomplicated. We could get a very traditional account of the person— one Saint Augustine would have recognized—with social pressures, standing in for God, cultivating external incentives that give long-range interests a fighting chance against selfish short-range ones. This would in turn suggest a recovery of *very* conventional neoclassical foundations, Robinson Crusoe and all: we would have a motivational core of the individual maximizing short-range hedonic satisfaction. Sen's picture would then become quite natural, since we'd also have a clear way of justifying the claim that the individual could be assisted by socially (externally) encoded values in realizing her "real" (long-range) interests over and against her narrow (short-range) preferences.

However, this is not the model of subpersonal dynamics that Ainslie develops. As mentioned in chapter 5, the most pressing threats to a short-range interest come from other short-range interests that directly compete with them for resources. Furthermore, short-range interests themselves typically have stakes in the projects of long-range interests, since they depend on the resources that long-range interests accumulate. As Ainslie says, "Some of a person's short-range interests may lie in simply replacing her longer-range ones, as drug addiction beats out social-reward seeking in an addict's mental economy. More often, though, a short-range interest is not in killing but in parasitizing longer-range ones, like an addiction to credit-card abuse that preys on a person's longer-range interest in saving money. In that case, the longer-range interest provides money for the short-range interest to consume" (2001, p. 62). Thus the dynamic relations among interests are, as stressed in chapter 5, characterized by logrolling among shifting coalitions. Consider a person whose short-range interest in the thrill of gambling has become very powerful. Needing to crowd out other short-range interests that require money, the gambling interest might exploit the saving interest to suppress a shopping interest. This might be reflected in the self-narrative of the whole person as a rationalization of gambling by reference to the idea that every person should have one recreational vice, and that she spends no more on gambling than others do on spontaneous shopping, or than she herself might spend on shopping if she didn't gamble. The claims struck by such rationalizations are often true, or at least partly true.

Ainslie (2001, pp. 90–94) characterizes the bargaining games between short-range and long-range interests as repeated PDs. This is useful insofar as it focuses his attention on commitment mechanisms, which long-range interests need to find in order to credibly threaten short-range interests into limited cooperation. To invoke one of Ainslie's standing examples, a short-range interest in binging on fatty foods risks wholesale suppression by a coalition of a long-range interest in dieting and a short-range interest in preening if it presses for and wins too much indulgence. At the same time, the long-range interest might increase its risk of losing if it tries to suppress the binging interest altogether. Thus equilibrium might be found in which a personal rule is established that allows a visit to the Burger Den every Friday lunchtime but not otherwise. So long as the long-range interest's threat to impose a more severe diet if the short-range interest succeeds in weakening the rule with further exceptions is credible, equilibrium might be maintained. Of course, the credibility of the short-range interest's threat to pounce greedily on any exogenous weakening of resolve is equally essential, since this is what makes establishment of a personal *rule* necessary in the first place.

Useful though it is as a generator and organizer of examples, Ainslie's emphasis on PDs as the basic games among interests seems exaggerated. In a complex legislature populated with many interests, the range of games that will be going on at any one time will typically be large: there will be assurance games, pure and impure coordination games, inspection games, and many others. Ainslie's own clinical concentration on the dynamics of addiction no doubt gives PDs special salience for him, since unless an addiction is to something truly harmless—in which case it's not clear it can meaningfully be regarded as an addiction in the first place—its relationship with the long-range interests it must prey on without killing will indeed have the preference-structure of a repeated PD. However, if Ainslie's model is to be worked up into a picture of the whole subpersonal marketplace, rather than just being an analysis of the special-interest tactics of addictions, then the entire apparatus of the public-choice literature on legislative games (see Ordeshook 1997 and Stratmann 1997 for surveys) will call for deployment. This is not really a criticism of Ainslie's approach, however. His model's success in accounting richly for one complete and important, but antecedently very puzzling and highly complex, phenomenon, addiction, is the principal source of its empirical persuasiveness.

It is worth emphasizing how precisely the logrolling model characterizes the dynamics of addiction and its control. If long-range interests keep, or try to keep, addictions within bounds by establishing personal rules that allow them limited expression in cooperative equilibria, then a crucial tactic for long-range success will be bundling. The example above of the burger lover can be used to illustrate the point. If she relaxes her rule and also allows binging on public holidays, this might not disrupt equilibrium if holidays are sufficiently special relative to normal days that they set no precedent for further relaxation to include Sundays and days when the weather is especially nice. But all relaxations of equilibrium rules carry this risk. Thus the holiday extension might need to be bundled with other habits, implicated in other subpersonal games, that emphasize the pervasive specialness of holidays; if the person allows occasional sleep-ins or drinking sessions, perhaps these should also be scheduled only for holidays, or only for holidays and Fridays. Of course, this is risky too: as holidays become occasions for general bacchanalia, more short-range interests will be attracted to lobby for the most liberal possible personal definition of "holiday." Other long-range interests circle about looking for niches to exploit too. If a personal rule is overly rigid, equilibrium might be destroyed by the intervention of a long-range interest in preventing the personality from becoming too dull and inflexible for pleasant social fluidity.

It is noteworthy that bundling is a basic logrolling device in legislatures, such as the U.S. Congress, in which party discipline is weak. Commitment in deals among members of Congress is typically achieved by collapsing the products of compromises along multiple dimensions into omnibus bills that prevent destruction of equilibria by endless attempts at marginal renegotiation, and which also impede the president's ability to exploit his veto power by "cherry picking" only his favorite legislation.[8] Presidents periodically seek to enhance their bargaining power by pressing for line-item vetoes. Members of Congress, in turn, signal their appreciation of the important reduction in their influence this change would bring by generally resisting it independently of party affiliation. Ironically, members of the president's party are likely to support line-item veto power only when they're least able to bring it about, that is, when they are in a legislative minority and so prefer to be in a coalition with a more powerful president as a second-best alternative to being steamrollered by the majority legislators from the other party. These sorts of dynamics are *exactly* analogous to those by which dominant long-range interests in a person—say, an interest in winning an Olympic medal, or being the top diva in an opera company, or making CEO—must work to preserve equilibrium among coalitions of other interests. Very difficult ambitions of this sort will need line-item vetoes just like presidents who aim to effect substantial institutional shifts. But neither can simply be a dictator sitting in a command bunker and issuing orders; the less powerful bargainers will gang up and stage a coup if they are just disregarded. I emphasized "exactly" a moment ago for a reason. The systematic mathematical logic of many-person dynamic game theory is the *only* tool we know of that has both the expressive range for describing all of this, and the axiomatic rigor for allowing us to prove real theorems about it.

But, the reader may be worrying, isn't this *still* just a complex of metaphors? And isn't that signaled by an apparent arbitrariness in our ability to individuate and reindividuate interests as it suits our modeling purposes, especially if the interests don't reduce to cognitive modules whose boundaries can be fixed by independent empirical means? The answer to this worry is fundamental to the argument of this chapter, and indeed to that of this whole book. *Subpersonal interests are real bargainers because the underlying ontological framework on which the model rests is interpreted through RPT. All we individuate for the application of economics are behaviorally revealed utility functions.* Some further remarks from Ainslie should help to make the point clear:

Regularly recurring rewards create interests in the same way that economic opportunities create businesses to exploit them.... The process I have described is simply an example of selection by reward, as that process is conventionally understood.

Interests are separated when the goods on which they are based are mutually incompatible. Interests that could be based on compatible goods cannot be practically distinguished from each other, and there would be no point in trying to do so. Interests may coalesce or divide over time, because they need not have an institutional life of their own. (1992, p. 90)

This can be glossed (though Ainslie does not do so) as: the interacting units in this, as in any other marketplace, are individuated by reference to their utility functions. Furthermore, we will infer their existence from their revelation in market outcomes and bargaining dynamics:

... the concept of internal interests is convenient simply because contradictory goals that are preferred at different times are not weighed against each other to produce a single, unambivalent purpose, but rather tend to produce conflicting sets of processes that persist as long as they sometimes obtain their respective goals. (Ibid.)

If, though, we're free to individuate interests by inference from equilibria in games, we will face vicious underdetermination problems—too many games compatible with the behavioral evidence—unless we can independently constrain our choices of particular models by reference to something other than our hunt for application of our formal tools, RPT, and game theory. One key source of constraints is scarcity: if we know which resources are depleted by activity, we can estimate the budget constraints that make economics the relevant logical perspective in the first place. Then some careful deployment of MISF is in order to independently determine a utility-maximization rule (i.e., EUT or something else). Ainslie implicitly marks a distinction like the one I have drawn between MISF and OISF when he notes that

internal interests ... may seem to be a set of little homunculi within the person, like the ego and id, or angels and devils. Such personifications of higher and lower motives have reemerged so often ... that they probably refer in some way to actual observation, but they have been defined only vaguely and have tended to deteriorate into allegory. However, the problem with homunculi has not been their personlike qualities . . .

(Gloss: this is not "the problem" *insofar as* we're telling an OISF account rather than following the project of MISF.)

. . . but the lack of a principle that could relate them to the whole person, on the one hand, and to the known elements of motivation, on the other.

In temporary-preference theory, a person's motivation in general is divided into interests by the operation of the matching law. (Ibid., p. 94)

That is to say, evidence from experimental economics as reviewed in chapter 5, that isolates both framing effects and the specific patterns in preference reversal discussed there, motivates replacement of EUT by the matching law in modeling the utility maximization of the whole person, and in analyzing subpersonal dynamics at the horizontal (OISF) level. As explained earlier, there is no incompatibility between doing this while using EUT as the utility-maximization rule in the *vertical* decomposition of MISF analysis. Straightforward economic agents (neurons and/or modules) that track expected utility can provide information output to dynamics of systems that are molded by evolutionary pressures to follow heuristics like matching. Again: MISF and OISF decompositions are not in competition. Ainslie anticipates this:

[I]nterests are limited in their duration of dominance, but not necessarily in their access to any of the functions that compose the "self" in any of its definitions. Again, like parties trying to rule a country, internal interests gain access to most of a person's resources when they prevail. The person who wants to stay up later at night and the person who wants to rest in the morning are indeed entire personalities, in the sense that they have the whole person's psychic apparatus at their disposal; and yet they are clearly in conflict with one another. When an intelligent person is acting in his long-range interest not to smoke, he may use that intelligence to devise better stratagems to precommit his future behavior; but when he acts in his short-range interest to have a cigarette, he can marshall that same intelligence to evade these devices. (Ibid.)

I submit that Ainslie's descriptions of the cases above are richly adequate to the phenomena; but they make little sense (absent a dualist interpretation that is ruled out) unless the distinction between MISF and OISF is drawn—that is, unless we recognize that MISF and OISF analyses of a system need not identify isomorphic subpersonal networks. Brains are additively composed of bugs, but people aren't.

Neurons, and maybe modules, are straightforward economic agents, but coalitions of interests aren't.

The implication of this, about which I'll say more in the next—and final—chapter, is that the seam between (Samuelsonian) microeconomics and macroeconomics (in which the aims, if not the methods, of general equilibrium analysis are to be cashed out game-theoretically) happens at the site of the person, rather than in the composition of people into societies as traditionally taken for granted. (Put another way: one informs a theory of how microeconomics, as applied to human behavior, relates to macroeconomics partly by saying how people are related to their brains.) That this is a radical proposal is patent; and that's why a whole second volume will be needed for working it out.

Before saying any more about this portentous idea, however, we need to discharge the immediate promised target of this section, which was the biologically proper function of the self. Let us begin by referring back to Ainslie's account of the use of bundling to control addiction. The dieting burger lover must avoid overrelaxation of her Fridays-and-holidays rule not, of course, because one Tuesday's burger will make her fat, but because having a burger on a Tuesday *predicts* a whole series of future Tuesday burgers—and, catastrophically, Monday, Wednesday, and Thursday burgers as well, because once the bright line between all these days and Fridays (and holidays) is crossed, there isn't another salient distinction around which to stabilize equilibrium. (I'm of course just assuming this for the sake of the example. Things might be different if, say, Tuesday is half-price day at the Burger Den.) But predicts *to whom*? The answer is, obviously: to all of the interests in the repeated game. Very well, but then on whose behavior does the success of the prediction depend? The answer to this is: on the behavior of the whole self.

In that answer lies the *other* function—that is, the nonsociological function—of the self. Precisely because each interest is fully as clever as a person, as Ainslie emphasizes, their strategic cunning will tend to unravel all equilibria, at least in PDs and other dilemma-type games. (Pure coordination equilibria will be fine, of course, in the absence of exogenous shocks.) One obvious downside of this is that if the assets that feed addictions aren't irremediably very scarce—as they perhaps are for elephants[9] and monkeys, but not for modern people—everyone might become addicted to something biologically destructive. (This may explain why groups of people whose budget constraints around narcotic substances suddenly relax—aboriginal North Americans and Australians when Europeans arrived, or American blacks in the twentieth century—often encounter unusually severe addiction problems. Cultural evolution will swiftly build self-narrative defenses against the threat, in the form of moralization of sobriety, but generations caught in the lag will suffer.) This special problem is an instance of a more general one. We can best focus on it by fulfilling a promise left open from chapter 5, where I considered and rejected various possible uses that have been suggested for money-pump arguments, but said I would eventually arrive at a sound one. Here it is.

What it means to say that a person hyperbolically discounts is that she will value the same commodity differently depending on whether she's far away from or close to it in time. Thus, as Ainslie (2001, p. 40) points out, a straightforward hyperbolic discounter will tend to spend resources today undoing what she did yesterday—like a national legislature that struggles to reduce the budget deficit its spending last year created, and which was foreseeable at the time. This is, of course, just the situation of the money-pump victim. Fortunately, long-term interests will be politically active at the subpersonal level trying to produce overall discounting behavior that is more exponential. However, as in legislatures, this is an inadequate solution in itself, because long-range interests have conflictual relationships with one another. Even a person usually dominated by one long-range interest or another may still be a money pump if alternating long-range coalitions keep churning the elements of her investment portfolio. But a further analogy with national legislatures offers the clue as to why traditional neoclassical economists have long sniffed something generally relevant in the region of money-pump arguments. Famously, legislatures that seem relatively incompetent at managing the fiscus can suddenly turn into effective economic agents when faced with obvious national crises; think of the British and American legislatures during World War II, or the New Zealand parliament when the country went bankrupt in the 1980s. National will tends often to manifest just when it's truly needed, that is, when national survival is visibly at risk.

A person is typically a more fragile corporate entity than a country (or, at least, a modern first-world country).[10] Agents who will use her as a money pump if they can are almost always around looking for opportunities. This effects her subpersonal bargaining situation in important ways. For one thing, it degrades the fall-back positions of her short-range interests if equilibrium breaks down, which will make them more impatient for deals with long-range interests. It also gives particular long-range interests access to a new currency with which to recruit coalitions of supporting short-range interests: a long-range interest can attract some short-range interests to support it not just by offering it periodic gratification, but by offering it security—so long as it helps ensure not only that the long-range interest in question keeps its project active, but retains standing dominance over other long-range interests. Just as a national leader in a crisis will emphasize his value as a coordination focus by "wrapping himself in the flag," so a long-range subpersonal interest campaigning as a guardian against money pumps is incentivized to "wrap itself in the self." The analogy goes still deeper (of course: at the abstract level of economics it's less an analogy than a structural *identity*). The symbolic activity of politicians and their cultural cheerleaders is the main activity in which national identities *consist*—something historical figures as diverse as Louis XIV and Ronald Reagan have often grasped explicitly. Similarly, successful promotion by some long-range interests of themselves as *being* the self *is* the basic self-creating activity, implemented in the spinning and reinforcing of narratives.

What I have called the "sociological" function of selves—the way in which their existence and maintenance supports social coordination in complex communities—probably accounts for most of their actual dynamics, which is why I concentrated on this first. But sociological functions can only explain maintenance of traits and dispositions, not their biological origins. Our reflections on picoeconomics suggest possible explanations of how self-narrating got selected to begin with. As social organisms become more complex in their computational capacities, and as their conspecifics simultaneously become more sophisticated also, the value of being able to simulate an exponential discounter rises. We must be careful, however, not to smuggle foresightedness on evolution's part into our assumptions. If all the political communities housed in *H. sapiens* individuals were incapable of controlling preference cycling at the aggregate level, then no one would be capable of money-pumping anyone else, and so that form of pressure to evolve selves would not arise. Most other social animals are probably hyperbolic discounters, and thus vulnerable to being money-pumped (if only by the parametric environment) but most other social animals don't narrate selves. To locate a possible proper function for the self, we thus need to find a historical triggering condition specific to humans.

As Ainslie (2001, p. 46) points out, an evolutionary explanation of hyperbolic discounting needs to represent its problematic aspects as costs that, for one reason or another, weren't high enough in the actual evolutionary career of a lineage to be filtered out, given the positive value conferred by speedy attention to cues of immediate, but only briefly available, prospects for reward. A salient respect in which people are unusual animals is our degree of control over parametric factors. Since hyperbolic discounting seems to have evolved prior to our emergence, in wondering about the cost-benefit analysis of hyperbolic discounting, we should consider the circumstances of creatures who are substantially at the mercy of their parametric environments. By comparison with our situation, this is a two-edged sword. On the one hand, such animals are much less vulnerable to being *strategically* money-pumped. Even if a mutant dog arose who could marshal his internal interests into an implementation of pumping ability, he simply couldn't control enough of the contingencies around his own or any other dog's budget constraints to actually implement pumping. As David Spurrett (personal communication) points out, hyperbolically discounting animals can suffer disasters of bad luck in some environmental contingencies; if my drug supply lies along the best path between my optimal nesting site and my food source, I might starve to death. This just means, of course, that the existence of hyperbolic discounting shows such accidents to have been tolerably rare from natural selection's perspective. But animals who did not evolve under the rigors of *strategic* pumping threats are at a severe disadvantage when they meet *H. sapiens*. The famous stupidity of the sphex wasp (Wooldridge 1968) splendidly illustrates the point. The wasp lays its eggs only after paralyzing and burying a cricket for its larvae to feed on. A rigid preference has evolved for placing the cricket inside the burrow only after the burrow has been inspected. The cricket's presence on the burrow threshold, to which the wasp has brought it, is the cue for inspection. The human scientist can set the wasp into a sad loop by simply moving the cricket a few inches from the threshold while the wasp is inspecting. She will then emerge, put the cricket back where it belongs, and repeat the whole procedure, endlessly. (Note that, superficial resemblance notwithstanding, this is not a case of money-pumping because no utility is being transferred. More significantly, the futile cycling does not result from any preference reversal on the wasp's part. Quite the opposite: the scientist is exploiting the wasp's total inability to make her *rigid* preference structure interact sensibly with a contingent change in market conditions.)

The origins of selves might thus lie in the possibilities for strategic money-pumping that arose with human mastery of parametric contingencies. It is a commonplace in evolutionary anthropology that humankind took an immense step away from the tyranny of the parametric when it developed communal agriculture. At the very same time, the fact that harvests were *communal,* and thus open to distribution through many possible institutional structures (and mediated by different possible reciprocal insurance schemes), vastly increased the relevance to biological fitness of marginal advantages in nonparametric behavior. On this hypothesis, domestication of food supplies created the conditions for an arms race in which anyone's improvement in ability to control preference cycling at the level of the whole organism put enough pressure on other individuals' abilities for natural selection to "notice" and so genetically wire in capacities to narrate selves (that is, to play G' and G-level games).[11] This mechanism need only have provided an initial wedge into the process. Thereafter, group-selection dynamics at the cultural level, operating on the sociological function of selves, could accelerate the process.

The second hypothesis—which could well be complementary to the first—rests on emphasizing that the basic technological prerequisite for creating selves is a recursive public-signaling system. Dennett (1991b, 1995) has emphasized this in arguing that human language must have evolved prior to, and as the basis for, the distinctively human kind of consciousness that comes with the capacity for selfhood. Of course, any explanation of the origins of a communication system must itself rest on an analysis of social games. In this respect, Dennett has himself been most attracted to the Machiavellian intelligence hypothesis discussed in chapter 7. But Machiavellian advantages are potentially relevant to all social animals, so this suggestion in turn must lead us in search of a special feature of the early hominid environment that made Machiavellian competition unusually important. Perhaps, as Dennett has suggested, hominid ecological circumstances made lying possible to an extent not encountered in other social ancestral lines. Alternatively, perhaps our ancestors grew their *weirdly* large brains (weirdly, that is, even relative to those of other social animals) for reasons not directly related to social dynamics, and thereby acquired unprecedented levels of Machiavellian cunning as a side-effect.

Again, the point here is not to embark on the fraught task of combing speculative haystacks for needles of evidence that might tip the probability of one particular story against another. (I am not saying this that is not worth doing at all, as ideological opponents of evolutionary psychology often maintain. I am just not going to do it here.) What bears emphasis in the present context is what all of the possible stories have in common: they rest on the idea that selfhood complements its sociological function with the additional functional property of allowing nonstraightforward economic agents to try to money-pump each other, and to in turn defend themselves against being pumped. Unlike the sociological function, this function can be biologically selected without group selection *having* to be generally operative. Since group-selection dynamics surely *were* operative once competition between political communities of people became a primary ecological circumstance of *H. sapiens*, the two functions could thereafter reinforce and amplify one another.

One aspect of these dynamics that is especially interesting in the traditional context of economics is that, as Ainslie (1992, pp. 228–242) has discovered, the development of fiat money seems to facilitate the ability of nonstraightforward economic agents to simulate straightforward ones. (That is, people act like exponential, rather than hyperbolic, discounters in many circumstances involving earning, spending, and saving money.) Ainslie offers a plausible part of the explanation for this when he suggests that

cash pricing makes a wide variety of transactions conspicuously comparable, and hence invites an encompassing personal rule about the value of money generally. It's easy to interpret any financial transaction as a precedent for all others. That is, if a person sees what she spends for food, clothes, movie tickets, toys, postage stamps, and so on all as examples of wasting or not wasting money, she'll add thousands of examples to her interdependent set of choices, each flattening her effective discount curve a little more. The ease of summing and comparing all financial transactions lets the value of purchasable goods fluctuate much less over time than, say, the value of staying up late versus getting enough sleep or of angry outbursts versus holding your temper. Accordingly, it's rare to see someone swayed by her immediate emotional comfort by only a tiny fraction more than by next year's, but common to see her behave as if her immediate wealth were worth only a tiny fraction more than next year's. (2001, p. 101)

This account emphasizes the functionality of economic agency in what I have been calling the "biological" sense: use of monetary accounts by long-range interests helps to keep short-range interests behaving in line with coalition policies. Monetary accounting also serves the sociological function of economic agency (as Ainslie 2001, p. 157, recognizes), since it allows agents to easily keep books—in computerized society, increasingly detailed and increasingly retrievable books—on one another's preference consistency over time. (Consider the rising tyranny of credit ratings.) This, of course, greatly increases the risk of one's being money-pumped—literally—if subpersonal coalitional equilibria break down, while increasing one's own ability to pump others if it doesn't.

This point invites a reinterpretation of the results reported by Frank, Gilovich, and Regan (1993) that training in neoclassical economic theory seems to cause people to behave more like individual-utility maximizers. Dupré (2001) echoes a regularly heard refrain that interprets these data as suggesting that neoclassicism is a self-reinforcing ideology. What the data may instead point to is a standing fact about the whole evolutionary trajectory of *H. sapiens*: as interpersonal dependency grows more complex by its own natural dynamic, the isolated microeconomies of typical animals cohere into macroeconomic systems. Neoclassical economics of the Samuelsonian (as opposed to the mature anthropocentric or semi-Aristotelian) variety becomes increasingly empirically applicable, not because economists promote it but because it captures the dynamics that have been favoring the evolution of selves since our ancestors started talking. Montague and Berns's (2002) discovery of a match between brains' valuation of monetary reward under varying attitudes to risk, and Black–Scholes financial option pricing, discussed above, is further striking evidence in this regard.

And that, of course, is this book's central thesis. Here is what a person is: a set of basically compatible long-range interests that have co-opted a sufficient army of short-range interests into their coalition to maintain stable equilibrium. A person is *that* person just so long as her revealed preferences at the whole-person level don't significantly cycle. This is why we can model people as (nonstraightforward) economic agents—just as we sometimes can, and should, model countries. Of course, a biological *H. sapiens* individual goes through changing external circumstances during its biography, so no one coalition of interests will stay in power forever. Becker and other mature anthropocentric neoclassicists have missed this point, whereas a Samuelsonian neoclassicist can accept it without difficulty. At the same time, the social pressures that discipline self-narratives tend to make people more and more like straightforward economic agents for increasing stretches of their biographies. These pressures are not *external* to their personal utility functions, as Sen supposes. They are what make (whole-) personal utility functions possible in the first place. Society does not struggle to civilize inner Robinson Crusoes, for people don't biologically have such things. Instead, human society gives rise to something new under the evolutionary sun: creatures that act increasingly like the economic agents familiar among our asocial relatives, who nevertheless turn the trick of achieving the powerful network efficiencies that the asocial cannot.

As I intimated earlier, the evolution of sociality involves a fundamental trade-off, as a result of which sociality is not the typical trajectory for a genomic line. Individual organisms gain the fruits of network efficiencies at the expense of their economic rationality. We are assured that this trade-off is unavoidable by Arrow's impossibility theorem (see Sen 1979 for a magnificently clear discussion), which shows that no procedure for aggregating the preferences of a community's members can be simultaneously democratic and cycle proof. The significance of "democratic" here does not rest on appeal to individualistic norms; *some* level of democracy is what avoidance of control bottlenecks has to *mean*, and network efficiencies require avoidance of bottlenecks.

The political philosopher Gregory Kavka (1991) rightly emphasizes that if individuals are modeled by analogy to political communities, as Ainslie and I urge, then Arrow's theorem must apply to them. This does not impugn the analogy. The behavior of national legislatures, after all, *does* routinely cycle. As we saw in chapter 5, so does the behavior of whole people. Incidence of cycling can only be reduced (but never eliminated) by limitations on the freedom of the community's constituents to switch coalitions with low cost whenever a potential gain in marginal utility appears. Dictatorship—dominance of the community by one or a few members—is the most familiar way of limiting democracy, but as stressed a moment ago, in the context of a large brain this amounts to revoking the very decentralization of information processing that makes large brains effective in the first place. Evolution should not be expected to build biological equivalents to the Soviet Union. But there is another source of potential constraints on democratic freedom that lies *outside* of systems: scarcity itself, and the risks (to individuals) that this associates with policies. As we saw earlier in this section, this is what induces Ainslie's communities of interests to preserve such coherence as they do. The same is obviously true for corporations and, much less effectively in the present world, for nations. This again shows us why we will need to involve something like macroeconomic analysis irreducibly in models of microeconomic realms: identification of exogenous constraints on a community's actions is the macroeconomist's mission. It is then the job of the microeconomist to explain how these constraints feed back into the incentives of a community's constituent agents. None of this will surprise any economist who is not ideologically devoted to reductionism. Given my expressed confidence in what mainstream economic theory has achieved, I would be distinctly uncomfortable if it would. The interesting work to be done in the second volume of this study will consist in setting the bidirectional feedback relations between the microeconomic and the macroeconomic into the more general setting of evolutionary behavioral dynamics.

In the context of the present volume, however, the point that communities of agents *must* encounter the formal limitations raised by the Arrowian impossibility of perfect economic rationality draws our attention back to a question that has been touched on repeatedly, but has still not been adequately addressed. In an evolutionary context, appeal to concepts of rationality in behavioral explanation must be related to some sort of adaptationist model. The empirical relevance of RPT, with its emphasis on consistency and optimization, is necessarily parasitic on such adaptationism. What kind of adaptationism, if any, can be defended as empirically significant, if the conjunction of Arrow's theorem and the impossibility of implementing the ultimate refinement as a game-theoretic solution concept shows us that nature can't build literal maximizers, either collective or individual, with large brains?

Rationality and Explanatory Adaptationism

The above challenge returns us to Sugden's (2002) argument for eliminativism as introduced at the end of chapter 5. I have been building a case for the empirical significance of a microeconomics based on the Robbins–Samuelson argument pattern, shorn of its namesakes' introspectionism and individualism. However, Sugden's contention is that in an account of behavior based on (biological and cultural) evolutionary dynamics like the one I have been defending, the concepts of "rationality," "utility," and "maximization" no longer do any useful analytical work and should be junked. This is one *sense* of eliminativism that has not been met by the arguments I have given so far. The other sense of it—the one that concerns Davis and Mirowski—in which selves are eliminated from our ontology, has been dealt with over this chapter and the previous two. But this aspect of eliminativism is not the one promoted by Sugden, or by the most prominent advocate of eliminativism (by name) among philosophers, Rosenberg (1992). It is incumbent on me to reply to eliminativism in their sense, because to credit a construction of microeconomics to Robbins and Samuelson that accords no genuine role to rationality, utility, or maximization would be silly—like crediting Jefferson Davis as a good democrat except for his lapse into the endorsement of slavery. It's true, strictly speaking, but rhetorically perverse. I didn't devote a long chapter to the interpretation of Robbins and Samuelson as a pure exercise in *rebranding* an utterly different conception.

As noted when Sugden's argument was briefly discussed in chapter 5, his target is slightly ambiguous. Many of his critical points are directed against the specific claim that individual people are expected-utility maximizers. Obviously, I am in entire agreement with that claim. We have seen, in this chapter, reasons for thinking that neurons and perhaps modules are expected-utility maximizers, and for thinking that this is relevant to explaining the fact that people are at least sometimes capable of tracking NE. But we know how to substitute tracking of various possible alternative (heuristic) functions for maximization into models when and as we're empirically motivated to do so. Sugden is historically correct in his explanation of why economists have treated EUT as part of the *foundations* of postwar neoclassicism (rather than as something added to it for particular uses). As he says, "von Neumann and Morgenstern produced their axiomatic formulation of expected utility theory to persuade a skeptical economics profession of the meaningfulness of the cardinal utility indices that game theory needs" (2001, p. 119). However, I have argued here that such skepticism was most rationally based on internalism about preferences, which is dissolved in a version of economic theory that interprets preference by application of intentional-stance functionalism. The sense of "preference" relevant in models of agents who are selves, and whose preferences are therefore products of game-determining coordination, is obviously cardinal, in a stronger sense than von Neumann and Morgenstern's, because it licenses interpersonal comparisons. (See Binmore 1994, 1998 for an account of interpersonal preference comparison in a revealed-preference framework.)

Of course, we can't apply game theory in any particular case without using some explicit theory or other of utility maximization, either EUT or one of its rivals. Sugden's skepticism goes deeper than doubt about whether people maximize expected utility; it's based on doubts about whether models that make use of maximization are likely to be relevant (at all) to the study of any real behavior. In particular, Sugden's complaint about economists is that they have nothing but a preference for a priori theorizing that leads them to expect such models to be relevant. People do what they do—no doubt because they have some native dispositions that give them goals, and because they have some particular capacities or other for adaptive learning and mimicry that lead them to modify their understanding of good means to these goals and to often revise the goals themselves. We should turn to cognitive science to find out about these dispositions and capacities, and then seek to explain patterns in economic behavior by reference to them. But why suppose that there is consistent maximization of *anything*? Sugden concedes (2001, pp. 123–124) something I have emphasized, that "in the case of animal behavior, we *already know* what is being selected for, namely reproductive success, and so we are entitled to infer that selection will favor learning heuristics that serve reproductive success." But, he then rightly says, human behavior doesn't maximize reproductive success, or anything else we can derive directly from biology—or, perhaps, he implies, anything (in general) at all.

There is, throughout Sugden's argument, a strong hint of hyperempiricism that would discard all systematic theory in favor of a simple collection of behavioral facts. I don't imagine Sugden intends to promote that, since it's never how effective science is done. His argument is driven by the assumption that the only possible justification for deploying Samuelsonian economics would have to be that either people maximize something general, or that we can use an assumption that they do as an idealization we can then systematically and usefully relax under empirical guidance. He thinks that neither of these things is true. What I want to question here is his assumption. In trying to understand human behavior, one of the things we need to do is model people as marketplaces of subpersonal interests (and as themselves embedded in social marketplaces). These subpersonal interests just *are* utility functions. (Which heuristic functions they maximize we must indeed do empirical work to discover; see below.) The utility functions are only revealed in behavior. So their analysis calls on Samuelsonian economics. Another thing we need to do in trying to understand human behavior is neuroeconomics; and neurons and modules might actually be expected-utility maximizers. So there is another arena where Samuelsonian economic theory will be needed. Finally, the dynamics that stabilize selves lead people to approximate economic agency. We thus need that concept to characterize the basins of attraction at the population level that, under conditions to be determined by evolutionary analysis, contribute to stabilizing *sets* of selves. Young (1998) demonstrates the power of several such analyses in application to cultural evolution.[12]

I have been arguing that we should try to understand people in the way we try to understand the economies of countries, whatever, exactly, that should be in the light of behavioral science—my topic for the next volume. For the moment, however, we can say this much: it's possible to understand national economies at all only to the extent that we can think of their constituent citizens and social associations as having stable utility functions *to some extent*. People may be easier to model because the straightforward economic agency of parts of their brains implies more readily discoverable boundaries on the informational dynamics of the games among their interests. This is for cognitive science, including neuroeconomics, to study. Sugden complains that "within evolutionary game theory, surprisingly little work has been done to investigate how imitation and learning actually work, or even (a project which might be more congenial to game theorists) how these processes *might* work" (2001, p. 123). The program of neuroeconomics, along with Camerer's (2003b) "behavioral game theory," directly addresses the complaint.

The core of Sugden's objection to what he sees as mere pseudoempiricism in economists' embrace of evolutionary game theory (EGT) is his justified contention that many economists assume that we can reasonably model people just as we can asocial animals. (That is, by assuming that individual utility functions track expected fitness.) I have agreed with him that we cannot, and have provided additional reasons to his for thinking so. But in light of the objection it is incumbent on me to explain why, even where people are concerned, reference to maximization and rationality are implicit in the *appropriate* application of EGT. I will now provide this explanation. Its basic foundation is the claim that EGT is best understood as the application of intentional-stance functionalism to interacting systems collectively confronting scarcity.

The argument from EGT to eliminativism as it was sketched in chapter 5 relied on accepting a premise implicitly assumed by classical game theorists, to the effect that such rationality as players display must be embodied in internal computational capacities and dispositions with which they are endowed. An ideal of "full rationality" is then understood as implying dispositions to perform unbounded internal computations over belieflike representations of strategies. "Fully rational" strategic expectations are thus interpreted as being those that take account of *all* information that *could* be computed, using some finite procedure, from the structure and play of the game. Since general dispositions to use such expectations are not naturally possible—that is, could not be built by natural selection—they should be eliminated. Intentional-stance functionalism denies the premise that rationality is best understood in terms of internal computations over propositional structures, and thereby avoids the conclusion. Intentional-stance ascription infers beliefs and desires from strategic play at equilibrium, rather than the other way around.

This answers the argument given for eliminativism in economics by Rosenberg (1992) (for more details see Ross 1994b); but it doesn't answer Sugden. A general consideration that is supposed to make the new argument for eliminativism a better argument than Churchland's (1979, 1981) more familiar ones is that it relies on an actual, available strategy for predicting and explaining behavior, rather than on abstract metaphysical hypotheses about the sorts of objects beliefs might be. In this context, to say that we *can* think of beliefs in terms that don't require their explicit representation and computation by players cuts little ice: if our best models of games among people don't require them, on any interpretation, and if modeling the history of behavior as a series of games is the most productive way to represent human economic behavior, then the philosophical issues can be argued to turn out as just irrelevant. If we are to resist the eliminativist conclusion to the argument as outlined, then we must do something stronger than simply trot out Dennett's, or anyone else's, alternative conception of beliefs. We must, instead, show that modeling the history of behavior as a series of games requires the continued evocation of rationality assumptions. Furthermore, these must be invoked in a way that does not imply the modeling of perfectly rational players who do not exist and are not even idealizations of agents who do exist (since the idealizations can't be relaxed without vitiating the models).

As Sugden (2001, pp. 121–122) implicitly recognizes[13] when criticizing Binmore's (1994, 1998) use of RPT, one route by which rationality would be recovered in the specific context of EGT is if we expected natural and/or cultural selection to weed out inconsistent preferences. This is indeed what Binmore supposes, and it amounts to treating selection as a generator of adaptations that are optimal given specific environmental and other constraints. (Optimally adapted systems might be only boundedly rational, in light of search or information-retrieval costs.) Such rationality would be only behavioral, rather than (in general) representational and computational. But this is the only sort of rationality required for the relevance of RPT, and the only kind recognized as *generally* relevant to natural behavior by an intentional-stance functionalist.

Dennett (1995) is well-known for defending the use of optimality assumptions in modeling evolutionary processes. Mirowski, as we saw in chapter 1, describes this aspect of Dennett's thought as a "bungee jump" and joins Sugden in also criticizing Binmore for it. This attitude is common. Dennett's approach to adaptationism is frequently misunderstood by his critics because, detaching it from the wider context of intentional-stance functionalism, they fail to understand what motivates it. Adaptationism is typically glossed as the view that natural selection builds perfect individual products. Now, if "perfect," in each particular case, is understood relative to a given ecological equilibrium, then the hypothesis that selection builds perfect organisms raises complex questions, both philosophical and biological (see the papers in Orzack and Sober 2001); it is not just the indulgence of Panglossian optimism as which it is often mocked.[14] However, as we will see in a moment, this is not quite the version of adaptationism to which Dennett appeals. Before we come to that, we should note that his talk of natural selection as an algorithm for searching design space has led some critics to read him as promoting the much stronger idea that evolution builds *logically* optimal creatures. Since this would recapitulate the assumption that plagued the refinement program, if this were Dennett's view we would have to agree with Sugden that it is fanciful.

Ross (2002b) discusses Dennett's view of selection in relation to a distinction between "causal" and "diagnostic" versions of adaptationism, arguing that Dennett maintains only the latter but has often been criticized as if he maintained the former. Godfrey-Smith (2001) captures essentially the same insight, but with a more refined, threefold, schematization of kinds of adaptationism, so here I will follow his typology. First we have *empirical* adaptationism. This is, very roughly, the thesis that most biological change is explained by reference to natural selection. (To make this less rough, one would need to consider different possible interpretations of "biological change," and ask whether "exclusively" or "mainly" or some other restrictive operator should precede "explained by," but I will pass over these technicalities here.) One could produce a variant of empirical adaptationism for cultural evolution by substituting "changes in widespread human behavioral patterns" for "biological change" and "cultural selection" for "natural selection." Second, Godfrey-Smith distinguishes *explanatory* adaptationism. This is the version of adaptationism he attributes to Dennett, and he says it is "the most misunderstood" adaptationist thesis (ibid., p. 336). An explanatory adaptationist is someone who supposes that explanation of apparent design in nature is the crucial explanandum for evolutionary theory, and that the only effective logical devices for resolving that explanandum are Darwinian argument patterns. Third and finally, we have *methodological* adaptationism. This is the view that the data of biology are best organized by reference to selection hypotheses. In a less generic expression, it is advice to biologists to begin specific inquiries by hypothesizing optimal natural design, and then progressively relax that hypothesis as new data come in. On this version of adaptationism, adaptive accounts are pragmatic idealizations.

There is no question that Dennett is an explanatory adaptationist. As we will see shortly, he is also a methodological adaptationist. But although, as Godfrey-Smith shows, one can produce quotes from Dennett that, out of context, appear to endorse empirical adaptationism, his explicit disavowals of that thesis are clear and frequent, and have been so from his first writings on evolutionary theory (see immediately below). This is not because he takes sides in the disputes among biologists over the relative causal significance of mutation and genetic drift to changes in gene frequencies; rather, it is because he denies that there is a privileged, objective grain of analysis for function attribution that can be brought to bear across all particular cases. "Mother Nature," he wrote in his first systematic discussion of the topic, "doesn't commit herself explicitly and objectively to *any* functional attributions; all such attributions depend on the mind-set of the intentional stance, in which we assume optimality in order to interpret what we find. The panda's thumb was no more *really* a wrist-bone than it was a thumb. We will not likely be discomfited, in our interpretation, if we consider it a thumb, but that is the best we can say, here or anywhere" (Dennett 1987, p. 320). Anyone who doubts that this has remained Dennett's considered position is referred to his (2000) debate with Ruth Millikan, in which he reiterates, and produces new arguments for, his contention that there are no facts of the matter concerning the right level of precision with which adaptations should be identified. Since he certainly *does* believe that there are facts of the matter, in every case, concerning the molecular-level causes of changes in gene frequencies, it follows that, for him, selection is not to be construed as one member of a vector of causes, some of whose other competing members are mutation and drift. The causal events in the history of phylogeny are just the actual conceptions and births of organisms, and the causal processes at the molecular level that directly drive events of meiosis. Natural selection is then the organizing principle, *just conceptually equivalent to* taking the intentional stance toward evolution, from which explanatory patterns that would otherwise be invisible emerge from this biographical data about organisms. Reference to it permits us to recover the reasons, as opposed to the causes, in nature. This is explanatory and methodological adaptationism, but it is not empirical adaptationism.

An explanatory adaptationist must be prepared to justify his claim that questions about apparent design are the big issues of evolutionary theory. Godfrey-Smith (2001, pp. 349–351) suggests that, in Dennett's case, the justification appeals to the pervasive contribution to a person's general intellectual worldview that typically accompanies the recognition of mindless, rather than deliberate, design as the general source of biological order. There is no doubt that the battle against intelligent design and other "skyhooks" has been an (increasingly) important motivation for Dennett's philosophy. However, Godfrey-Smith does not mention the original, explicit basis for Dennett's explanatory adaptationism, a basis much more directly related to the issues of this book: that explanatory adaptationism is a crucial part of the justification of intentional-stance functionalism itself. Explaining this will take a few paragraphs.

Dennett's antireductionism in behavioral science is based on emphasizing that the restriction of analytical attention to purely causal microdynamics blocks access to patterns in interaction that are "substrate-neutral," that is, products of relationships between *types* of environmental pressures and broad *types* of selection vehicles. Such patterns can often be identified only by asking what an agent seeking to achieve certain outcomes generated by its selection environment would optimally do. The optimizing perspective is useful because the existence of multiple causal means to a given end is the norm in selection-driven processes, including both agent-directed outcome engineering *and* environment-driven selection. Identification of recurrent, counterfactual-supporting patterns in such processes requires that we abstract away from particular causal histories to focus on functions that selection would likely have stumbled across one way or another.

The logic of the intentional stance is essentially the same. Recall from chapter 2 that the intentional stance involves the use of referential indices that *triangulate* among the idiosyncratic learning and representational histories of both analyst and subject, and norms of public reference.[15] If the analyst fails to consistently triangulate—if, on the one hand, he insists on referring to only one corner of the triangle through a policy of elimination (or intentionalist microcausalism), or, on the other hand, attends exclusively to another corner by treating the subject as a robotically programmed representative of a social type—then he will simply miss the real patterns necessary for predicting and explaining the things the subject does. All strategies that focus exclusively on one corner of the triangle or another—introspectionism, microcausalism (with eliminativism as one of its subspecies), and Watsonian behaviorism—are attempts to reduce the vector of intentional causation to one or another component. It is because such reductions lose real information that we can identify the intentional stance as (sometimes) tracking real patterns.

Most philosophers of mind and language, as noted back in chapter 2, are externalists these days. But, as Dennett (1987, chapter 8, and many other places) argues, many also think it is still a sensible project to ask questions about how *particular* intentional states in brains semantically contribute to intentional states individuated by environmental triangulation. That is, many philosophers are still quasi internalists, imagining that brains—or, one level of abstraction higher, inner representational agents, who might be Robinson Crusoe—have beliefs about the same subjects as whole people do, which can be usefully considered as part of a project of determining what a person "really" believes. (Dretske 1988 is an exemplary instance.) Dennett—along with Clark, and Binmore, and me—*denies that there are quasi people inside people, or, therefore, quasi-personal beliefs underlying the triangulated personal-level attributions.* Beliefs rationalize the behavioral patterns of whole people in environmental contexts, given histories. There is no place to look "inside" the person—not to the brain, and not to a presocialized bearer of a utility function—for deeper facts of the matter about what people believe.

One can, of course, take the intentional stance toward a brain, or a module, or a neuron—as in neuroeconomics, and in MISF applications more generally—but then the beliefs one identifies will not generally be about any objects *people* have beliefs about.[16] This is because the intentional stance just *is* application of explanatory adaptationism. Use of it therefore requires sensitivity to the particular kind of selection history that produced the system being intentionally conceived. Application of the intentional stance consists in wondering about, and offering explanations about, *the ways in which organs or behavioral dispositions in systems constitute solutions to problems.* Where do the problems in question come from? In the case of brains and neurons, from the history of biological evolution. If you take the intentional stance toward a brain, you are thereby emphasizing that the brain is an organ designed by natural selection. You are not thereby denying that brains and their structures are also *caused by* (among other things) environmental accidents and mutations and recombinatorial constraints. When you are studying those accidents, you needn't have regard for brains' *beliefs* at all. However, if you *do* adopt the intentional stance toward a brain for *other* explanatory purposes—explaining, for example, why in human brains processing of information about social relations is closely linked to the auditory processing cortex—then these beliefs must be based on informational discriminations that natural selection (and not drift or random mutation) could find.

But *people* are products of *cultural* selection. Thus, taking the intentional stance toward them is an application of explanatory adaptationism about culture. I pointed out above that, according to intentional-stance functionalism, one can't usefully try to settle questions about people's belief contents by looking "deeper inside" them. But if uses of the intentional stance are not to be pure exercises in free confabulation, there had better be *some* sources of constraints on intentional interpretation. Of course, there are. First, belief attributions are constrained by considerations of the information subjects have been exposed to. Second—the constraint of main interest here—people's status as intentional systems in the first place is derived from the fact that we know natural selection has endowed them with *desires*. The point is not that people's "real" or "core" desires are those that might maximize their reproductive fitness. This, the mistake of some evolutionary psychologists who I criticized earlier, is another form of residual internalism. Rather, the point is that *because* we know that people are adapted cognitive systems and adapted pursuers of goals—some of these relatively hardwired, to be sure, but others impressed upon people by their social histories and modified by their self-stabilization dynamics—we know they are problem solvers, sites for explanation by appeal to reasons. Their histories *as* problem solvers constrain interpretations of what their beliefs and desires can plausibly be about. Explanatory adaptationism explains why the intentional stance delivers useful predictions and explains real patterns in the first place.[17]

Is the question of how the intentional stance arises a sufficiently "big" one, in Godfrey-Smith's terms, to justify explanatory adaptationism? I suggest that, at the very least, it surely is if our interests are economic. What discipline has a more fundamental connection with *problems* faced by systems than economics?

The account just given deepens our understanding of why OISF individuations of system components cross-classify MISF individuations of components.[18] Brains and neurons (and probably modules) play causal roles in personal behavior, just as people play causal roles in corporate and national behavior. But a person is a solution to a series of strategic problems posed by cultural (G'- and G-level) games. A brain is (among other things) a solution to a series of problems posed by biological (G''-level) games. Here are a few slogans, pronounced earlier in this book, that are all expressions of this: brains are not proper parts of people; people have no inner Robinson Crusoes; there are no such things as "internal" personal preferences. In economics, humanistic semi-Aristotelianism rests on a failure to appreciate any of this. Economic eliminativism rests on a failure to appreciate that adaptationism need not be of the empirical variety; or so I will now argue.

First, it should now be clear that the intentional-stance functionalist's belief in beliefs is in no tension with the rejection by Gintis of the classical game theorist's notion of belief. Classical game theorists were led down their path toward the ultimate refinement because they reason *forward* from assumptions about the rational structure of putative internal-belief systems to the equilibria of games in which agents with such belief structures would engage. The agents' beliefs are therefore supposed to be fixed points in internal computational dynamics. The intentional-stance functionalist, by contrast, works *backward* from the equilibria of plausible evolutionary games to belief ascriptions that would rationalize them in light of facts about evolutionary histories and information-processing capacities. For Dennett, all belief ascription, just like all function ascription in adaptationist explanation, is of this retrospective character, and "beliefs" do not denote internal computational states. This, fundamentally, is why the label "neobehaviorist" fits the Dennettian stance. It helps to make clear that what Gintis is rejecting when he abolishes references to "beliefs" from game theory are not the same kinds of things Dennett refers to when he affirms the existence and scientific significance of "beliefs."

This much of the response to eliminativism recapitulates points that have been made at earlier moments in this book, from a number of angles. I want now to press the difference between empirical and explanatory adaptationism further, in an effort to explain why, contra Sugden, I do not see turning to EGT as a basic economic modeling tool as recommending retirement of the concept of utility, or of models of economic agents as utility maximizers.

Sugden (2001, p. 118), as part of his contention that economists adopting EGT are generally being insufficiently revolutionary, complains that "When game theorists profess to be interested in biology, they are not thinking of biology as biologists would, as an empirical science struggling to make sense of the facts of the natural world. They are thinking of a small body of mathematical techniques that have proved useful in some of the more theoretical branches of biology." Indeed. But there is a sound justification for this. Applications of EGT to populations of organisms—or, for that matter, to communities of selves, or communities of Ainslie's interests—are exercises in OISF, based on taking the intentional stance toward the systems that their dynamics instantiate. When population geneticists, evolutionary theorists, or systemacists study groups of animals and sort them into species, they are doing MISF (or, if they build cladograms entirely by reference to molecular data, may not use the intentional stance at all). Therefore, the sets of players in evolutionary games should not be expected, in general, to map onto the sets of kinds into which biologists sort organisms.

How, in general, should strategies be individuated in applications of EGT? In building a classical game, the only individuation issue arises around the agents. Once we have fixed them, and so specified a set of utility functions, there is no further scope for judgment in the individuation of strategies. Every agent that has at least one move has exactly as many distinct strategies as they have combinations of information sets in the extensive form of the game, and these are fully inferable from the game's structure. Nothing so clear can be said about strategy individuation in EGT, however, because no elements entirely exogenous to such games need stay constant through their course. Individuals of course change with generations, as do fitness constraints and, possibly, the environmental parameters that fix the space of the game itself. One might casually suppose that a constraint can at least be imposed on strategy identities by requiring players of strategies to be identified with their own descendents. However, in many EGT investigations of equilibrium stability, especially those modeling cultural dynamics, violation of this constraint is precisely the source of the most interesting stability properties. For example, Skyrms (1996, chapter 2) discusses a simple game in the replicator dynamics in which the equilibrium strategies reliably survive through early, risky rounds of the game with a plethora of rivals because the introduction of recombination enables them to go temporarily extinct but return through the matings of less initially unfortunate types of players. Monophylicity is thus violated: there may be strategies present in equilibrium who had none of their own kind as ancestors. In the biological realm, species, identified by reference to genetic structure, cannot pull off this sort of Lazarus act. But that is just the point: strategies as elements of the formalism of EGT cannot *in general* be identified with species, or with lineages.

The point here is not, of course, that in any particular model one can't or shouldn't map strategies onto objects individuated independently from outside the formalism. (If one didn't, it wouldn't be a model *of* anything.) The point, rather, is that evolutionary strategies, like interests and other OISF objects, are retrospective constructs for rationalizing outcomes.[19] As with interests, we can just let our individuation principles be driven by the requirements of the formalism itself. Treating game theory as a branch of mathematics denies us wiggle room on what evolutionary strategies can be *formally*, if evolutionary games are not to be games only metaphorically. It must be possible to construct, at any given time, a static snapshot of the evolutionary game as a classical game. The prior dynamics that generated this game, along with exogenous mutations, will have determined the range of moves available to its players. A strategy is then simply any possible path through the tree of the game. This has the perfectly reasonable effect of relativizing evolutionary strategies to particular evolutionary games. I say reasonable because, if Dennett is right, we don't find strategies in nature independently of interpreting evolution using the intentional stance—that is, adopting an explanatory adaptationist perspective.

And what should be our principles for individuating games themselves? Games as *syntactic* structures are individuated (in extensional form) by reference to their underlying directed graphs. How do we go about adding a semantics (that is, a biological or cultural-dynamical interpretation)? In classical game theory, the assignment of payoffs, interpreted as distributions of real assets, to terminal nodes does this; and thus we say that a game changes whenever its payoff structure does. Payoff assignments, of course, are derived from utility functions. In an evolutionary game payoffs are interpreted as fitness coefficients; but these will not and cannot stay constant as games evolve. Now, typically the whole point of an EGT model is to understand dynamic change in relevant parameters—including strategy frequencies, the topology of the adaptive landscape, and fitness coefficients—as games evolve. In these circumstances, if game individuation is not to be entirely discretionary, some quantity has to be conserved. What might this be? Brown (2001) shows how to generalize EGT as an extremum theory, in which selection is conceptually unified as maximization of an abstract "fitness-generating function" that takes different specific interpretations in different sorts of selective regimes (density independent, density dependent, or frequency dependent). Like the neoclassical utility function, the fitness-generating function is of interest precisely because it does not have a predetermined empirical interpretation.

Sugden (2001, p. 128), in urging economists to shuck off their commitment to a familiar formal superstructure and behave like real biologists, is not explicit about what he thinks "real" biologists do. (They mainly measure things they find and grow. No doubt Sugden thinks economists should gather more data. One can't argue with that, but it's always true in every science.) It is his suspicion of the systematizing power of formalism, going even beyond his suspicion of "rationality," that leads me to read him as a more radical eliminativist than the kind whose campaign against "rationality" is merely a rejection of the refinement program. So let me venture a suggestion as to what his intuition (or that of some hypothetical, self-conscious economic eliminativist who borrows his arguments) about a truly "biological" economics might be.

The intuition will start from a certain image about biology. Imagine that we first approach the history of life as hyperstrict cladists. That is, we insist that each evolutionary novelty, however minor its degree of variance, occupy a unique place on a single cladogram where strict monophyly is imposed. The resulting tree will of course be densely packed with clades—uselessly dense from the perspective of anyone seeking explanatory generalizations beyond very small scales. The structure will be useful to a systemacist trying to chart, for example, the molecular development within a group of closely related mosses; but this is a fundamentally descriptive rather than explanatory enterprise. How might we try to find useful patterns here, in a principled way? It seems that we will require some notion of "evolutionary novelty that makes a difference," if only to first reduce the bewildering array of clades on the tree. But: makes a difference *to what*? Keeping to the cladist spirit, we might answer just: a difference to the distribution of clades at the end of the process (or the present, if that is what you are trying to explain, or some point in the evolutionary past that interests us). However, this furnishes only data for explanation; from a perspective that seeks to explain evolutionary patterns it is perfectly circular. Now, perhaps EGT could be brought in at this point to help us explain why clades occur where they do, and in which clusters. Strategies would be identified with lineages. The highly structured data we've imagined assembling would be the main source of constraints on our selection of games; no hunches about "problems faced by natural selection" would play a role. No reasons, anywhere, would enter the explanatory picture at all.

This might be a valuable and productive way to use EGT. But the eliminativist's intuition seems to push further and suggest that it would thereby contribute to our understanding of *all there is to explain.* Philosophically, what does this intuition amount to? It expresses a hyperempiricism about what we want from science that is incompatible with the need for explanation by reference to real patterns. Attaching a consistent semantics to the classes of objects in evolutionary game theory will clearly, like all projects in semantic interpretation of formal structures, require some reference to the world. But we should not impose a priori restrictions that this must be the world as described by reductionist approaches. This exactly recapitulates the reason why neuroeconomics, however important and helpful it is, does not potentially displace or discharge picoeconomics. Again, MISF and OISF approaches to individuation are not competitors.

I am urging, against the eliminativist intuition, that games are, fundamentally, *problems*, and strategies are candidate ways of coping with them. But what empirical motivation do we have for thinking that we ought to represent the history of life in terms of problem solving? The answer, as urged by Glimcher (2003, chapter 7), Conway Morris (2003), and others, is: the fact of widespread convergence in evolution. Knowing that two groups of organisms occupy economically similar niches predicts morphological similarity over and over again in ecology and ethology, independently of phylogeny. Conway Morris (2003), in particular, piles up hundreds of instances in which unrelated animals who face similar ecological pressures have evolved nearly identical morphological structures. To cite a nice summary tableau from Ray (1992, p. 396): "Among dinosaurs, the *Pterosaur, Triceratops, Tyrannosaurs* and *Ichthyosaur* are ecological parallels, respectively, to the bat, rhinoceros, lion and porpoise of modern mammals. Similarly, among modern placental mammals, the grey wolf, flying squirrel, great anteater and common mole are ecological parallels, respectively, to the Tasmanian wolf, honey glider, banded anteater and marsupial mole of the marsupial mammals of Australia." These sets of pairs, though they vividly illustrate the point, are slightly crude. As Conway Morris documents, however, convergent patterns are often sufficiently robust and detailed enough to allow successful *quantitative* predictions of highly surprising refinement and accuracy. Nor does convergence just denote gross similarities, such as all predators of large fleshy prey having sharp teeth; as Conway Morris indicates, ecological similarity often predicts common structures down to the level of chemical facilitators and pathways. Here, with a vengeance, are strategies more abstract than species or lineages, and as wholly unrestricted by monophylicity. The ubiquity of convergence as an overwhelming reason for modeling evolution as a problem solver is in no way impugned by Gould and Lewontin's (1979) famous point that evolution builds "spandrels," that is, parts of organisms that are side effects of design strategies rather than contributors to optimization. Quite the contrary: spandrels are precisely side effects of solving *problems*, and can only be understood *as* spandrels relative to that perspective.

Gintis and Sugden are of course right to say that the beliefs of the classical game theorist and the refinement program have no place in evolutionary games. There is nobody in the picture with either the relevant foresight or the relevant computational capacities. However, this does not eliminate problems and solutions, and therefore it does not eliminate reasons. The relevant problems, solutions, and reasons are faced by natural selection. They existed long before there was anyone around who was capable of appreciating them. The rationales by which the history of life sorts itself into games are, as Dennett would put it, "free-floating" (that is, entertained by neither the players nor the designer); but the theorist who therefore tries to deny that they are real patterns will be forced into the deeply irrealist position of holding that there were no evolutionary games in progress before evolutionary game theorists came along. Yes, we analysts, we intentional-stance-takers, must interpret data as games and strategies to turn them into formal objects that permit deployment of our mathematical techniques. But the ubiquity of convergence is an empirical fact that forces us to engage in such interpretation if we want to understand biological phenomena.

Economic Adaptationism

In deploying Godfrey-Smith's typology of forms of adaptationism in the previous section, I acknowledged, without providing any details, that Dennett is both an explanatory and a methodological adaptationist. It would be odd for anyone to endorse the first without endorsing the second. If investigations of leading questions about evolutionary histories require that data be organized by reference to games and strategies, then at least where these leading questions are concerned, sound method must obviously involve performing that organization.

Dennett's methodological adaptationism is expressed in his endorsement of reverse engineering as a basic epistemological procedure in the behavioral sciences. Let us examine one of his leading examples:

When Raytheon wants to make an electric widget to compete with General Electric's widget, they buy several of GE's widgets, and analyze them: that's reverse engineering. They run them, benchmark them, x-ray them, take them apart, and subject every part of them to interpretive analysis: Why did GE make these wires so heavy? What are these extra ROM registers for? Is this a double layer of insulation and, if so, why did they bother with it? Notice that the reigning assumption is that all these "why" questions have answers. Everything has a *raison d'être*, GE did nothing in vain.

Of course if the wisdom of the reverse engineers includes a healthy helping of self-knowledge, they will recognize that this default assumption of optimality is too strong: sometimes engineers put stupid, pointless things in their designs, sometimes they forget to remove things that no longer have a function. Sometimes they overlook retrospectively obvious shortcuts. But still, optimality must be the default assumption; if the reverse engineers can't assume that there is a good rationale for the features they observe, they can't even begin their analysis. (1994, p. 685)

The explanatory adaptationist in biology is urged to reverse engineer natural selection's designs in just this way.

Note that the assumption of the reverse engineer here is not that the *product* is perfect for any and all purposes, but that the *designer* had *some* purposes in mind. Invitation to reflect on the designer's purposes implies invitation to also reflect on her constraints. Where naturally designed systems are concerned, reverse engineering must recognize that they were produced by a designer without foresight, required at each stage to tinker with preestablished platforms rather than work from scratch to functional specifications. Equally important, nature does not develop her designs in isolation from one another, issuing them from the factory, as it were, one at a time. She instead designs, in increments, entire macroeconomies, in which the constraints on optimal function of any one product are provided partly by equilibrium considerations across the whole range of competing brands. The optimizing idealization, as applied to Mother Nature, is thus not the claim that she builds a set of rational economic creatures, but rather that she computes information in the way a market does, finding open niches for competitive strategies and then (eventually) filling them. This is the intended sense in which Dennett (1995) characterizes natural selection as "algorithmic." It is precisely analogous to the kinds of assumptions about markets with which economists studying aggregate systems typically begin. This procedure does not require any assumption to the effect that each individual agent, or even any individual agent, in the ensemble is a perfect computer of its ideal utility maximization. The relevant adaptationist assumption, as applied to natural selection, is instead that selection pressures will tend to dampen the aggregate impacts of suboptimal individual dispositions, *relative to* whatever market microstructure nature has implemented in the case of a given ecological system.

Dennett is of course not an economist, and I think is open to being accused of a certain innocence about the potential for variation among market types. That is, there is some justice in one antiadaptationist point that has been made against him, namely, that he makes an assumption that can be expressed in economic terms as the view that nature necessarily moves toward general equilibrium. In biological terms, this would be expressed as: there is a unique equilibrium set of niches, and nature (eventually) fills them all. Mirowski's worry about "bungee-jumping" may derive such appropriateness as it has from this point.[20] In this context, we need not critically evaluate the complicated issues raised by Mirowski's insistence that Gödel's theorem implies that general equilibrium can never be effectively computed. Simply because nature is a dynamic system it obviously will never be *at* general equilibrium, but this isn't what Dennett's assumption amounts to. The assumption, instead, is that wherever a selectionist account finds an unfilled niche, that account faces a burden of argument in explaining why nature has failed to find it.

A homely economic example will help to illustrate the point. Suppose an economist came across the following data about a city. It has several competing businesses profitably selling golf equipment. Consumer spending patterns show nontrivial levels of aggregate demand for golfing tours to other areas. The city is surrounded by large, flat farms that face recurrent financial crises and are kept afloat only by regular, and highly controversial, government subsidies. Yet there are no golf courses within motoring range of the city. This set of facts would constitute an economic anomaly and demand special explanation. (Perhaps it's impossibly expensive to maintain lawn grass, because of the soil or climate.) After discovering it, we would not be satisfied with *any* account of the municipal economy that failed to suggest an explanation, not because we think this minor distortion in its leisure market is so economically significant in itself, but because we know there's something odd about the city's circumstances that might be important to a general economic model in all sorts of ways. That the absence of golf courses is anomalous doesn't depend on an assumption that the city's citizens and investors are individually perfectly rational. It depends on the assumptions that we know approximate things about their utility functions *and that information about preferences and prices flows reasonably efficiently within the system.*

Dennett's model of evolution as algorithmic expresses the idea that because natural selection faces no time constraints and is a massively parallel processor, it must be a highly efficient information processor, to a degree that justifies the kind of economic adaptationism I have just described. We might add as another point in favor of this hypothesis that natural selection is not regulated by any rent-seeking institutions. However, this reference to institutions also reveals the rub in the hypothesis. Regulation can both impede information flow and facilitate it. Furthermore, the market represented by nature may be free, but it is far from perfect (in the economist's sense). Since it builds products that evolve their own interests—that is, that will do what they can to perpetuate themselves—it spontaneously throws up entry and exit barriers. That is, groups of organisms are incentivized, by natural selection's own operations, to blockade niches and to destroy niches that might otherwise be occupied by others. (They need no foresight to do this. Lions devote substantial time to hunting and killing cheetah cubs when cheetahs are in their area, so much so that this seems to be contributing to cheetah extinction in several parts of Africa.)

This is, of course, all just vague and speculative teasing of an analogy so far. The point, for now, is not that Dennett's implicit economic adaptationism is necessarily misguided. Rather, it is that it is primitive. Information no more flows costlessly in nature than it does in human markets. As Mirowski (2002) points out, we have a burgeoning formal exploration of the systematic ways in which particular interactions of information-flow dynamics influence the evolution of types of market structures, which goes by the name of "market microstructure theory" (see O'Hara 1995 for a survey). If economic adaptationism is an interesting idea, then it deserves to be investigated using the resources of this analytical tool. Furthermore, a new branch of behavioral science, artificial life (Langton 1995; Boden 2001), that devotes itself to creating new evolutionary dynamics, not investigated by the history of actual life on earth, amounts to the study of wider possibilities and limitations on dynamic information flow among economic agents in general. Exploration of these two paths of investigation, mutually informing each other, is a specific strategy for combining behavioral science and economic theory in the style suggested by intentional-stance functionalism.

Indeed, artificial life research as it is already carried out can be thought of as standing to the study of market typologies as traditional microeconomics stands to traditional macroeconomics. In one of the most profound artificial life projects developed to date, Thomas Ray (1992) has triggered the evolution of parasitism, hyperparasitism, and sociality in strings of self-replicating computer code merely by placing them in a low-structure simulated environment where they compete for scarce CPU time and memory. Further attempts to generate features of complexity, such as the evolution of sex, essentially involve manipulating the microeconomic parameters on the environment. Another artificial life researcher, David McFarland (1992) has argued that a fundamental modeling assumption for the discipline should be to conceive of animals as "cost-based robots." The idea—which McFarland formally develops—is that microeconomic pressures, as the domain of unavoidable *problems* for active systems with goals—agents, that is—

are the source of the real dynamics characteristic of self-evolving life, what distinguishes its products from the "dead" robots of classical AI.

If economic adaptationism is a bungee jump, as Mirowski alleges, then we might remind ourselves that bungee jumping isn't ruinous if the cord is attached. Is Dennett's untethered to the bridge? Young (1998) provides a series of demonstrations that, if we can empirically justify models of the learning dispositions of agents in populations, we can prove theorems that represent the local equilibria on which they converge as asymptotic functions with equilibria of classical game theory as their limits. This is promising, in the present context, because classical game theory is the formal language of industrial organization theory, and that theory is, in turn, the descriptive apparatus for distinguishing between types of markets. The major limitation of that formalism is that it doesn't represent informational dynamics; but this is just what Young's models, along with market microstructure theory, address. It is obviously part of the mission of cognitive science to discover the kinds of learning dispositions that Young shows us how to include in the picture. As noted above, neuroeconomics promises crucial help in enabling us to formally reconstruct learning models in the conceptual vocabulary of Samuelsonian economics. Indeed, if we are persuaded by Glimcher's main argument then this will be essential to empirical success in choosing among learning models for application to biological individuals.

Young's program, harnessed to input from neuroeconomics, thus yields promise for what we might think of as "Marshall's revenge" (to employ a Mirowskian rhetorical gambit): in place of Dennett's implied general equilibrium model of natural selection as a designer, we would instead work with a family of partial equilibrium models in which we use data from evolutionary ecology and artificial life to individuate populations of interactors for the application of market microstructure theory. Industrial organization theory can then be used to compare relative efficiencies. I will evaluate the prospects for all of this in detail in the companion volume to this study, by asking how well it can be made to comport with Sutton's (2000) recent defense of a Marshallian program in empirical macroeconomics. The founders of neoclassicism will thus still be with us.

Sugden (2001, pp. 125–127) worries about the adequacy of Young's approach because of its failure to take time fully seriously. As Dennett (1995) has himself emphasized, natural selection can be evaluated with respect to equilibria—general *or* partial—only in the long run. Young's approach capitalizes on this. By introducing small noise terms into otherwise deterministic models, he permits stochastic perturbations to gradually wash out the influence of historical contingencies. This is what enables particular equilibria as dominant basins of attraction in evolutionary games to be selected as limits in the models; *eventually* the operation of the noise shakes systems out of local minima into which they happen to fall. Sugden objects to this exactly as Keynes objected to Marshall: ". . . in many of Young's models the long run seems to be extraordinarily long, perhaps even a matter of billions of years. (How long would it take Britain to switch to driving on the right if we waited for a coincidence of random mistakes by individual drivers? And that would be just *one* transition between individual equilibria: Young's long run is a period which contains a very large number of transitions)" (2001, p. 127). (To make the point of the objection fully intelligible, Sugden's footnote to this remark must be quoted as well: "In a rare historical aside, Young [1998, pp. 16–17] summarizes the actual history of 'keep left' and keep right' conventions in Europe, and claims that this exhibits the patterns predicted by his theory. But he has to use a model in which nations, not individuals, are players; the French Revolution counts as a single exogenous shock" [2001, n. 10, p. 129].)

It is not clear what the force of this objection is quite supposed to be for efforts to *understand* the dynamics of economic processes scientifically. But even where matters of policy are concerned, attention to equilibria might be directly relevant in the way suggested—in a somewhat different context—by Binmore (1998), as long as we have an associated dynamics that enables us to isolate local features of equilibrium *paths.* To apply again the lessons from natural selection as discussed in this chapter, consider the payoff of Dennett's version of adaptationism for complex organisms. Nature is obviously not "at" the kind of general equilibrium Dennett's algorithmic interpretation of selection implicitly suggests. Nevertheless, it is its local stability identified by reference to that equilibrium concept that makes the intentional stance possible, that is, that enables us to interpret behavior by reference to reasons. Economic analysis, for both explanatory and policy purposes, has as its task the interpretation of systems by reference to structures of reasons, namely, games. We now have at hand a conceptual framework that should at least give us some grounds for optimism about that task.

I will now regard eliminativism, in both its manifestations, as answered. This means that the only source of philosophical foundations for economics left standing is intentional-stance functionalism.

Because we have not yet shown how to inform it with the insights of market microstructure theory, we cannot yet apply it to build new foundations for macroeconomics. And since the microeconomics of interactions among whole people are partly constrained by the macro-economic pressures that impinge on them, we can't finish that story yet either. Enough is on the table, however, to complete the description of the Robbins–Samuelson argument pattern that specifies the domain and form of microeconomic theory. That, with some parting reflections on the foils from chapter 1, will be the subject of the remaining chapter to close this volume.

9

The Robbins–Samuelson Argument Pattern and Its Foils

The Robbins–Samuelson Argument Pattern

In chapter 4 I started to sketch what I called the "Robbins–Samuelson argument pattern" (RASP) for explanation of microeconomic phenomena. It is now time to complete it. Let us begin, then, by reiterating its first part:

Suppose you want to explain and/or predict what happens when the members of a group of one or more goal-directed systems, in causal interaction wherever the group is larger than one, pursue ends that cannot all be satisfied given available common resources that have alternative uses. In that case, use as much evidence as you should (according to pragmatically governed but scientifically rigorous standards) gather about their behavior to represent the schedule of ends pursued by each system as a (ordinal or VNM, depending on the intended application and purpose of the solution) utility function, defined as per axioms that admit of solution by simultaneously maximizing each utility function for a given allocation of resource constraints.

Note first that this makes two features fundamental to a phenomenon's being "economic": *scarcity* (Robbins) and *agency* (Samuelson). It also identifies the basic object of generalization as the interacting *group* of agents rather than the individual, although the individual may be the limiting case of the group in Robinson Crusoe situations.

However, it was argued over the past few chapters that Robinson Crusoe, given his internal complexity, doesn't implement a classical Robinson Crusoe situation. The study of a single neuron in Glimcher's program, or an insect, focuses on a "pure" Robinson Crusoe situation. In such cases, absence of complexity implies that intentionality can be discharged in the model of that system. With the discharge of intentionality, specifically economic ontological principles cash out and admit of translation into physical principles. However, this doesn't imply that the real pattern identified by economics is reduced away or found to have been just a methodological heuristic, since the system's individuation *as* a system depends on the irreducibly economic model of its environmental context.[1]

All the first step of the RASP does is tell us how and when to individuate economic agents. This can yield no predictions about their behavior until we have empirically justified a particular maximization function for each of them. Are they maximizing expected utility, or the target of a matching law, or what? For this, the economist must work in direct collaboration with the cognitive-behavioral scientist, in the way well exemplified in neuroeconomics. That is, constraints on the maximization function will be found by working toward reflective equilibrium between top-down (economic) derivations from the structure of the games the agents play (see below), and bottom-up (cognitive science) characterizations of their information-processing capacities and dispositions. Conceptual commensurability of the two approaches, in a given application, is to be expected because both presuppose a shared MISF decomposition of a wider system. MISF decomposition takes the design stance to the system under study, which implicates it in the intentional stance toward whatever sort of selection process produced it.

Therefore, the next step of the RASP is:

Empirically identify a maximization function for each agent in the network of interactors.

As yet, this says nothing about how to aggregate the agents into a network. This will involve constructing their interaction as a game or a set of games. However, saying this by itself is not helpful without guidance as to what sorts of games the evolutionary history of the agents has generated. If the information-processing dynamics of the agents restrict them to G''-level games—that is, if their strategy sets given any distribution of resource constraints cannot be modified— then microeconomic modeling by itself can complete the model. Thus the final steps of the RASP, considered just as the argument pattern for *microeconomics*, are:

Identify the constraints on G''-level games playable by the agents. Identify the specific scenario to be explained with one such game, and find that game's Nash equilibria.

The game thus solved might, of course, have multiple NE. However, attempts to achieve further selection by refinement would have to imply a conviction that either (i) something—the assignment of the utility functions, or the identification of the maximization functions—supposedly achieved earlier was in fact left uncompleted, or (ii) the agents are in fact capable of going beyond G''-level games.

It will at once be objected that the argument pattern as described can't be unfolded as a simple "feed-forward" sequence, because identification of maximization functions and identification of games mutually depend on each other. However, this simply points to the particular places in which the microeconomic modeler depends on exogenous data for constraints that enable her to avoid (actual, practical, as opposed to purely philosophical and in-principle) underdetermination problems. Information-processing dynamics discoverable independently by the cognitive scientist constrain the maximization function, and ecological models of carrying capacities in environments, along various dimensions, constrain the games. Of course, there is no guarantee that, in any given case, these constraints will be sufficient to inspire confidence in the model. But that's how it goes in empirical science—the point made by the philosopher who reminds us that underdetermination problems can't be made to go away by logic alone. They can only be mitigated by having plenty of data. Pragmatically, one should stop worrying that one's model is underdetermined at the point where it would take superogatory levels of ingenuity to find a competing one.

Solving a well-justified G''-level game is as much as microeconomic analysis *all by itself* can accomplish. Now, lots of possibilities for what *else* one might be motivated to do in aiming at fuller understanding of the phenomena are open. If the agents are not (except in the indefinitely long evolutionary run) capable of getting past G''-level games, then one can apply evolutionary game theory at the population level to identify the relative stabilities of the identified NE. This is what should be done in the case of populations of asocial organisms. The result, if all goes well, will be a model that furnishes quantitative ecological predictions.

But, of course, all the serious philosophical, methodological, and ideological problems that have beset the history of economics concern what to do with agents who *can* go beyond G''-level games. *Radical*—"antieconomic"—answers have consisted in different sorts of claims to the effect that this is where economics ceases to be useful altogether;

it's time for sociology or anthropology or hermeneutics or some combination of them, and economists should wait in the other room with the biologists. *Conservative* answers—Becker's, for example—have denied that the sociologists, and so forth, have anything important to contribute because (interpreting what they say in my conceptual terms), G''-level dynamics causally swamp G' and G-level dynamics. (Models in evolutionary psychology that try to explain too much by reference to Pleistocene utility functions effectively make this sort of claim too.)

Rejecting these scorched-earth perspectives, as I have in this book, leaves a variety of conciliatory approaches on the table. Semi-Aristotelianism—Jevons, Sen, Davis—is one of them. It supposes that the agents identified by the microeconomist constitute "cores" around which real people build important excretions that "rise above" the economic. At this point, I can gloss my opposition to this approach by saying: it ignores the fact that the objects of basic study in microeconomics are games, not individuals. People are functions of the games they play, not the other way around. They thus don't reduce to aggregates of G''-level game players plus some add-ons, even if analysis of such games is required in the early steps of explaining how people in general came to be, phylogenetically, or how specific people come to be, ontogenetically. G''-level games are basic only historically, and analytic ontologies do not, in general, map onto historical ones.

As for eliminativists like Rosenberg, Gintis, and Sugden, it would be presumptuous of me to try to say where their position stands with respect to mine because (except in the case of Rosenberg) their eliminativism isn't self-consciously intended as such. I have argued against eliminativist suggestions on the basis of claiming that they result from failure to fully appreciate the important distinction between agents and selves, as this impacts on game-theoretic modeling. If present eliminativists are persuaded to accept this distinction, then perhaps they will wish to retreat from the eliminativist spins they give to their methodological remarks (as Gintis indeed seems inclined to do).

So who's left at the table when we ask how economics applies to social agents, and to people in particular? For one, Marx; not because there is anything persuasive in the labor theory of value or the hypothesis of the falling rate of profit, of course, but because no broadly Marxist microeconomics could be independent of macroeconomics, if we set out to anachronistically explicate Marx in terms of that distinction. I suggested in chapter 7 that market processes tend to turn people, over time, into beings who act more like economic agents. This is obviously redolent of some aspects of Marx's thought (though, unlike Marx, I feel no compulsion to deplore the process or think we should try to arrest it in general).

I will have a bit more to say about Marx in the next volume. But pointing out this affinity between the account of people given here, and Marx's understanding of them, is a useful basis for summarizing what can be said about people before our attention turns to macroexplanation. People, like countries—and for the same reason—are, from the economic perspective, *macroeconomic* objects in the first place. The first-order properties of these objects, as will be explained in the next volume, are things like savings rates, personal accounts and balances of payment, average system-level interest rates, and so on. *Microeconomic* analysis will have useful things to say about people just insofar as their behavior sometimes, or in some kinds of situations, approximates that of economic agents, neoclassically conceived. There are such times and situations, and ways of trying to identify them. This brings me back, in rounding out this book, to my two foils.

Imperialism and Resistance: Dupré

After encountering most of this book's arguments in draft form, Harold Kincaid (personal correspondence) asked " 'Economics' equals what for you, and why? On good naturalist grounds I would take 'economics' to refer to a complex social practice changing over time, in which neoclassical theory and offshoots are only a component. So what is the standing of your 'economics is about' claims?" I of course said quite a bit about this very general philosophical question in chapter 1, but it must be returned to now, in light of all the detailed argument that has been put forward since then. It is most useful to revisit the question in tandem with another of Kincaid's: "Why are bugs agents but humans not? Is it just an empirical fact that there is a central locus of control in the former and not the latter? Or am I confused in taking that as the criterion?"

That's the criterion, all right. The basic "good naturalist" grounds for any philosophical claim about science must be some set of empirical facts or other. But why make *this* fact so important? The answer is that our ability to derive successful quantitative predictions about asocial animals—and neurons, and maybe cognitive modules—from neoclassical maximization models isn't an *isolated* fact about them, stemming from peculiarities of their nature: it's a function of very general, structural facts about how information can and can't flow in systems of different levels of complexity. It's because there are such general facts—facts the neoclassicals, but not Aristotle or Smith or Marx, glimpsed—that economic theory, and neoclassical economic theory in particular, is a domain of systematic theory and not just "social practice over time."

Of course, the early neoclassical economists glimpsed this general structural feature of the world only hazily. To the extent that we are persuaded by Mirowski's (1989) history of their thought, they were in fact clear about very few details. They had an abiding faith in the virtues of systematicity; they thought systematicity should be grounded in a field theory of some sort; they were suspicious of claims about intrinsic or objective value; and that's about it. On my telling in chapter 3, Jevons and Marshall weren't even consistent about this, since their ad hoc distinction between higher and lower wants suggested that, for them, human urges for beauty and goodness aren't susceptible to systematization within the field theory they favored. Their impulse toward the systematic, however, survived their hesitations; Robbins and the others of his generation took major steps toward extending its thrust, and Samuelson displayed absolute devotion to it—perhaps his only consistent philosophical intuition. In this book, I have followed this fundamental neoclassical motivation in light of what we are coming to know, and which Jevons, Robbins, or Samuelson could not know, about information-processing dynamics in biological and cultural systems. These dynamics are the basis for the most general equivalence classes of phenomena we find in the behavioral sciences. Therefore, they are—as an empirical matter—the grounds of recourse for pursuit of systematicity in the behavioral domain. That is why my account privileges them, instead of old intuitions about people as prototypical agents, or old intuitions about the "natural" domain of economic theory, in sorting out the ontological framework for economic inquiry.

My arguments won't persuade someone who doesn't care about systematicity as a value, let alone someone like Dupré, who positively celebrates disorder. This is as deep a divide as can be found in the general philosophy of science, with a large continuing literature. A person who is as yet uncommitted in this conflict of basic impulses might reasonably be swayed in one direction or the other by reference to the implications of systematicity versus disunity with respect to other norms and purposes. The reader of Dupré (2001) is supposed to find disunity attractive because it helps to "free" people from an imperialistic and tyrannical scientism, based on association between economic theory and evolutionary cognitive science. Let me here, therefore, briefly consider how persuasive this appeal should be in light of the specific theses I have defended in this book.

In arguing with Dupré, I will not try to catalog the many misleading things he says about what both economists and evolutionary cognitive scientists actually think. Dennett (forthcoming) has made a good start on this, but the full indictment would be very long. Let me here add just one item to it that Dennett misses, an addition worth noting because it is so portentously general, and directly contrary to a central point I have relied on throughout this book. Having more or less conflated neoclassical economics with rational choice theory, Dupré criticizes economists for presenting too much of human life as if it were explicit cost-benefit calculation. We are reminded (2001, p. 118) that much human behavior simply involves conformity to social norms, and told that "only" when requests for explanations of human behavior "go to the specific projects of the individual" do "questions of rationality in the sense of rational choice theory arise at all." He thereby assumes that individualism is necessarily built into the very firmament of economic logic. This in turn seems to be based on assuming internalism, since in a footnote on the same page, urging that the intentional stance can be dropped when "we go straight to biology," he asks "Does a cow believe that putting grass into its mouth will relieve its hunger?" and answers "Surely not" (n. 2). There is no conceivable basis for this confident assertion except internalism about intentional states. Yet not only is externalism about belief the dominant view in cognitive science, it seems to be Dupré's view too, since he elsewhere (1993, chapter 7) defends intentional psychology against eliminativism while simultaneously denying dualism, reductionism, and supervenience. That package either amounts to intentional-stance functionalism or it is incoherent.

The version of the partnership between economics and cognitive science that alarms Dupré characterizes both activities in a way that denies every main thesis about them I have advanced in this book. Dupré's imperialistic hegamon combines an individualistic economics, using EUT as its core foundational theory of the agent and taking maximization of the individual's material wealth as its model for everything, and joins it to an evolutionary cognitive science that derives personal utility from expected fitness and models the mechanisms that support this derivation by decomposing people additively into modules. I don't know whether we should be frightened, as Dupré is, by a possible social science that bolts all these assumptions together; but in any case he'd be right that we should reject it, if it exists, because its leading assumptions are all false. Does it actually exist, though? Do leading theorists in either economics or cognitive science in fact herald Dupré's distopia, or is he attacking a straw person?

In important respects, the evolutionary psychologists who attempt to reduce people to modules that maximize utility functions evolved for our Pleistocene ancestral environment come closest to putting flesh on Dupré's target. Indeed, Tooby and Cosmides (1992), the leading promoters of this research program, specifically exempt economics from their critique of standard social sciences *because* it alone has hung on to a healthy individualism that sociologists and anthropologists dissolved in a Durkheimist haze. It is abundantly clear from his text that Dupré is in fact disproportionately motivated by an image of these evolutionary psychologists as the vanguard of the nasty imperial legions.

I say "disproportionately" because closer attention to the details of Cosmides's and Tooby's arguments for their approach—as opposed to high-minded rhetoric aimed in its general direction and hitting every nearby associate in evolutionary behavioral science for good measure—shows that the bugbear contains the seeds of its own self-correction. As pointed out in Ross (2002a), the argument of Cosmides and Tooby for modular decomposition of people, along with that of Pinker (1997), relies crucially on appeal to the frame problem in AI, and related objections to the possibility of governing complex systems like people through central-control bottlenecks. I have of course laid heavy stress on this theme too. However, Cosmides, Tooby, and Pinker, at least in their methodological manifestos of the 1990s, simply seem not to have fully absorbed the fact that modularity doesn't solve bottleneck problems if the integration of modules is all bottom-up and *additive*. They partly see this, since they recognize that a collection of well-functioning modular optimizers may build an organism that optimizes poorly as soon as its environment shifts significantly. They don't equate the utility function of a typical contemporary person with expected reproductive fitness; indeed, they argue that modern people get themselves into individual and social messes by using optimization tools sculpted for one class of utility functions in attempted service of a different set. Their view is thus much of the way along the road to breaking the conceptual identity between people and biological individuals. All they tend to miss is the last step in this disidentification, that of recognizing that the units into which people decompose under behavioral analysis should not be expected to map onto cognitive modules (though of course the modules may well be there, and playing an important role in generating behavioral patterns). That is, in my terms, the evolutionary psychology literature of the 1990s doesn't distinguish between MISF and OISF analysis.[2]

This is hardly a devastating criticism of that literature. MISF analysis is useful and important, regardless of whether strong modularity hypotheses will in the end be justified by it. (I expect they won't be, at least with respect to cognition in general; see Karmiloff-Smith 1992.) OISF analysis doesn't tell us the *only* things worth knowing about ourselves. Dupré might, in criticizing the early proclamations of evolutionary psychology, have criticized it just for overgeneralizing its implications. Most nascent research programs trying to carve out niches for themselves do that at first. Yet Dupré doesn't even attempt such close criticism (which involves respect for a principle of charity in interpretation, something he eschews altogether where evolutionary psychologists are concerned, and to which he pays bare lip service in the case of neoclassical economists).

Instead, what Dupré resorts to is a sweeping denunciation of the *general* project of trying to understand human behavior systematically. He says:

It may be said to be of the essence of scientific understanding that it requires concentrating on a very small number of factors and treating other factors as fixed. It is also sometimes suggested that a central feature that distinguishes science from prescientific modes of understanding is the commitment to quantitative techniques. And quantification, finally, requires abstraction. To decide to measure one feature of a class of objects is to privilege that feature over others. This combination of abstraction and quantification is characteristic of the modeling techniques found in much of biology and the social sciences, is signaled by the *ceteris paribus* condition on scientific laws, and is perhaps most strikingly exemplified in many attempts at microreductive explanation. Perhaps it is this combination of abstraction and mathematical representation that is distinctive of the most uncontroversially scientific practices of enquiry. But if this is so, it indicates a limit to the possibility of scientific understanding of phenomena as complex and multicausal as human behaviour. This is the most general moral to be drawn from the deficiencies and absurdities of imperialistic economism. (2001, p. 136)

If science must falter as soon as it encounters complex and "multi-causal" (meaning, presumably, just "complex" again—what else could it mean?) phenomena, then most science is just impossible. Kepler and Newton, perhaps, nailed the relations among the large bodies in the solar system because these are among the few salient networks of phenomena in our environment that aren't complex. Ever since then, if Dupré is right, we've been engaged in a quixotic pursuit, because pretty much everything else has turned out to be complex. Perhaps most of this was innocent—a few nuclear weapons aside—but now we risk subjecting ourselves to false tyranny by spinning epistemic fantasies about ourselves.

This is a familiar complaint, one heard before from Carlyle, Ruskin, and many others. Economics, of course, knows it specifically in the form of "dismal science" labels. As Robbins's definition of economics emphasizes, one of the things objective economic analysis often—perhaps even generally—aims at showing us is which combinations of outcomes we can't have simultaneously or at unachievable bargain rates. Perhaps cognitive science adds further discouraging news; for example, that people can't order their brains around like captains of Cartesian ships. I will not condescend to the reader by offering a long speech in rejoinder about the dangers of wishful thinking or making policy choices in blissful ignorance. Which has caused more misery in recent human experience: falsely thinking there are things we *can't* do, because scientists, particularly economists, psychologists, and biologists, have discouraged us with gloomy pessimism, or attempting collective stunts whose implausibility could have been foreseen through more effective institutionalization of systematic thought? This is of course a deep political judgment—the deepest of them all. Everyone must assess the inductive record for themselves. In my own case, I line up here with Binmore's (1994, 1998) whiggery: in a world not only of general scarcity but of grotesque and widespread poverty, it is obligatory to try to change the status quo, but foolish and counterproductive to leap blindly off equilibrium paths in doing so. Of course, in the absence of details, this declaration isn't much more useful than advising people to buy low and sell high. Some such details must also wait for the next volume.

I have not had much respectful to say about one of my foils, because I think that raising populist alarms against systematic science is morally irresponsible. This, in turn, is because I doubt that we can improve the lives of people in destitute parts of the world without a great deal *more* systematic science. It is thus with some relief that I turn, in conclusion, back to my other foil, whose analysis aims at improving economic science rather than choking it.

Economic Theory and Cognitive Science in Mirowski's Mirror

I mentioned in chapter 1 that, as Dennett's work in the foundations of cognitive science has been the leading inspiration for the thesis defended in this volume, Binmore's way of understanding economics as a social science will play a foundational role in the next one. I'll lead into this baton passing now, in the course of closing off this volume's dialogue with Mirowski. Mirowski (2002, pp. 514–516), after discussing Binmore, asks a series of rhetorical questions about his psychological assumptions that I, on the basis of the last seven chapters, will now presume to answer (not, of course, claiming to do so on Binmore's behalf).

"It would appear," Mirowski begins, "that Binmore's fundamental ambition is to defend the neoclassical program to the hilt, or, as he puts it, 'Find the boundaries up to which neoclassical theory works'" (ibid., p. 514). Whether this is or isn't an accurate characterization of Binmore's aims, it well describes an aspect of the present book. However, since neoclassicism has had a complex history involving important shifts in its underlying philosophical foundations, the idea of defending "neoclassicism" *simpliciter* must be an underdescription of any particular ambition. Neoclassical economics grew up in tandem with empiricist psychology and analytic philosophy. In the case of all three enterprises, commitment to systematicity ultimately triumphed over initial adherence to phenomenology. Empiricist psychology finds maturity in third-person evolutionary cognitive science that denies introspection and turns people into complex communities of agents and interests. Analytic philosophy escaped its origins in Kant and became broadly Humean and naturalistic. Neoclassical economics started by trying to model people whose unified rationality is transparent to them, and ended up, with Samuelson, describing abstract equilibrium machines in which people aren't even mentioned except by incidental implication. Thus one cannot try to locate the core commitments of neoclassicism just by scrutinizing the words of Jevons or Walras, any more than one could sensibly insist that empiricist psychologists stay true to Wundt or analytic philosophers remain loyal to Frege.

However, closing his interrogation of Binmore, Mirowski (ibid., p. 516) asks us to consider the concept of an evolutionary stable strategy and then says "if Nash equilibria embody rationality, then it is the entire population, and not the individual agents, that can be graced with the honorific of rationality in those models. But if it is the population that is rational, we are returned to the group mind of sociology, the anathema that neoclassical economics had set itself against." It would be much more accurate to say that the group mind was anathema to Locke and Kant, and that some early neoclassicals were Lockeans or Kantians, like lots of their contemporaries.[3] Putting aside the cloud of ideological propaganda about rugged individuals that has often hovered over neoclassicism—but surely not over Pigou, Bergson, or Samuelson— why should the fact that neoclassicism swallowed big gulps of Locke and Kant with its bottle be taken to restrict its present ambit?

As I discussed in chapter 6, Robinson Crusoe pedagogy, which is still useful, has had a great deal to do with this image. Very large numbers of people in higher- and middle-income countries take Economics 101 and then stop. This no doubt contributes greatly to the idea, promoted in the semipopulist announcements of revolutions in economics (or the need for them) mentioned at the end of chapter 7, that incorporating behavioral and evolutionary factors into the discipline overthrows a fundamental allegiance to an empirical thesis that people are selfish individual maximizers. As noted repeatedly in this book, although many economists of course have defended that idea, it is not clear they ever had a good empirical or theoretical reason to. Evolutionary considerations do not threaten inner Robinson Crusoes because they had no plausible ontological significance in the first place. In turn, the ontological importance of selves does not rest on the model of the inner Robinson Crusoe and is not called into question when we abandon the latter idea.

I suggest, therefore, that no one need lose much sleep over Mirowski's worry for Binmore that "the more he took the cyborg sciences seriously, the more he reduced the Self to rubble" (ibid., p. 516). Binmore explicitly (see his 1998, p. 193) disavows eliminativism, while simultaneously abjuring internalism on the same page. His view of mind is clearly intentional-stance functionalist; and we have seen over the past few chapters the important role and irreducible ontological status that intentional-stance functionalism assigns to selves.

These observations should lower the temperature around Mirowski's main question for Binmore, but they don't specifically answer his question, at least all by themselves. The question is: "What precisely is the interpretation of replicator dynamics which Binmore propounds? Does the meme soup exist in the bowl of the individual cranium?" (2002, p. 514). Reading "the meme soup" here as just a vivid name for the network of basins of attraction in social-imitative learning, the generic answer given by the intentional-stance functionalist is by this point in our story patently obvious: it certainly does *not* exist "in the individual cranium," though it profoundly influences much that goes on there. Although this much is self-evident, there is justice in Mirowski's suggestion that we need far more details about the specific ways in which meme soups relate *Homo economicus* to *Homo sapiens* before we should expect people to agree that Binmore and Dennett together show us how to stitch neoclassical economics and evolutionary cognitive science together.

Once again, that is the job for my next volume. However, before leaving this one, let us see how much we can now say, just on the basis of *this* volume's conclusions, about the prospects for economic theory in the context of Mirowski's "five futures" from chapter 1. To spare the reader annoying thumbwork in paging back, I will reintroduce each future by quoting my own description of it from the first chapter.

1. Judd's Revenge.   *In this future, economics pays essentially no attention to cognitive science. It uses computational technology to study, with increasing intricacy, what would happen to rational agents if they could access and crunch all the information that our newest machines can, at least as quickly as they do (or, for some applications, instantaneously). As Mirowski puts it (2002, p. 451), this future implements the idea of conflating rationality with econometric inference.* Economists will obviously remain interested in what paths to equilibrium *can* be computed by a physically possible machine, regardless of what the cognitive and behavioral sciences have to say about what *is* computed in real time by actual and evolved systems (both individual and social). Abstract computability considerations at least give us a benchmark for systematizing our purely statistical-normative theory of optimization, and that is interesting in itself. However, my thesis in this book must have the consequence that Mirowski is right to regard this as being of very limited empirical relevance. I suggested in chapter 8 that as societies develop more, and more widely accessed, tools for bookkeeping the activities of selves, selves under threat of being money-pumped will come increasingly to approximate straightforward economic agents. However, this doesn't imply that societies themselves will come to approximate such agents. What is computed by societies as economic information processors are outcomes of complex bargaining dynamics, and *nothing* has as a utility function the minimization of cycling among social preferences (see Hardin 2004). Samuelsonian welfare economics, in its macroeconomic aspect, must undergo massive transformation in the light of behavioral science—as it has indeed been doing (see Bowles 2003).

What about particular, sophisticated, markets in which traders might be incentivized to hire game theorists as agents to recommend strategies for them, based on the best data that computers can crunch? Might pursuit of Judd's revenge not yield the appropriate idealization of them (for purposes of MISF-style analysis)? Present empirical evidence from the field of behavioral finance (see Barberis and Thaler 2002) offers little encouragement for the view that financial asset markets, the most obvious domain for such an implementation, are evolving into perfect equilibrium calculators. There are at least three reasons for doubting that, in principle, they could. The first is essentially Mirowski's reason: the ultimate refinement is noncomputable. Second, financial markets are not, and cannot be, encapsulated from wider networks of social games, because no one and nothing has a standing incentive to try to so encapsulate them. Third, as suggested by the recent history of markets in which game theorists have played dominant roles—such as the telecommunications bandwidth auctions market—to the extent that arms races among mechanism designers are set into motion, the game theorists themselves tend to undermine Pareto improvements by bidding up their own rents (Lane 1999, pp. 308–313). (As good game theorists, how could they not?) The third reason is really a specific institutional manifestation of the second.

These reasons explain my agreement with Mirowski, expressed in chapter 1, that [*t*]*here isn't much room for doubt, given the allocation of person hours in economics now, that* [Judd's revenge] *will be at least* part *of the future of economics. To the extent that it dominates that future, it represents the regime in which economics remains most proudly separate from disciplines that might, on other conceptions, be thought to be its neighbors. [But this is] the path by which economics could drift most completely away from all relevance to anything outside of itself, including actual human economies.*

2. Lewis Redux.   In this future, economists make heavy use of computation theory while largely ignoring other, biologically connected, parts of cognitive science. (This might be glossed as: they treat computation theory as if it weren't *relevantly integrated into cognitive science.) They use results in the theories of functional relations and of topology to try to engineer their way around the implications of Gödel's proof. Mirowski depicts Kenneth Arrow's current perspective as the leading representation of the view, which takes heart from such results as Scarf's (1973) procedure for computing approximations to general equilibrium under special restricted circumstances.* Among Mirowski's futures, this is the one on which his assessment is most essentially tied to his worries about the implications of Gödel's theorem. In this book, I have repeatedly shied away from endorsing these worries, but I have never explained why. My remarks in chapter 8 about the conditions of relevance for evolutionary game-theoretic approaches like Young's (1998) provide the hint, however. To the extent that a real market is relatively isolated from others, evolutionary analysis can permit us to compare the extent to which it will converge to a partial equilibrium without the participants having to compute it. There is no reason to discourage economists, working as applied computer scientists, from building abstract computational representations of such processes. A variety of techniques, at different levels, are potentially relevant to this. These include "swarm intelligence" models of learning in networks of myopic agents (Kennedy and Eberhart 2001), and applications of nonformal but operationally powerful proof techniques ("cut" functions and so forth; see Lloyd 1984) that, in the engineering domain, save theorem provers from being crippled by formal incompleteness. Note, however, that to the extent that computational models are taken to simulate evolutionary learning, as in swarm intelligence, this future shades into Mirowski's second one. To the extent that computationalists remain fixated on theorem proving and general equilibrium, they risk the same isolation from empirical science as practitioners of Judd's revenge.

3. Simulatin' Simon. *In this scenario, economics integrates itself massively with artificial intelligence research, emulating the biography of the program's celebrated inspirer. . . . The motivation for the approach is straightforward: let us assume that biological brains are the basic causal engines of economic behavior, and then see what they can do under specific constraints by simulating them at various levels of abstraction.* In commenting on Mirowski's attitude to this future in chapter 1, I said that *Mirowski does not doubt that this sort of integration between economics and cognitive science will be an essential* part *of any future in which economics makes progressive contributions to our understanding of behavior. Behavioral science cannot, as* *a practical matter, thrive on a strict diet of observations of biological systems plus top-down theory. However, Mirowski affirms that economics cannot just consist in such work.* I added my own extension of this point as follows: [*A*]*n additional problem with simulation alone, at least as it has often been engineered in AI and also in some a-life modeling, is that it attempts to find the basis for behavioral patterns as "emerging" from, or even being decomposable into, the internal dynamics of modular parts of simulated systems.* The discussion of the relationship between neuroeconomics and picoeconomics in chapter 8 now permits this point to be put in more specific detail. There is every reason to expect simulations of brains to play an important role in the continuing integration of neuroscience with behavioral science, including behavioral economics (see Camerer 2003a). Neuroeconomics will in turn be an important source of empirical constraints for OISF models of irreducibly intentional systems like people and communities. Once again, some swarm intelligence models are relevant here: Kennedy and Eberhart (2001, pp. 370–381) effectively engage in Simonesque neuroeconomics when they seek to select learning algorithms for connectionist systems by assigning tasks to networks of simple units that maximize local expected utility. In the context of Glimcher's work, this might have more direct relevance to the study of biological brains than Kennedy and Eberhart themselves suggest. However, as they fully appreciate (ibid., pp. 255–263), constraints on models of social phenomena can no more be all bottom-up then they can be all top-down. This follows, in my discussion, from the emphasis on nonisomorphism between MISF and OISF decompositions of intentional systems. Mirowski's third future will be an important part of the partnership between economic theory and cognitive science, but it cannot be the whole future.

4. Dennett's Dangerous Idea. *This names the program by which economic theory is genuinely and fully integrated with the main current research front in evolutionary cognitive science. Rather than merely using artificial computational devices to simulate biological agents, it involves modeling these agents as literally being specific instances of computational devices.* This of course describes the ideal basis of the partnership for economic theory and cognitive science as I have described it over the past few chapters. Of course, it is a drastically truncated summary. Furthermore, the picture of "DDI" I have given departs from Mirowski's characterization of it in crucial ways. Far from "rubbishing the self," it denies that selves reduce to agents. In chapter 1 I quoted Mirowski as saying that DDI maintains *"that all human endeavor is constrained maximization 'all the way down.'"*[4] This is accurate, but only given the deep twist that although people are products of pressures to achieve constrained maximization, trade-offs among the different irreducible levels of complex organization that biological and cultural evolution builds prevent them, in principle, from pulling it off. (I trust it is clear by now that saying this constitutes no kind of normative criticism of them. I don't think that people should be *trying or hoping* to emulate bugs; but at the same time I recognize that they frequently get themselves into awful messes, both individual and social, because they can't.) It is the job of economic theory to identify the *extent* to which various kinds of real systems achieve constrained maximization in different sorts of circumstances. Bugs and neurons do it reliably. People are under increasing social pressure (with consequences both good and ill) to do it better as informational networks expand. The stories of attempts by whole societies to do it, as we will examine in the next volume, are farces or tragedies, depending on political and moral taste.

5. Vending von Neumann.   *It involves taking fully seriously the idea that types of whole markets—Walrasian tatonnement, Shapely-Shubik, one-sided unified quasi auctions of various types, two-sided clearinghouse or double auctions, and so on—implement different formal types of computational devices. Just as with the different types of devices sorted into hierarchies with respect to logical power by the mathematical theory of computation, or the different types of grammars sorted into a generative-power hierarchy in Chomsky's work on the foundations of formal linguistics, we can try to develop a generalizing theory that tells us which markets can simulate or beget which others, and compare them with respect to both information-processing capacity, and differential efficiency given particular allocation problems. That is, economic theory could be developed into a computational theory of markets.* This is an exciting and promising future indeed. It recognizes the artificiality of the seam between microeconomics and macroeconomics—at least where intentional units under study aren't straightforward economic agents that can be aggregated by additive functions—because it genuinely shucks off reductionist impulses. Further exploration of it, in relation to a behavioral macroeconomics informed by work on artificial life, will be a major aspect of my next volume.

I went on to say, in chapter 1, that *the von Neumann vision as sketched by Mirowski is in fact not a competitor to Dennett's dangerous idea, as he imag-*

ines, but is fully compatible with it. Indeed, by drawing on my own and collaborators' work on the underlying metaphysics necessary to make Dennett's theory of intentional behavior fully consistent with the social and physical sciences (Ross 2000; Ross and Spurrett 2004a; Ross et al. forthcoming), I aim to show that the prospects for successfully vending von Neumann look much better if we are persuaded by Dennett's theories of the self and of intentional behavior, and by Binmore's game-theoretic model of the wider social dynamics in which markets arise. I thereby combine Mirowski's futures four and five into a comprehensive model of economic theory as part of a unified science. That task remains unfinished at this point. But the reader should at least now be able to see how and why Dennett's account of the person meshes with a microstructural account of markets.

Mirowski (personal communication) doesn't welcome my suggestion that his futures four and five can and should fuse. "Of course," he says, "I won't concede that von Neumann can be subsumed under the Dennett–Binmore program. (How could this happen when they *just don't get it?*)." The second volume of *Economic Theory and Cognitive Science* will explain how it can happen—indeed *is* happening.

Notes

Chapter 1

1. By this I don't mean that a good postmodernist scholar operates by pure whimsy. Some metaphorical tropes can be sustained and will produce illuminating narratives, and others won't. I mean only that the level of justification a postmodernist will demand for selecting a trope will typically be analytically shallow compared to those of more traditional scholarship.

2. Binmore reacts with scorn to the example of Mirowski's treatment of Nash which I'm about to describe. As my coming remarks will indicate, I am, although wishing to keep everything calm and diplomatic, in accord with Binmore on this case. However, Binmore's general account of Mirowski's thesis is inaccurate, as Mirowski rightly says in his reply in the same issue of the *Journal*.

3. As Mirowski (personal communication) points out, the association of Arrow with Lewis in my extreme condensation of Mirowski's history risks being misleading. On Mirowski's telling, Arrow was among the people whose work buried the novelty of Lewis's approach. But, also according to Mirowski, Arrow and others did this by *taming* it, that is, domesticating its radicalism for compatibility with neoclassicism. It is the domesticated version of Lewis's strategy that Mirowski considers as a possible future for economics.

4. To an approximation, we can: some connectionist models of mind simulate input-output functions characteristic of biological-system behavior without our being able to understand what they're doing because relevant functional decompositions can't be articulated. Such models can be useful for confirming hunches about what general kinds of learning systems can do what, but without supplementation by further work of a different kind, they can't constitute resolved explanations of phenomena even in their own narrow domain. See Kennedy and Eberhart 2001 for some detailed examples.

5. Of course, these futures are incompatible only if future number three is interpreted as a regime in which no one does anything but piecemeal simulations. Mirowski clearly does not intend his futures to be exclusive in that way. He simply describes their limiting cases for expository purposes.

6. Dennett would be delighted to have his ideas regarded as "dangerous" in a different sense, the sense in which he calls Darwin's idea "dangerous": that is, as dangerous to entrenched but simplistic and stultifying ideologies about people and the limitations of their existential situation. Let us have all we can of *that* sort of danger.

7. Mirowski (personal communication) adds here: "Dennett as 'dangerous' is of course a play on his own title, but it derives not simply from problems concerning the 'self.' It comes from his helping foster the impression, which I maintain is fallacious, that bits of AI and garbled bits of (supposed) evolutionary theory buttress the scientific veridicality of neoclassical theory, when in fact, they are all just projections of one another, which split off from OR [Operations Research] in the 1950s, have been nurtured in the bosom of the computer, and became instituted for some time as separate research communities, before now experiencing the shock of recognition upon re-encountering one another. The danger is mistaking family resemblance (which has historical explanations) for validation (which doesn't)." This book will be one long argument that there is deep logic behind this family resemblance after all. So I hope that Mirowski will also regard it as dangerous.

8. The philosophical reader is apt to take this as indicating a policy of "eliminativism." For reasons to be made clear in the later chapters of the book, it is not. Though I expect science to massively revise, and sometimes eliminate *aspects of*, basic folk intentional and social ontologies, I do not anticipate their wholesale elimination.

9. The best case against Dupré's metaphysical thesis is Spurrett 2000.

10. A philosophically careful and self-conscious engineer—or a historian—might of course use concepts of space and time once systematized by an earlier theory, such as Newton's. But in such cases we would expect the concepts to be implicitly indexed to Einstein's, since Einstein's system, not Newton's, correctly describes the world as far as we can tell now.

11. The term "causal capacities" is used here following Cartwright (1989). I use it here as a conceptual placeholder, because, for reasons explored at length in Ross and Spurrett 2004a, b and Ross et al. forthcoming, I think that belief in any systematic, *general* notion of causation rests on a mistaken picture of science. In the sources just cited, I and my coauthors seek to analyze the idea of causal capacity in other, more systematic terms. Going into these details in the present work would, however, require a very long digression that would not pay back, in illumination of my subject matter of economics, the investment demanded from the reader.

12. This view has its most important philosophical origins in Wittgenstein's famous "private language argument." I recommend and endorse the treatment of that argument given in Pettit 1993, chapter 2.

Chapter 2

1. It is a disputed question among philosophers as to whether other propositional-attitude markers, such as "fears," "worries," "doubts," and so forth, are subspecies of beliefs and desires, or separate but less central species. I will bypass this issue here, as it doesn't matter to anything that will arise in the book. Something else I will avoid are the special issues around "knows," which grammatically and often pragmatically operates like an attitude, but which has the special and strange property that it is supposed to denote commitments on its users' part to justification, truth, and maybe certainty. The philosophical literature on this subject is gigantic, but I bypass it because I think that the concept of knowledge is of no relevance to naturalistic philosophy or to science.

2. Note that what matters here is whether a person has these *concepts*, not, at least directly, whether they use these *words* for the concepts. "Politicians, financiers, CEOs, and bureaucrats" might be many contemporary western people's way of thinking or saying "oligarchy."

3. In connectionist systems, it is often unclear how to interpret the meanings of local state transitions.

4. Philosophers say that one type of thing or property or relation X "supervenes" on another type Y if, for any instance x_i there exists a y_i such that there can't be a change in the state of x_i without a change in the state of y_i. The idea is popular as a way of describing the relation of dependence that seems to exist between minds and brains, without committing all the way to the reductionist thesis that minds just *are* brains. Though I can leave this concept alone for purposes of the present argument, I in fact doubt that it does any useful metaphysical work; Ross and Spurrett 2004b explains why.

5. Readers who suspect there will turn out to be some relationship between methodological solipsism in cognitive science and the venerable doctrine of methodological individualism in economics are correct, as we'll see much later.

6. Putting this argument in a fully convincing form is a delicate business. For the reader who is skeptical, I recommend the elaboration in Pettit 1993, pp. 76–106.

7. The qualification is necessary here to allow for one meaning of "internalism" used in linguistics that isn't directly relevant to the present discussion. Chomsky (2000) advocates "internalism," in explicit opposition to "externalist" philosophers. However, he does so in the context of thinking that all of semantics as philosophers understand it is impossible as a distinct branch of inquiry. I leave this position out of consideration here, because it would seem to rule out the prospects for any social science except formal linguistics itself, given the restrictive concept of science Chomsky requires for his argument, and given that most social sciences surely must traffic in semantically individuated types.

8. We will see in chapter 5 that eliminativism is proving persuasive to some important economists on such grounds. Rosenberg (1992) applies a Kim-type metaphysical argument for eliminativism to economics, but he does so as part of his philosophical explanation of an eliminativist conclusion he first reaches on the basis of arguments about the actual scientific track record of economics.

9. Let this not stand, as it so often does in discussions of such things, as an assumption by a westerner that nonwestern cultures must incorporate exotic ideas into everything they say. The Zulu translation of "There's an elephant in the road," "Kukho indlovu emgwaqini," is transparent on its surface as deriving from "Kunenkinga enkulu ekubhekile," which in turn refers to a "big problem." This, it will be seen, is *specifically* relevant to the philosophical issue under discussion. The semantics of the Zulu sentence directly packs in practical human problems from which the English translation abstracts. To attribute the relevant belief *using Zulu* is automatically to sympathize with the driver, whereas the attributor using English need merely empathize with her cognitive state. It would, however, be an error—the error of the internalist—to think that this difference must pick out a relevant difference between an English-speaking and a Zulu-speaking *person*. The Zulu driver is not (necessarily) "exotic." Her culture just invites different emphases in capturing situations, which anybody can readily appreciate in performing linguistic translations if they try.

10. I'm not sure how better than this to label former semantic internalists who still insist on causally active internal "concepts," as Fodor does.

11. These are the main alternative models of representation that each had their proponents in classical AI. Hayes (1979) advocates the first approach, and Newell and Simon (1976) promote the second.

12. As we will see in chapter 4, Friedman doesn't turn out, under careful philosophical analysis, to actually be a consistent instrumentalist after all. But it takes some work to unearth this from beneath his rhetoric.

13. See Dennett 1993 for explicit reflections on the dialectic around instrumentalism.

14. Although there are apparently nonlocal connections in quantum phenomena, it is not possible to use them to send classical bits of information.

15. New string-theoretic representations of black holes suggest that they might not be after all.

Chapter 3

1. This statement might seem to imply denial of Nancy Cartwright's (1989) thesis that where generalizations apply to relations among classes of empirical events, they must always be hedged with ceteris paribus clauses in order to be true. However, it has no such implication. x and y here could refer to what Cartwright calls "causal capacities." If an instantiation of a set of causal capacities denoted by x triggers an environmental change in which y capacities are present, then this could be true of an instance even if, in that instance, *all* the typical and measurable effects of y are blocked by the presence of countervailing influences.

2. For a very preliminary direct defense, consistent with the much fuller story to be told in this volume and its successor, see Ross and Bennett 2001.

3. For Aristotle's main extended discussions of economics, see the *Nicomachean Ethics* 5.5, and the *Politics* 1, pp. 8–10.

4. As Mirowski (1989) emphasizes, a key moment in the history of economics came when, as a result of developments in classical physics, our notion of the resources to be spent were homogenized as "energy."

5. See Meikle 1995, 2001.

6. Smith and Hume were deeply interested in the psychological foundations of economics, Ricardo and Marx much less so.

7. Mirowski (1989, pp. 205–207) disagrees with this common view. This is partly because Bentham was far more important to one of neoclassicism's founders, Jevons, than to its other one, Walras, or to Edgeworth, Pareto (p. 221), or Fisher (p. 235). However, for reasons best made clear by the plausibility of spinning the history in the way I will be doing, I think psychological subjectivism about value should be regarded as a core neoclassical commitment. This automatically makes Bentham generally important, even if much of the route of his influence was more roundabout—for example, through Mill and then Ayer back to the postwar neoclassicists, rather than via the straight path through Jevons—than standard histories often suppose.

8. Mirowski (1989) reduces Bentham's distance from the classical political economists, and increases it from the neoclassicists, by pointing out that, according to Bentham "money was the best measure of pleasure or pain" (p. 206). This seems to make exaggerated use of Bentham's remarks on that subject, since lots of neoclassicists have regarded money as, in many circumstances, the most practical proxy for utility, while certainly not equating money prices, metaphysically, with subjective value coefficients. Mirowski also makes much of the fact that Bentham, unlike the neoclassicists, didn't care

much about making economics over in the image of contemporary physics. This is true, but it's unclear how this is supposed to show that his value-subjectivism wasn't an important philosophical influence on economists.

9. See Ross 1991.

10. I think this is evidence that Bentham did not intend his familiar claims about utility being a matter for "calculation" by policymakers to be taken too literally. The economists of the 1930s who criticized him (see below) paid little attention to this point; but then they *were* trying to find principles susceptible to literal calculation. This is a main part of the explanation of how Mirowski (1989) and I, reading the same sources, can have such diametrically opposed takes on Bentham's relationship to neoclassicism. Yes, Pareto, Fisher, etc., rejected Benthamite foundations by name in the course of distancing themselves from sensationalism, as Mirowski notes (p. 235). But my point is that they, like Robbins and Hicks later (see below), were importantly misreading Bentham; *he* didn't care very much about psychology *either*.

11. As explained in note 10 above, Mirowski (1989) in effect accepts this too; but he follows Pareto and Fisher in not seeing that this *was* Bentham's attitude.

12. The qualification here is important. I do not disagree with Mirowski's (1989) thesis that the neoclassical program was also about rendering an economic field theory after the style of mid-nineteenth-century physics. This is fully compatible with what I have said. Presumably, the early neoclassicists believed that if psychology could ever become a respectable science, it would have to produce a field theory too, and that measurements of points in their fields would measure properties of individual agents commensurable with their economic properties.

13. See Castañeda 1975 and Aune 1977 for examples.

14. I again follow Mandler (1999) here. His analysis of this history is, in my opinion, the currently authoritative one, though I also think it should be supplemented by attention to Mirowski (1989). Their stories might be thought incompatible—indeed, *are* incompatible unless some of Mirowski's claims about psychology being irrelevant to neoclassical intellectual history are toned down—but I in fact think that their very different emphases allow each to explain what the other leaves unsatisfactory. Showing this must be a project for another occasion, however.

15. One of Mirowski's (1989) main theses is that a core commitment of neoclassicism is that it's *literally* supposed to be energy, on an understanding of that idea as physics abandoned it in the late nineteenth century. This is a fruitful and interesting possibility, in my view, but not one on which the very idea of an indifference curve logically depends.

16. Put technically: we assume only that measurement of relative utility is unique up to monotone transformation.

17. Different psychological interpretations of this are possible; see Mandler 1999, pp. 117–120.

18. See Bergson 1938, Samuelson 1938, Hicks 1939, Kaldor 1939, and Robbins 1938.

19. Robbins (1938) is clear on this point, arguing that normative utilitarianism, which he elliptically endorses, is independent of psychological cardinalism, which he rejects.

20. See, for example, Addleson 1997, where he rejects an entire project associated with mainstream economics that he calls "equilibrium explanation," just *because* it rests (he

says) on positivism. As I argue in a review of Addleson's book (Ross 1998), however, he gives little indication of understanding what positivism as a historical moment in epistemology and metaphysics actually was, and he seems to imagine that by rejecting one or two theses associated with some versions of positivism, one thereby disposes of *any other* philosophical idea one can also associate with positivism, and then of anything one can claim was motivated by any of these ideas. This is shockingly bad history, and equally deplorable logic, but it is all too representative of much of the current anti-neoclassical literature.

21. The 1935 edition of Robbins's *Essay* was in fact the second, following a first edition of 1932. The revisions Robbins made for the second edition are philosophically significant. The present general treatment must pass over these issues, however. For present purposes, I therefore take the 1935 edition—the one most economists have read—as the canonical one.

22. The internal coherence of Caldwell's organization of this history is further strengthened by emphasizing Robbins's association with the Austrian school of economic methodologists, who were deeply Kantian in their views. But once the gulf between Kantians and positivists is erased, as it is by Friedman, all this makes sense.

23. One of the strongest suggestions of this is found in a long footnote on pp. 102–103, in which he carefully criticizes Marshallian partial equilibrium analysis for obscuring possibilities for rigorous axiomatic demonstration. This is Robbins at his most charming, since he *morally* praises Marshall for keeping practically minded readers on board by eschewing a level of rigor that, Robbins acknowledges, Marshall could readily have demonstrated; but Robbins regrets this approach from the perspective of concern for scientific foundations. The implied contrast between the systematic and the practical as a basis for distinguishing true science, along with deference to axiomatization as the hallmark of the latter, could not be made more transparent without risking irreverence toward Marshall, which Robbins will not allow himself.

24. If I were, I would flesh out the following general story about influences. Robbins was directly influenced by the Austrian methodologists, as Caldwell (1982) stresses. They in turn were part of the same milieu in which the Vienna circle arose; that is, they were scientific omnivores of technical competence, steeped in Kantian epistemology and metaphysics, and anxious to demarcate science from nonscience in the nightmare of political irrationalism that came early to Austria before engulfing the world. The relationship between Robbins's views and "official" positivism is thus a tale of common causes.

25. In case the reader now fears that Robbins here takes back his disavowal of economics' commitment to consistency, note that his next sentence after this one is: "But this is not to say that it is necessary *ab initio* that it always is consistent or that the economic generalizations are limited to that, perhaps, tiny section of conduct where all inconsistencies have been resolved."

26. See, e.g., Robbins 1935, p. 56, note 2.

27. Hicks and Allen were aware that the principle as stated cannot be perfectly general; it typically fails in the case of complementary goods, such as gin and vermouth for martini drinkers. But if one assumes, as they did, that the basis of the principle is empirical rather than logical, there can be no decisive objection to simply treating this as a contingent set of limiting cases.

28. See preceding note.

29. In deference to Mirowski, it should be added that the engineer who likes Samuelson's machine must be an engineer who can appreciate devices independently of what they actually do, or, indeed, of whether they can do *anything* clearly worthwhile. Well, there are different sentimental types of engineers. The kind who will appreciate Samuelson is the one who delights in the large, deliberately useless, gadgets that solipsistically whirl and turn beside the National Palace in Stockholm.

30. This certainly does not apply uniformly throughout the *Foundations*. A number of its chapters and sections are critical reviews of the literature on economic topics given prominence by Hicks and other contemporaries, for example the price of money and the problems of rationing. These are certainly inspired by worldly problems. However, Samuelson's objective is often to dissolve, from the mathematical point of view, their supposed special significance.

31. Mirowski (1989, chapter 6) argues that neoclassicism's failure to *consistently* borrow field theory from classical physics, or to keep up with physicists as they radically amended that theory, emerged most damagingly as incoherence on the subject of production. Though I am making a different point with it here, the quoted passage of Samuelson's should be interpreted in light of recurrent controversies over the treatment of capital and production in neoclassicism. These topics will be deferred until the next volume of this study, after a new model of the relationship between people and agents has been worked up in this one.

32. See Romanos 1983.

33. And should not altogether abandon them, as I urged in the previous chapter.

34. Here I follow Blaug 1980, pp. 164–168, and 1985, pp. 348–350.

35. I avoid saying *causal* variables here because, as discussed previously, positivist economists of Hicks's and Samuelson's sort were officially agnostic about causation. We can note in passing, however, that in the absence of intuitions about causation, it's hard to see why we're supposed to be so sure that a distinction between income and substitution effects is even meaningful, let alone important.

36. I owe this note of clarification, and recognition of the need for it, to Dan Hausman.

37. Mirowski (1989, p. 369) suggests with textual evidence that Samuelson fudged these implications only after Houthakker's work had made them clear. However, the fudge was already being anticipated right in the *Foundations*. After his demonstration in chapter 5 that "all of consumer theory" boils down to the principle that, given the right functionalization of demand, a consumer's demand for a commodity always changes in the same direction as his income, Samuelson says "Many writers have held the utility analysis to be an integral and important part of economic theory. Some have even sought to employ its applicability as a test criterion by which economics might be separated from the other social sciences. Nevertheless, I wonder how much economic theory would be changed if either of the two conditions above were found to be empirically untrue. I suspect, very little" (1947, p. 117). If this remark were accepted, it would constitute a blank check for avoiding any possible concerns about the empirical implications of utility analysis.

38. "The utility analysis rests on the fundamental assumption that the individual confronted with given prices and confined to a given total expenditure selects that combination of goods which is highest on his preference scale. This does not require (a) that the individual behave rationally in any other sense; (b) that he be deliberate and

self-conscious in his purchasing; (c) that there exist any *intensive* magnitude which he feels or consults."

39. It is closely related, on this interpretation, to a concept much in vogue in the sciences of dynamic processes, viz., "self-organization."

40. Davis (2003, pp. 53–61) considers the "time-allocation" model of Stigler and Becker (1977) as the basis for one such possible new concept, but then subjects it to what he considers a decisive criticism. I will consider that model, along with Davis's and other criticisms, in chapter 4.

41. As Hausman (2000) notes, "RPT" has recently also been used to refer to theory that shows how to infer preferences from choices *plus restrictions on agents' cognitive states* (Green and Osbard 1991; Border 1992). In this book, "RPT" will *never* refer to that.

42. Economists will be most used to expressing the point as follows: theorists of Hicks's and Robbins's day equated cardinality with *measurability* (unique determinateness up to linear transformation). Von Neumann and Morgenstern showed that these concepts are in fact not equivalent (Lewin 1996, p. 1308).

43. I say this despite an explicit demurral from Samuelson himself, who says in a footnote of the *Foundations* that Robbins's definition is "too broad from one point of view, and much too narrow from another" (1947, p. 22, n. 3). But Samuelson's basis for saying this is puzzling in the extreme. It's supposed to somehow follow from the fact that we can learn things about economic systems by studying stability properties in addition to maximizing properties. I couldn't agree more about the interest of stability conditions to economics, as will be clear later; but I confess to being baffled as to how exactly Samuelson is interpreting Robbins in thinking that this undermines his definition. And before the reader leaps to thinking that my bafflement here admits of easy relief by reference to "satisficing behavior in evolutionary equilibria," etc., she should know what Samuelson says immediately after the footnoted passage: "Nevertheless, many of these stability conditions rest implicitly upon maximizing behavior." Yes, indeed, again. I think Robbins can rest undisturbed over these remarks.

Chapter 4

1. My formulation here is not intended to suggest that my account *conflicts* with Mirowski's. I think the two accounts are complementary.

2. Note carefully that I am restricting attention to *reasons*, and to reasons *widely entertained by economists*. Thus, the dimunition of previous confidence in the power of general equilibrium theory as a result of the excess demand literature of the early 1970s (Sonnenschein 1972, 1973; Mantel 1974, 1976; Debreu 1974) has probably backwashed and dimmed the luminescence of everything from the postwar period; but since RPT is quite independent of general equilibrium theory, this is a possible *causal* factor rather than a *reason*. If Mirowski were right that RPT is flawed because it is built on existence proofs rather than constructive procedures, this *would* count as a reason; but not as a reason for *economists'* disenchantment with Samuelson, since, as Mirowski precisely complains, few economists have taken constructivist objections seriously.

3. The PD is so ubiquitously discussed in the literature of so many disciplines that I will assume familiarity with it here. Its most thorough and accurate discussion, in direct application to the kind of use Sen tries to make of it, is Binmore 1994, pp. 95–256.

4. The idea that *perfect*, and perfectly general, Kantian morality can, through logical symmetry, produce socially inferior equilibria equivalent to those that perfect narrow selfishness would generate, is an old one. It is vividly explored in a classic satirical novel by the nineteenth-century Canadian writer James De Mille (1888/1969).

5. In the experiments, this has to be the problem, because the other possible sources of error—misspecification of information, unnoticed strategic commitment, or uncertainty as to whether the players are maximizing expected utility or something else—will certainly have been controlled in any decent experimental setup *intended to unequivocally induce a PD*.

6. Davis 2003 must also be cited for spotting, indeed emphasizing as its main point, the connection between internalism and models of economic agency. However, Davis precisely fails to see that his own critique of internalist assumptions threatens the basis of Sen's attack on neoclassicism; Sen is instead the main hero of Davis's book. This is perhaps because Davis doesn't devote attention to Sen's early, technical, work, but only to his more recent reflections on concepts of freedom and flourishing.

7. The defense I recommend is Joyce 2001.

8. At least, partly; Sen obviously can't justify his general set of policy recommendations without help from metaethical arguments against metaphysical subjectivism about value (as Davis 2003, pp. 174–177, recognizes). I am just referring here to shared views on the relationship between preferences and persons.

9. "Utilities can, of course, be defined in many different ways . . . The richness of the utilitarian perspective relates to this versatility. However, some defenders of utility-based calculation seem to have been tempted to re-define the term 'utility' to cover whatever it is that we wish to value. As a defense of utility-based ethical calculation this is tautologous and adds little to the discussion" (Sen 1987, p. 40, n. 13).

10. I am not here endorsing the wider use to which Fodor puts this argument; see Ross 2002b. Fodor assumes that it's impossible to usefully make the possible worlds move at all; this assumption is false.

11. For rigorous development of the concept of a problem-solving strategy, see Kitcher 1976, 1981, and 1989.

12. I must simply refer the curious reader over to Kitcher and Thagard here, rather than more helpfully provide one of their examples, because the point of the examples lies in their full details. As a result, all interesting examples take many pages to lay out.

13. If there is anyone reading this book who is a stranger to the literature and is looking for an up-to-date place to jump into it, I recommend Paul, Miller, and Paul 1997.

14. I will here be describing those aspects of "the" model common to this whole literature; so the description should not be read as a précis of Becker per se.

15. Dupré in fact never challenges the hypothesis itself. He criticizes the style in which it is derived on grounds that it is too mathematical, and must thus abstract away from many or most aspects of the psychological and psychosocial dynamics of family life. He also heaps scorn on a minor, highly particular, side consequence concerning the relationship between equality and some possible income tax schemes that Becker derives from one special case of the general model. I take it as self-evident that neither of these criticisms jeopardizes the significance of the general model in the least. This sort of

argument is unfortunately typical of Dupré's levels of fairness and logical rigor in criticizing views he doesn't like; see Dennett forthcoming.

16. On this point I am in agreement with Becker, though our reasons differ. See Becker 1976, pp. 153–168.

17. Having said this, I can't resist relating one extension of the anecdote. One of the goals of the project was to avoid having game outcomes be determined by accidental features of my designs; I wanted to be able to run good historical experiments. So I kept packing more and more real causally relevant variables (e.g., contingencies of weather, the engineering of transport infrastructure for movement of supplies, etc.) into the endogenous structures of the games. The limit of the enterprise was of course Borgesian: my last design was a board simulation of the Napoleonic wars that would have taken as long to play out as the actual wars took to fight. A friend and I played for one entire day, and by nightfall my sole accomplishment as Napoleon was to have got one small company outfitted and on its way from its marshalling quarters. It got bogged down on a bad road in heavy rain. I take it that a number of philosophical lessons for sensible modeling are self-evident here.

18. See Ross and Spurrett 2004a, b for a full discussion of this.

19. It seems highly likely, as Mäki suggests, that Friedman shares in the misunderstanding of his own text, for reasons to be discussed below.

20. For example—this is a note for philosophers—Bas van Fraassen's "constructive empiricism" is, in Mäki's taxonomy, a variety of commonsense realism.

Chapter 5

1. My historical remarks here follow the standard survey in Roth 1995.

2. An example: a physicist, a chemist, and an economist are stranded on a desert island. Hungry, they find a crate of canned food that fell off a ship washed up on the beach. Alas, they have no can opener. The physicist sets to work figuring out how she can induce increased pressure inside the cans to pop them. The chemist looks for naturally occurring volatile elements he could use to create reactions that will eat through the lids. The economist sits down to calculate their newfound well-being, saying "First, assume a can opener."

3. See Johnson-Laird 1988 for a survey written after this point had become clear to most workers.

4. I have put "moods" in scare quotes to emphasize that the careful cognitive scientist (as opposed to the folk psychologist) will want to slow way down here to wonder very seriously what, if anything, "mood" really refers to.

5. This is, of course, just a way of putting Kuhn's point about "normal science" without all the exciting noise about incommensurability.

6. See Davidson, McKinsey, and Suppes 1955.

7. The anthropocentric neoclassicist might object that they've learned that they lived long enough to have realized the savings. However, given the magnitude of the discount rates revealed by empirical studies of appliance purchases, this hypothesis would require deeply implausible levels of risk aversion or beliefs in probabilities of personal disaster not consistent with other behavior.

8. Very sophisticated students of rationality do this. A recent field subject I can report as having exhibited the behavior was Dan Dennett in December 2002. Another is my wife, a South African philosopher of education, every time she dines out in the United States.

9. Value = Amount / Constant$_1$ + (Constant$_2$ × Delay) (Ainslie 2001, p. 35).

10. I am unaware of, but would be interested in, methodically gathered empirical data on the behavior of elderly people with respect to this phenomenon. It seems implausible that people are so quixotic as to keep climbing the ever-steeper investment mountain they'd need to scale to maintain expectations of rising utility *all the way* to an end point whose location they can reliably predict. Perhaps widespread belief in afterlives is a way of pulling off this kind of self-narrative. However, I am doubtful that *reported* belief in afterlives is often consistent with actual consumption-and-savings patterns. Or perhaps they aim for continuously rising expectations by themselves plus their children, so that there is no anticipated end point. In that case we should observe strikingly different behavior from the childless.

11. In the succeeding installments, 6:30 Hobbes and 8:30 Hobbes, realizing that they'll also be sucked into this dilemma by the endless temporal multiplication of Calvins, team up to do the homework.

12. The game theory novice should note that this game does *not* resemble a one-shot prisoner's dilemma, in which the socially efficient outcome is unavailable to rational players because it isn't a NE in the first place.

13. This is what Mirowski associates with paranoia, as mentioned in chapter 1. His idea is that the player internalizes, so as to try to control, the whole strategic world in his own head. Well, perhaps. But if we must psychoanalyze, a delusion of grandeur seems equally appropriate as a diagnosis. I don't feel the call to psychoanalyze in the first place, however.

14. Hausman (2000, pp. 111–112) makes this argument explicitly. Taking for granted, unlike me, that the point of game theory is to extend normative decision theory into strategic contexts, Hausman validly interprets the point as undermining RPT. As I'm throwing EUT overboard, however, here is one of those cases where one person's *modus ponens* is another person's *modus tollens*. The game theorist, I say, can give these players no advice beyond: here are the NE of this game. Good luck to you.

15. The noneconomist is apt to be a bit bewildered here. Since outcomes in classical games are partly functions of what players know *would* happen for each possible vector of strategies (i.e., complete strategic paths through game trees), a solution to a game must specify a move for each player at *every* node, regardless of which nodes are actually reached in the play of that solution. Thus the NE specification just given must include a move—in this case, r_2—for player II, even though, since player I plays L, II never actually has a move. The rationality of I's and III's moves can only be evaluated by reference to what II *plans to do* if the game moves off the equilibrium path.

16. Put technically: if the game beginning at node 4 could be treated as a subgame, Lr_2l_3 would not be a subgame perfect equilibrium (SPE).

17. Note, again following Hausman (2000): here is a direct violation of RPT.

18. As Kincaid (1997, chapter 7) argues, it's not even clear that letting our players know all of mathematics would get them to the ultimate refinement, since not even all of the mathematical facts are sufficient to decide fundamental issues in epistemology presupposed by the assumption that it's rational to apply Bayes's rule.

19. Gintis, in personal correspondence in 2004, now says he regrets this remark. This confirms my earlier suggestion that his eliminativist tendencies, while following from the logic of his general views, are not intended.

20. For outstanding introductions to the replicator dynamics, and demonstration of it at work on some deep and long-standing philosophical problems, see Skyrms 1996, 2004.

Chapter 6

1. My discussion of the template will follow Robertson 1957, pp. 33–39.

2. Elster (1985) argues that, earlier, Marx was explicit in defense of the principle.

3. Von Mises probably has some significant part of this responsibility, which he inherits, via Menger, from the Kantian elements in his thinking. I follow Binmore (1994, 1998)— and Nietzsche—in seeing the massive influence of Kant in the history of modern Western thought as having been largely disastrous. Hayek is frequently attributed responsibility for the popularity of methodological individualism, in its noninnocent forms, but Caldwell (2003) argues convincingly that this is undeserved.

4. Following Binmore (1994, 1998), and for exactly his reasons, I would find it much easier to clearly declare my general political views if the term "Whig" came back into more common circulation.

5. I say *pseudo*experiments because they involved researchers using themselves as subjects, without use of what any contemporary psychologist would regard as adequate controls. See the first half of Lyons's book for details (although Lyons does not use the phrase "pseudoexperiments").

6. See, for representative instances, both professional and popular (respectively), Block 1993 and Malik 2000. Neither Block nor Malik is directly interested in the issue I have identified as important to the foundations of economics. I thus think it highly suggestive that their misunderstanding of Dennett is just the one into which Mirowski and Davis, who are entirely motivated by concerns over economics, also fall.

7. For economists: this is a philosopher's term of art denoting such things as the qualitative (distinctive) redness of a particular red patch, the qualitative (distinctive) Miles-ness of a Davis trumpet solo, and so on.

8. The difficulty that many philosophers have had in swallowing Dennett's view lies, I think, right here. Philosophers of mind have traditionally divided the labor in seeking accounts of thought *processes* and thought *content*. Faced with that tradition, Dennett pragmatically divided his own labor: *The Intentional Stance* (1987) is officially his theory of content, and *Consciousness Explained* (1991) is officially his theory of process. But, as I've just indicated, neither theory is complete without the other.

9. For a model that builds in distribution of control for standard functioning, but then stops short of what I'm calling the "subtle" step, see Anderson 1983.

10. At least, so psychoanalysis claims. It's clearly true that people acquire information they can't subsequently retrieve. What's more tendentious is the claim that there are active processes of *suppression*. Anxiety might simply lead to more generalized *ignoring* as the logical flip side of *concentrating*.

11. The material in this section is drawn, with modifications, from Ross 2002c.

12. An important exception is Juarrero 1999.

13. The sort of work I have in mind here is well exemplified by Aune (1977) and Castañeda (1975).

14. If the importance of this distinction is doubted, note that different projects are implied by the two ideas. If humans are not prototypical agents then we will want to know which properties allow them to approximate agency. If they are prototypical agents then in analyzing agency we directly analyze people.

15. This is the basis on which I would argue that Marxists are misguided in treating socioeconomic classes as agents. They're not wrong because methodological individualism is true in general. This all gets very complicated, though, because *Marx* thought that methodological individualism is true in general. (See Elster 1985.)

16. Ainslie (2001, chapter 8) is correct in diagnosing Ryle's mistake as trying to eliminate the *will*, rather than the mind *tout court*. I'm fairly sure that neither Dennett nor anyone else would have put the point this way, however, until Ainslie showed, in the context of his own new theory of motivation, why it's still a good idea to talk about "the will" after all.

17. This does not preclude the use of specific organs, such as skin, that sort stimuli into broad equivalence classes with respect to source, where "equivalence" is referenced to particular functions of general importance.

18. I'm speaking anachronistically here. When Dennett wrote his paper, none of the extant attempts by philosophers to capture the distinction had yet achieved the level of clarity that Lloyd's account subsequently established. This meant that Dennett himself couldn't reach the degree of exactness in his distinctions that can be read back into his paper with the benefit of hindsight. See Ross and Zawidzki 1994 for a discussion aimed at sorting out some of the logical priorities in this dialectic.

Chapter 7

1. Let me remind them again that those dreaded positivists—Neurath and Carnap, for example—liked people a lot too. They thought it supremely important to try to feed and house them better, using the best possible science—which entailed, in the circumstances of their day, defeating irrational fascist stupidity.

2. A different way is by asking whether a given animal can compute second-order abstractions, that is, relations between relations. Such evidence as we now have suggests that this operationalization makes the intelligence club very small: humans, chimps, bonobos, and possibly toothed whales.

3. In discussions of animal intelligence, attention is often drawn to the cephalopods, especially octopi, as the geniuses among the invertebrates. That they seem to be. But it is not established that their intelligence, by the measure suggested above, approaches the levels found in the social birds and mammals. See Boal 1991 for reasons for doubt. Furthermore, octopi might be more intensely social than their living patterns suggest to observation. And perhaps, in any case, octopus intelligence evolved in the sorts of social conditions still evident among many species of squid—who might well, for all we know now, be as or more clever than octopi. These are all interesting research questions that follow from the hypothesis that individual intelligence is an adaptive response to going social without going cusocial.

4. We don't know, for example, whether there were intelligent dinosaurs.

5. This is intended only as a sketch of how to attempt a definition. Much fussy work would need to be done, ruling out viral effects on DNA, handling the problem of distinguishing sibling clones, and specifying restrictions on what "common" information means, to promote it into a definition. If this were philosophy of biology, I'd have to stop right here and do that work. However, for present purposes the definition sketch is sufficient, because all the argument needs is the claim that there is a general set of conceptual resources for individuating organisms without appeal to any economic properties.

6. I have *more* information than you do, of course, thanks to observing myself in far more detail. The point is that my evidence about myself isn't different *in kind* from yours. It consists, like yours, in the record of judgments about behavior organized from the intentional stance.

7. Jean-Paul Sartre (1943) was right to reject the belief that selves are metaphysical essences. But the normative conclusion he drew from this fact, which then formed the basis for both his philosophy and his deplorable political life, is one I regard as outright lunacy. This is the thesis that "good faith" lies in deliberately striving to undermine one's own self, buttressed by the claim that psychological honesty depends on resenting oneself, whatever specific characteristics that self has. The idea that the best state of being a person can aim at is adolescent romanticization of psychic suicide is stunningly silly, if nothing worse. My obvious disrespect for Sartre stems not from this normative judgment itself, though, but from the fact that I doubt Sartre's sincere belief in his own thesis. If I am right about this, his philosopher's card should be taken away.

8. So here is something Sartre was right about, although the insight wasn't original to him. "The other" *is* the enforcer of social oppression, when it's actually oppressive, and the order the other enforces is logically bound to be whatever the approximate local status quo is. However, the idea that, if you're a reformer, simple psychic rebellion is a worthwhile response to this fact is something *effective* reformers grow out of.

9. Most of the discussion in this section is drawn from Ross and Dumouchel 2004a,b, and Ross 2004.

10. I think this way of technically interpreting Hobbes is consistent with the definitive account of his work given in Hampton 1986. It is because Hobbes's analysis occurs at the S-level that it isn't obvious, in advance of Hampton's careful application of the principle of charity to his argument, whether the people in his state of nature are solving a coordination game or a repeated PD when they anoint the sovereign.

11. To show just how closely, I'm following Binmore here: since the players of G_i' don't know with certainty who they'll become as a result of playing some game G_l, they negotiate behind a "Binmore veil of ignorance" as discussed at length in Binmore 1998. Unlike agents behind the more traditional veils of Rawls (1971) and Harsanyi (1977), Binmore-veiled agents can make their contracts contingent on the expected noncooperative dynamics of G_l, because Binmore veils are *actual* and descriptive, rather than hypothetical and normative like Rawls veils and Harsanyi veils.

12. LaCasse and Ross (1998), in criticizing Danielson, also assume that Robinson Crusoes are the "real" players of repeated social games, and then show that, if the outcomes of Danielson's games are interpreted in terms of the utility functions of Robinson Crusoes playing $G!$, Danielson's attempt to find a strategic role for morality fails. Because LaCasse and Ross don't question the reality or usefulness of Robinson Crusoes, this drives them to conclude moral nihilism from their critique. I was set back onto the righteous path by the analysis of Binmore (1998).

13. This point in no way takes back my present silence on the systematic economic relationship between biological individuals and selves. *Of course* there is an *ontogenetic* relationship between the history of the species from which the individuals are drawn and the distribution of selves they produce, which is all I am appealing to here. This implies nothing in particular about the *economic* relationship between any given biological individual and any given self.

14. It should be noted at this point that my three-level framework of game levels (now including long-run evolutionary games) is somewhat arbitrary; in many contexts, a modeler might want to resort to a more refined set of levels. Here, however, as my concerns are restricted to the general relationships between analog metalinguistic signaling and digital signaling in people, I can restrict detailed attention to just the relationships between the G and G' levels. How many more, at ranges of increasing metalevels, might be constructed for the various purposes of ethnologists, historical anthropologists, primatologists, zoologists, and so forth, is open, and an issue I will bypass.

15. ... except very crude ones, like upraised middle fingers to other drivers, that often make things worse.

16. The idea behind this concept is that people couldn't, in general, successfully coordinate around projects with distributive consequences if they couldn't evaluate outcomes from one another's perspectives with reasonable accuracy. On Binmore's scheme, an agent behaviorally reveals, in negotiation, her assignment of preferences to her negotiating partners by choosing strategies that imply outcomes she doesn't expect to be vetoed given that assignment. If all agents do this, and their expectations are generally accurate, then, Binmore shows, the society they constitute will reach "empathy equilibrium," in which no agent has an incentive to pretend that her empathetic preferences are other than what they really are. Binmore argues that prevalence of approximate empathy equilibria in societies is the basis for stable interpersonal comparisons of utility, without which complex social bargains would be impossible. This idea is nicely complementary to my account of game determination dynamics, a point to which I will return in detail in the next volume.

17. They may reemerge as serious problems, tragedies of the commons, when independently evolved cultures at different G'-level equilibria "globalize." A good theory *should* predict this, since it's what actually happens until and unless global institutional frameworks evolve to dampen the problem.

18. I will not try to produce a catalog here. See Dasgupta 2002 for a short list, and a civilized rebuttal.

19. Rosenberg 1992 is the best argued.

20. I will qualify this by saying that some of Lawson's epistemological concerns about econometric inference are justified; see Kincaid 2004. However, even here, where there is firm ground available for him Lawson goes too far in his hostility to economists' pragmatic practices, as Hoover (2002) argues.

Chapter 8

1. Again, the reader is referred to Ross and Spurrett 2004a, and Ross et al. forthcoming, where the argument for that that has been described in this book is actually given.

2. This of course doesn't *eliminate* the underdetermination of theory by evidence—nothing in empirical science can. The philosophical critique of a particular scientific

enterprise should stop once *all* the specific evidence for a theory is not being mainly interpreted through the very theory for which it is taken as evidence. This ineliminably requires some judgment concerning the domains of theories; but reference to well-articulated models can lift such judgments out of the domain of the purely subjective. See Giere 1988.

3. This condition doesn't, in general, select a unique NE for a given inspection game. Furthermore, not all NE for a given inspection game will be equally efficient. Interesting questions about the NE sets for inspection games center on probabilities of their finding (or, in evolutionary models, remaining in) efficient equilibria versus risk-dominant equilibria, since these often come apart. However, none of these issues are relevant to the experiments of Glimcher that I'll be discussing, since what will be of interest is whether his monkeys track *any* NE, and then *how* their brains implement the tracking they do.

4. Although perhaps the fact that Glimcher successfully predicted monkey-neuron utility maximization using unrefined EUT, while Breiter et al. (2001) found prospect theory predicted the target for human neuron utility maximization, reflects the fact that people play G-level games while monkeys just play G'-level ones.

5. Note carefully: this is a different problem from the problem of assigning value to what is already taken as salient, the problem studied by the neuroeconomists.

6. The sentence doesn't report a straightforward "research fact." It summarizes Ainslie's (2001, pp. 25–26) interpretation of many facts. The forensically inclined reader is therefore referred back to Ainslie here.

7. Ainslie (personal communication) is carefully tentative about this interpretation, calling the relationship of surprising events to expected events in producing reward "tantalizingly unclear." See his 2003 for deeper reflections.

8. Ainslie (personal communication) reminds me not to introduce analogies between subpersonal dynamics and political structures that include presidents without reiterating clearly that, on the model of the person I share with him and Dennett, there is no chief executive in the person. So, reiteration duly made. Note, furthermore, that in the analogy to follow I appeal not to the U.S. president's general executive role, but only to his occasional function of casting vetoes on proposals of other political agents. Some agents in people *do* sometimes have that sort of limited and temporary authority. And, like U.S. presidents, they can't actually use it unless some other agents agree that it's wise to do so.

9. Bush anecdote has it that African elephants are prone to short-term addiction to narcotic marula berries, on which they gorge to the point of becoming falling-down drunk. However, the berries are only ripe during short seasons, and there's nothing elephants can do to increase their availability. If elephants could develop agriculture they might have a serious problem.

10. By fragile I don't mean that a person is more prone to preference cycling. Quite the opposite: no normal person could be money-pumped by a country; people are closer to straightforward economic agency than countries. I mean "fragility" in something closer to its literal sense: people's mistakes are far more likely to kill them.

11. This hypothesis of course implies that preagricultural people lacked the sorts of selves we have. That hypothesis has been defended independently by Jaynes (1976), but I need not endorse a version of the idea as radical as his. This is because the account of the self in chapter 7 reserves the (fully developed) sense of "self" for the products of processes that are plausibly very new in history: the playing of G-level games as distinct

from G'-level ones. This has probably been accomplished entirely by cultural evolution, so it is possible that even some contemporary people, if their cultures drastically suppress expressions of individual differences, play only G-level games whose equilibria are readily predictable from idealized models at the G'-level. Many social scientists speak of "individualism" as a modern phenomenon; there is even a long tradition in some literatures of regarding it as a modern (postagricultural) *pathology* (although I don't endorse that tradition).

12. Sugden (2001, pp. 125–127), as part of his argument, criticizes Young's work directly. I will return to this below.

13. I have to say "implicitly" here because Sugden reserves the explicit term "rationality" for processes of representation and computation, and so says that Binmore "does not appeal to rationality at all, but only to evolutionary selection" (2001, p. 120). However, he then proceeds to criticize Binmore's use of traditional economic consistency conditions. This is "rationality" as the intentional-stance functionalist must understand it, and so is the sense relevant to the present discussion.

14. As so often, Dupré (2001, pp. 42–43) emerges from his glass house with an armful of stones here.

15. See Pettit 1993 for a very careful defense of this point.

16. To reiterate a crucial point from the previous section, there will be zones of convergence as social dynamics lead people to more closely approximate economic agency. The match between brain valuation of monetary reward and Black–Scholes asset pricing, as discussed there, is a sharp case in point.

17. One of Dennett's few critics to have clearly understood the relationship between his explanatory adaptationism and the intentional stance is Fodor (1996). Fodor is deeply skeptical of the whole picture. For a reply to Fodor, see Ross 2002b.

18. Where real patterns capturable only by an OISF analysis are concerned, the indeterminacy of perfectly precise content ascription at the level of MISF analysis of the same system blocks the appeal to what philosophers call "nomological supervenience relations." This is important in light of Kim's (1998) argument that such relations imply eliminativism wherever local reductions won't go through. See Ross and Spurrett 2004a,b.

19. This is, incidentally, relevant to oft-heard complaints about appeal to "memes" in attempts to justify the application of evolutionary game theory to cultural evolution. These complaints are typically based on the fact that there seem to be no available stable principles for individuating memes. But memes are plausibly just on all fours, ontologically, with OISF objects generally. They too should be *inferred* from equilibrium models that are predictively and explanatorily successful, rather than built up independently from reductionist bases.

20. The objection applies even more clearly to previous claims I have made in print (see Ross 2002a). I say "more clearly" because I, not Dennett, have explicitly glossed his adaptationism in terms of market structure. Of course, if my interpretation of Dennett, both in earlier work and here is correct, than the objection must also be an objection to him.

Chapter 9

1. In Dennett's terms, all of this means, exactly: you can account for the system's behavior from the design stance.

2. This is my diagnosis of why Tooby and Cosmides exaggerate their criticism of the "standard social science model" of behavioral explanation. They discount the value of OISF analysis that takes social influences on the identities of people fully seriously.

3. In fact, Mirowski himself, in his 1989 study of early neoclassicism, minimizes the importance of philosophical psychology to Jevons and Walras. I think he is right to do so. Obviously, as I discussed in chapter 3, Jevons had views about philosophical psychology, and these played an important role in the subsequent history of neoclassical methodology. But for Jevons himself—and for Marshall—the model of people they imbibed by way of Bentham and Mill was incidental in comparison with their concern for systematicity, as expressed in their concern to emulate physics; or so Mirowski persuasively argues.

4. Tangential reference to the next sentence of Mirowski's I quoted is in order. He says "The theory of rational choice (perhaps simple optimization, perhaps game theory) is unselfconsciously treated as the very paradigm of information processing for biological organisms and machines . . ." Well, yes and no. The mathematical theory of rational choice—if we're liberal about using alternatives to expected utility theory wherever we're empirically motivated to do so—can be called the "paradigm" of intentional-stance functionalism if one likes. But the use of "choice" in this label has deeply misleading connotations. According to my account, insects are prototypical economic agents. On the popular conception of "choice," insects enjoy little or none of it.

References

Addleson, M. 1997. *Equilibrium versus Understanding*. London: Routledge.

Ainslie, G. 1992. *Picoeconomics*. Cambridge: Cambridge University Press.

Ainslie, G. 2001. *Breakdown of Will*. Cambridge: Cambridge University Press.

Ainslie, G. 2003. Uncertainty as wealth. *Behavioral Processes* 64: 369–385.

Aizenberg, J., A. Tkachenko, S. Weiner, L. Addadi, and G. Hendler. 2001. Calcitic microlenses as part of the photoreceptor system in brittlestars. *Nature* 412: 819–822.

Amit, D. 1989. *Modeling Brain Function*. Cambridge: Cambridge University Press.

Anderson, J. 1983. *The Architecture of Cognition*. Cambridge, Mass.: Harvard University Press.

Aristotle. 1992. *The Politics*. T. Sinclair, ed. and trans. Harmondsworth: Penguin.

Aristotle. 1998. *Nicomachean Ethics*. D. Ross ed., W. D. Ross, trans. Oxford: Oxford University Press.

Arnett, D. 1996. *Supernovae and Nucleosynthesis*. Princeton, N.J.: Princeton University Press.

Aune, B. 1977. *Reason and Action*. Dordrecht: Reidel.

Baars, B. 1988. *A Cognitive Theory of Consciousness*. Cambridge: Cambridge University Press.

Barberis, N., and R. Thaler. 2002. A survey of behavioral finance. NBER working paper no. 9222. http://www.papers.nber.org/papers/W9222.

Barwise, J., and J. Seligman. 1997. *Information Flow: The Logic of Distributed Systems*. Cambridge: Cambridge University Press.

Batterman, R. 2000. Multiple realizability and universality. *British Journal for Philosophy of Science* 51: 115–145.

Baumol, W. 1972. *Economic Theory and Operations Analysis*. 3rd edition. Englewood Cliffs, N.J.: Prentice Hall.

Becker, G. 1976. *The Economic Approach to Human Behavior*. Chicago, Ill.: University of Chicago Press.

Becker, G. 1981. *A Treatise on the Family*. Cambridge, Mass.: Harvard University Press.

Beer, R. 1990. *Intelligence as Adaptive Behavior*. San Diego, Calif.: Academic Press.

Bell, W. 1991. *Searching Behaviour*. London: Chapman and Hall.

Ben-Nur, A., and L. Putterman, eds. 1998. *Economics, Values, and Organization*. Cambridge: Cambridge University Press.

Bentham, J. 1859/1954. The psychology of economic man. In W. Stark, ed., *Jeremy Bentham's Economic Writings*, pp. 421–450. London: Allen and Unwin.

Benzion, U., A. Rapaport, and J. Yagil. 1989. Discount rates inferred from decisions: An experimental study. *Management Science* 35: 270–284.

Bergson, A. 1938. A reformulation of certain aspects of welfare economics. *Quarterly Journal of Economics* 52: 310–334.

Berns, G. 2003. Neural game theory and the search for rational agents in the brain. *Behavioral and Brain Sciences* 26: 155–156.

Binmore, K. 1987–1988. Modeling rational players I and II. *Economics and Philosophy* 3: 179–214 and 4: 9–55.

Binmore, K. 1992. *Essays on the Foundations of Game Theory*. Oxford: Blackwell.

Binmore, K. 1994. *Game Theory and the Social Contract, volume 1: Playing Fair*. Cambridge, Mass.: MIT Press.

Binmore, K. 1998. *Game Theory and the Social Contract, volume 2: Just Playing*. Cambridge, Mass.: MIT Press.

Binmore, K. 2004. Review of *Machine Dreams*, by Philip Mirowski. *Journal of Economic Methodology* 11: 477–483.

Bishop, J. 1989. *Natural Agency*. Cambridge: Cambridge University Press.

Blaug, M. 1980. *The Methodology of Economics*. Cambridge: Cambridge University Press.

Blaug, M. 1985. *Economic Theory in Retrospect*. 4th edition. Cambridge: Cambridge University Press.

Block, N. 1993. Review of *Consciousness Explained*, by Daniel Dennett. *Journal of Philosophy* 90: 181–193.

Boal, J. 1991. Complex learning in Octopus bimaculoides. *American Malacological Bulletin* 9: 75–80.

Boden, M., ed. 2001. *The Philosophy of Artificial Life*. Oxford: Oxford University Press.

Border, K. 1992. Revealed preference, stochastic dominance, and the expected utility hypothesis. *Journal of Economic Theory* 56: 20–42.

Bowles, S. 2003. *Microeconomics: Behavior, Institutions, and Evolution*. Princeton, N.J.: Princeton University Press.

Breiter, H., I. Aharon, D. Kahneman, A. Dale, and P. Shizgal. 2001. Functional imaging of neuronal responses to expectancy and experience of monetary gains and losses. *Neuron* 30: 619–639.

Brinck, I., and P. Gärdenfors. 2003. Co-operation and communication in apes and humans. *Mind and Language* 18: 484–501.

Brook, A. 1994. *Kant and the Mind*. Cambridge: Cambridge University Press.

Brook, A., and D. Ross, eds. 2002. *Daniel Dennett*. New York: Cambridge University Press.

Brooks, R. 2002. *Robot*. Harmondsworth: Penguin.

Broome, J. 1990. Should a rational agent maximize expected utility? In K. Cook and M. Levi, eds., *The Limits of Rationality*, pp. 132–145. Chicago, Ill.: University of Chicago Press.

Broome, J. 1991. Rationality and the sure-thing principle. In G. Meeks, ed., *Thoughtful Economic Man*, pp. 74–102. Cambridge: Cambridge University Press.

Brown, J. 2001. Fit of form and function, diversity of life, and procession of life as an evolutionary game. In S. Orzack and E. Sober, eds., *Adaptationism and Optimality*, pp. 114–160. Cambridge: Cambridge University Press.

Buchanan, R. 1979. *What Should Economists Do?* Indianapolis, Ind.: Liberty Press.

Burge, T. 1986. Individualism and psychology. *Philosophical Review* 95: 3–45.

Byrne, R., and A. Whiten, eds. 1988. *Machiavellian Intelligence: Social Expertise and the Evolution of Intellect in Monkeys, Apes, and Humans*. Oxford: Oxford University Press.

Caldwell, B. 1982. *Beyond Positivism: Economic Methodology in the Twentieth Century*. London: Unwin.

Caldwell, B. 2003. Hayek and cultural evolution. In U. Mäki, ed., *Fact and Fiction in Economics*, pp. 285–303. Cambridge: Cambridge University Press.

Camerer, C. 1995. Individual decision making. In J. Kagel and A. Roth, eds., *The Handbook of Experimental Economics*, pp. 587–703. Princeton, N.J.: Princeton University Press.

Camerer, C. 2003a. Strategizing in the brain. *Science* 300: 1673–1675.

Camerer, C. 2003b. *Behavioral Game Theory*. Princeton, N.J.: Princeton University Press.

Camerer, C. 2003c. Behavioral game theory: Plausible formal models that predict accurately. *Behavioral and Brain Sciences* 26: 157–158.

Candland, D. 1993. *Feral Children and Clever Animals*. Oxford: Oxford University Press.

Cartwright, N. 1989. *Nature's Capacities and Their Measurement*. Oxford: Oxford University Press.

Castañeda, H.-N. 1975. *Thinking and Doing*. Dordrecht: Reidel.

Chalmers, D. 1996. *The Conscious Mind*. Oxford: Oxford University Press.

Cheney, D., and R. Seyfarth. 1990. *How Monkeys See the World*. Chicago, Ill.: University of Chicago Press.

Chew, S., and K. MacCrimmon. 1979. Alpha-nu choice theory: A generalization of expected utility theory. Working paper no. 686, University of Columbia Faculty of Commerce and Business Administration.

Chomsky, N. 2000. *New Horizons in the Study of Language and Mind*. New York: Cambridge University Press.

Chung, J. W. 1994. *Utility and Production Functions*. Oxford: Blackwell.

Churchland, P. 1979. *Scientific Realism and the Plasticity of Mind*. Cambridge: Cambridge University Press.

Churchland, P. 1981. Eliminative materialism and the propositional attitudes. *Journal of Philosophy* 78: 67–90.

Churchland, P. 1988. *Matter and Consciousness*. 2nd edition. Cambridge, Mass.: MIT Press/Bradford.

Churchland, P. 1995. *The Engine of Reason, the Seat of the Soul*. Cambridge, Mass.: MIT Press/Bradford.

Clark, A. 1989. *Microcognition*. Cambridge, Mass.: MIT Press/Bradford.

Clark, A. 1997. *Being There*. Cambridge, Mass.: MIT Press/Bradford.

Clark, A. 2002. That special something. In A. Brook and D. Ross, eds., *Daniel Dennett*, pp. 187–205. New York: Cambridge University Press.

Coase, R. 1988. *The Firm, the Market, and the Law*. Chicago, Ill.: University of Chicago Press.

Collier, J. 1986. Entropy in evolution. *Biology and Philosophy* 1: 5–24.

Collier, J. 1988. Supervenience and reduction in biological hierarchies. In M. Matthen and B. Linsky, eds., *Philosophy and Biology*, pp. 209–234. Calgary: University of Calgary Press.

Collier, J. 2002. What is autonomy? *International Journal of Computing Anticipatory Systems* 12: 112–121.

Collier, J., and C. Hooker. 1999. Complexly organised dynamical systems. *Open Systems and Information Dynamics* 6: 111–136.

Collier, J., and S. Muller. 1998. The dynamical basis of emergence in natural hierarchies. In G. Farre and T. Oksala, eds., *Emergence, Complexity, Hierarchy, and Organization: Selected and Edited Papers from the ECHO 3 Conference, Acta Polytechnica Scandinavica, MA91*. Helsinki: Finnish Academy of Technology.

Colman, A. 2003a. Cooperation, psychological game theory, and limitations of rationality in social interaction. *Behavioral and Brain Sciences* 26: 139–153.

Colman, A. 2003b. Beyond rationality: Rigor without mortis in game theory. *Behavioral and Brain Sciences* 26: 180–192.

Constantinides, G. 1988. Habit formation: A resolution of the equity-premium puzzle. Unpublished working paper, Graduate School of Business, University of Chicago.

Conway Morris, S. 2003. *Life's Solution*. Cambridge: Cambridge University Press.

Cook, K., and M. Levi, eds. 1990. *The Limits of Rationality*. Chicago, Ill.: University of Chicago Press.

Cox, J., and S. Epstein. 1988. Preference reversals without the independence axiom. *American Economic Review* 79: 408–426.

Cubitt, R., and R. Sugden. 2001. On money pumps. *Games and Economic Behavior* 37: 121–160.

Cummins, R. 1975. *The Nature of Psychological Explanation*. Cambridge, Mass.: MIT Press/Bradford.

Damasio, A. 1994. *Descartes's Error*. New York: Putnam.

Danielson, P. 1992. *Artificial Morality*. London: Routledge.

Dasgupta, P. 2002. Modern economics and its critics. In U. Mäki, ed., *Fact and Fiction in Economics*, pp. 57–89. Cambridge: Cambridge University Press.

Davidson, D. 1980. *Essays on Actions and Events*. Oxford: Oxford University Press.

Davidson, D., J. McKinsey, and P. Suppes. 1955. Outlines of a formal theory of value. *Philosophy of Science* 22: 140–160.

Davis, J. 2003. *The Theory of the Individual in Economics*. London: Routledge.

Dawkins, R. 1976. *The Selfish Gene*. Oxford: Oxford University Press.

Dawkins, R. 1982. *The Extended Phenotype*. Oxford: Oxford University Press.

De Mille, J. 1888/1969. *A Strange Manuscript Found in a Copper Cylinder*. Toronto: McClelland and Stewart.

Debreu, G. 1959. *Theory of Value*. New York: Wiley.

Debreu, G. 1974. Excess demand functions. *Journal of Mathematical Economics* 1: 15–23.

Dennett, D. 1969. *Content and Consciousness*. London: Routledge.

Dennett, D. 1978. Artificial intelligence as philosophy and as psychology. In D. Dennett, *Brainstorms*, pp. 109–126. Montgomery, Vt.: Bradford.

Dennett, D. 1981. Three kinds of intentional psychology. In R. Healey, ed., *Reduction, Time, and Reality*. Cambridge: Cambridge University Press. Reprinted in Dennett 1987, pp. 43–81.

Dennett, D. 1987. *The Intentional Stance*. Cambridge, Mass.: MIT Press/Bradford.

Dennett, D. 1991a. Real patterns. *Journal of Philosophy* 88: 27–51.

Dennett, D. 1991b. *Consciousness Explained*. Boston, Mass.: Little Brown.

Dennett, D. 1993. Back from the drawing board. In B. Dahlbom, ed., *Dennett and His Critics*, pp. 203–235. Oxford: Blackwell.

Dennett, D. 1994. Cognitive science as reverse engineering: Several meanings of "top-down" and "bottom-up." In D. Prawtiz, B. Skyrms, and D. Westerstahl, eds., *Logic, Methodology and Philosophy of Science*, pp. 679–689. Amsterdam: Elsevier Science BV.

Dennett, D. 1995. *Darwin's Dangerous Idea*. New York: Simon and Schuster.

Dennett, D. 2000. With a little help from my friends. In D. Ross, A. Brook, and D. Thompson, eds., *Dennett's Philosophy: A Comprehensive Assessment*, pp. 327–388. Cambridge, Mass.: MIT Press/Bradford.

Dennett, D. 2003. *Freedom Evolves*. New York: Viking.

Dennett, D. Forthcoming. Holding a mirror up to Dupré. *Philosophy and Phenomenological Research*.

Dixit, A., and S. Skeath. 1999. *Games of Strategy*. New York: Norton.

Dowding, K. 2002. Revealed preference and external reference. *Rationality and Society* 14: 259–284.

Dowding, K. Forthcoming. A defence of revealed preference analysis. *Economics and Philosophy*.

Dretske, F. 1988. *The Explanation of Behavior*. Cambridge, Mass.: MIT Press/Bradford.

Dugatkin, L., and H. Reeve, eds. 1998. *Game Theory and Animal Behavior*. Oxford: Oxford University Press.

Dukas, R., ed. 1998. *Cognitive Ecology*. Chicago: University of Chicago Press.

Dumouchel, P. 1999. *Emotions: Essai sur le corps et le social*, second revised edition. Paris: Synthelabo.

Dupré, J. 1993. *The Disorder of Things*. Cambridge, Mass.: Harvard University Press.

Dupré, J. 2001. *Human Nature and the Limits of Science*. Oxford: Oxford University Press.

Edgeworth, F. 1881/1932. *Mathematical Psychics*. London: London School of Economics.

Elster, J. 1979. *Ulysses and the Sirens*. Cambridge: Cambridge University Press.

Elster, J. 1985. *Making Sense of Marx*. Cambridge: Cambridge University Press.

Elster, J. 1999. *Alchemies of the Mind*. Cambridge: Cambridge University Press.

Elster, J. 2000. *Ulysses Unbound*. Cambridge: Cambridge University Press.

Epstein, J., and R. Axtell. 1996. *Growing Artificial Societies*. Cambridge, Mass.: MIT Press.

Ewert, J.-P. 1987. Neuroethology of releasing mechanisms: Prey-catching behavior in toads. *Behavioral and Brain Sciences* 10: 337–368.

Fisher, I. 1892. *Mathematical Investigations in the Theory of Value and Price*. New Haven, Conn.: Yale University Press.

Flanagan, O. 2002. *The Problem of the Soul*. New York: Basic Books.

Fodor, J. 1975. *The Language of Thought*. Cambridge, Mass.: Harvard University Press.

Fodor, J. 1980. Methodological solipsism considered as a research strategy in cognitive science. *Behavioral and Brain Sciences* 3: 63–73.

Fodor, J. 1983. *The Modularity of Mind*. Cambridge, Mass.: MIT Press/Bradford.

Fodor, J. 1987a. Modules, frames, fridgeons, sleeping dogs, and the music of the spheres. In Z. Pylyshyn, ed., *The Robot's Dilemma*, pp. 139–149. Norwood, N.J.: Ablex.

Fodor, J. 1987b. *Psychosemantics*. Cambridge, Mass.: MIT Press/Bradford.

Fodor, J. 1994. *The Elm and the Expert*. Cambridge, Mass.: MIT Press/Bradford.

Fodor, J. 1996. Deconstructing Dennett's Darwin. *Mind and Language* 11: 246–262.

Frank, R. 1988. *Passions within Reason*. New York: Norton.

Frank, R. 2004. In defense of sincerity detection. *Rationality and Society* 16: 287–305.

Frank, R., T. Gilovich, and D. Regan. 1993. Does studying economics inhibit cooperation? *Journal of Economic Perspectives* 7: 159–171.

Friedman, M. 1953. *Essays in Positive Economics*. Chicago, Ill.: University of Chicago Press.

Friedman, M. 1999. *Reconsidering Logical Positivism*. Cambridge: Cambridge University Press.

García-Arrarás, J. E., M. Rojas-Soto, L. Jimenez, and L. Diaz-Miranda. 2001. The enteric nervous system of echinoderms: Unexpected complexity revealed by neurochemical analysis. *Journal of Experimental Biology* 204: 865–873.

Gardner, E. 1997. Brain reward mechanisms. In J. Lowinson, P. Ruiz, R. Millman, and J. Langrod, eds., *Substance Abuse: A Comprehensive Textbook*, pp. 51–85. Baltimore, Md.: Wilkins and Wilkins.

Gardner, E. 1999. The neurobiology and genetics of addiction: Implications of the "reward deficiency syndrome" for therapeutic strategies in chemical dependency. In J. Elster, ed., *Addiction: Entries and Exits*, pp. 57–119. New York: Russell Sage.

Gauthier, D. 1986. *Morals by Agreement*. Oxford: Oxford University Press.

Giere, R. 1988. *Explaining Science*. Chicago, Ill.: University of Chicago Press.

Gigerenzer, G., P. Todd, and the ABC Research Group. 1999. *Simple Heuristics That Make Us Smart*. Oxford: Oxford University Press.

Gilbert, M. 1989. *On Social Facts*. Princeton, N.J.: Princeton University Press.

Gintis, H. 2000. *Game Theory Evolving*. Princeton, N.J.: Princeton University Press.

Gintis, H. 2003. A critique of team and Stackelberg reasoning. *Behavioral and Brain Sciences* 26: 160–161.

Glimcher, P. 2003. *Decisions, Uncertainty, and the Brain*. Cambridge, Mass.: MIT Press.

Godfrey-Smith, P. 1996. *Complexity and the Function of Mind in Nature*. Cambridge: Cambridge University Press.

Godfrey-Smith, P. 2001. Three kinds of adaptationism. In S. Orzack and E. Sober, eds., *Adaptationism and Optimality*, pp. 335–357. Cambridge: Cambridge University Press.

Goodie, A., and E. Fantino. 1995. An experimentally derived base-rate error in humans. *Psychological Science* 6: 101–106.

Goodin, R. 1990. De gustibus non est explanandum. In K. Cook and M. Levi, eds., *The Limits of Rationality*, pp. 217–221. Chicago, Ill.: University of Chicago Press.

Gould, S. J., and R. Lewontin. 1979. The spandrels of San Marco and the Panglossian paradigm: A critique of the adaptationist program. *Proceedings of the Royal Society of London B: Biological Sciences* 205: 581–598.

Green, E., and K. Osbard. 1991. A revealed preference theory for expected utility. *Review of Economic Studies* 58: 577–596.

Greenspan, P. 2000. Emotional strategies and rationality. *Ethics* 110: 469–487.

Grether, D., and C. Plott. 1979. Economic theory of choice and the preference reversal phenomenon. *American Economic Review* 75: 623–638.

Griffiths, P. 1997. *What Emotions Are*. Chicago, Ill.: University of Chicago Press.

Guala, F. 2000. Artefacts in experimental economics. *Economics and Philosophy* 16: 47–75.

Hacking, I. 1983. *Representing and Intervening*. Cambridge: Cambridge University Press.

Hacking, I. 1999. *The Social Construction of* What? Cambridge, Mass.: Harvard University Press.

Hampton, J. 1986. *Hobbes and the Social Contract Tradition*. Cambridge: Cambridge University Press.

Hardin, R. 2004. *Indeterminacy and Society*. Princeton, N.J.: Princeton University Press.

Harsanyi, J. 1977. *Rational Behavior and Bargaining Equilibrium in Games and Social Situations*. New York: Cambridge University Press.

Hartl, J., and E. Fantino. 1996. Choice as a function of reinforcement ratios in delayed matching to sample. *Journal of Experimental Analysis of Behavior* 66: 11–27.

Hausman, D. 1992. *The Inexact and Separate Science of Economics*. Cambridge: Cambridge University Press.

Hausman, D. 2000. Revealed preference, belief, and game theory. *Economics and Philosophy* 16: 99–115.

Hayek, F. 1960. *The Constitution of Liberty*. Chicago, Ill.: University of Chicago Press.

Hayes, P. 1979. The naïve physics manifesto. In D. Michie, ed., *Expert Systems in the Microelectronic Age*, pp. 242–270. Edinburgh: Edinburgh University Press.

Heilbroner, R., and W. Milberg. 1995. *The Crisis of Vision in Modern Economic Thought*. Cambridge: Cambridge University Press.

Heinrich, J., R. Boyd, S. Bowles, C. Camerer, E. Fehr, H. Gintis, and R. McElreath. 2001. In search of homo economicus: Behavioral experiments in fifteen small-scale societies. *AEA Papers and Proceedings* 91: 73–78.

Herrnstein, R. 1961. Relative and absolute strengths of response as a function of frequency of reinforcement. *Journal of the Experimental Analysis of Behavior* 4: 267–272.

Hicks, J. 1939. The foundations of welfare economics. *Economic Journal* 49: 696–712.

Hicks, J., and R. Allen. 1934. A reconsideration of the theory of value. *Economica* 1: 52–76, 196–219.

Hogarth, R., and M. Reder, eds. 1986. *Rational Choice*. Chicago, Ill.: University of Chicago Press.

Hollerman, J., L. Trembley, and W. Schultz. 1998. Influence of reward expectation on behavior-related neuronal activity in primate striatum. *Journal of Neurophysiology* 80: 947–963.

Hollis, M. 1998. *Trust within Reason*. Cambridge: Cambridge University Press.

Hoover, K. 1988. *The New Classical Macroeconomics*. Oxford: Blackwell.

Hoover, K. 2002. Econometrics and reality. In U. Mäki, ed., *Fact and Fiction in Economics*, pp. 152–177. Cambridge: Cambridge University Press.

Houthakker, H. 1950. Revealed preference and the utility function. *Economica* 17: 159–174.

Houthakker, H. 1961. The present state of consumption theory. *Econometrica* 29: 704–740.

Hull, D. 1988. *Science as a Process*. Chicago, Ill.: University of Chicago Press.

Hutchins, E. 1995. *Cognition in the Wild*. Cambridge, Mass.: MIT Press/Bradford.

Jaynes, J. 1976. *The Origins of Consciousness in the Breakdown of the Bicameral Mind*. New York: Houghton Mifflin.

Jevons, W. S. 1871. *The Theory of Political Economy*. London: Macmillan.

Johnsen, S. 1994. Extraocular sensitivity to polarized light in an echinoderm. *Journal of Experimental Biology* 195: 281–291.

Johnson, S. 2001. *Emergence*. New York: Scribner.

Johnson-Laird, P. 1988. *The Computer and the Mind*. Cambridge, Mass.: Harvard University Press.

Joyce, R. 2001. *The Myth of Morality*. Cambridge: Cambridge University Press.

Juarrero, A. 1999. *Dynamics in Action*. Cambridge, Mass.: MIT Press/Bradford.

Kagel, J., and A. Roth, eds. 1995. *The Handbook of Experimental Economics*. Princeton, N.J.: Princeton University Press.

Kahneman, D., P. Slovic, and A. Tversky. 1982. *Judgment under Uncertainty: Heursitics and Biases*. Cambridge: Cambridge University Press.

Kahneman, D., and A. Tversky. 1979. Prospect theory: An analysis of decision under risk. *Econometrica* 47: 263–291.

Kalai, E. 1990. Bounded rationality and strategic complexity in repeated games. In T. Ichiishi, A. Neyman, and Y. Tauman, eds., *Game Theory and Applications*, pp. 131–157. San Diego, Calif.: Academic Press.

Kaldor, N. 1939. Welfare propositions in economics and interpersonal comparisons of utility. *Economic Journal* 49: 549–551.

Karmiloff-Smith, A. 1992. *Beyond Modularity*. Cambridge, Mass.: MIT Press/Bradford.

Karni, E., and Z. Safra. 1987. "Preference reversal" and the observability of preferences by experimental methods. *Econometrica* 55: 675–685.

Kavka, G. 1991. Is individual choice less problematic than collective choice? *Economics and Philosophy* 7: 143–165.

Keller, E. 1985. *Reflections on Gender and Science*. New Haven, Conn.: Yale University Press.

Keller, E. 2001. *The Century of the Gene*. Cambridge, Mass.: Harvard University Press.

Kennedy, J., and R. Eberhart. 2001. *Swarm Intelligence*. San Fransisco, Calif.: Morgan Kauffman.

Kim, J. 1998. *Mind in a Physical World*. Cambridge, Mass.: MIT Press/Bradford.

Kincaid, H. 1997. *Individualism and the Unity of Science*. Lanham, Md.: Rowman and Littlefield.

Kincaid, H. 2004. Development theory and the philosophies of science. In M. Ayogu and D. Ross, eds., *Development Dilemmas*, pp. 107–144. London: Routledge.

Kirby, K., and R. Herrnstein. 1995. Preference reversals due to myopic discounting of delayed reward. *Psychology Science* 6: 83–89.

Kitcher, P. 1976. Explanation, conjunction, and unification. *Journal of Philosophy* 73: 207–212.

Kitcher, P. 1981. Explanatory unification. *Philosophy of Science* 48: 507–531.

Kitcher, P. 1982. *Abusing Science*. Cambridge, Mass.: MIT Press.

Kitcher, P. 1984. 1953 and all that: A tale of two sciences. *Philosophical Review* 93: 335–373.

Kitcher, P. 1989. Explanatory unification and the causal structure of the world. In P. Kitcher and W. Salmon, eds., *Scientific Explanation*, pp. 410–505. Minneapolis: University of Minnesota Press.

Krebs, J., and N. Davies. 1984. *Behavioral Ecology: An Evolutionary Approach*, second edition. Sunderland: Sinauer.

Kreps, D. 1990a. *Game Theory and Economic Modeling*. Oxford: Oxford University Press.

Kreps, D. 1990b. *A Course in Microeconomic Theory*. Princeton, N.J.: Princeton University Press.

Kripke, S. 1972. *Naming and Necessity*. Cambridge, Mass.: Harvard University Press.

LaCasse, C., and D. Ross. 1998. Morality's last chance. In P. Danielson, ed., *Modeling Rationality, Morality, and Evolution*, pp. 340–375. Oxford: Oxford University Press.

Ladyman, J. 2004. Supervenience: Not local and not two-way. *Behavioral and Brain Sciences*, in press.

Lane, P., ed. 1999. *Economics: Making Sense of the Modern Economy*. London: The Economist.

Langton, C., ed. 1995. *Artificial Life: An Overview*. Cambridge, Mass.: MIT Press.

Lawson, T. 1997. *Economics and Reality*. London: Routledge.

Levy, S. 1992. *Artificial Life*. New York: Pantheon.

Lewin, S. 1996. Economics and psychology: Lessons for our own day from the early twentieth century. *Journal of Economic Literature* 34: 1293–1323.

Lewis, D. 1969. *Convention*. Cambridge, Mass.: Harvard University Press.

Lichtenstein, S., and P. Slovic. 1971. Reversals of preference between bids and choices in gambling decisions. *Journal of Experimental Psychology* 89: 46–55.

Lichtenstein, S., and P. Slovic. 1973. Response-induced reversals of preference in gambling: An extended replication in Las Vegas. *Journal of Experimental Psychology* 101: 16–20.

Lloyd, D. 1989. *Simple Minds*. Cambridge, Mass.: MIT Press/Bradford.

Lloyd, J. 1984. *Foundations of Logic Programming*. Berlin: Springer Verlag.

Loewenstein, G. 1988. Frames of mind in intertemporal choice. *Management Science* 34: 200–214.

Loomes, G., C. Starmer, and R. Sugden. 1991. Observing violations of transitivity by experimental methods. *Econometrica* 59: 425–439.

Loomes, G., and C. Taylor. 1992. Non-transitive preferences over gains and losses. *Economic Journal* 102: 357–365.

Luce, D. 1959. *Individual Choice Behavior: A Theoretical Analysis*. Westport, Conn.: Greenwood.

Lyons, W. 1986. *The Disappearance of Introspection*. Cambridge, Mass.: MIT Press/Bradford.

Machina, M. 1982. Expected utility analysis without the independence axiom. *Econometrica* 50: 277–323.

Maes, P. 1991. A bottom-up mechanism for behavior selection in an artificial creature. In J.-A. Meyer and S. Wilson, eds., *From Animals to Animats*, pp. 238–246. Cambridge, Mass.: MIT Press/Bradford.

Mäki, U. 1986. Rhetoric at the expense of coherence: A reinterpretation of Milton Friedman's methodology. In W. Samuels, ed., *Research in the History of Economic Thought and Methodology*, volume 4. pp. 127–143. Greenwich, Conn.: JAI Press.

Mäki, U. 1992. Friedman and realism. In W. Samuels and J. Biddle, eds., *Research in the History of Economic Thought and Methodology*, volume 10, pp. 171–195. Greenwich, Conn.: JAI Press.

Malik, K. 2000. *Man, Beast, and Zombie*. London: Weidenfeld and Nicolson.

Mandler, J. 1984. *Stories, Scripts, and Scenes: Aspects of Schema Theory*. Hillsdale, N.J.: Lawrence Erlbaum.

Mandler, M. 1999. *Dilemmas in Economic Theory*. Oxford: Oxford University Press.

Mantel, R. 1974. On the characterization of aggregate excess demand. *Journal of Economic Theory* 7: 348–353.

Mantel, R. 1976. Homothetic preferences and community excess demand functions. *Journal of Economic Theory* 12: 197–201.

Marr, D. 1982. *Vision*. San Francisco, Calif.: Freeman.

Marras, A. 2002. Kim on reduction. *Erkenntnis* 57: 231–257.

Marshall, A. 1890. *The Principles of Economics*. London: Macmillan.

May, L., M. Friedman, and A. Clark, eds. 1996. *Mind and Morals*. Cambridge, Mass.: MIT Press/Bradford.

Maynard Smith, J. 1982. *Evolution and the Theory of Games*. Cambridge: Cambridge University Press.

McClamrock, R. 1995. *Existential Cognition*. Chicago, Ill.: University of Chicago Press.

McFarland, D. 1992. Animals as cost-based robots. *International Studies in the Philosophy of Science* 6: 133–153.

McFarland, D., and A. Houston. 1981. *Quantitative Ethology: The State-Space Approach.* London: Pitman.

McGeer, V. 2001. Psycho-practice, psycho-theory, and the contrastive case of autism. *Journal of Consciousness Studies* 8: 109–132.

Meikle, S. 1995. *Aristotle's Economic Thought.* Oxford: Oxford University Press.

Meikle, S. 2001. Quality and quantity in economics: The metaphysical construction of the economic realm. In U. Mäki, ed., *The Economic World View*, pp. 32–54. Cambridge: Cambridge University Press.

Meyering, T. 2000. Physicalism and downward causation in psychology and the special sciences. *Inquiry* 43: 181–202.

Miller, R. 1987. *Fact and Method.* Princeton, N.J.: Princeton University Press.

Millero, F. J. 2001. *The Physical Chemistry of Natural Waters.* New York: Wiley-Interscience.

Millikan, R. 1984. *Language, Thought, and Other Biological Categories.* Cambridge, Mass.: MIT Press/Bradford.

Minsky, M. 1985. *The Society of Mind.* New York: Simon and Schuster.

Mirowski, P. 1989. *More Heat Than Light.* New York: Cambridge University Press.

Mirowski, P. 2002. *Machine Dreams: Economics Becomes a Cyborg Science.* Cambridge: Cambridge University Press.

Montague, P. R., and G. Berns. 2002. Neural economics and the biological substrates of valuation. *Neuron* 36: 265–284.

Muller, J. 1993. *Adam Smith in His Time and Ours.* New York: Free Press.

Nagel, T. 1974. What is it like to be a bat? *Philosophical Review* 83: 435–450.

Nagel, T. 1986. *The View from Nowhere.* Oxford: Oxford University Press.

Needham, P. 2002. The discovery that water is H_2O. *International Studies in the Philosophy of Science* 16: 205–226.

Newell, A., and H. Simon. 1976. Computer science as empirical inquiry: Symbols and search. *Communications of the Association for Computing Machinery* 19: 113–126.

Noë, R., J. van Hooff, and P. Hammerstein, eds. 2001. *Economics in Nature.* Cambridge: Cambridge University Press.

North, D. 1990. *Institutions, Institutional Change, and Economic Performance.* Cambridge: Cambridge University Press.

Nussbaum, M. 1981. *The Fragility of Goodness.* Cambridge: Cambridge University Press.

Nussbaum, M. 1994. *The Therapy of Desire.* Princeton, N.J.: Princeton University Press.

O'Hara, M. 1995. *Market Microstructure Theory.* Oxford: Blackwell.

Oppenheim, P., and H. Putnam. 1958. Unity of science as a working hypothesis. In H. Feigl, M. Scriven, and G. Maxwell, eds., *Minnesota Studies in the Philosophy of Science*, volume 2, pp. 3–36. Minneapolis: University of Minnesota Press.

Ordeshook, P. 1997. The spatial analysis of elections and committees: Four decades of research. In D. Mueller, ed., *Perspectives on Public Choice*, pp. 247–270. Cambridge: Cambridge University Press.

Ormerod, P. 1994. *The Death of Economics*. New York: Wiley.

Orzack, S., and E. Sober, eds. 2001. *Adaptationism and Optimality*. Cambridge: Cambridge University Press.

Oyama, S. 2000. *Evolution's Eye*. Chapel Hill, N.C.: Duke University Press.

Pareto, V. 1909/1971. *Manual of Political Economy*. New York: Augustus Kelley.

Paul, E., F. Miller, and J. Paul, eds. 1997. *Self-Interest*. Cambridge: Cambridge University Press.

Peacocke, C. 1979. *Holistic Explanation: Action, Space, Interpretation*. Oxford: Oxford University Press.

Pettit, P. 1993. *The Common Mind*. Oxford: Oxford University Press.

Pettit, P. 2001. The virtual reality of *Homo economicus*. In U. Mäki, ed., *The Economic World View*, pp. 75–97. Cambridge: Cambridge University Press.

Pinker, S. 1994. *The Language Instinct*. New York: Morrow.

Pinker, S. 1997. *How the Mind Works*. New York: Norton.

Platt, M., and P. Glimcher. 1999. Neural correlates of decision variables in parietal cortex. *Nature* 400: 233–238.

Polanyi, L. 1989. *Telling the American Story*. Cambridge, Mass.: MIT Press/Bradford.

Ponce, V. 2003. *Rethinking Natural Kinds*. Doctoral dissertation, Duke University.

Putnam, H. 1975. *Mind, Language, and Reality*. Cambridge: Cambridge University Press.

Pylyshyn, Z. 1987. *The Robot's Dilemma*. Norwood, N.J.: Ablex.

Quartz, S., and T. Sejnowski. 2002. *Liars, Lovers, and Heroes*. New York: William Morrow.

Quiggin, J. 1982. A theory of anticipated utility. *Journal of Economic Behavior and Organization* 3: 323–343.

Quine, W. V. 1953. Two dogmas of empricism. In W. V. Quine, *From a Logical Point of View*, pp. 20–46. Cambridge, Mass.: Harvard University Press.

Quine, W. V. 1969. Epistemology naturalized. In W. V. Quine, *Ontological Relativity and Other Essays*, pp. 69–90. New York: Columbia University Press.

Quine, W. V. 1991. Two dogmas in retrospect. *Canadian Journal of Philosophy* 21: 265–274.

Rabin, M. 1998. Psychology and economics. *Journal of Economic Literature* 36: 11–46.

Rawls, J. 1971. *A Theory of Justice*. Cambridge, Mass.: Harvard University Press.

Ray, T. 1992. An approach to the synthesis of life. In C. Langton, C. Taylor, J. D. Farmer, and S. Rasmussen, eds., *Artificial Life II*, pp. 371–408. Redwood City, Calif.: Addison-Wesley.

Redman, D. 1997. *The Rise of Political Economy as a Science*. Cambridge, Mass.: MIT Press.

Reichenbach, H. 1957. *The Philosophy of Space and Time*. New York: Dover.

Ritzman, R. 1984. The cockroach escape response. In R. Eaton, ed., *Neural Mechanisms of Startle Behavior*, pp. 93–131. New York: Plenum Press.

Robbins, L. 1935. *An Essay on the Nature and Significance of Economic Science*, second edition. London: Macmillan.

Robbins, L. 1938. Interpersonal comparisons of utility: A comment. *Economic Journal* 43: 635–641.

Robbins, L. 1998. *A History of Economic Thought*. Princeton, N.J.: Princeton University Press.

Roberts, C. 1996. *The Logic of Historical Explanation*. University Park: Pennsylvania State University Press.

Robertson, D. 1957. *Lectures on Economic Principles*, volume 1. London: Staples Press.

Romanos, G. 1983. *Quine and Analytic Philosophy*. Cambridge, Mass.: MIT Press/Bradford.

Rosenberg, A. 1983. If economics isn't science, what is it? *Philosophical Forum* 14: 296–314.

Rosenberg, A. 1992. *Economics: Mathematical Politics or Science of Diminishing Returns?* Chicago, Ill.: University of Chicago Press.

Rosenberg, A. 1994. *Instrumental Biology, or The Disunity of Science*. Chicago, Ill.: University of Chicago Press.

Ross, D. 1991. Hume, resemblance, and the foundations of psychology. *History of Philosophy Quarterly* 8: 343–356.

Ross, D. 1993a. Quining qualia Quine's way. *Dialogue* 32: 439–459.

Ross, D. 1993b. *Metaphor, Meaning, and Cognition*. New York: Peter Lang.

Ross, D. 1994a. Dennett's conceptual reform. *Behavior and Philosophy* 22: 41–52.

Ross, D. 1994b. Real patterns and the ontological foundations of microeconomics. *Economics and Philosophy* 11: 113–136.

Ross, D. 1997. Critical notice of *Existential Cognition*, by R. McClamrock. *Canadian Journal of Philosophy* 27: 271–284.

Ross, D. 1998. Review of *Equilibrium versus Understanding*, by M. Addleson. *Economics and Philosophy* 14: 163–168.

Ross, D. 1999. *What People Want: The Concept of Utility from Bentham to Game Theory*. Cape Town: University of Cape Town Press.

Ross, D. 2000. Rainforest realism: A Dennettian theory of existence. In D. Ross, A. Brook, and D. Thompson, eds., *Dennett's Philosophy: A Comprehensive Assessment*, pp. 147–168. Cambridge, Mass.: MIT Press/Bradford.

Ross, D. 2002a. Dennettian behavioral explanation and the roles of the social sciences. In A. Brook and D. Ross, eds., *Daniel Dennett*, pp. 140–183. New York: Cambridge University Press.

Ross, D. 2002b. Dennett and the Darwin wars. In A. Brook and D. Ross, eds., *Daniel Dennett*, pp. 271–293. New York: Cambridge University Press.

Ross, D. 2002c. Why people are atypical agents. *Philosophical Papers* 31: 87–116.

Ross, D. 2004. Meta-linguistic signaling for coordination amongst social agents. *Language Sciences* 26: 621–642.

Ross, D., and F. Bennett. 2001. The possibility of economic objectivity. In U. Mäki, ed., *The Economic World View*, pp. 246–272. Cambridge: Cambridge University Press.

Ross, D., and P. Dumouchel. 2004a. Emotions as strategic signals. *Rationality and Society* 16: 251–286.

Ross, D., and P. Dumouchel. 2004b. Sincerity is just consistency: Reply to Frank. *Rationality and Society* 16: 307–318.

Ross, D., and C. LaCasse. 1995. Towards a new philosophy of positive economics. *Dialogue* 35: 1–27.

Ross, D., J. Ladyman, D. Spurrett, and J. Collier. forthcoming. *What's Wrong with Things: Information-Topological Structural Realism.* Oxford: Oxford University Press.

Ross, D., and D. Spurrett. 2004a. What to say to a skeptical metaphysician: A defense manual for cognitive and behavioral scientists. *Behavioral and Brain Sciences.*

Ross, D., and D. Spurrett. 2004b. The cognitive and behavioral sciences: Real patterns, real causes, real unity but no supervenience. *Behavioral and Brain Sciences*, in press.

Ross, D., and T. Zawidzki. 1994. Information and teleosemantics. *Southern Journal of Philosophy* 32: 393–420.

Roth, A. 1995. Introduction to experimental economics. In J. Kagel and A. Roth, eds., *The Handbook of Experimental Economics*, pp. 3–109. Princeton, N.J.: Princeton University Press.

Rothschild, E. 2002. *Economic Sentiments: Adam Smith, Condorcet, and the Enlightenment.* Cambridge, Mass.: Harvard University Press.

Ryle, G. 1949. *The Concept of Mind.* London: Hutchinson.

Salmon, W. 1984. *Scientific Explanation and the Causal Structure of the World.* Princeton, N.J.: Princeton University Press.

Samuelson, P. 1938. A note on the pure theory of consumer's behavior. *Economica* 5: 61–72.

Samuelson, P. 1947. *Foundations of Economic Analysis.* Enlarged edition, 1983. Cambridge, Mass.: Harvard University Press.

Samuelson, P. 1972. Maximum principles in analytical economics. *American Economic Review* 62: 249–262.

Sartre, J.-P. 1943. *L'être et le néant.* Paris: Galimard.

Satz, D., and J. Ferejohn. 1994. Rational choice and social theory. *Journal of Philosophy* 91: 71–87.

Savage, L. 1954. *The Foundations of Statistics.* New York: Wiley.

Scarf, H. 1973. *The Computation of Economic Equilibria.* New Haven, Conn.: Yale University Press.

Schank, R., and R. Abelson. 1977. *Scripts, Plans, Goals, and Understanding.* Hillsdale, N.J.: Lawrence Erlbaum.

Schelling, T. 1960. *The Strategy of Conflict.* Cambridge, Mass.: Harvard University Press.

Schelling, T. 1978. Economics, or the art of self-management. *American Economic Review* 68: 290–294.

Schelling, T. 1980. The intimate contest for self-command. *Public Interest* 60: 94–118.

Schelling, T. 1984. Self-command in practice, in policy, and in a theory of rational choice. *American Economic Review* 74: 1–11.

Schlick, M. 1933/1979. Positivism and realism. In H. Mulder, ed., *Moritz Schlick: Philosophical Papers, volume II (1925–1936)*, pp. 259–284. Dordrecht: Kluwer.

Schrödinger, E. 1943. *What Is Life?* Cambridge: Cambridge University Press.

Schultz, W., P. Dayan, and P. Montague. 1997. A neural substrate of prediction and reward. *Science* 275: 1593–1599.

Searle, J. 1980. Minds, brains, and programs. *Behavioral and Brain Sciences* 3: 417–458.

Searle, J. 1992. *The Rediscovery of the Mind.* Cambridge, Mass.: MIT Press/Bradford.

Searle, J. 1997. *The Construction of Social Reality.* New York: Free Press.

Sen, A. 1969. Quasi-transitivity, rational choice, and collective decisions. *Review of Economic Studies* 36: 381–393.

Sen, A. 1971. Choice functions and revealed preference. *Review of Economic Studies* 38: 307–317.

Sen, A. 1973. Behavior and the concept of preference. *Economica* 40: 241–259.

Sen, A. 1977. Rational fools. *Philosophy and Public Affairs* 6: 317–344.

Sen, A. 1979. *Collective Choice and Social Welfare.* Amsterdam: North-Holland.

Sen, A. 1987. *On Ethics and Economics.* Oxford: Blackwell.

Sen, A. 1999. *Development as Freedom.* New York: Random House.

Seyfarth, R., and D. Cheney. 2002. Dennett's contribution to research on the animal mind. In A. Brook and D. Ross, eds., *Daniel Dennett*, pp. 117–139. New York: Cambridge University Press.

Shackleford, J. 1989. Neural data structures: Programming with neurons. *Hewlett Packard Journal* (June): 69–78.

Shannon, C. 1948. The mathematical theory of communication. *Bell System Technical Journal* 27: 37–423, 623–656.

Shizgal, P., and K. Canover. 1996. On the neural computation of utility. *Current Directions in Psychological Science* 5: 37–43.

Sibly, R., and D. McFarland. 1976. On the fitness of behavior sequences. *American Naturalist* 110: 601–617.

Sigmund, K. 2003. "Was you ever bit by a dead bee?"—evolutionary games and dominated strategies. *Behavioral and Brain Sciences* 26: 175–176.

Simon, H. 1947. *Administrative Behavior*. New York: Macmillan.

Simon, H. 1978. Rationality as process and as product of thought. *American Economic Review* 68: 1–16.

Skog, O.-J. 1999. Rationality, irrationality, and addiction—Notes on Becker's and Murphy's theory of addiction. In J. Elster and O.-J. Skog, eds., *Getting Hooked*, pp. 173–207. Cambridge: Cambridge University Press.

Skyrms, B. 1996. *Evolution of the Social Contract*. Cambridge: Cambridge University Press.

Skyrms, B. 2002. Signals, evolution, and the explanatory power of transient information. *Philosophy of Science* 69: 407–428.

Skyrms, B. 2004. *The Stag Hunt and the Evolution of Social Structure*. Cambridge: Cambridge University Press.

Slovic, P., D. Griffin, and A. Tversky. 1990. Compatibility effects in judgment and choice. In R. Hogarth, ed., *Insights in Decision Making: Theory and Applications*, pp. 5–27. Chicago, Ill.: University of Chicago Press.

Sober, E. 1984. *The Nature of Selection*. Cambridge, Mass.: MIT Press/Bradford.

Sober, E., and D. Wilson. 1998. *Unto Others*. Cambridge, Mass.: Harvard University Press.

Sonnenschein, H. 1972. Market excess demand functions. *Econometrica* 40: 549–563.

Sonnenschein, H. 1973. Do Walras identity and continuity characterize the class of excess demand functions? *Journal of Economic Theory* 6: 345–354.

Spurrett, D. 2000. *The Completeness of Physics*. Doctoral dissertation, University of Natal (Durban), now University of KwaZulu-Natal. Available at http://cogprints.ecs.soton.ac.uk/archive/00003379/.

Starmer, C., and R. Sugden. 1991. Does the random-lottery incentive system elicit true preferences? *American Economic Review* 81: 971–978.

Stein, E. 1996. *Without Good Reason*. Oxford: Oxford University Press.

Stich, S. 1990. *The Fragmentation of Reason*. Cambridge, Mass.: MIT Press/Bradford.

Stigler, G., and G. Becker. 1977. De gustibus non est disputandum. *American Economic Review* 67: 76–90.

Stratmann, T. 1997. Logrolling. In D. Mueller, ed., *Perspectives on Public Choice*, pp. 322–341. Cambridge: Cambridge University Press.

Sugden, R. 2000. Team preferences. *Economics and Philosophy* 16: 175–204.

Sugden, R. 2001. The evolutionary turn in game theory. *Journal of Economic Methodology* 8: 113–130.

Sugden, R. 2002. Beyond sympathy and empathy: Adam Smith's concept of fellow feeling. *Economics and Philosophy* 18: 63–87.

Sunder, S. 1995. Experimental asset markets: A survey. In J. Kagel and A. Roth, eds., *The Handbook of Experimental Economics*, pp. 445–500. Princeton, N.J.: Princeton University Press.

Sutton, J. 2000. *Marshall's Tendencies.* Cambridge, Mass.: MIT Press.

Taylor, C. 1989. *The Sources of the Self.* Cambridge: Cambridge University Press.

Thagard, P. 1992. *Conceptual Revolutions.* Princeton, N.J.: Princeton University Press.

Thaler, R. 1981. Some empirical evidence on dynamic inconsistency. *Economic Letters* 8: 201–207.

Thaler, R. 1992. *The Winner's Curse.* New York: Free Press.

Thurstone, L. 1931. The indifference function. *Journal of Social Psychology* 2: 139–167.

Tommasi, M., and K. Ierulli, eds. 1995. *The New Economics of Human Behavior.* Cambridge: Cambridge University Press.

Tooby, J., and L. Cosmides. 1992. The psychological foundations of culture. In J. Barkow, L. Cosmides, and J. Tooby, eds., *The Adapted Mind*, pp. 19–136. Oxford: Oxford University Press.

Tversky, A., P. Slovic, and D. Kahneman. 1990. The causes of preference reversal. *American Economic Review* 80: 204–217.

van Brakel, J. 2000. The nature of chemical substances. In N. Bhushan and S. Rosenfeld, eds., *Of Minds and Molecules: New Philosophical Perspectives on Chemistry*, pp. 162–184. Oxford: Oxford University Press.

van Fraassen, B. 1980. *The Scientific Image.* Oxford: Oxford University Press.

Wallace, D. 2004. Protecting cognitive science from quantum theory. *Behavioral and Brain Sciences*, in press.

Wallis, W., and M. Friedman. 1942. The empirical derivation of indifference functions. In O. Lange, ed., *Studies in Mathematical Economics and Econometrics*, pp. 175–189. Chicago, Ill.: University of Chicago Press.

Walras, L. 1874/1954. *Elements of Pure Economics.* W. Jaffé, trans. London: Richard Irwin.

Wegner, D. 2002. *The Illusion of Conscious Will.* Cambridge, Mass.: MIT Press/Bradford.

Weibull, J. 1995. *Evolutionary Game Theory.* Cambridge, Mass.: MIT Press.

Wheeler, Q., and R. Meier, eds. 2000. *Species Concepts and Phylogenetic Theory.* New York: Columbia University Press.

Whiten, A., and R. Byrne. 1997. *Machiavellian Intelligence 2.* Cambridge: Cambridge University Press.

Wicksteed, P. 1910. *The Common Sense of Political Economy.* London: Macmillan.

Willams, B. 1976. Persons, character, and morality. In A. Rorty, ed., *The Identities of Persons*, pp. 184–205. Berkeley: University of California Press.

Wittgenstein, L. 1953. *Philosophical Investigations.* Oxford: Blackwell.

Wong, S. 1978. *The Foundations of Paul Samuelson's Revealed Preference Theory*. London: Routledge.

Wooldridge, D. 1968. *Mechanical Man: The Physical Basis of Intelligent Life*. New York: McGraw Hill.

Yaari, M. 1987. The dual theory of choice under risk. *Econometrica* 55: 95–115.

Young, H. P. 1998. *Individual Strategy and Social Structure*. Princeton, N.J.: Princeton University Press.

Index

Page numbers in *italic* type indicate figures or tables.